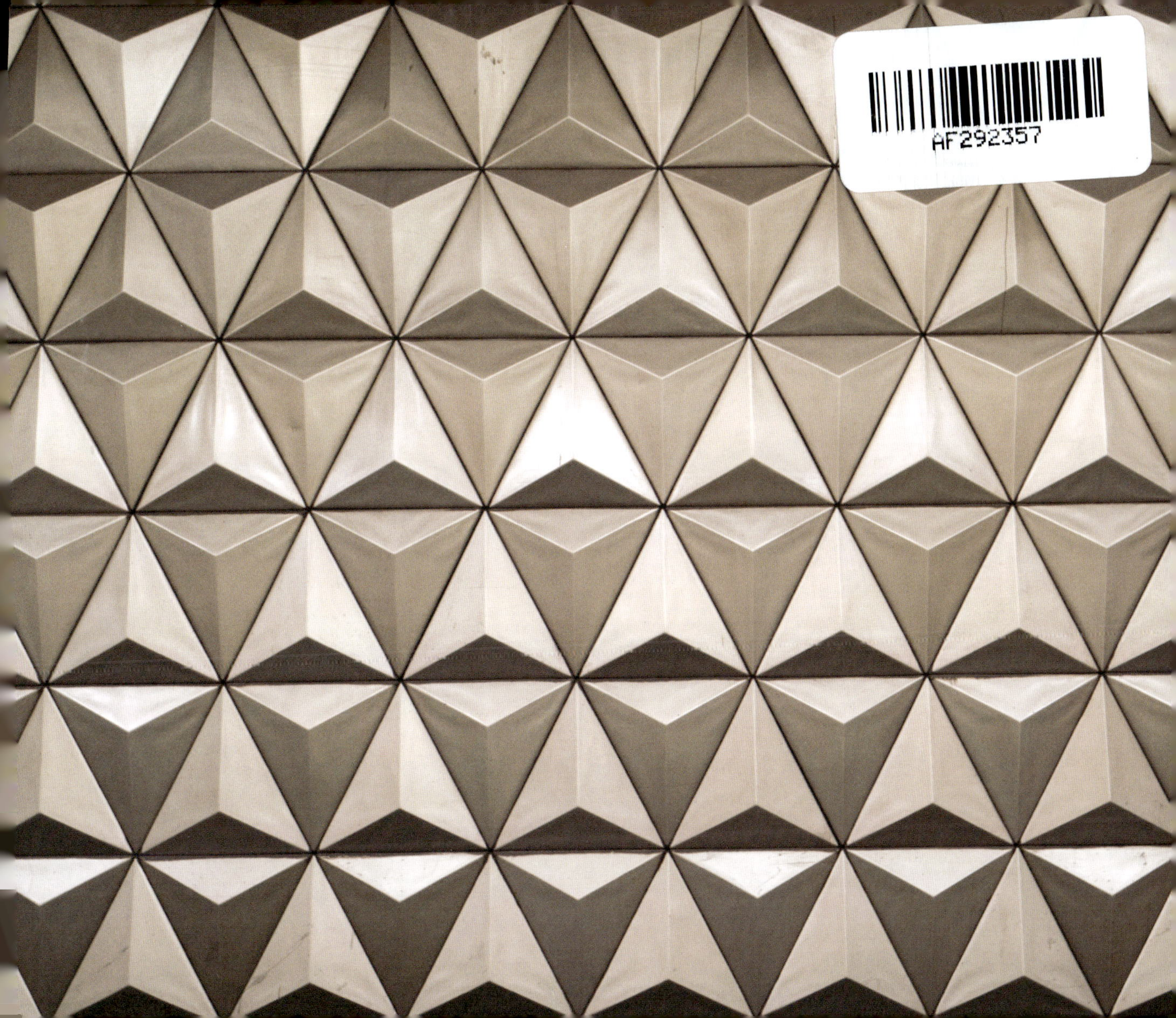
AF292357

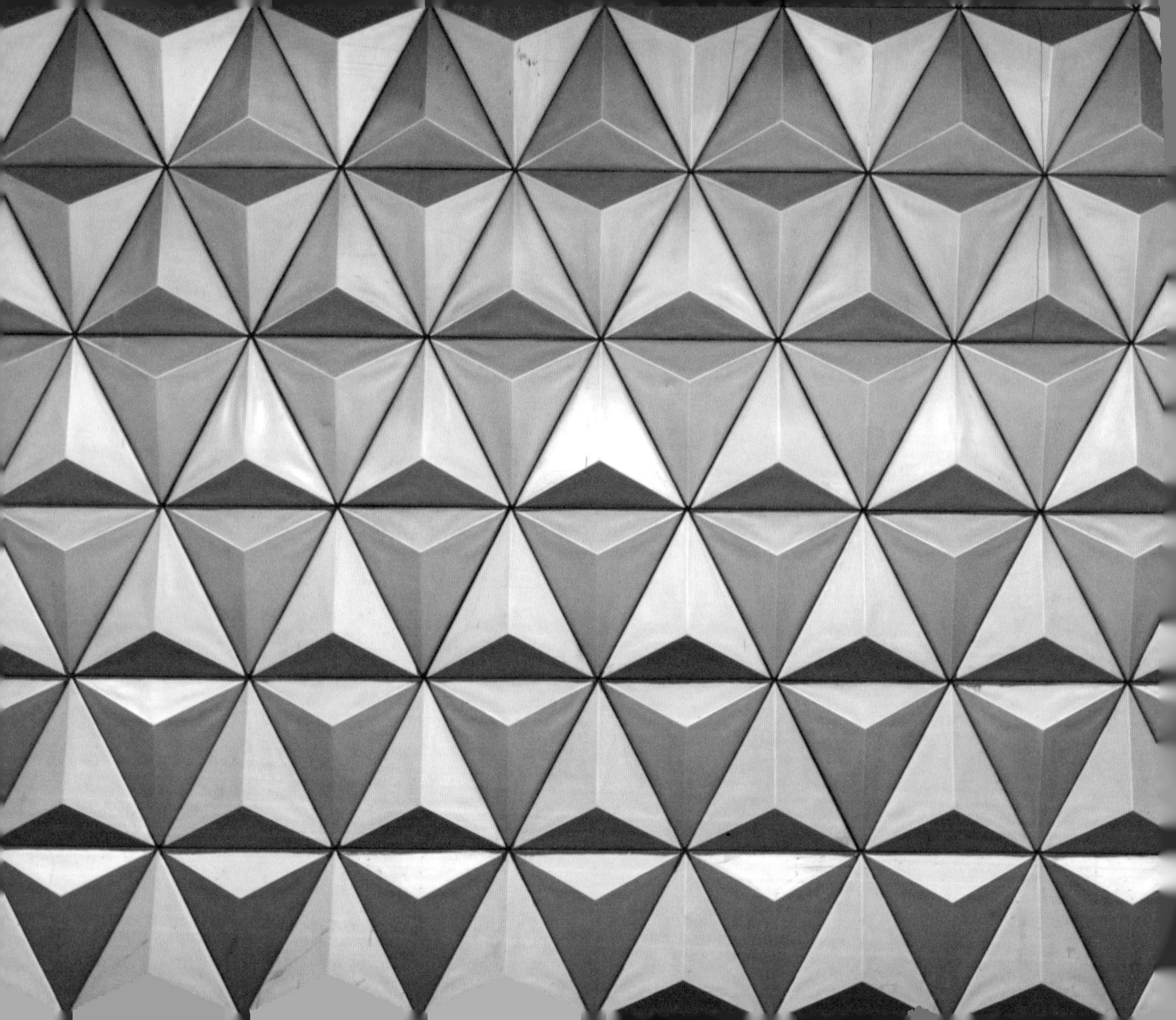

СТАНЦИИ СОВЕТСКОГО МЕТРО

SOVIET
METRO
STATIONS

CHRISTOPHER HERWIG

OWEN HATHERLEY

FUEL

OWEN HATHERLEY

The Heavens Underground
The Metro Architecture of the Soviet Union, 1935–1995

**'Their palaces are for Pharaohs,
but ours are for the people.'**

Alexey Dushkin
Moscow Metro architect, 1935

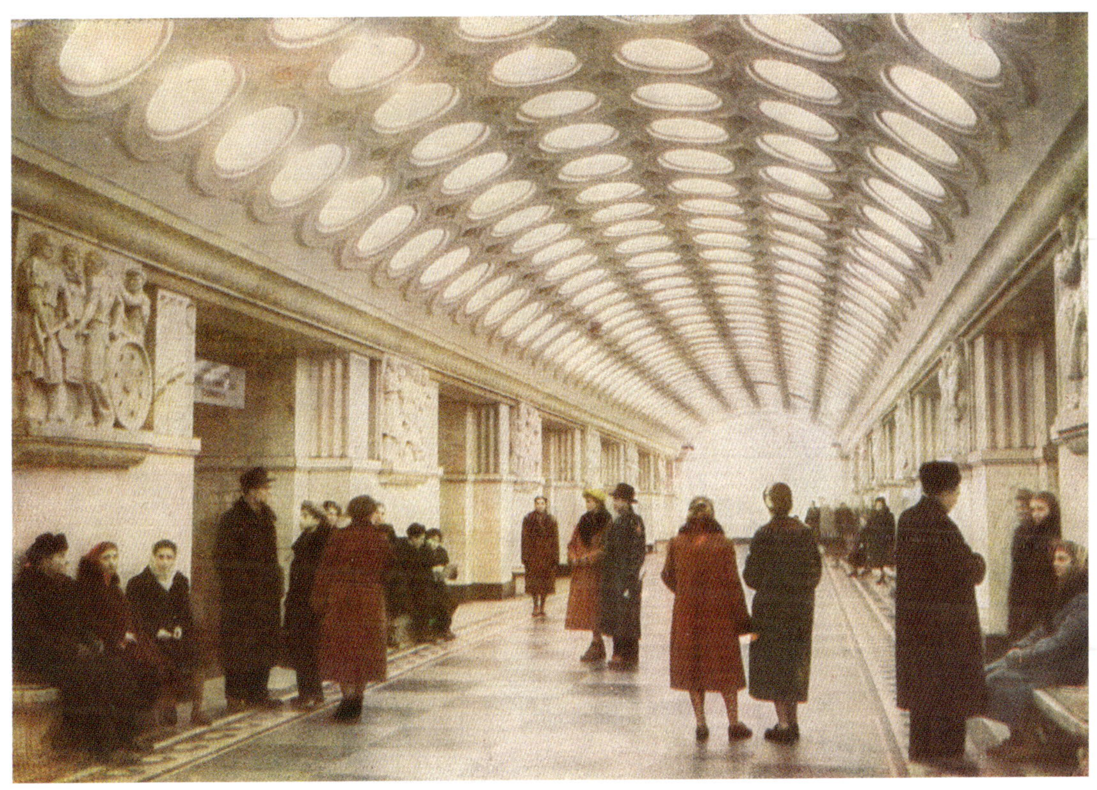

Postcard Elektrozavodskaya, Moscow, 1961

A Collective Unconscious
How they built the Metro

The young Stalinist and former miner Nikita Khrushchev was the head of the Communist Party of the City of Moscow in the mid-1930s. Effectively, this made him Mayor of the capital, and the head of construction, in which capacity he was the politician in charge of building the Moscow Metro. Writing his memoirs many decades later, he would recall that 'we were very unsophisticated. We thought of a subway as something almost supernatural'. He continued: 'I think it's probably easier to contemplate space flights today than it was for us to contemplate the construction of the Moscow Metro in the early 1930s.'[1] In part, Khrushchev was saying that nothing so complex in engineering terms had been built in the capital of the 'Workers' and Peasants' State'. This wasn't just about whether you could build large projects without the instruments of capitalism; it was the measure of a cultural cringe. Could 'the Bolsheviks' – as they referred to themselves, even as most of the original Bolshevik leadership were shot or sent to concentration camps – really build a project as ambitious as an Underground system? But he was also talking about the fact that it couldn't just be another public transport system. It had to be built in a new way. It had to be a Communist space, not just a functional one. It had to articulate the values of the socialist state. And it had to incarnate the Soviet 'family of nations'. Like so much else, this soon got very out of hand.

Anyone who knows a bit about Soviet state socialism knows about the Moscow Metro and its system of underground palaces; these awesome, opulent spaces have been a fixture of travel guides since the 1930s, and now they're equally prevalent on Instagram accounts. Much less known is that these marble-clad portals in the centre of the capital are just the most visible elements of a gigantic Metro-building project that would gradually expand into more than a dozen different systems across several Republics – Russia, Ukraine, Belarus, Georgia, Armenia, Azerbaijan, Uzbekistan. After Moscow came Saint Petersburg, Kyiv, Tbilisi, Baku, Kharkiv, Tashkent, Yerevan, Minsk, Nizhny Novgorod, Samara, Novosibirsk, Yekaterinburg, Dnipro. 'Metro-Trams' with palatial underground halls were built in Krivyi Rih and Volgograd; and a miniature 'Cave Metro' was built for the tourist site of New Athos, Abkhazia. Soviet experts were also responsible for engineering Metro systems outside the USSR – in Prague, Budapest, Warsaw, Sofia, Pyongyang, and Calcutta (as it then was), India's first Metro system in the capital of Communist-governed West Bengal.[2] Soviet Metro building was an enormous project, spanning two continents. An early slogan had it that 'the whole country is building the Moscow Metro', but between the 1960s and '80s this could have been rephrased as 'the Moscow Metro is being built in the whole country'. Why, then, was this particular kind of Metro building so important?

Some of this was a political choice, and one which now looks very astute – a privileging of public over private transport, a choice that many cities in the West are now trying to reverse-engineer as they dismantle their 1960s' road schemes and put back the tram lines they tore out. But there's so much more than that. Both the internationalism and the tragedy of the Soviet Metro are subtexts of Hamid Ismailov's novel *The Underground* (2014), in which a part-African, part-Khakass Soviet citizen, 'without papers' and hence disqualified from actually living in the capital, finds refuge underground from the violent, racist and small-minded reality above. In Sokol, one of the most gorgeous of all the Moscow stations, he reflects on how a system that got it so wrong above, got it so right below: 'The Metro is the subconscious of Soviet building; its collective unconscious, its archetype. What was left unrealised – or never fully realised – on the surface was achieved underground', with channelled movement, clear entry points and exits, and a strict division between controllers, drivers, conductors and obedient passengers.

'The whole of that totally controlled system could only exist at a remove from the world. It was as if it had been taken out of the equation, deleted from the face of the earth; it existed and at the same time remained invisible; the ideal was achieved, yet it remained otherworldly'.[3] On this, Khrushchev and Ismailov, the Stalinist city boss of the 1930s, and the Uzbek liberal novelist in the 2010s, can agree. The Soviet Metro was not entirely of this earth.

Subterranean Palaces
Moscow, Saint Petersburg

The decision to build the Moscow Metro was made in the early 1930s as part of the second Five-Year Plan, and early sketches and outlines show a project in the spirit of international modernism – the nearest comparable project being the elegant tile-covered stations designed by Alfred Grenander for the Berlin U-Bahn. The shift towards the palaces we know was actually the result of enthusiasm for London's Piccadilly Circus station, designed by Charles Holden in 1928, which combined super-deep escalators with spacious, travertine-clad public spaces. (Holden was given a USSR state prize for his work as an adviser on the Metro, returning the favour in the 1940s when he designed Gants Hill station on the Central Line as a tribute to Moscow.) The London-style deep platforms were intended to double

as bomb shelters, which is why Soviet Metro systems have always been classified as 'military objects' – something that can still cause problems should you want to take photographs in them, although the most opulent systems have reconciled themselves to the inevitable.

In Moscow's first line, opened in 1935, you can actually watch the Metro become less modernist and more classical, less lightweight and heavier, as you travel into the centre from the first station, Sokolniki, where thin, blue marble pillars still have some of the crystalline clarity of constructivism, through the classical halls of Krasnye Vorota, the Pantheon-like coffered space of Biblioteka imeni Lenina, the Egyptian-inspired columns of Kropotkinskaya, and ending with the art deco suavity of Park Kultury. Most of these stations had a grand entrance building and in some this was part of a clearly programmed journey. At Krasnye Vorota, Nikolai Ladovsky's shell-like avant-garde entrance was the mouth into which you descended, to find yourself in Ivan Fomin's underground hall, so full of red marble it can feel practically radioactive.

Spatially, some of these stations have similar proportions to those in Berlin, and most are reached by steps rather than long escalators. What was new, though, was the opulence of the facing materials, a dazzling showcase of rich surfaces. 'More marble', noted one historian, 'went into the stations of the first line than into all the palaces of the Tsar in the fifty years before the revolution.'[4] This was, of course, a matter of pride, but it was already possible to see that priorities were somewhat warped. The first line was built, as the great oppositionist Communist Victor Serge pointed out, without certain basic human necessities. Returning to the city after years in forced exile, and about to be expatriated to his native Belgium, he finds that while he's been in an unheated hut

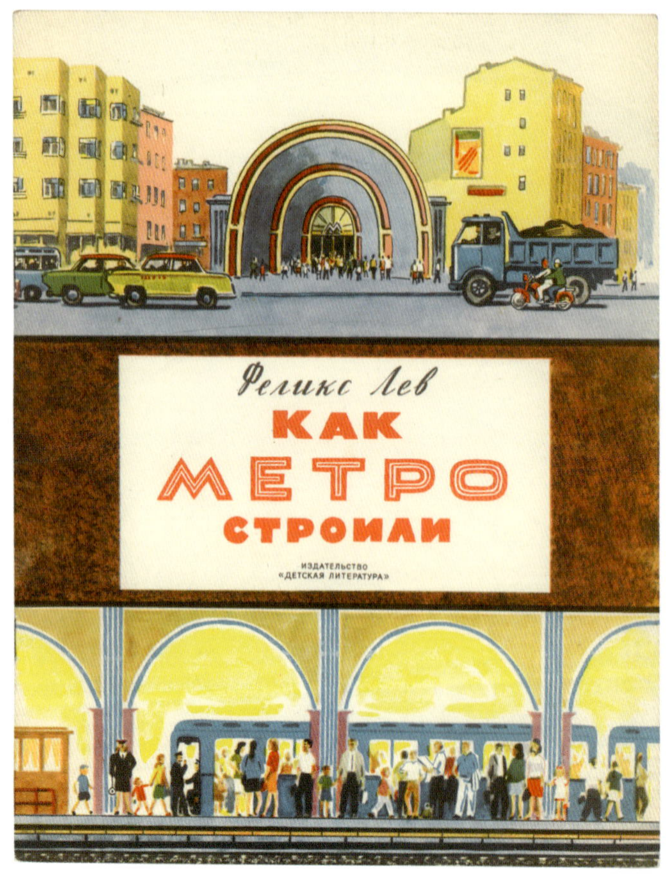

How the Metro Was Built, illustrated children's book, 1973

8

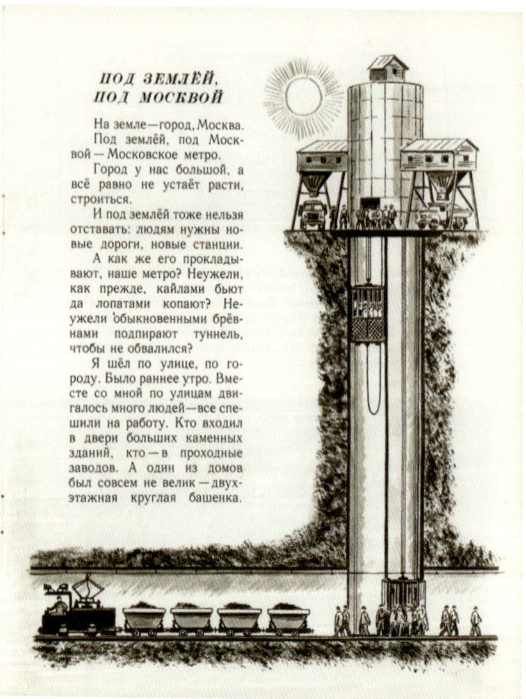

opposite *Metro*, illustrated children's book, 1957

without a toilet in Central Asia, they've built 'the luxurious Metro, with its granite paving, its walls of Ural stone, its exits, huge under-ground avenues – but without benches, and expensive. We know how to build subterranean palaces, but we forget that a working-class woman coming home from work would love to be able to sit down beneath all these rich-hued stones'.[5]

If the workers' experience was often ignored at this basic level, their contribution formed a central part of the propaganda associated with the Metro project. Komsomolskaya station featured a mosaic of enthusiastic young Metro builders. Books were published almost immediately – *Stories of Metro Builders* (1935), came out while the line was under construction; *How the Metro Was Built* (1935), followed when it opened. In these, according to the historian Tijana Vujosevic, 'the Metro was a magical, glorious and magnificent world, built by people whose fervour for labour was matched only by their fervour for beauty'. The peculiar combination of functional and fantastical means that 'prosaic passages with statistics and descriptions of construction operations are interrupted, as if by wells of electric light, by poetic descriptions of ecstatic experiences, of enchantment with the Metro's light and beauty'.[6] Escalators are referred to as 'living staircases' or the 'magic stairway'. In *How the Metro Was Built*, writers describe how the workers react as they visit their completed stations for the first time, on the night before they open. 'The builders, for whom the only thing left to do was to go to bed, could not take their eyes off their child', we are told; the workers 'loomed about, from corner to corner, caressing their well-made environment with their eyes'.[7] This was possible precisely because the Metro was not built on modernist lines. Each station used different marbles, each one had different decorative details – coffering, capitals, cartouches, finials, friezes, mosaics,

majolica, some of it traditional, much of it newly invented – so a worker could point and say, 'I did that', the opposite of the mechanised labour imagined by Soviet modernists.

But even here, there is a deeply sinister underside to the Soviet Underground, and it comes out especially in the work of the Metro's most talented designer, the Ukrainian architect Alexey Dushkin. On the first line, he designed what is now Kropotkinskaya, but was originally Palace of the Soviets, intended to serve a preposterous and never-built skyscraper

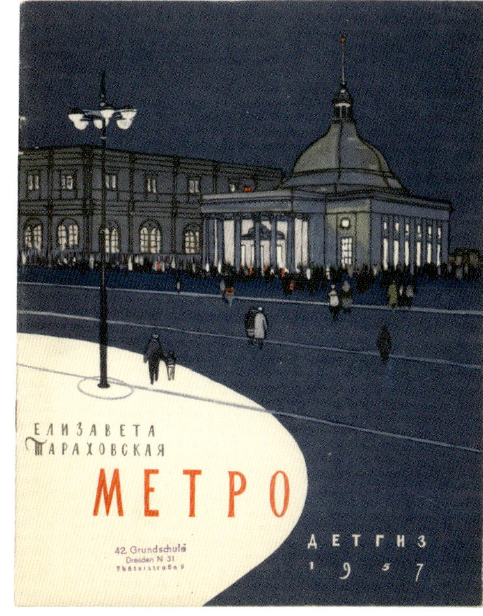

that was supposed to surpass New York's Empire State Building. When the project was shown off to the Party bosses, Stalin's right-hand man Lazar Kaganovich objected that the architects had, as Moscow Metro historians Egor Larichev and Anastasia Uglik put it, 'paraphrased the house of the Pharaohs, i.e. the Great Temple of Ammon at Karnak. But Dushkin denied the charge with words that have become a household phrase: "Their palaces are for Pharaohs, but ours are for the people."'[8] A lovely story – but there was much more happening in Dushkin's stations than this transvaluation of the architecture of power. This didn't just look like the architecture of the Pharaohs, it was built using their methods.

The story of the Metro from the perspective of its workers is one of staggering negligence towards the lives and livelihoods of its 'owners'. In Khrushchev's own account, the Metro was the future leader's baby, its construction enforced with the utmost brutality. Here, as Underground-railway historian Benson Bobrick puts it, 'negligence was sometimes perversely portrayed as heroic';[9] there were dozens of collapses, floods and fatal accidents, and after 1938 the Metro would be built in large part by prisoners. Workers were not the only problem. In a speech on the Metro's opening, Kaganovich complained of 'old-regime geology', which 'proved to be a pre-revolutionary part of the old regime, incompatible with the Bolsheviks, working against us.'[10]

Many stories of the Metro's construction feature accounts – often apocryphal – of the uncovering of horrifying remnants of the Russian past. In one tale, the builders of Ploshchad Revolyutsii – Revolution Square, just outside the Kremlin – excavate one of Ivan the Terrible's torture chambers. What isn't apocryphal is the panic that some of the station designs induced. In Dushkin's design for Ploshchad Revolyutsii,

sculptures of revolutionary figures by Matvei Manizer crouch in the arches between the main concourse and the platforms. Given that the Great Terror that began in 1937 was still raging, this was potentially a risky move. One of the many Metro stories that have something of urban myth about them describes the designers' terror of their work being interpreted as showing the Soviet people 'on their knees'. If so, what saved them was the realism of the monumental sculptures of revolutionaries, workers, peasants, sportsmen and sportswomen. Stalin apparently spent some time at the opening looking at and caressing Manizer's statues, murmuring: 'They look alive, almost alive'.[11]

In stations such as Kropotkinskaya, Ploshchad Revolyutsii and Mayakovskaya, Dushkin maintained the delicate balance between the demand for heroic revolutionary rhetoric and iconography and the expression of space and construction. Other architects, like Vladimir Shchuko and Vladimir Gelfriekh at Elektrozavodskaya (one of several superb stations opened during the war, when the Metro was used as a bomb shelter, as intended), also combined sculpture and space with great drama, creating atmospheric lighting effects that are as cinematic as they are religiose. That balance breaks down in two post-war projects that were intended to celebrate the glory of the Soviet state in its victory over Nazi Germany – the Circle Line of the Moscow Metro, and Line 1 of the new Leningrad Metro, both of which were being built right at the end of Stalin's reign and completed just after it, in 1954 and 1955 respectively; just in time, as we'll see.

Every station on the Circle Line and Leningrad's Line 1 tells a story, and some of them do so consecutively. Eventually, in both cases, an entire Metro line comprises one continuous epic, an awesome and terrifying propaganda blockbuster

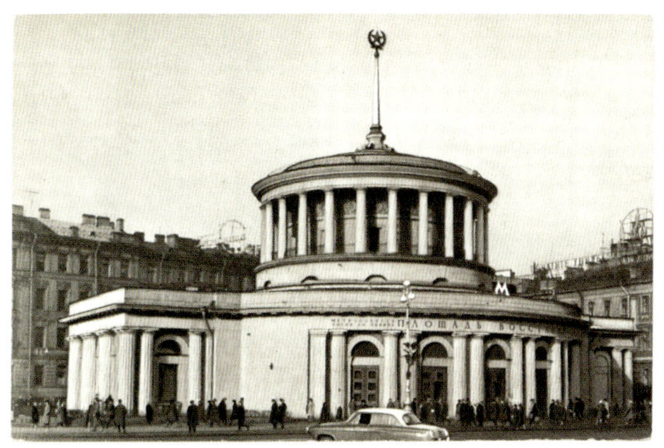

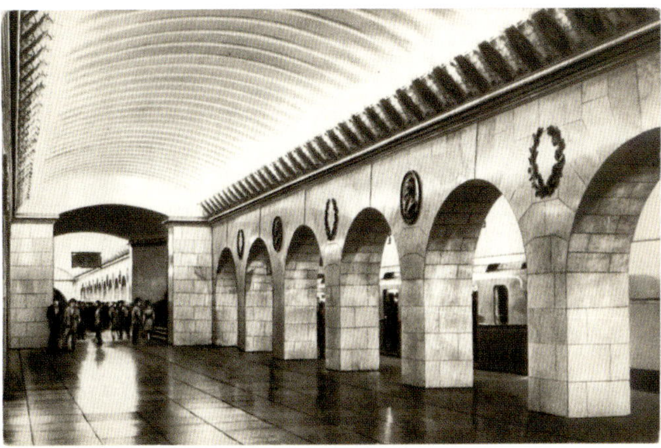

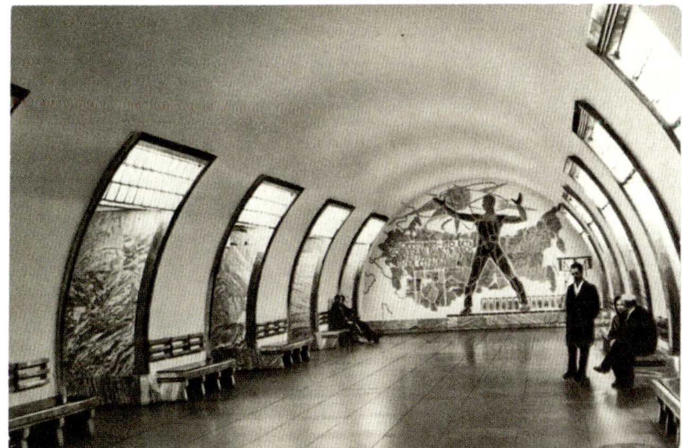

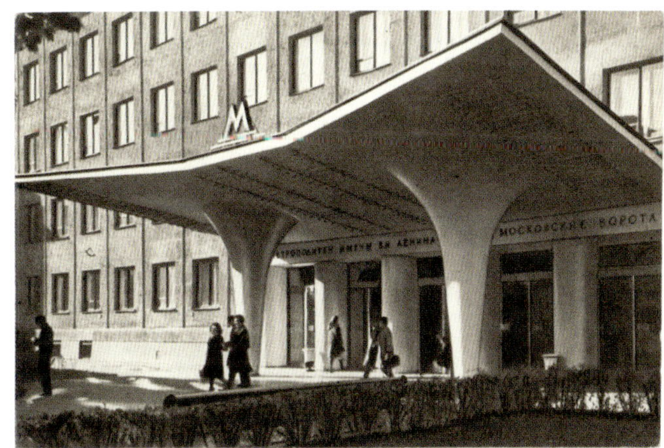

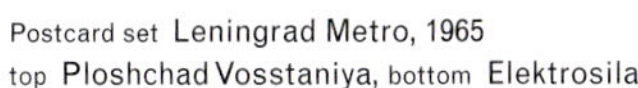
Postcard set Leningrad Metro, 1965
top Ploshchad Vosstaniya, bottom Elektrosila

top Tekhnologichesky Institut, bottom Moskovskiye Vorota

dripping with heroism, stupidity and kitsch. On the Moscow Circle Line, the ornamentation and elaboration in a station like Belorusskaya can be so intense that you might worry you'll fall over a sculpture or a mosaic – although at least by this point the architects had heeded Victor Serge's complaints and started to provide benches. Kievskaya, with its Renaissance mosaics, is intended to tell the story of Ukraine, and was the subject of a difficult competition, as Khrushchev decided various entries didn't 'express Ukraine'; Krasonopresnenskaya tells the story of the 1905 revolution, which was fought intensely in the area the station serves; Novoslobodskaya, in which Dushkin created one of his strangest grottoes, is lined with gold and punctuated with stained-glass panels depicting the sciences and professions, using glass taken from churches in newly annexed Latvia; Park Kultury has ceramic medallions showing sportsmen and women in Gorky Park; Oktyabrskaya treats of military victory, and is notorious for its end-of-hall motif of a blue sky beyond a closed gate; and the titan of all the stations, Komsomolskaya Koltsevaya, recounts the whole of Russian history up to the 1940s, in a gigantic hall intended to awe new arrivals from the three mainline railway stations above it.

Similarly, on Leningrad's Line 1, each station tells a propaganda tale in bronze, gold, mosaic and the usual polychrome marbles. In the city centre, Pushkinskaya focuses on the work and world of the national poet; Baltiiskaya uses icy marble, mosaic and ceramic to showcase the glories of the Soviet fleet; and Ploshchad Vosstaniya uses bronze medallions to tell the story of the October Revolution in Lives of the Saints style, right down to Lenin's nights in the wilderness of Finland. But the real drama is found in three stations of the industrial suburbs – Kirovsky Zavod (Kirov Factory), Narvskaya, and Avtovo. In Aleksandr Andreev's Kirovsky Zavod, the capitals of the pale-blue marble pylons are miniature metal sculptures based on the machinery and products of the factory it served, creating a weird and unique techno-classicism; the station above is a miniature Parthenon, a severe take on this 'Athens of the North'. Narvskaya, designed by David Goldgor, Sergei Sporansky and A. V. Vasiliyev, follows suit, with arched strips of electric lighting between red marble; each column features a highly detailed relief sculpture of working life in the district, one figure even carrying a model of the domed station above. But nothing can quite prepare you for the stupendous, stupefying Avtovo, famous for its colonnade of sculpted frosted glass. Yevgeny Levinson and Andrei Grushke reverse the way that the first Moscow stations used stone so light and ethereal it almost felt like glass; here, glass is used as if it were as heavy and thick as stone – but still translucent and opalescent. The effect is jaw-dropping, but walk to the end of the station hall and you'll see that after a while it stops, and the last columns are faced in a cream marble – marking the exact point when the effects of a sudden shift in Soviet design policy hit the station.

This book is not just about the famous, appalling, magnificent palaces of Stalinism, but about the entire life of the Soviet Metro, and here the story is much more complicated than conventional histories will tell you. Moscow-Metro historians Egor Larichev and Anastasia Uglik claim that all the stations built after 1954 were like 'two peas in a pod' until the Stalin style was fully revived in the 2003 station Park Pobedy. This, as we'll see, is far from the truth, but the Stalin style certainly came under heavy attack soon after the dictator's death. The historian Alexander Zmeul claims that within months architectural critics were denouncing the excess of the Circle Line stations, their denunciations given an official stamp by Khrushchev's decree a year later, condemning 'excess' and 'superfluous' detail in architecture, as the government finally decided to concentrate on human rather than purely propagandistic needs. And these needs were very great – in *An Economic History of the USSR* (1969), Alec Nove points out that in the years when 'Stalin seemed more concerned with prestige projects, such as the lavishly decorated Moscow underground railway, than with ordinary housebuilding or the maintenance and repair of existing houses', a full 5 per cent of Muscovites lived in kitchens and corridors, while 25.6 per cent occupied only part of a room.[12] Architects themselves were often the target of the shift away from excess, as the state was not liable to blame itself – in 1954, Leonid Polyakov was stripped of the Stalin Prize he had only just won for Oktyabrskaya station.[13]

The immediate consequence was that stations clearly designed as Stalin-era palaces were completed without the decorative details originally planned; VDNKh in Moscow or Ploshchad Lenina in Leningrad are the most obvious of these, with the grandeur in the space rather than the details. And from 1961 onwards, the many mosaics and statues of Stalin in the Metros of both cities were replaced, covered up or taken away. But the first genuinely new fruits of the official shift in architectural policy really were minimal, a Berlin-style U-Bahn that could have been built in the early 1930s if the vainglorious values of Stalinism had not got in the way. The tile- and marble-clad halls lined with columns of this era were known as 'centipedes' by Muscovites, and these too have their defenders. When I ask Moscow architecture critic Anna Shevchenko for her first memory of the Metro, she points out, 'I grew up outside the Moscow centre, and my first memories would be about the modernist stations of the Filyovskaya Line, built in the 1960s, with their open air, clean lines and glass entrances'; here she points to the modernist surface hall of Molodezhnaya, and in this book you'll find Leninsky Prospekt and Shabalovskaya provide examples. By comparison, she says, 'The stations of central Moscow seemed somehow excessive and foreign', and notes with regret that the stations of the Filyovskaya Line are currently being renovated to make them more in keeping with the bombast of the city centre, through 'the thoughtless addition of cheesy patriotic paintings'.

It was actually Leningrad that managed to create a new style to express the modernism of the 'Thaw', both technologically and architecturally. Line 2, opened in the early 1960s, mostly in the city's Stalin-era Moscow District, is marked by features like the expressive concrete entrance to Moskovskiye Vorota, with its flying wings, and several increasingly modernist decorative mosaics; and Line 3, opened in the mid-1960s, has a series of central stations, like Lomonosovskaya and Mayakovskaya, that pioneered the automatic platform doors found decades later in ultra-modern systems like Seoul or London's Jubilee Line (where they're known by the macabre name 'suicide doors', designed to make sure there's never 'a person under a train'). But rather than today's glass screens, Line 3's doors are heavy metal shutters, opening and slamming closed between marble pillars. This was quite an engineering achievement in the 1960s, and it helps to explain the iron messages on the pillars of the interchange at Tekhnologicheskiy Institut station, celebrating the progress of automation. Subsequently, many Metro lines worldwide, from Warsaw to Calcutta, would be engineered by the city's Metro design institute, Lenmetrogipotrans.

But then, in 1970, yet another shift occurred. Again, Aleksandr Zmeul argues, it starts with an attack in an architecture journal, *Arkhitektura Moskvy*, harshly criticising the 'centipedes' of Moscow's suburban extensions; following this, an official decree condemns the lack of 'individuality' and local specificity of recent stations, and then a move starts with central stations Kuznetsky Most and Pushkinskaya towards a 'third way' between industrial standardisation and 1930s-style grandeur. This is how Moscow Metro stations have been built until very recently, with halls as late as the 2000s and the 2010s (Rimskaya, or Dostoevskaya) being semi-ironic but still deeply atmospheric continuations of Dushkin's subterranean marble grottoes. As we'll see, the advances in Metro design were by this point actually coming from outside Moscow, but their innovations were having an effect in the capital. This could lead to major incongruities, as dramatic stations serve very undramatic districts. Hamid Ismailov's narrator describes one of the most puzzling of these, Chertanovskaya, in the distant high-rise suburbs stretching for miles in the city's south. Ismailov describes it as:

> 'one of the rare stations not executed in the image of the columnar T or the parade of the Grecian pi. No, this station is unique, not mass made; it is stylish, special. I would have called it Snow Queen Station ... look at the noble coldness of the icy flooring, the crystalline embrace of the pillars, the hanging stalactite lamps – and all on a sultry summer's day!'

But this sense of arrival and anticipation is deceptive. 'Step outside, and you'll wonder what happened to that feeling. You'll find yourself in a normal Moscow suburb. It could be Teplii Stan or Altufyevo, Yugo-Zapadnaya, Yasenevo or Belyayevo.'[14] If these halls were once meant to be anterooms on the way to the future, triumphal portals showing the path to Communism, now the incongruities and gaps could no longer be ignored.

The Thaw Under the Surface
Kyiv, Tbilisi

The Moscow Metro's nationalist, imperial display was intended to represent the whole of the USSR, and there are references to the other Republics scattered all across the network. In a 1938 guide to the Moscow Metro, Egor Abakumov observes that 'thirteen different kinds of marble were used in the six stations of the Gorky Street [i.e. Line 2, including Ploshchad Revolyutsii and Mayakovskaya] line alone ... these marbles come from the Urals and Armenia, the Far East and Georgia, Uzbekistan and Siberia'.[15] The names of the marbles and other minerals used reveal their exotic provenance – Ufalei, Biryuk-Yankoy, Gazgan, Nizhny Tagil, onyx, porphyry. The first two lines to be built outside Russia, however, marked, at least at first, a sudden reduction in all of this sinister glamour. They would also be the first lines largely built after 1953, and hence 'clean', without Gulag labour; in terms of their extent, only Kyiv would come to rival that of the two Russian capitals. But in Kyiv, their story– initial grandeur gradually replaced with functionality – is totally reversed.

The Kyiv Metro, like Leningrad's, was an extremely demanding engineering task, with the boggy geology and archaeological complexity compounded by the city's unusual relief, with much of the historic centre standing on very high ground above a lower town on the riverside, and with the wide Dnieper river between. Because of this, the escalators were especially deep, often with domed underground anterooms lined with benches in between, as if to allow anyone exhausted by the journey to take an escalator break. The domes were often constructed outside in concrete before being literally sunk into the clay. From Arsenalna, still the deepest Underground station in the world, trains surge out

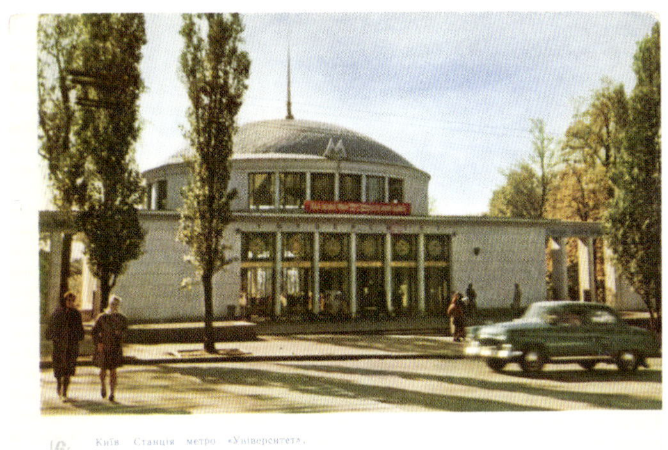

Postcard **Universitet**, Kyiv, 1963

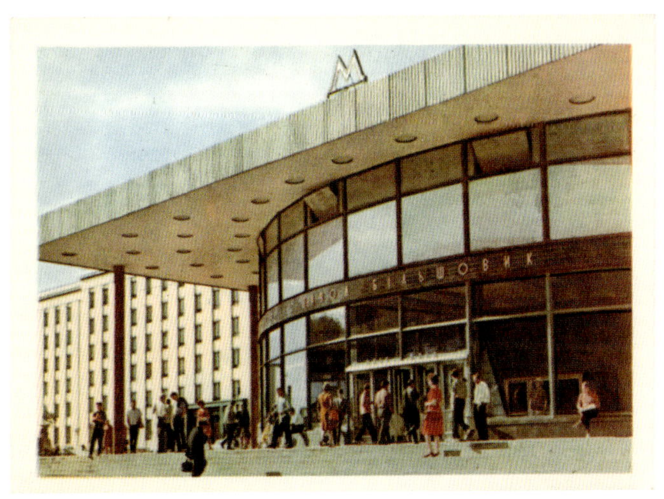

Postcard **Zavod Bolshevik**, Kyiv, 1960s

of a cave to reach the next station, Dnipro, on a two-level bridge over the river. For all this engineering melodrama, the actual stations opened in 1960 are relatively restrained.

Although Kyivites are liable to ask if you've been to Moscow when you express enthusiasm for their Metro, the extent to which the system was 'reduced' shouldn't be exaggerated – compared with anything in the West, it is staggeringly grand. The first line, from Vokzalna to Dnipro, has several stations that are obviously pared-down subterranean palaces, and some of the station entrances are still just as grand as anything in Moscow or Leningrad. Universitet and Vokzalna have heavy baroque buildings on the surface; and underneath, what were clearly once Circle Line/Leningrad Line 1 epics have been finished with relatively rudimentary chandeliers and bronze scenes of revolutionary actions (in Vokzalna, these depict both Cossacks and Communists); at Arsenalna, the budget was cut so severely that there is actually no central hall at all, like an ordinary London or Paris station. There is a partial exception at Universitet, where a lush red-marble hall with a terrazzo floor features inset busts of great scientists and writers – and there are the first signs of modernism reaching transport architecture, with the 'UFO' rotunda entrance to Kreschatyk, and the brutalist concrete stairwells at Dnipro, topped with a woman releasing doves and a man releasing Sputnik. The quickly opened first extension goes further with this, with the atomic-age mosaic at the polychrome-tiled Shuliavska (originally, Zavod Bolshevik), and the woman with Sputnik at Politekhnichnyi Institut.

After that, in Kyiv the 1970s were what the 1960s were to Moscow – 'centipedes', a 'normal' Metro. And then the shift announced in 1970 affected Kyiv much more than it did Moscow, with truly epic results – it could be said that the

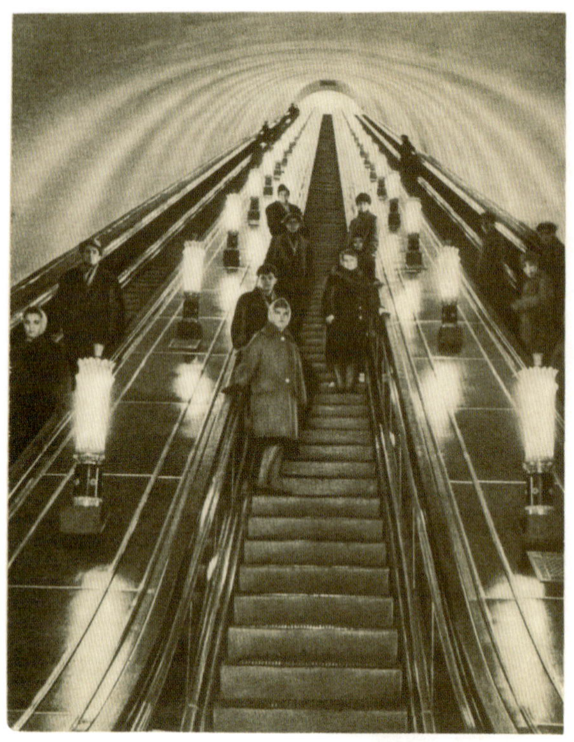

above and opposite **Kyiv Metro booklet**, 1961

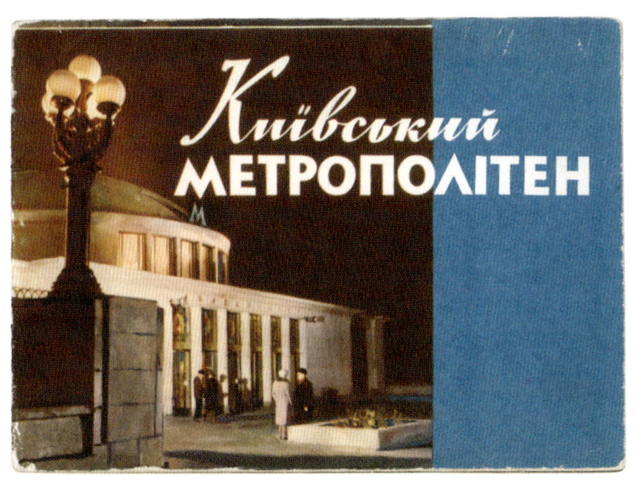

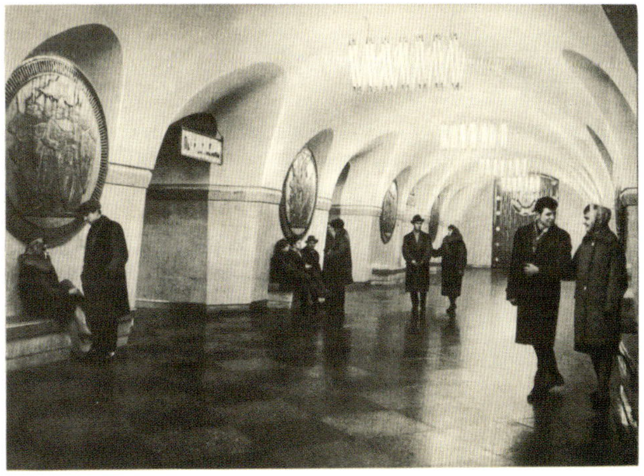

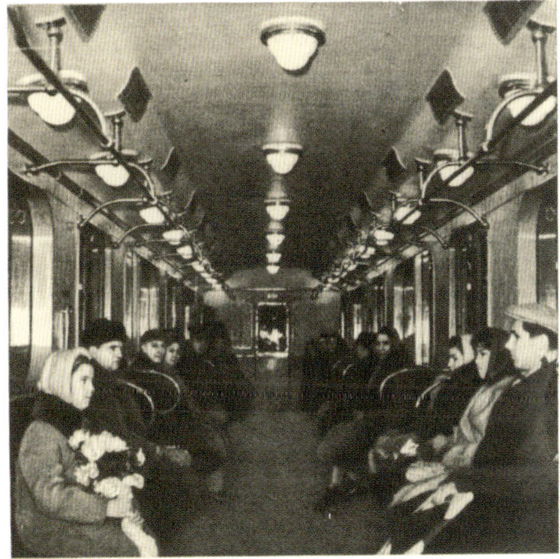

'1930s' happened in the Kyiv Metro in the 1980s. The partly opened Line 2 was extended with huge marble halls in which classicism and futurism are intermingled, like Lybidska (originally Dzherzhinska, after the KGB's founder), Olimpiiska, and the remarkable Palats Ukraina, designed like most of Kyiv's best stations by the team of Nikolai Alyoshkin, Tamara Tselikovskaya and Anatoly Krushinsky, and opened in 1984. This was built as Red Guard Station, and that's the theme of the decoration, with hammers and sickles and a revolutionary in mosaic at the end of the hall. But there's more – the free-flying modernist polygons that line the walls, created by the artist Stepan Kirichenko, resemble a tribute to Kasimir Malevich, the avant-garde painter who was born and raised in Kyiv. For the film-maker and writer Oleksiy Radynski, this represents 'the dialectical battle between the artistic avant-garde and Stalinism', as 'pure geometric forms, borrowed from El Lissitzky's "Beat the Whites with the Red Wedge" attack from all sides the gigantic socialist realist figure of a Red Army soldier'.[16] Another battle altogether can be found in Line 3. There are several impressive stations here, but the most famous is Zolotie Vorota, opened in 1989 outside the Golden Gate, one of the few survivals of the capital of Kyivan Rus', the cradle of Russian as well as Ukrainian civilisation. It is a shimmering tribute to the Byzantine architecture of that medieval state, with no attempt to tack on a Soviet theme. Looking at Zolotie Vorota, it's not so surprising that independence would follow soon after it opened.

As in Moscow, at first Metro design seems to have been totally unaffected by the empire's fall, with stations like Vydubichi and Slavutych (both of which you can find in this book) displaying a futuristic hauteur that quite clearly comes from the space-age optimism of earlier decades rather than the chaotic realities of the 1990s. And, again as in Moscow, those stations that were not already under construction when the USSR collapsed, like the double-level arcades and atomic chandeliers of Akademmistechko (2003), or the wide-arched spaces of Vystavkovyi Tsentr (2010), are hard to see as particularly post-Soviet, given that they were planned before 1989 and designed by the same team that had produced the epics of the 1980s. Here, if in few other places, the continuities of Soviet life in post-independence Ukraine can seem fairly positive. This is not a popular opinion.

One 1980s' station that became especially notorious here during the Maidan uprising of 2013–14 was Teatralna (originally Lenina), a station – not the only one in the USSR – dedicated to the thoughts and works of V. I. Lenin, with quotations in Ukrainian and Russian on either side and a giant bust at the centre, all in bronze, in a station of red and black marble. Lenin and the quotes were quietly removed in late 2013 out of fear that, with the fall of a nearby Lenin monument, Kyiv's last, the station would be vandalised; and in any case a law of 2015 on the 'de-Communisation' of public space in Ukraine would have made it illegal. Currently, the Kyiv Metro is a battleground for de-Communisation, with law and activism meeting preservation and commerce. In the end, it is hard to tell which is more damaging – the removal of various artworks from the stations, or their covering with advertisements, from large corporations and banks in the halls, from smaller businesses in the trains.

I asked Radynski if he granted much significance to the 'reduced' design of the Kyiv system, and whether or not this had much effect on its poor maintenance. He replied, 'I certainly do – however, I guess the omnipresence of ads in the Kyiv Metro has much more to do with barbaric business practices and a lack of restrictions on ads generally', which are draped across public buildings throughout the Ukrainian capital. And as he points out, the Metro stations of the 1980s, which have the full panoply of sculpture, mosaic and marble, are 'as covered with ads as the reduced ones'. Meanwhile, the lack of both finance and esteem for public spaces has meant that 'Soviet Metro stations are being redesigned in quite appalling ways, and this is not always related to de-Communisation *per se*', as at the redesign of Livoberezhna station. 'The obvious fact that stations need to be renovated at least once in several decades is used as a pretext for covering them in plastic while removing the ceramic reliefs and so on'. According to his argument, de-Communisation is just one of many forces gradually whittling away the grandeur of these civic spaces. 'Most of the surviving de-Communised artworks in Kyiv Metro are secure as long they are covered with white cardboard as a means of "soft" De-Communisation', he says. The Malevichian Red Guard at Palats Ukraina was simply 'hidden by the Metro administration rather than destroyed, as if they're waiting for these dark times to be over sooner or later'. The process is by definition endless 'in order to fully de-Communise the Soviet Metro, one would have to fill the tunnels and stations with soil'. Meanwhile, an extension promised since the 1990s founders on the stalled construction of the Podilsky Bridge over the Dnieper. The city's official population is just under 3 million, but unofficial estimates put it at 5 million, and the system can barely cope; as with St Petersburg, for all the grandeur, there are far too few stations for a city of this size. The bridge, says Radynski, 'would, at least in theory, make it possible to build the fourth Metro line', and the Mayor, Vitali Klitschko, who Radynski refers to as 'the Boxer', is 'now talking about launching the motorway part of the bridge first, and completing the Metro part "later" – in how many decades, no one knows.'

Curiously, Kyiv actually had a precedent for the radical de-Communisation of its Metro system, one that it has strangely ignored. After the 'Rose Revolution' of 2003 and especially the short war with Russia over the breakaway Georgian province of South Ossetia in 2008, public space in Tbilisi, the Georgian capital, was radically denuded of any remaining Lenins, revolutionary scenes, red stars, hammers and sickles – and the Tbilisi Metro had a fair few, since stripped out (the paradox that Georgia continued to have the last Stalin statues in the world is part of another story). But there was always less to take out here anyway; as in Kyiv, the Tbilisi system was the victim of Khrushchev's paring back of prestige projects. In his dictated memoir, Khrushchev points out that the construction of both was under way when he came to power, but he cut them back radically to pay for the social programmes neglected by Stalin, and, of course, to pay for all the rockets needed to compete in the nuclear-arms race with the United States. Most of Line 1, opened in 1966, lacks the pomp of Moscow, the futurism of Leningrad's Lines 2 and 3, or the residual grandeur of Kyiv's Line 1. What you have, in the stations dedicated to the epic poet Shota Rustaveli or the avant-garde theatre director Konstantin Marjanishvili, are simple marble halls with small relief sculptures. The bust of Marjanishvili is now a lone floating disembodied head; the revolutionary quotation that once featured beneath him has disappeared.

Some of this changed in the short second line, opened in 1979; at Technical University station, for instance, a pulsating multicoloured mosaic by Radish Tordia, Iden Tabidze and Apolon Kharebava shows off to full effect the remarkable part-Mexican muralist, part-Soviet avant-garde public sculptural reliefs so common in Georgia; and at Gurmagele station a bas-relief depicts the Metro's builders, lucky escapees from the de-Communisation laws (both stations are in this book). But much of the more interesting architecture in Tbilisi's early stations is on the surface rather than under the ground, where the budget cuts were much less decisive. So Rustaveli has a stone entrance pavilion in a wonderful invented ancient futurist style with mock-historical reliefs that one could call biblical brutalism, and at the slightly later Isani, designed by G. Modzamanishvili and N. Lomasadze and opened in 1971, there is a delicate shell construction in the shape of a concrete oyster. If all things were well, this would also have been included in this book, but Isani has been horrendously defaced with the cheapest opaque glass, making the delicacy of its design completely invisible.

In the de-Communisation of the Tbilisi Metro, it has been hard to separate ideology from material cheapening, with plastic, video screens and adverts liberally slathered over most of the stations in the 2006–07 renovation. However, no doubt many citizens of the Georgian capital would consider this a major improvement – in the 1990s, as war and economic collapse plunged Georgia into deep poverty, and even electricity became scarce underground, many questioned whether it would be possible to maintain the Metro at all. But I learned something about both Tbilisi people's politeness and the status of its Metro when I went to look at a mosaic in one station, and was usefully told 'the entrance is the other way'.

National in Form, Metropolitan in Content
Tashkent, Baku

Compared with the Metro in nearby Tbilisi, the Baku Metro, opened not long after in 1967, was architecturally much more ambitious, and with much more in the way of mosaics, gilding and general bling. This may have had something to do with the particular status of the majority-Muslim Soviet Republics in the architectural culture of the USSR. The art historian Boris Chukhovich, who was raised in the Uzbek capital, Tashkent, describes this phenomenon as a 'made-in-Moscow national style', where Moscow-trained – or often, just Russian – architects would be 'inspired' by the motifs of medieval architecture in the cities of the Soviet 'East', and would use them as appliqué decoration on what were otherwise quite standardised buildings. With a few exceptions, he argues that 'this "Modernism of the periphery"' was unable to extricate itself from 'the ancient Orient' as a place of reference.[17] Of course, the same could have been said about the auto-Orientalising of much of the Moscow Metro's architecture, which by the 1950s could verge on a sort of Ivan the Terrible despotic cosplay (built, of course, by a very real despotism), but here, in addition, imperial dynamics were brought to bear. If the relationship of Russia to Ukraine and Belarus could be said to resemble that of England to Scotland and Wales (and at worst, to Ireland), the relationship of Tsarist Russia to Central Asia and the Caucasus was colonial in a very similar way to that between the United Kingdom and India or Nigeria. The USSR repealed racial laws and promoted indigenous cadres to leading positions, but nobody doubted where the 'centre' and 'periphery' were located.

In Baku, 'inspiration' could come from the historic architecture of its old town, most of whose mosques, bathhouses, inns and fortress walls were built during its time as a Persian port city; later, in Tashkent, it could equally emerge from the exquisitely decorated Timurid architecture constructed when nearby Samarkand was the centre of Tamerlane's huge pan-Asian empire, much of which still survived in the Soviet Uzbek capital. That noted, some of the first stations opened in Baku in 1967 took the recent Soviet past, rather than anything more ancient, as their inspiration. Ganjlik station is a straightforward imitation of Dushkin's Pharaonic Kropotkinskaya, which the Baku station's Russian architects perhaps considered an apt return of a design originally taken from the Middle East. Somewhat more convincingly specific to the city was the Azerbaijani architect Mikeil Useinov's design for Narimonov station, with tall golden columns and Orientalist lotus-like capitals. This

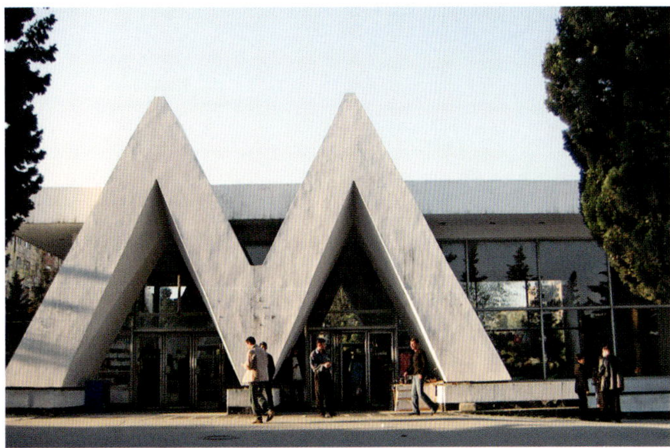

Memar Ecemi (formerly Mikrorayon), Baku, 1985

would be the model for later stations, particularly in the second line – as at Nizami, with its mosaics taken from works by the medieval poet Nizami Ganjavi, in the high, elegant columns and latticework lanterns of Z. Guliyeva's 1985 Inshaatchilar station, and the faceted gold colonnades of Khalglar Dostlugu (Friendship of Nations) station, opened in 1989. This flamboyance has, as in Moscow and Kyiv, been continued in recently opened stations, albeit with a certain luxury-shopping-mall shininess.

If Baku is richly decorated, then Tashkent is something else entirely – the most opulent of all the systems outside Moscow and Leningrad. This has been hard to document, especially since Uzbekistan's independence in the 1990s under the particularly authoritarian government of Islam Karimov; very few pictures of the system were published outside

Uzbekistan itself until a strictly enforced ban on photography was lifted in 2018. Now (as you can find here), it's possible to see what extraordinary things have been built beneath the city. These range from filigree Orientalist fantasies like Mustaqilik Maidoni (originally opened in 1977 as Lenin Square, designed by L. Adamov, A. Adilova, S. Adipov and L. N. Popov) and the intersecting Timurid domes of J. Mansurov's Alisher Navoi, along with more typical Soviet futurism, in the space-themed Kosmonavtilar, designed by S. Styagin and S. Sokolov and opened in 1984. The sheer size and richness of these stations are reminders that Tashkent was the fourth largest city in the USSR, after Moscow, Leningrad and Kyiv – a hugely important metropolis and a deliberately conceived model for visitors from post-colonial countries, showing what Soviet-style socialism could do for them.

Stagnation and Futurism
Kharkiv, Yerevan

In terms of construction rather than imagery, the most innovative systems built during the long Brezhnev era were in Ukraine and Armenia – that is, in the one-time Soviet Ukrainian capital, Kharkiv, opened in 1975, and in the Armenian capital, Yerevan, opened in 1981. Kharkiv radically changed how stations were built underground – and Yerevan did the same above ground, transforming entrances into magical multi-level squares. Both systems were the result of a decision made in the 1960s that any city with a population of one million would get a Metro to go along with the more workaday trams and trolleybuses. This ruling was, of course, open to abuse, given that statistics were a somewhat moveable feast in the Soviet Union. And belying the official designation under Gorbachev of the 1970s and early 1980s as 'the age of stagnation', the stations were often colourful, futuristic and sometimes outright individualist.

Kharkiv's contribution to Metro design – global, as it has been imitated far and wide – came in the 'Kharkiv type' of station hall, where an enormous continuous-span single vault is scooped out of the earth using a simple cut-and-cover technique, and is then secured with a steel armature between ground surface and construction. The great spaces created by this method can be found all over the Kharkiv system, and they would be imitated in Moscow, Tashkent, Kyiv and elsewhere by the start of the 1980s, and in Warsaw and Sofia in the 1990s. In a pamphlet published to accompany the opening of the system's second line in the mid-1980s, it is noted that 'the stations are characterised by their free space, colourful design of the interior, abundance of light and air', but that didn't mean there wasn't room for ideology

– 'the ideological and artistic decoration reflect the great revolutionary and fighting traditions of the city and its present day labour rhythm … the level of comfort of the Metro influences not only the passengers' mood, but their process of production and social activity'.[18] This Pavlovian claim points to the strange intensity of the Kharkiv Metro, the most Tarkovskyesque of all the systems, with many stations like miniature, subterranean spacecraft from *Solaris* (1972).

As well as the single-span vaults that were invented here, the Kharkiv-based architectural historian Ievgeniia Gubkina points to the importance of the 'complexity, as in "as a complex"' of the Kharkiv Metro's designs, the first to be clearly conceived as a coherent whole since the 1950s. 'All the three Metro lines are composed into an ensemble, where each line has its own stylistics'. It does this without reproducing Stalinist aesthetics: 'its asceticism and elegant restraint are the opposite of Moscow Metro pomposity'. It tells stories, still, but more subtly. Gubkina sees them as 'first and foremost a reflection of the era of "developed socialism"', as it was called in the Brezhnev period, when most problems had allegedly been solved. 'Some stations are distinctive by their imaginative solutions', she points out. 'For example, Moskovsky Prospect interprets the industrial landscape above the station. Zavod Malysheva reveals the topic of military production; but Sportyvna made by Plaksiev is the best of all', with 'its art deco citations, precise use of materials, high-quality implementation, and technological innovation'. You can find all these in this book, as well as several examples from the second part of the system, where the wide spans were supplemented with stations lined with radiant blue ceramics, weird, curvaceous directional signs and organic chandeliers, as at Universitet and Akademika Barabashova. At the astounding Akademika

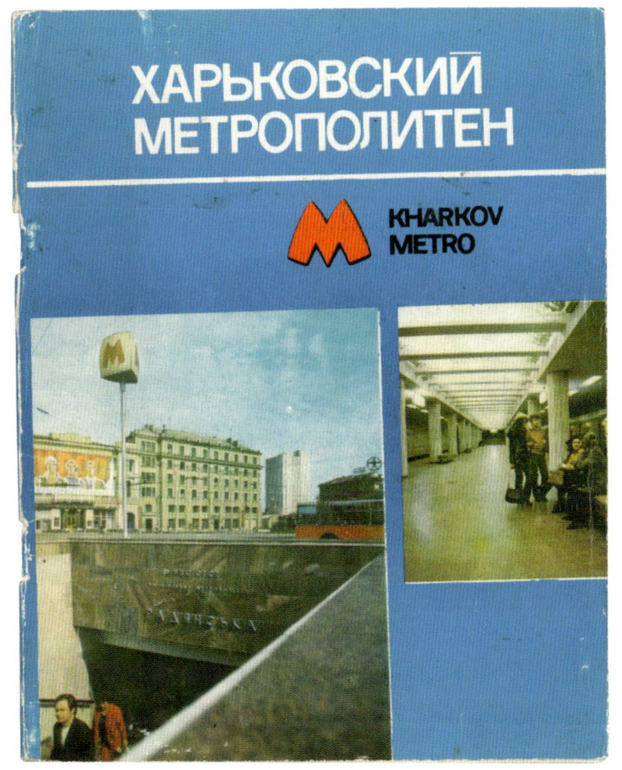

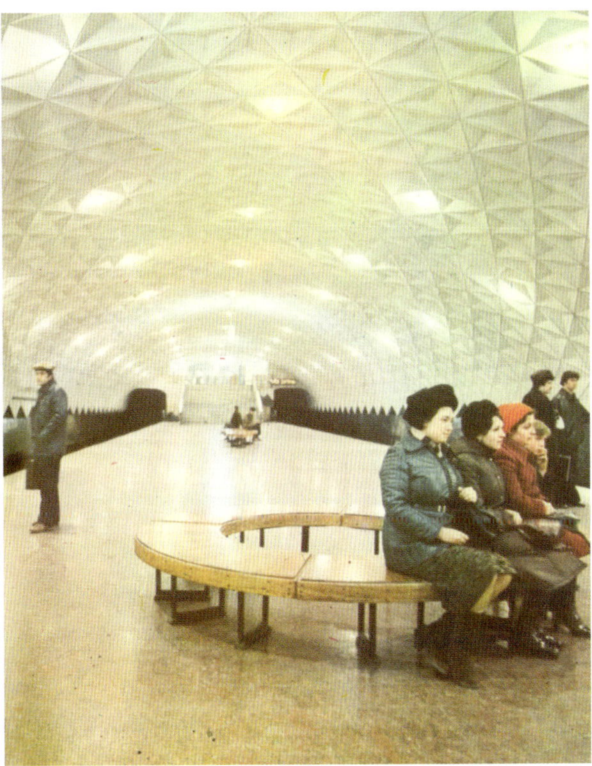

Kharkiv Metro booklet, 1980
right Sportyvna, Kharkiv

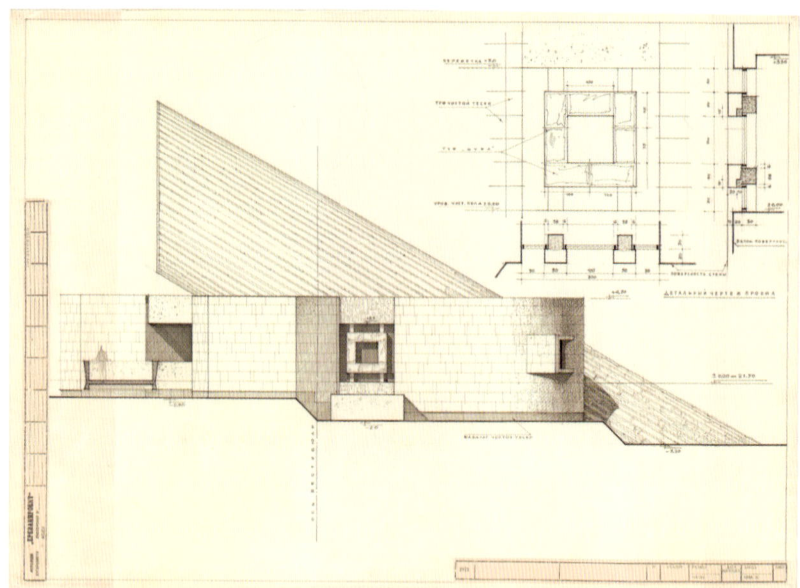

Design drawing by Stepan Kyurkchyan for Yeritasardakan, 1980

design elements', which have happened alongside the usual 'chaotic advertising' randomly applied to stations. 'The biggest enemy of our Metro is, above all, corruption and the market'. Even so, she still reckons that the Kharkiv Metro is 'the main pride of Kharkivites', alongside the immense KhTZ tractor works and Derzhprom, its internationally significant constructivist government centre. The decision to build it was always perceived by Kharkivites as the victory of Kharkiv and Kharkivites in the 'competition' of cities in the USSR, an achievement for which she gives much of the credit to the city's planner at the time, Viktor Antonov.

Pavlova station, designed by A. Z. Denisenko, V. A. Spivachuk and P. G. Chechelnitsky, these are combined with the wide spans, and the effect is as redolent of much of H. R. Giger's work on *Alien* (1979), as it is of Tarkovsky's *Solaris*.

Unlike the Kyiv system, Kharkiv's Metro has been only lightly de-Communised, with just the station names being changed – something that happened in Kyiv in the early 1990s. 'Much more harmful', Gubkina points out, have been the 'unprofessional repairs, changes in materials and

By any definition an impressive job was done – Kharkiv, a city of 1.4 million people, has three Metro lines, the same number as Kyiv, which at the lowest estimate has twice, and probably more than three times the population, although Kyiv has built much longer extensions to its lines. The Yerevan Metro has just the one short line for its 1.1 million people, and it had to resort to impressive levels of skulduggery to get it built at all. It is often claimed that in the early 1970s the city council, hosting a visit of the Ministry of Transport from Moscow to assess the city – which had not then reached the million mark – took drastic measures to make sure they got the money and the go-ahead to build. They organised the buses and cajoled their drivers to create massive traffic jams to convince the Moscow bureaucrats that a Metro was needed, and fast. I first heard this anecdote from the critic Ruben Arevshatyan, who confirms its authority: 'I have heard it from my father, and he was one of the organizers of those jams, working by that time at the architectural department of Yerevan Municipality. Other architects and urban planners from that period have also confirmed this story when I was doing the research interviews for *Soviet Modernism*' (which resulted in a book and exhibition, held in Vienna in 2013).

What little Metro architecture there is in Yerevan is made up for by its extreme individuality, particularly in two surface stations that have been treated as entire urban microcosms in themselves. The most central station in Yerevan is Republic Square, designed by Jim Torosyan and Mkrtich Minasyan, which opened in 1981. Underneath is an impressive hall of the 1970s' Moscow type, with a jagged and curved series of arches between the concourse and the platforms, and elegant expressionistic chandeliers. But above is something else. There are two layers; at the top is a canopy described by Tigran Hartunyan in his book on the city, as 'a flower made from orange tuff', with a spreading pale-stone fountain forming another flower underneath, a layered effect that 'cannot be appreciated from a human scale',[19] but only from

the upper levels of the buildings around, or, as you'll see, in the photographs in this book. This creates a much-needed and very popular shady public space in this dry southern city – at the time of writing, part of it is used as 'Damascus', a market run by refugees from the war in nearby Syria. Yeritasardakan ('Youth') station is similarly striking, though completely different in its approach. Designed by Stepan Kyurkchyan, it also opened in 1981, but here everything focuses on a large tilted tubular lightwell, with its windows arranged as a Metro 'M', looking right on to the long escalators below. If Republic Square is 'national', freely modelled on motifs from historic Armenian architecture, Yeritasardakan is wholly invented and purely modernist, though both share a spatial flamboyance.

Arevshatyan explains these differences not by something in Soviet Metro design itself, but in the very particular form of local modernism Armenian architects had developed in the Soviet period. 'The architecture in Yerevan and other cities of Armenia has been always distinct, even in different periods of Soviet history. That was conditioned by specific cultural as well as political premises, related to the development of a distinct national language in architecture'. He places these stations as part of a 'particularly intensive wave' in Soviet Armenian architecture, comparable to works like the Komitas Chamber Music Theatre, and the hillside 'Cascade', built during the 1970s and 1980s. 'Of course', he reminds me, 'this was related to the USSR's centre-periphery dynamics, but you should regard those dynamics through a much more complex prism – not black and white'. Those complexities, where the 'peripheral' Republics would attempt to carve out their own identities and locally Soviet, locally modern design cultures, are written across these Metro stations; the dynamics would fray as the 1980s went on.

From Acceleration to Collapse
Minsk, Volgograd, Nizhny Novgorod, Krivyi Rih, Samara, Novosibirsk, Yekaterinburg, Dnipro

The 1980s actually saw more Metro construction in the Soviet Union than any other decade – eight Metros were either completed or substantially built. They are relatively unknown compared with those we've encountered so far, perhaps because the Soviet system ended so soon after and they had no time to become either objects of local pride or state propaganda before all they stood for was discredited. They are also all relatively pared-down, as the Cold War detente of the 1970s, when most of them were planned, meant that they no longer had to be laid out as nuclear shelters with super-deep escalators. Extra decoration is mainly limited to walls, especially just above the stairwells into the main halls. But they have their own particular delights, with extensive use of the single-vault 'Kharkiv type'. One of the most coherently conceived of these systems opened in 1984 in Minsk, the Belarusian capital. According to Minsk architectural historian Dimitrij Zadorin, the distinctiveness of the Minsk Metro is subtle, but easily spotted – it is 'unified by the abundance of white colour into a kind of ensemble titled "White Russia"', the literal meaning of 'Belarus'. The result is 'uniform in quality', with 'neither masterpieces or faceless solutions, which is why each station deserves special attention'.[20] Typically, Soviet planning ideas have been maintained in the Minsk Metro's recent extensions, as have some of the practices – while in Moscow's Ploshchad Revolyutsii the nose of a bronze police dog was worn shiny by people rubbing it for luck, here the same is true of the bust of Lenin in the most central station, Ploshchad Lenina. Minsk is also relatively extensive for a 1980s system, with two long lines and a third nearly complete.

This is also the case in Russia's third largest city, Novosibirsk; this easternmost of Soviet Metros, opened in 1986, cleaves to the 1980s' Metro type, but has impressive murals and reliefs in its relatively simple stations.

Krivyi Rih, a steel town in south-eastern Ukraine, and the southern Russian city of Volgograd (still better known abroad as Stalingrad) both built combined 'Metro-Trams' in the mid-1980s – a rather successful model in terms of passenger use and extent, similar to the flexible 'Karlsruhe system' of tram-trains used widely in Germany, and in British cities such as Edinburgh, Manchester and Sheffield. But unlike these, it combines its segregated and street-running track with full-scale single-span underground stations in the Kharkiv mould; Krivyi Rih's subterranean stations are especially spacious and atmospheric. By contrast, full Metros have often underperformed. In 1985, Nizhny Novgorod – then named Gorky, after the writer – and in 1987, Samara – then Kuibyshev, after a Stalinist leader – both built short, single lines that were only extended decades later.

Samara is probably the richer of the two in design terms. The shimmering sky-blue cosmic murals and organic globular columns make Gagarinskaya one of the weirdest of all Metro stations (designed by A. N. Panin, it was part of a short 1993 extension). At Nizhny Novgorod, there is some interest in the murals and reliefs, and some vast Kharkivian halls, like Leninskaya and Chkalovskaya, but the wider project was clearly a failure. Kirill Kobrin, prolific author and editor of the journal *Emergency Rations*, grew up in the Avtozavod district of the city, which was initially almost all the Metro served – in an interesting reversal of much Western planning, the line taking the residents of a working-class housing estate into town opened first, with the rest to follow (it didn't). He points out that, while 'the initial idea was to construct in the next two to three years a line crossing the Oka river, from Avtozavod to the city centre, it happened only thirty years after that. The first line connected Avtozavod with the main train station and was pretty useless because people from this part of the city travelled outside Gorky pretty rarely – I have never seen this line crowded'. It happened to open 'on the very historical threshold between "stagnation" and *Perestroika*', a period when the old certainties were just starting to crumble. So 'when the Metro was opened, the authorities tried to sex up the event and organised a "people's competition" asking Gorkovites to write a song about the new Metro, a sort of anthem'. At the time, Kobrin was in a post-punk band, and they contributed the following song, solely in order to 'undermine the pompous propaganda rubbish':

'We dig a hole beneath the Earth
From Avtozavod to the train station.
To let a Worker dash as a rocket,
Invisibly and invincibly,
To let a Worker travel to his holiday destination.
To let the collective farmer bring to the market,
Stinking fruits of Mother Earth.'

They did not win the competition.

The last Metro built in the Union of Soviet Socialist Republics was in Yekaterinburg, or as it was then, Sverdlovsk, after the Bolshevik Yakov Sverdlov. It opened six months before the USSR's collapse and for a long time it was the shortest Metro line in the world, with just three stations. However, the underlying ideas derived from one of the forgotten parts of Gorbachev's proposed deal to the Soviet people – along

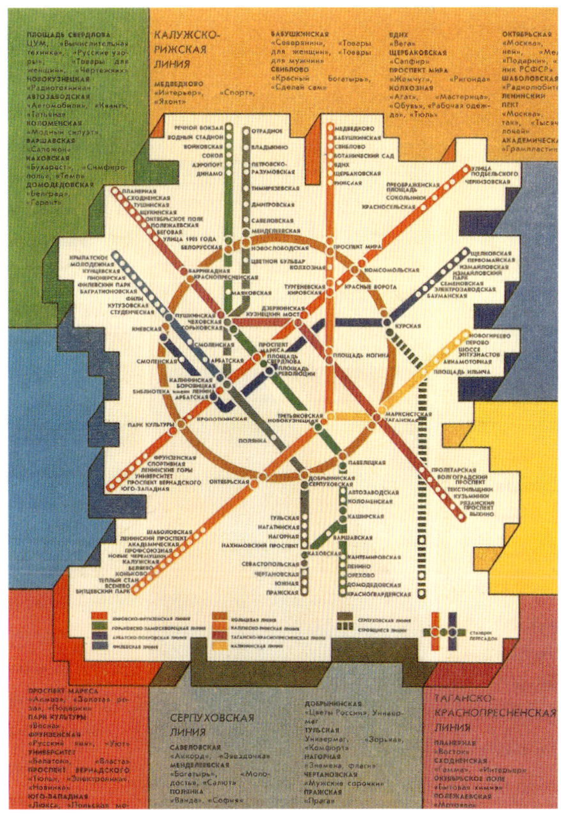

Moscow Metro map, 1991
Troy Litten collection

with *Perestroika*, reconstruction, *Glasnost*, openness, there would also be *Uskoreniye*, acceleration. Building projects would be bigger, better, higher-tech, and user-friendly, with consumption taking the place of the military-industrial complex. Of course, this never happened, but the Yekaterinburg Metro gives hints of it. The geographer Mikhail Ilchenko explains that the Metro 'expressed the expectations of the late Soviet period about this rapidly growing huge industrial megapolis in the Urals', so there are industrial sculptures and futuristic, chromium-plated light fittings everywhere, especially in N. A. Kudinova's Mashinostroiteley station, while the central Uralskaya and Ploshchad 1905 Goda returned again to the radiant Stalinist dungeons of 1930s' Moscow. The choice of surfacing materials, says Ilchenko, comes from 'the local traditions of the Urals region', where 'the use of different stones in the decoration stresses mining traditions and local history'. Much of the exotic marble in the Moscow Metro came from the Urals.

As in Nizhny Novgorod, the plan was to get people in and out of the centre to an industrial district built during the first Five-Year Plan, at the start of the 1930s – Uralmash, a huge machine-tool works. For Ilchenko, this 'actually opened the doors to the city' and 'gradually led to the loss of their local identity' for people who had previously lived in a self-contained city within a city. But in Dnipro, the Metro has still not reached the centre at the time of writing in 2019. The Dnipropetrovsk Metro – as it then was – was the fourth (counting Krivyi Rih) in Ukraine, and though it was almost entirely designed and built in the USSR – after it won out over Odessa to be the next Ukrainian million-citizen-city to get its Metro – it opened four years after the end, in 1995. As a transport artery, it still makes little sense, unless you live in the industrial suburbs strung along this linear route

by the Dnieper and want to go to the railway station. Many of the stations are variations on a theme, using for the first time a kit of parts, a common aesthetic, rather than a series of individual palaces. And yet, those few stations are utterly stupendous. Enormous halls, the largest of the Kharkiv-type spans, lined with coloured tiles in strange saturated blues, yellows and purples, and with station jingles that sound like Kraftwerk. They are truly incredible spaces, vast and mostly empty, with half the lights switched off to save electricity. That a collapsing system could have created something so extraordinary is perhaps surprising, but it would take some decades before this sort of deliberately excessive collective space would be valued again.

Afterlife
Kazan, Almaty, the Apocalypse, and Communism

Many Metros have been projected and left unbuilt in the post-Soviet space. The first cancellation was in Riga, where a Metro was fully designed and construction about to start when the struggle for Latvian independence took over, and urban growth started to be considered demographically problematic (i.e. leading to a Russian majority). Metros in Donetsk and Omsk have been partly constructed and then abandoned. Almaty, the largest city in Kazakhstan, and Kazan, capital of the Republic of Tatarstan in the Russian Federation, have built Metros that, like extensions in Moscow, Kyiv and Baku, are clearly continuations of Soviet design practices, although of course with explicitly Soviet symbols being mostly – if not entirely – absent. In the last couple of years, Moscow has abandoned even this, opting instead to break with continuity for the first time since Khrushchev, sometimes using design competitions and nods towards

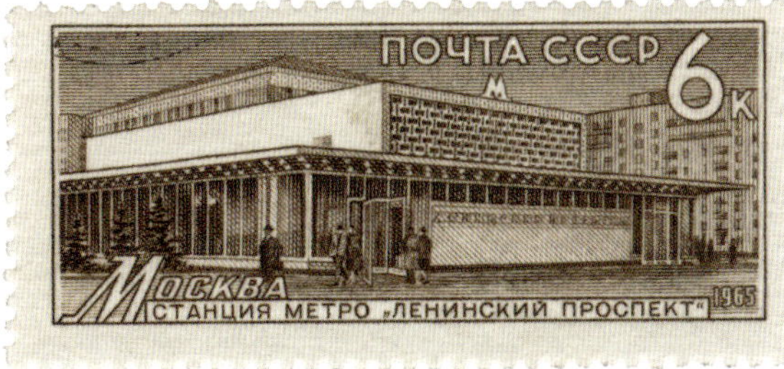
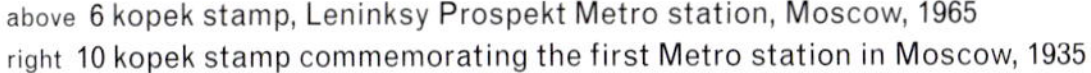
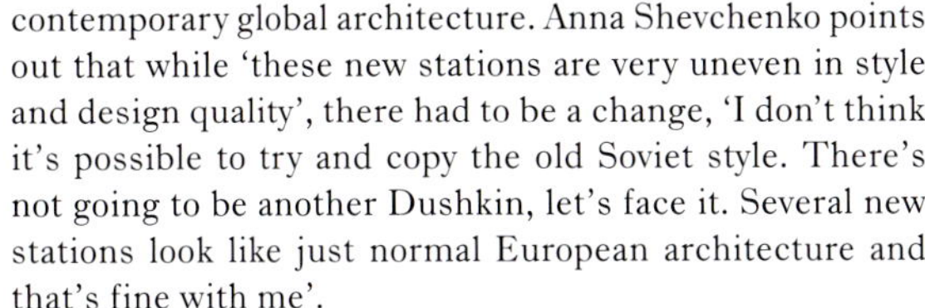
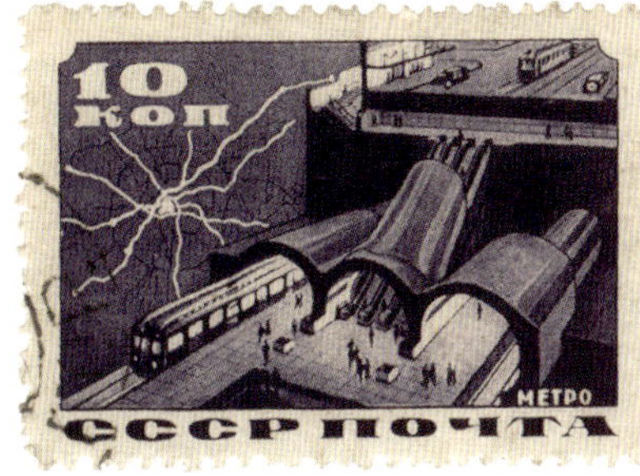

above 6 kopek stamp, Leninksy Prospekt Metro station, Moscow, 1965
right 10 kopek stamp commemorating the first Metro station in Moscow, 1935

contemporary global architecture. Anna Shevchenko points out that while 'these new stations are very uneven in style and design quality', there had to be a change, 'I don't think it's possible to try and copy the old Soviet style. There's not going to be another Dushkin, let's face it. Several new stations look like just normal European architecture and that's fine with me'.

It is perhaps foolish to try to reproduce the aesthetics of these extraordinary, haunting, overwhelming spaces in the present day, in such hugely different material and social conditions. But those old stations continue, and continue to be used for the straightforward purpose of getting around the city, just like any other tube network. Shevchenko reminds me that the 'total artwork' of the Moscow Metro is certainly ignored when the crowd is struggling to get through during peak hours, and sometimes it's clear that some areas are too narrow for today's flow. But it's a lot more than just an obstacle or a remnant. 'Still it's there, in the background, with socialist content in its democratic character, in the understanding that it was built for the people as the most beautiful of all Underground systems worldwide'.

Many futures have been imagined for the Soviet Metro. One of the most famous in recent years has been based on the system's other official function – as nuclear shelter. Dmitry Glukhovsky's series of science-fiction schlock novels, which have been adapted as video games, started in 2005 with *Metro 2033*, and are the contemporary equivalents of the many glowingly optimistic children's books explaining the Metro published between the 1930s and the 1980s. It's not hard to find the satirical elements in Glukhovsky's books; a map in the second volume, *Metro 2034* (2009), shows how the Metro has been divided up, as Communists take the 'Red Line' and oppositional Trotskyists stand bravely against the revolution betrayed from their base in Avtozavodskaya station. The elite rule an interconnected city-state made up of the stations around the Kremlin, such as Biblioteka Imeni Lenina, while the Circle Line has become the 'Hanseatic League', housing a population of traders in its opulent palaces. A Neo-Nazi 'Fourth Reich' occupies the stations on Tverskaya. In a reversal of the 1930s' 'civilising process', there are collective farms in the Metro, and mutants occupy the peripheral stations, especially those nearer to the uninhabitable surface. One of our troglodyte heroes stumbles on an urbex holy grail, the much-discussed but never-documented 'Metro 2' that allegedly runs around the Kremlin, solely for governmental use. 'The platform was so wide that it was impossible to see clearly what was on its other side. A cursory glance suggested that two thousand people could have waited here for a train'. But 'the rails were covered with a black rust and the rotted ties were covered with moss'.[21] He finds bronze letters, giving the station's name – Genshtab, a specialised Metro palace for the long-destroyed headquarters of the Red Army. The books' cult has spread across the former USSR, Eastern Europe and beyond – fan-fiction sequels and extensions have been set in most of the Metros in this book, and further afield, in Warsaw, Milan and Glasgow. There is a deep melancholy in all of this, as the pride and joy of Soviet socialism is literally covered in shit.

There's another way of looking at the Soviet Metro, one that is not nostalgic, but based at looking at urgent needs in the 21st century. We all know that urban economies based on private transport are completely unsustainable – wasteful of resources, poorly organised, and hugely destructive of urban and rural space – but we also know that the desire to have a car, to be in one, and to dream of the dubious delights of totally private transport is a powerful force. Rather than attempting to counter this with ordinary buses and shabby tubes, we need another dream to pose against the car. This is where the Soviet Metro truly comes in. It was built using methods as bad, if not worse, than those of capitalism at its most bloodthirsty – reading accounts of the Moscow Metro's construction is as shocking as those of India's railways, with the massive cost in human lives not offset by sculptures and murals of the Metro builders. But as existing spaces, these stations incarnate something important. That is, what Bini Adamczak, in her wonderful little book *Communism for Kids*

(2017), calls 'Communist desire' – the desire to live in a Communist way, in truly Communist spaces. These incredible halls, where some of the greatest art and architecture of the 20th century is just part of your daily routine, and where head-spinningly dreamlike communal spaces are also places you go through on your way to meet friends, go to work, go to the cinema or the football – these are much more than scattered remnants of a vainglorious empire. They're an unsurpassed vision of what the public spaces of the Communist future could be like everywhere.

1. Nikita Khrushchev, *Khrushchev Remembers*, volume 1 (Penguin, 1977), p. 87
2. On these partly Soviet-built systems outside the USSR, see the chapter 'Metro' in my *Landscapes of Communism* (Penguin, 2015) and the chapter of the same name in Oliver Wainwright's *Inside North Korea* (Taschen, 2018)
3. Hamid Ismailov, *The Underground* (Restless Books, 2015), pp. 182–83
4. Benson Bobrick, *Labyrinths of Iron: The Story of the Underground Railway* (Newsweek Books, 1982), p. 281
5. Victor Serge, *Memoirs of a Revolutionary* (NYRB, 2012), p. 374
6. Tijana Vujosevic, *Modernism and the Making of the Soviet New Man* (Manchester University Press, 2017), p. 157
7. *Modernism and the Making of the Soviet New Man*, p. 173
8. Egor Larichev and Anastasia Uglik, *Moscow Metro Travel Guide* (WAM, 2008), p. 24
9. *Labyrinths of Iron*, p. 275
10. *Moscow Metro Travel Guide* (WAM, 2008), p. 5
11. *Moscow Metro Travel Guide* (WAM, 2008), p. 20
12. Alec Nove, *An Economic History of the USSR* (Pelican Books, 1978), pp. 250–51
13. Sergey Kuznetsov, Aleksandr Zmeul, Erken Kagarov, *Hidden Urbanism – the Architecture and Design of the Moscow Metro* (Dom, 2016), p. 208
14. Hamid Ismailov, *The Underground* (Restless Books, 2015), p. 127
15. Egor Abakumov, *The Moscow Subway* (Trackie Press, 2010), p. 20
16. Oleksiy Radynski, 'Malevich's Territory', in Kateryna Mishchenko (editor), *The Book of Kyiv* (Medusa, 2015), p. 291
17. Boris Chukhovich, 'Building the "Living East"', in Katarina Ritter *et al.* (eds), *Soviet Modernism, 1955-1991 - Unknown History* (Park Books, 2013), p. 215
18. G. M. Voskresenskii, *Kharkivskii Metropoliten* (Prapor, 1980), p. 59
19. Tigran Hartunyan, Yerevan Architectural Guide (Dom, 2018), p. 94
20. Dimitrij Zadorin, *Minsk Architectural Guide* (Dom, 2018), p. 19
21. Dmitry Glukhovsky, *Metro 2033* (Gollancz, 2011) pp. 402–03

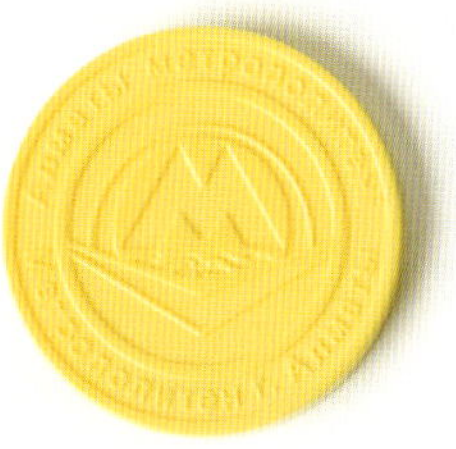

Almaty

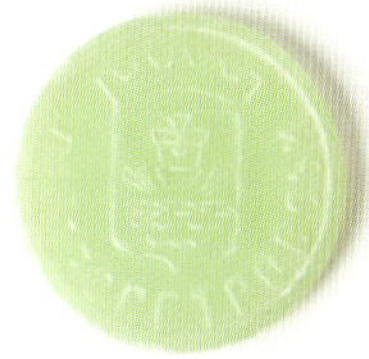

Dnipropetrovsk

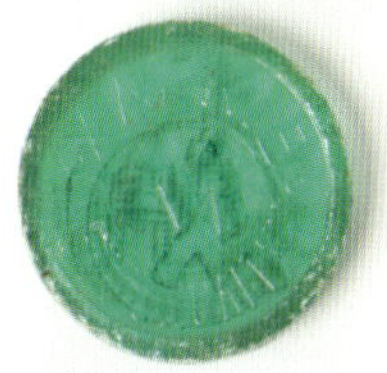

Kharkiv

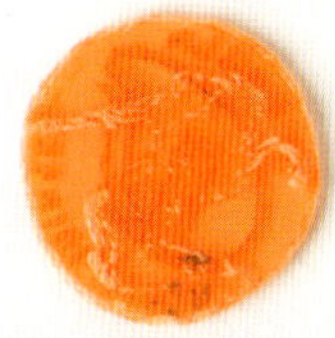

Yerevan

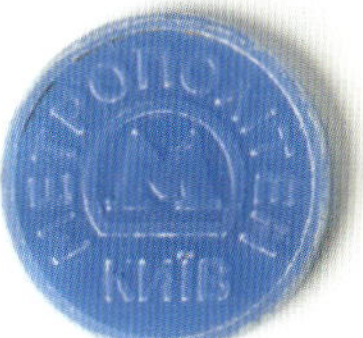

Kyiv

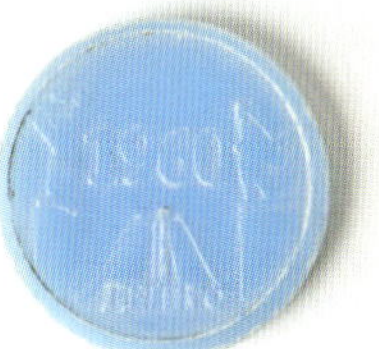

Kyiv

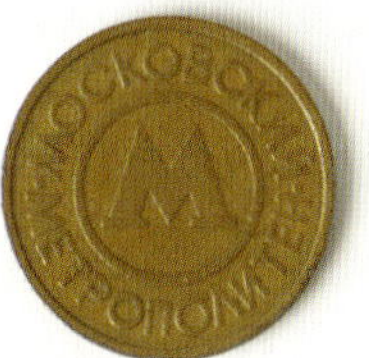

Moscow

Moscow

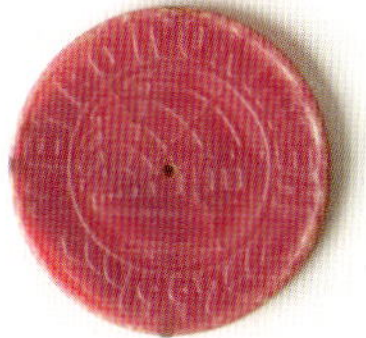

Minsk

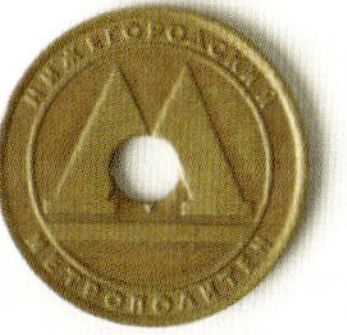

Nizhny Novgorod

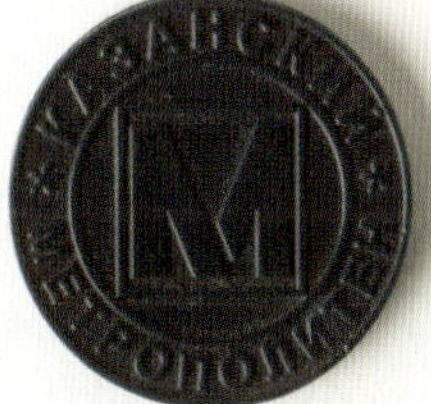

Kazan

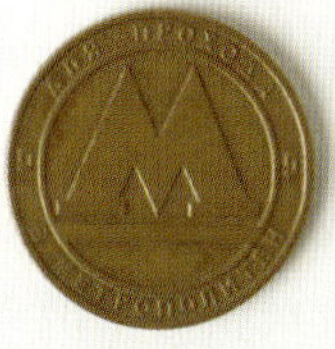

Saint Petersburg

ДНЕПР DNIPRO
УКРАИНА UKRAINE

OPENED 1995

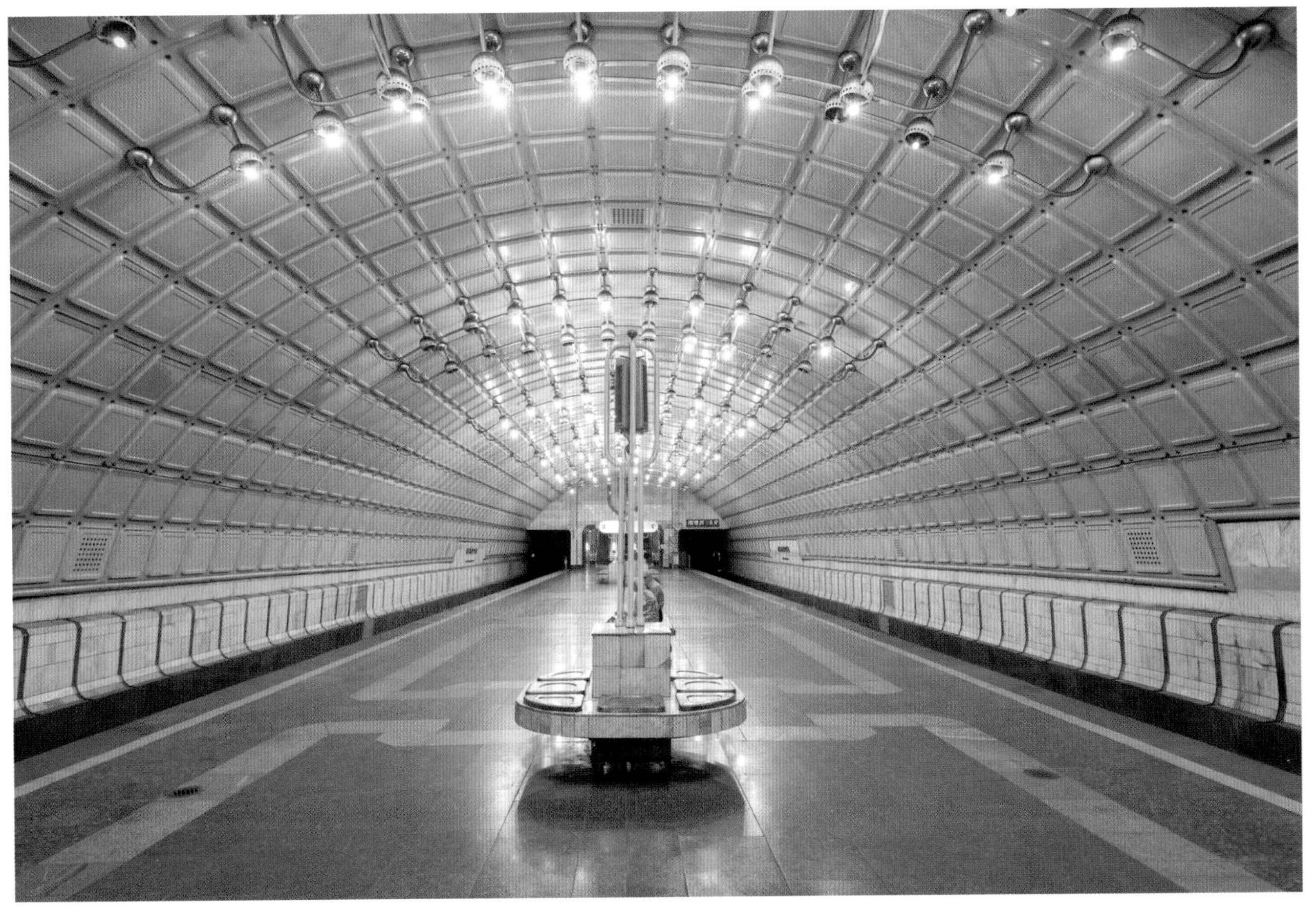

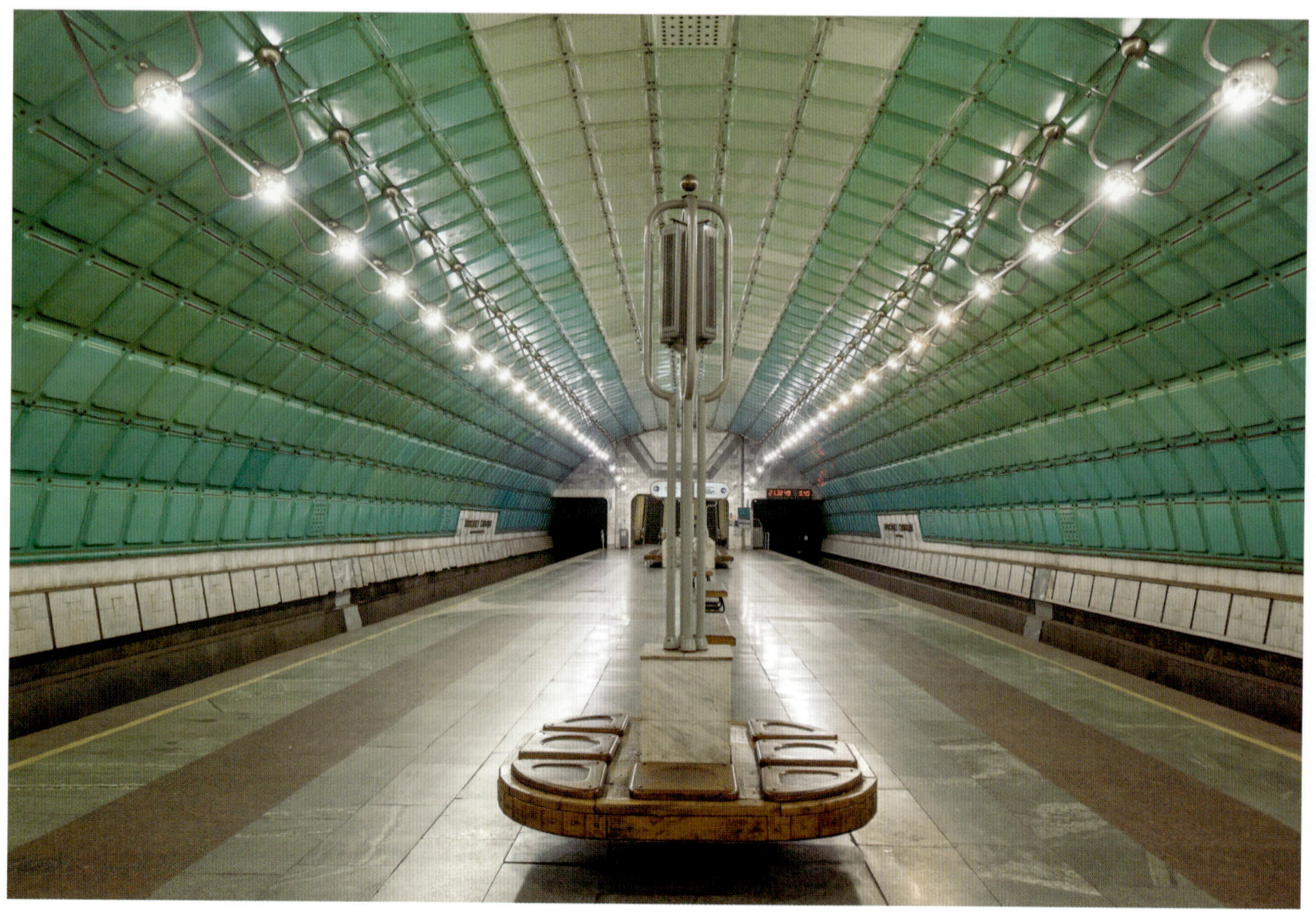

34　Prospekt Svobody, DNIPRO

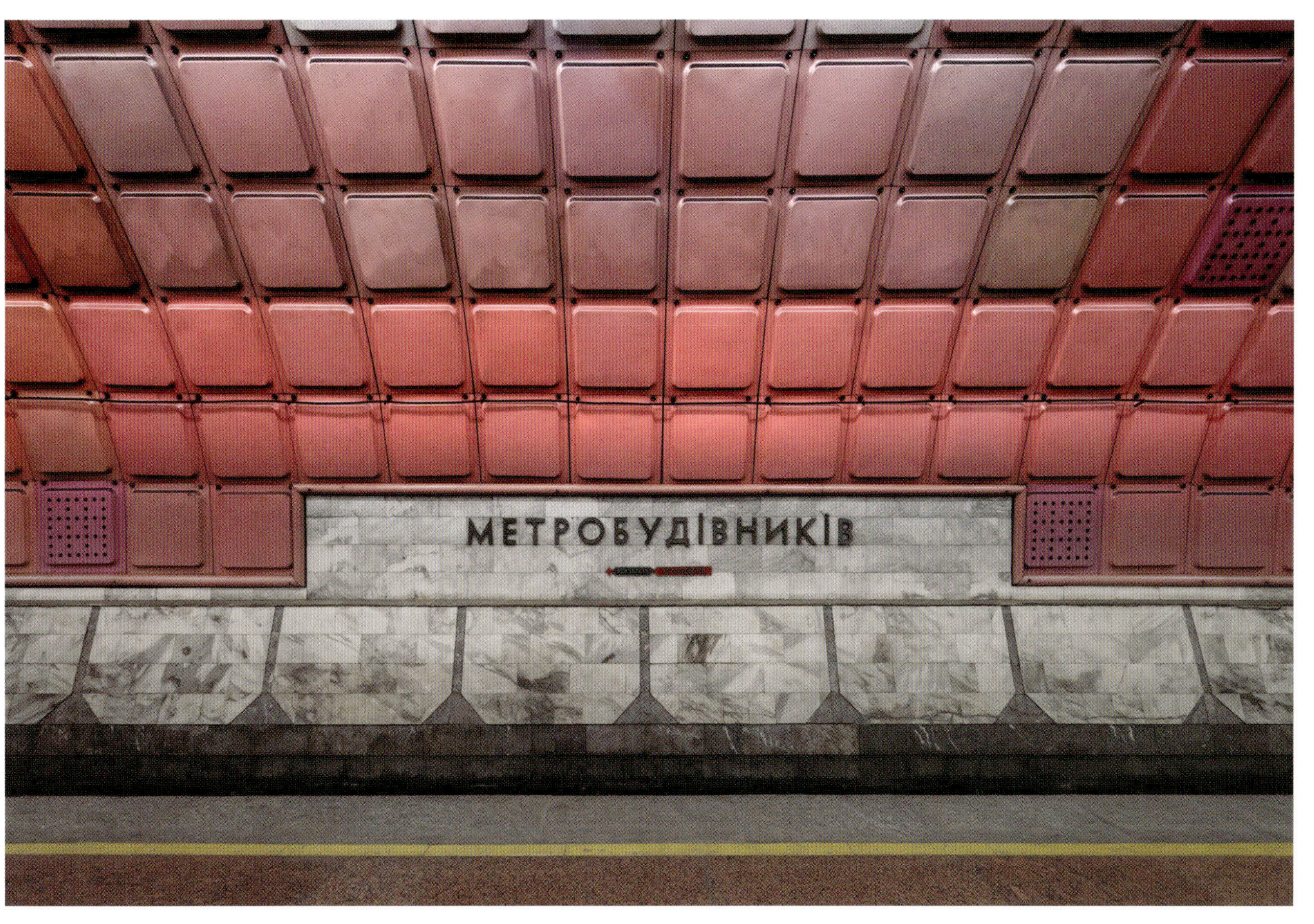
МЕТРОБУДІВНИКІВ

**ЕКАТЕРНБУРГ
РОССИЯ**

**YEKATERINBURG
RUSSIA**

OPENED 1991

   Prospekt Kosmonavtov, YEKATERINBURG

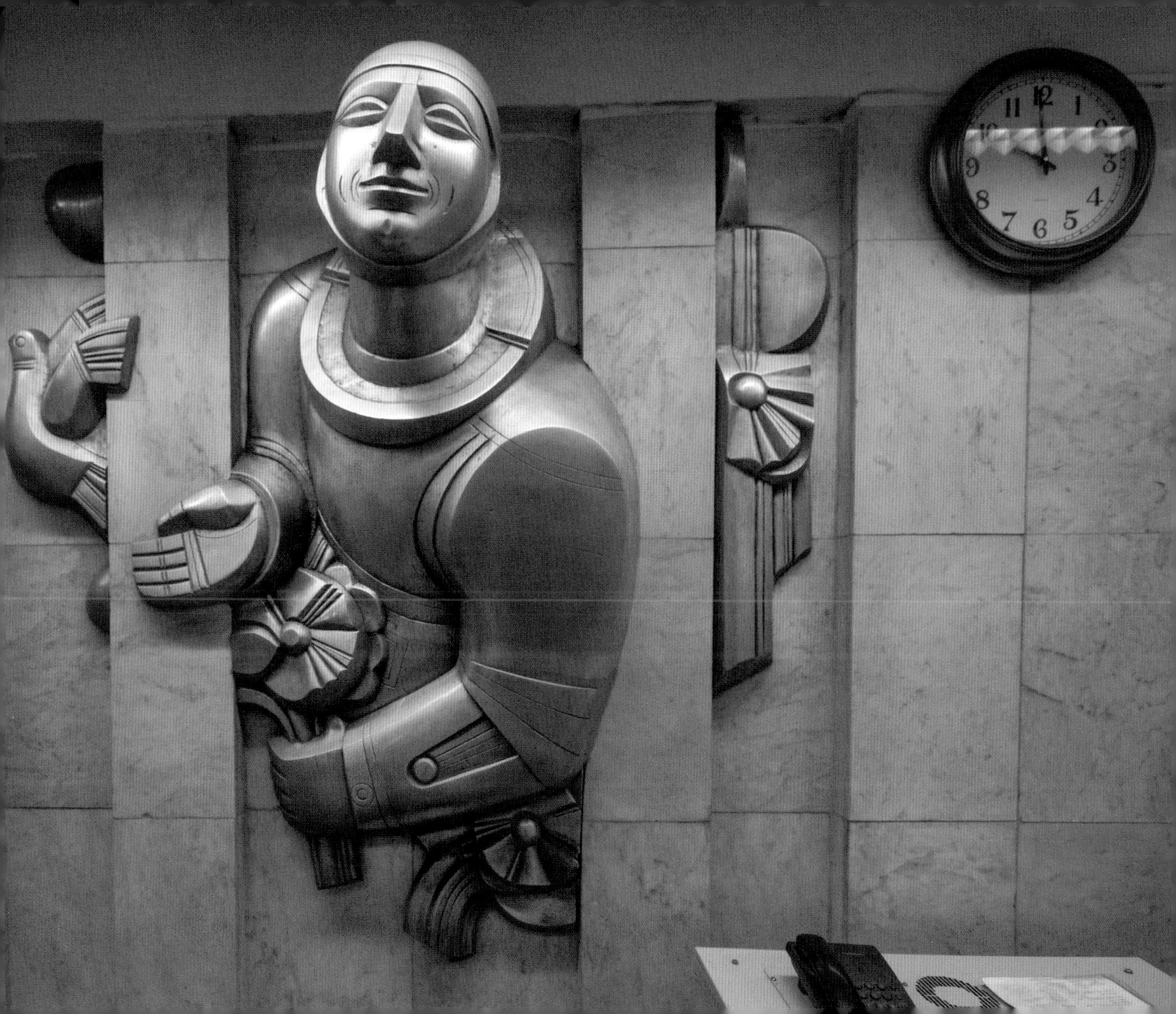

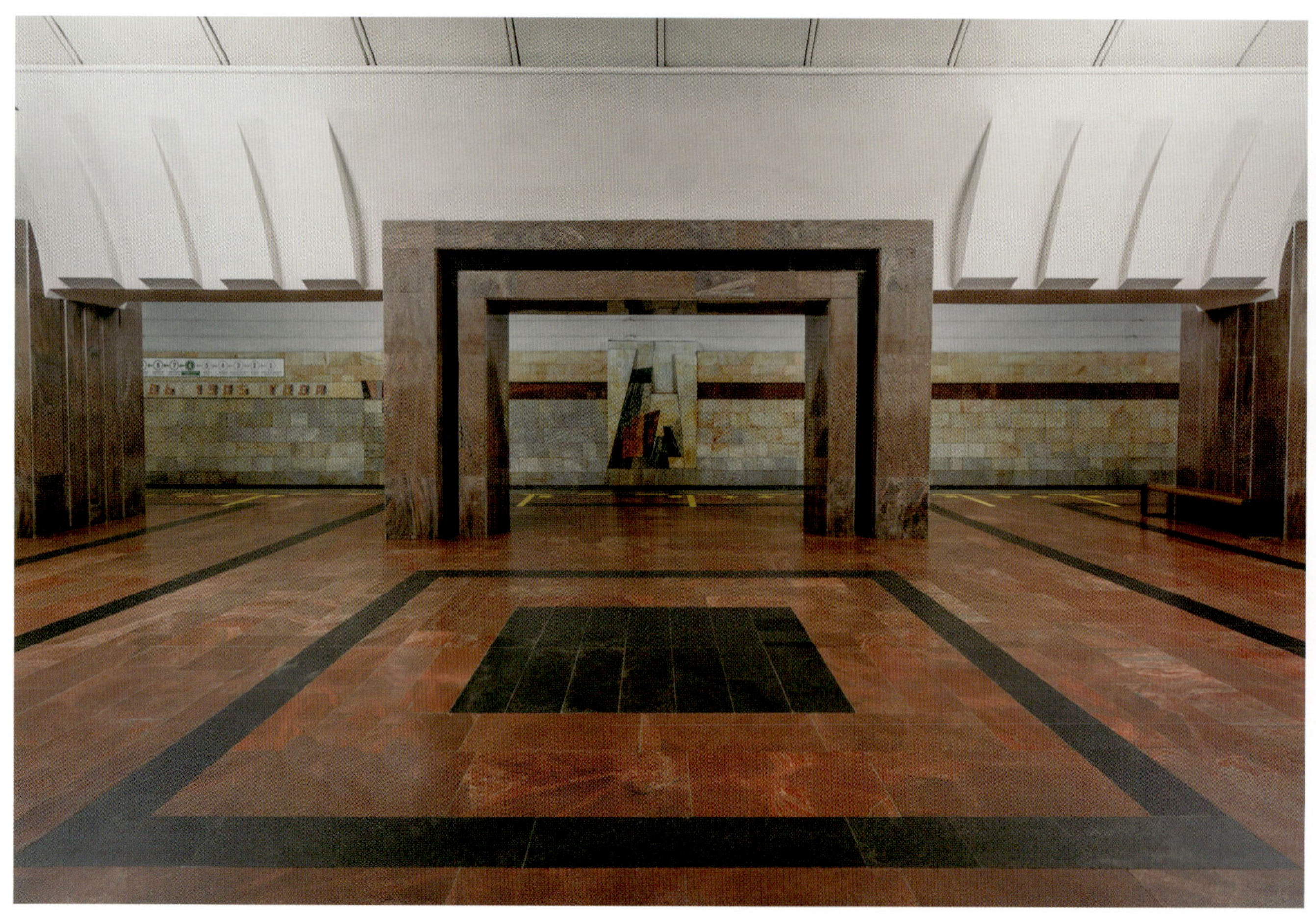

38 Ploshchad 1905 Goda, YEKATERINBURG

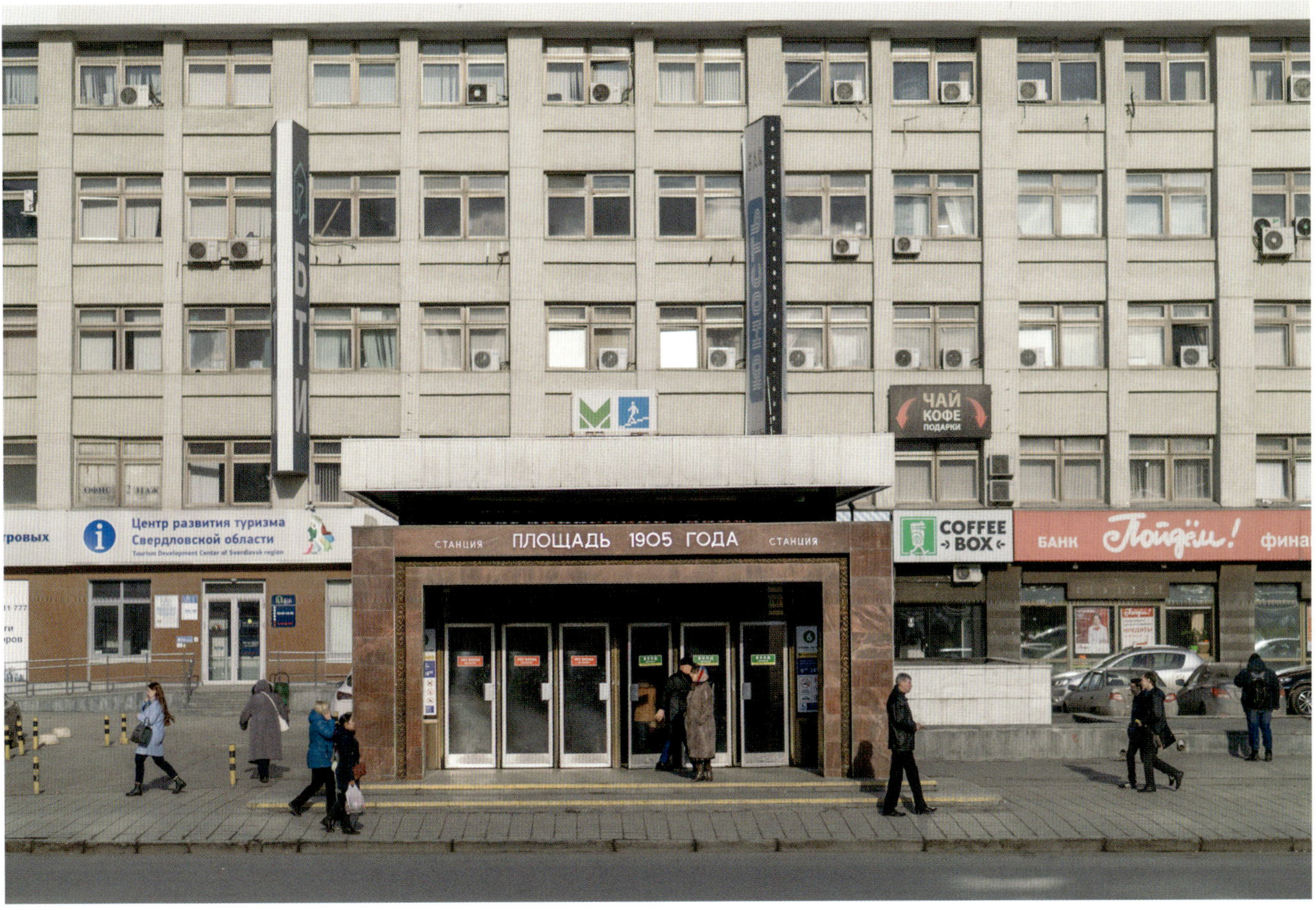
БТИ
ЧАЙ
КОФЕ
ПОДАРКИ
Центр развития туризма
Свердловской области
Tourism Development Center of Sverdlovsk region
COFFEE
BOX
БАНК
Пойдём!
фина
СТАНЦИЯ ПЛОЩАДЬ 1905 ГОДА СТАНЦИЯ
ОФИС 2 ЭТАЖ

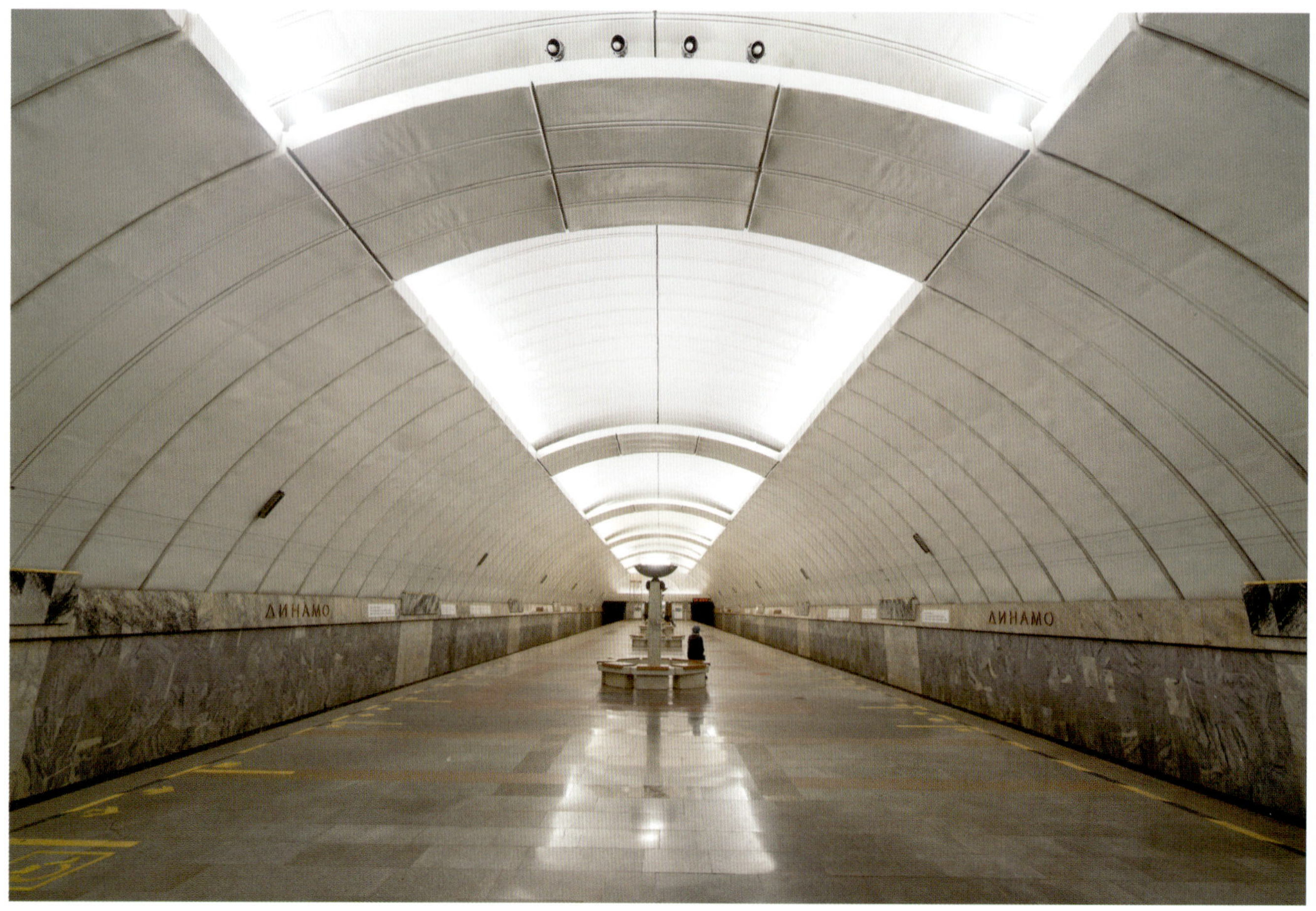

40   Dinamo, YEKATERINBURG

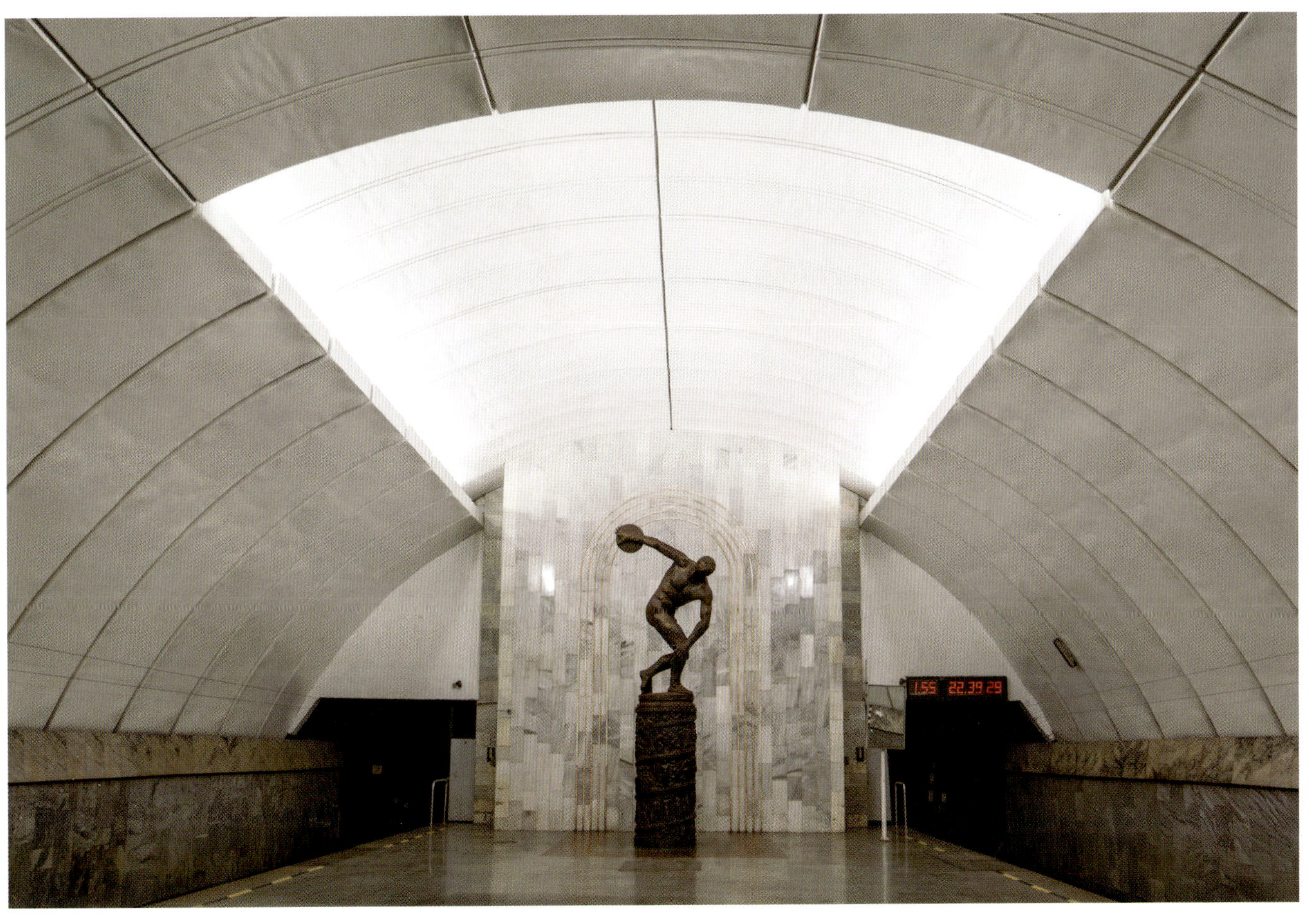
1.55 22.39.29

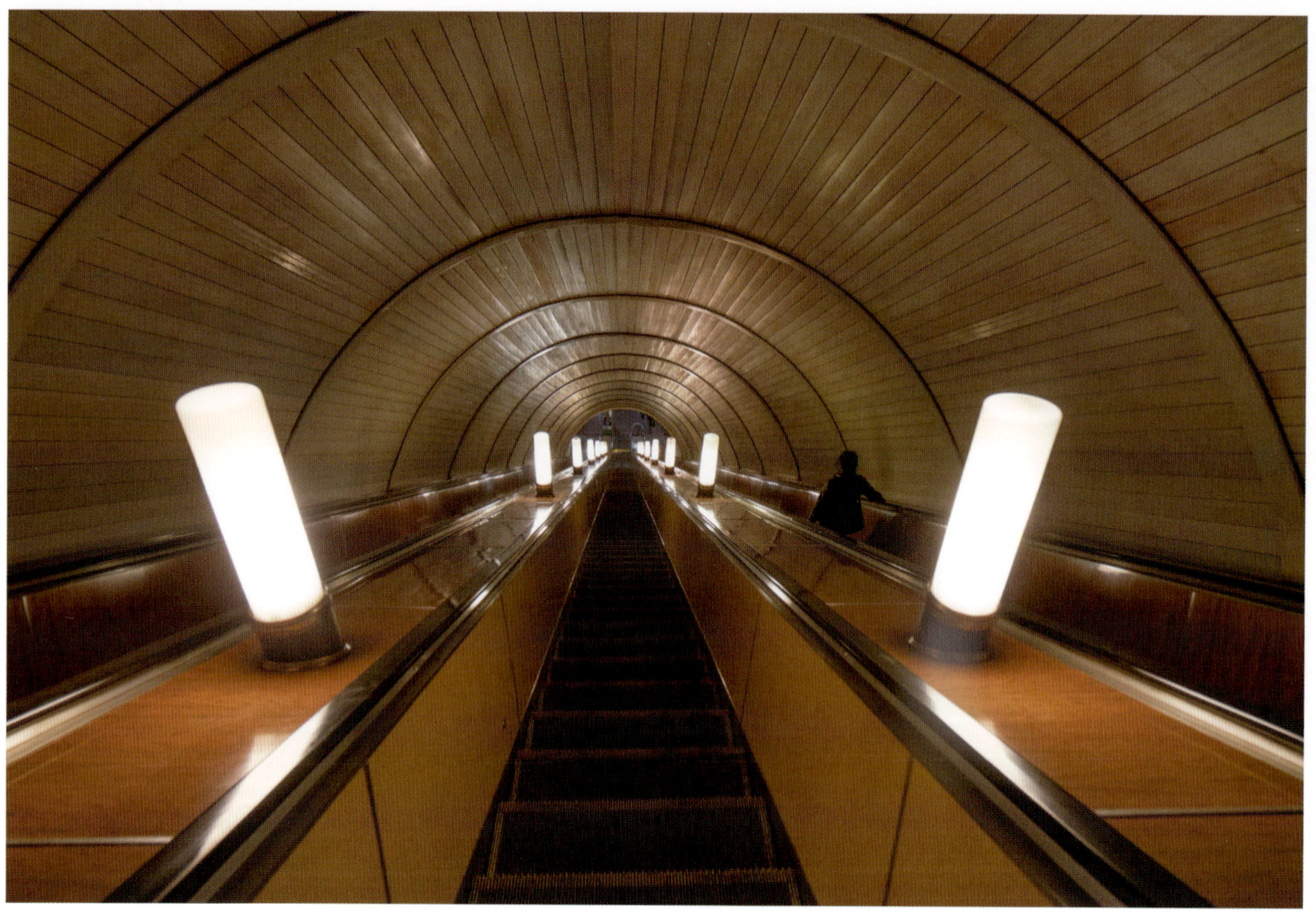

42   Dinamo, YEKATERINBURG

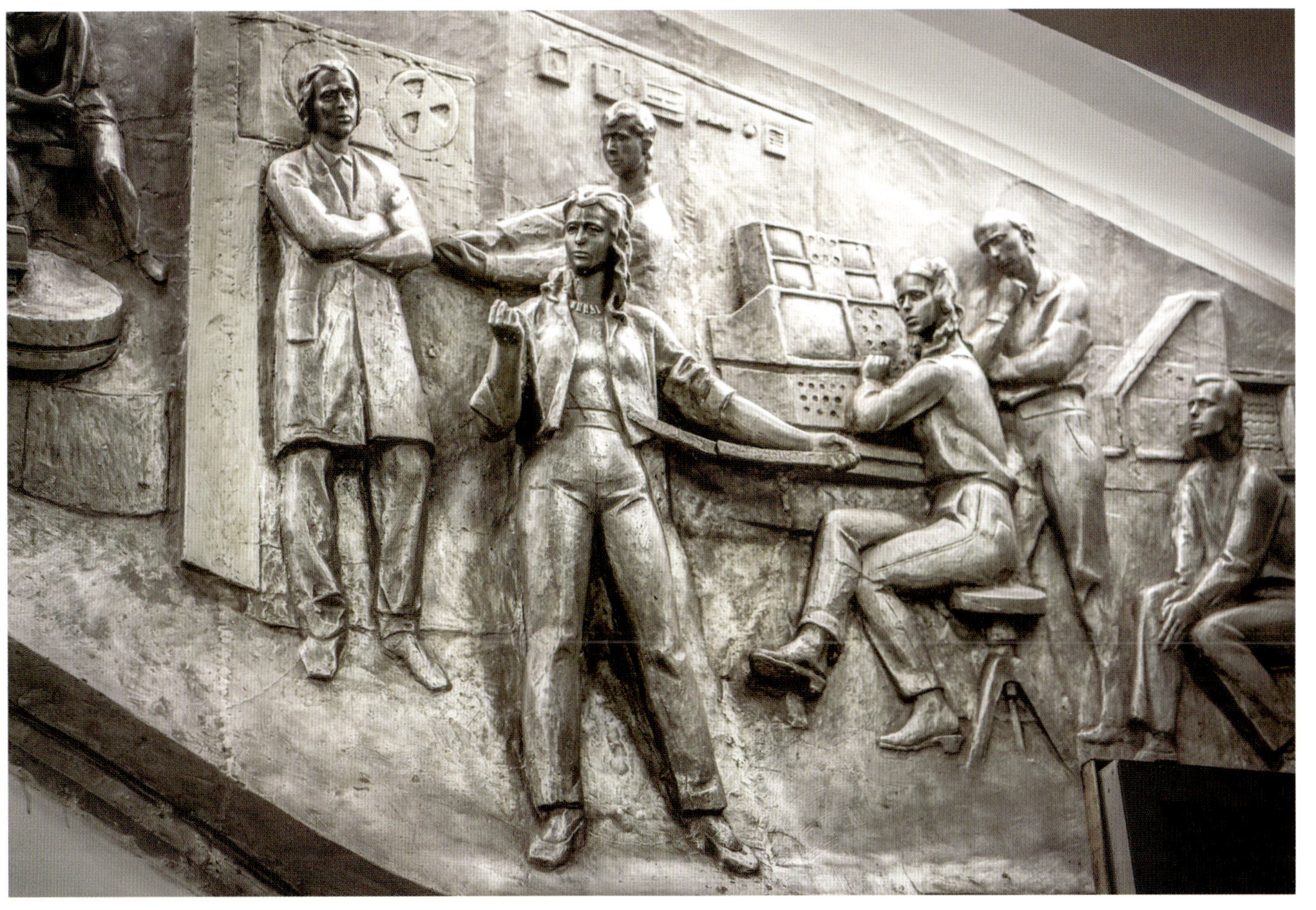

Uralmash, YEKATERINBURG   43

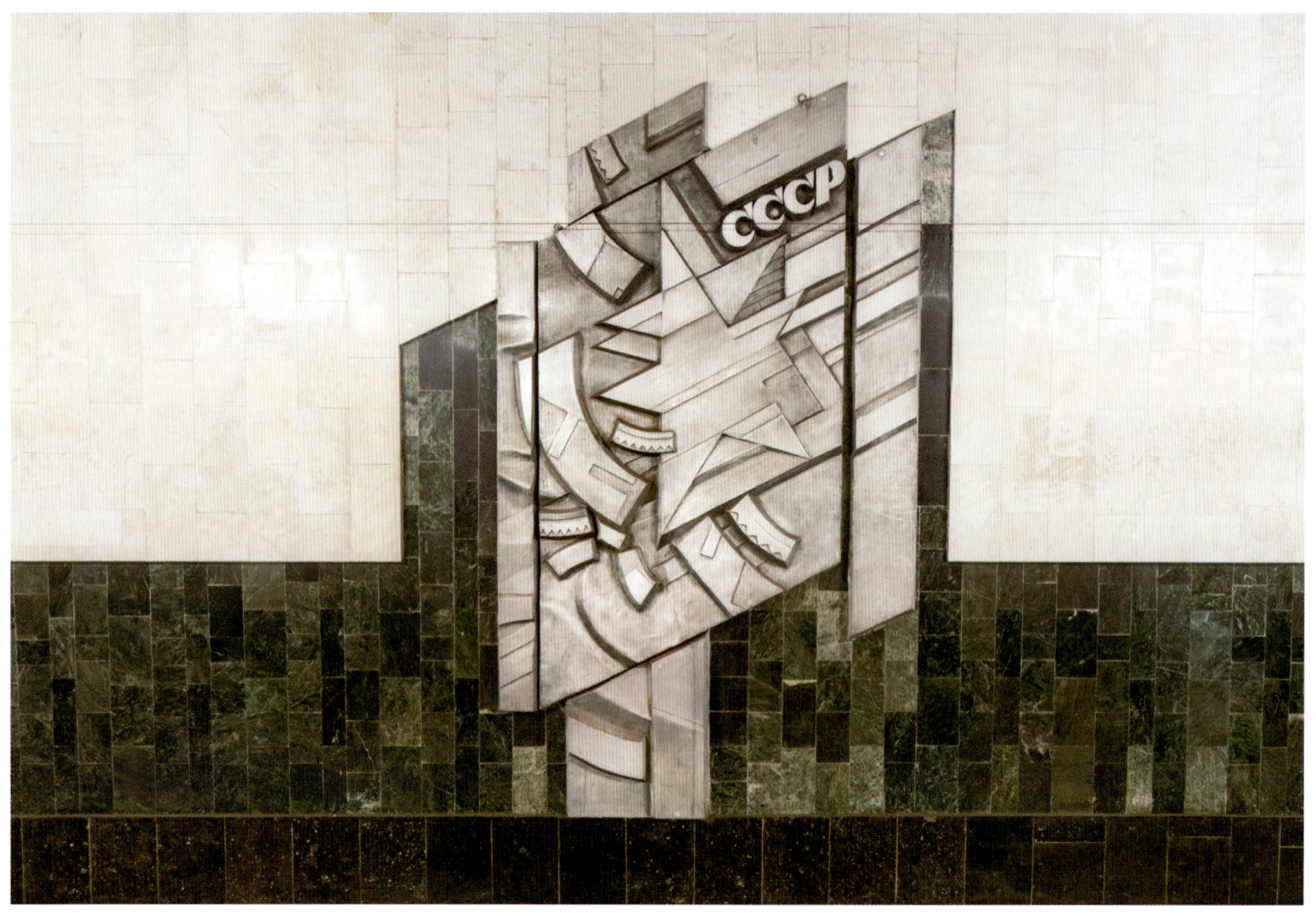

 Mashinostroiteley, YEKATERINBURG

overleaf left: Prospekt Kosmonavtov, YEKATERINBURG

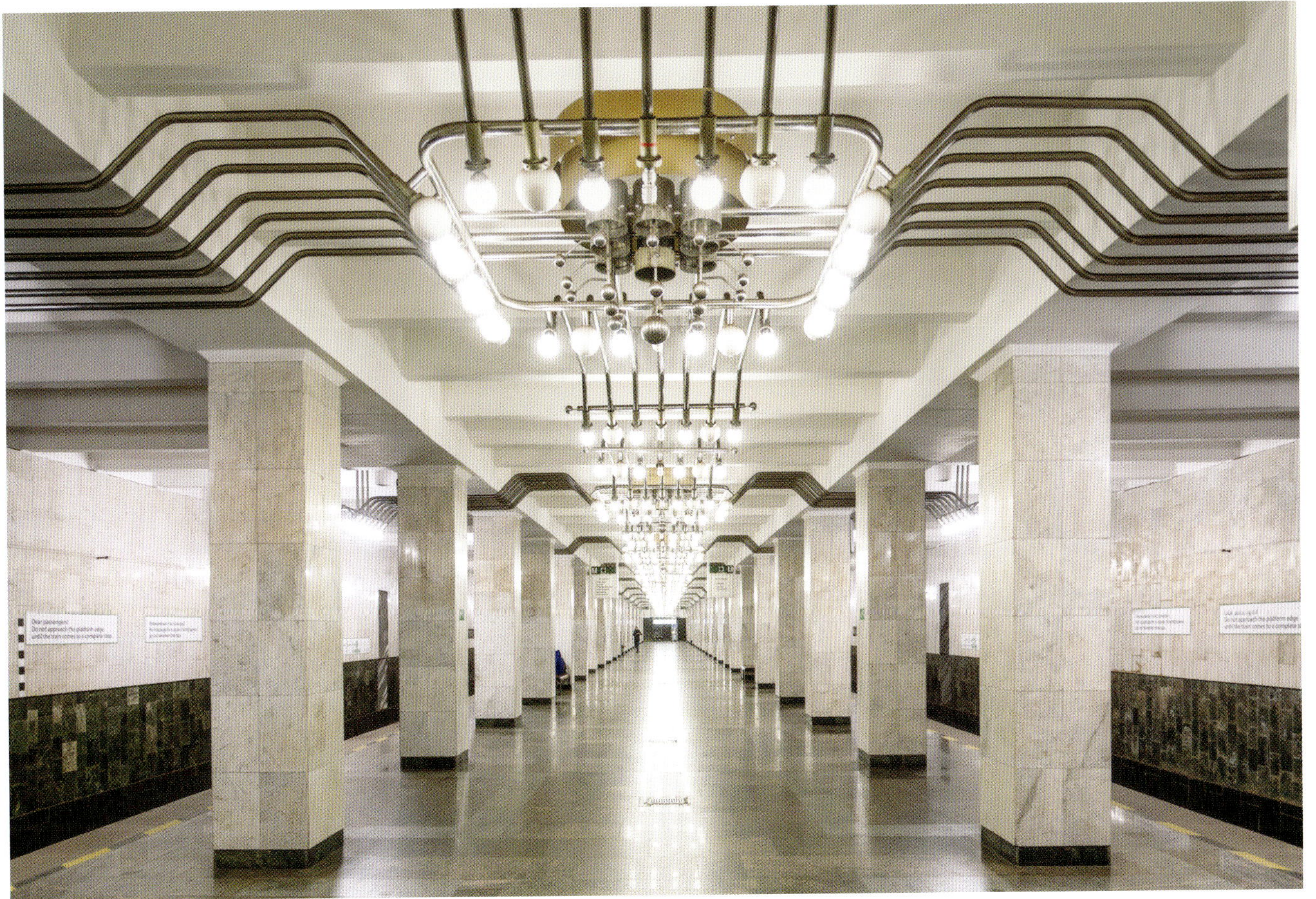

overleaf right: **Ploshchad 1905 Goda,** YEKATERINBURG

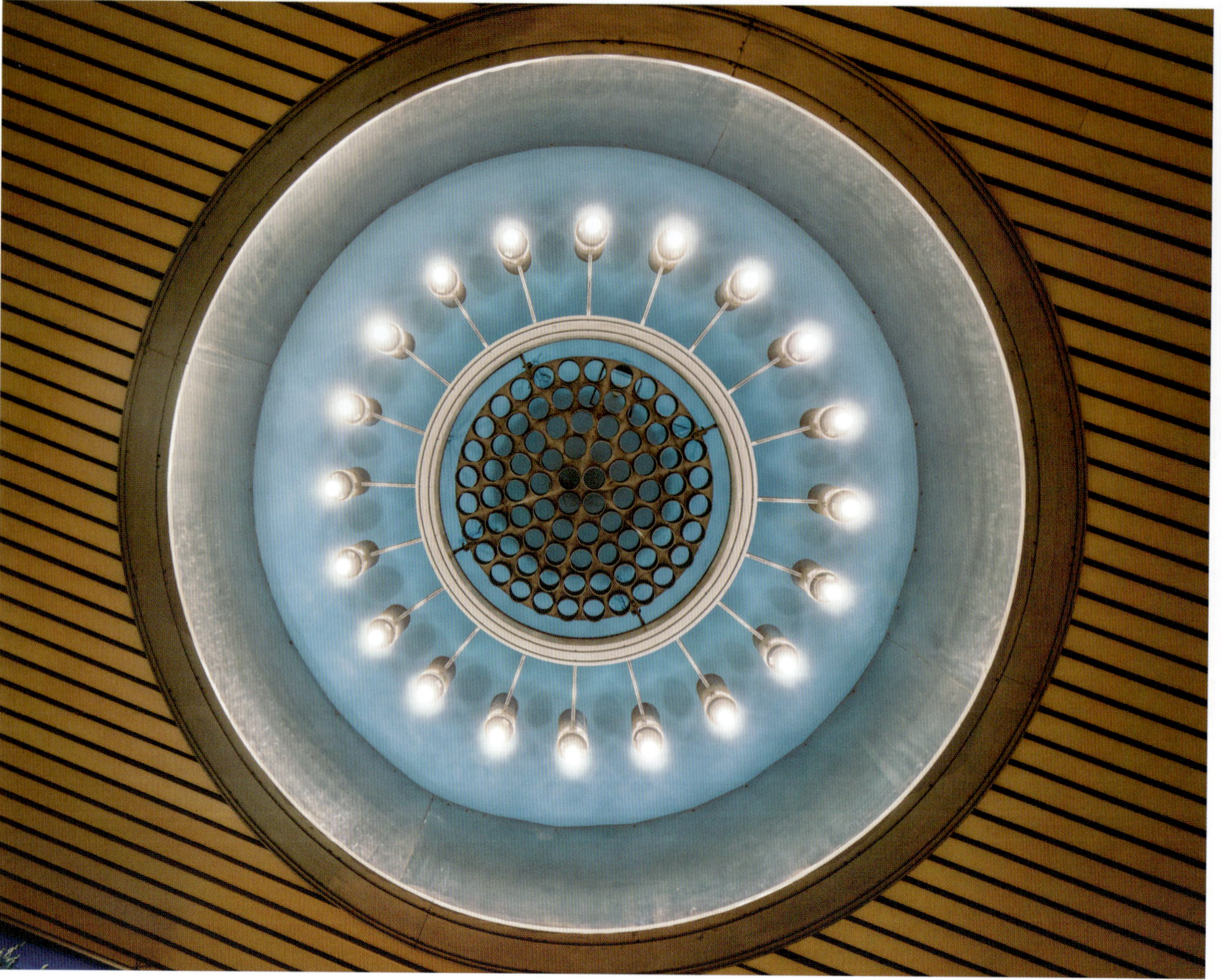

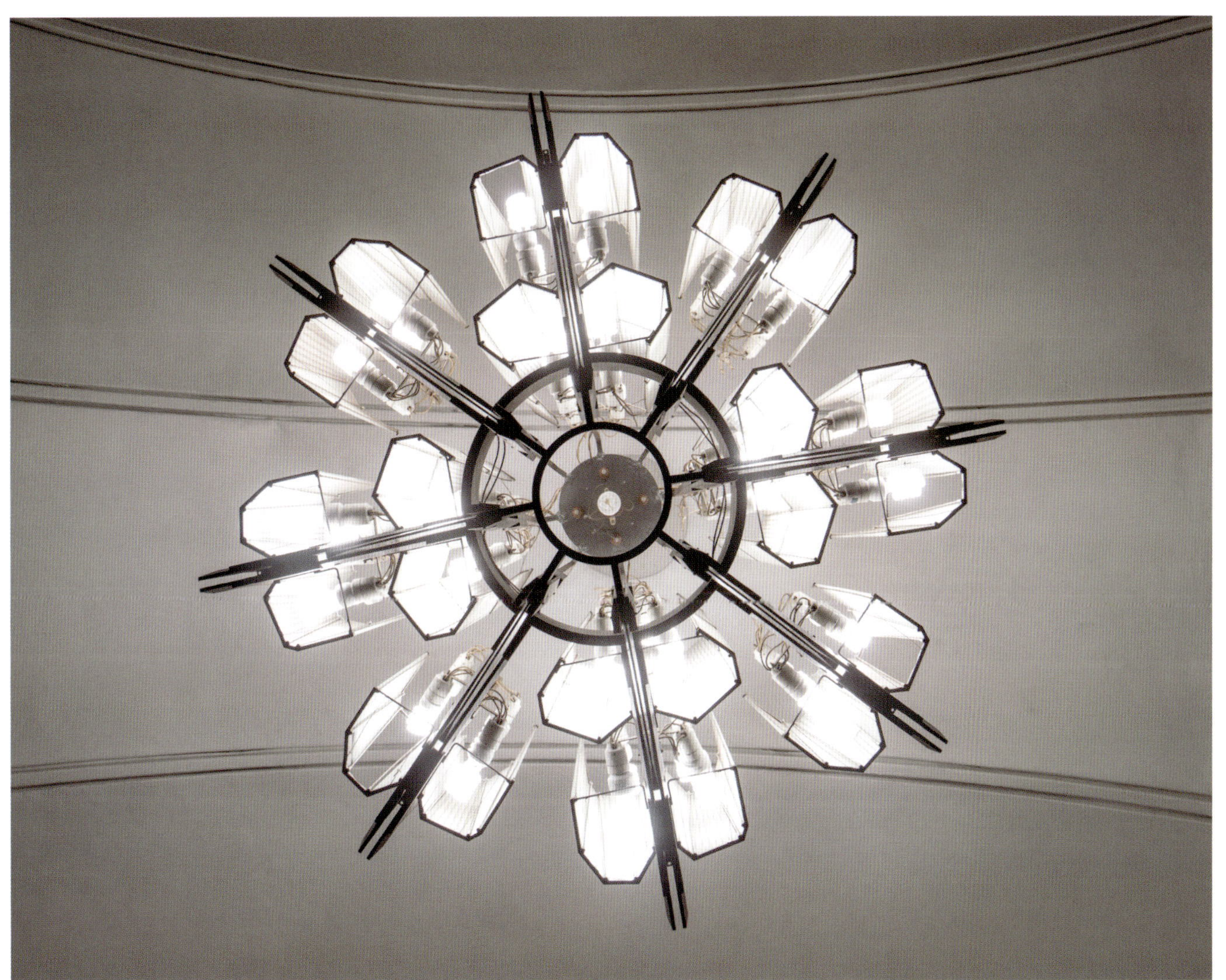

САМАРА   SAMARA
РОССИЯ   RUSSIA

OPENED 1987

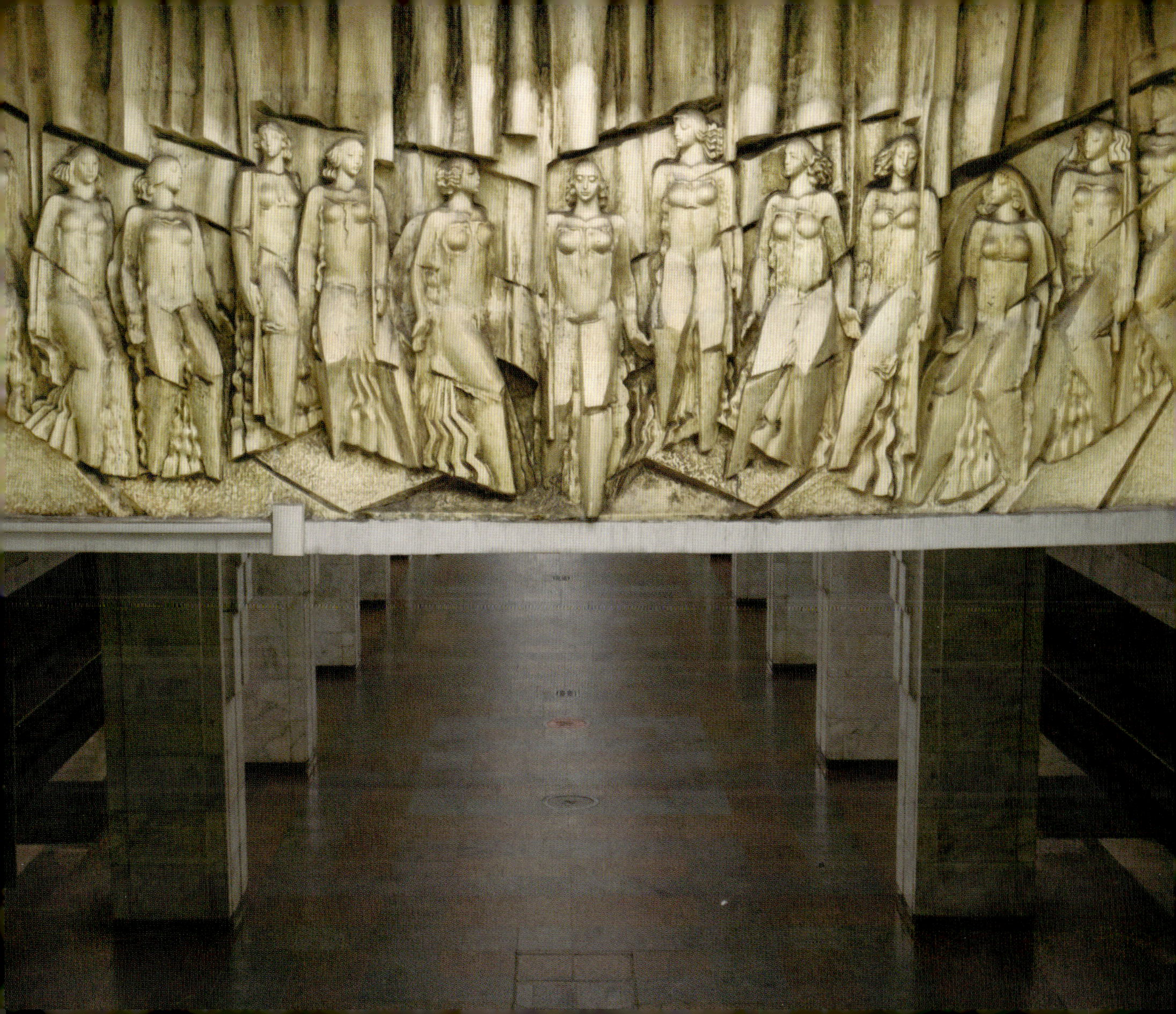

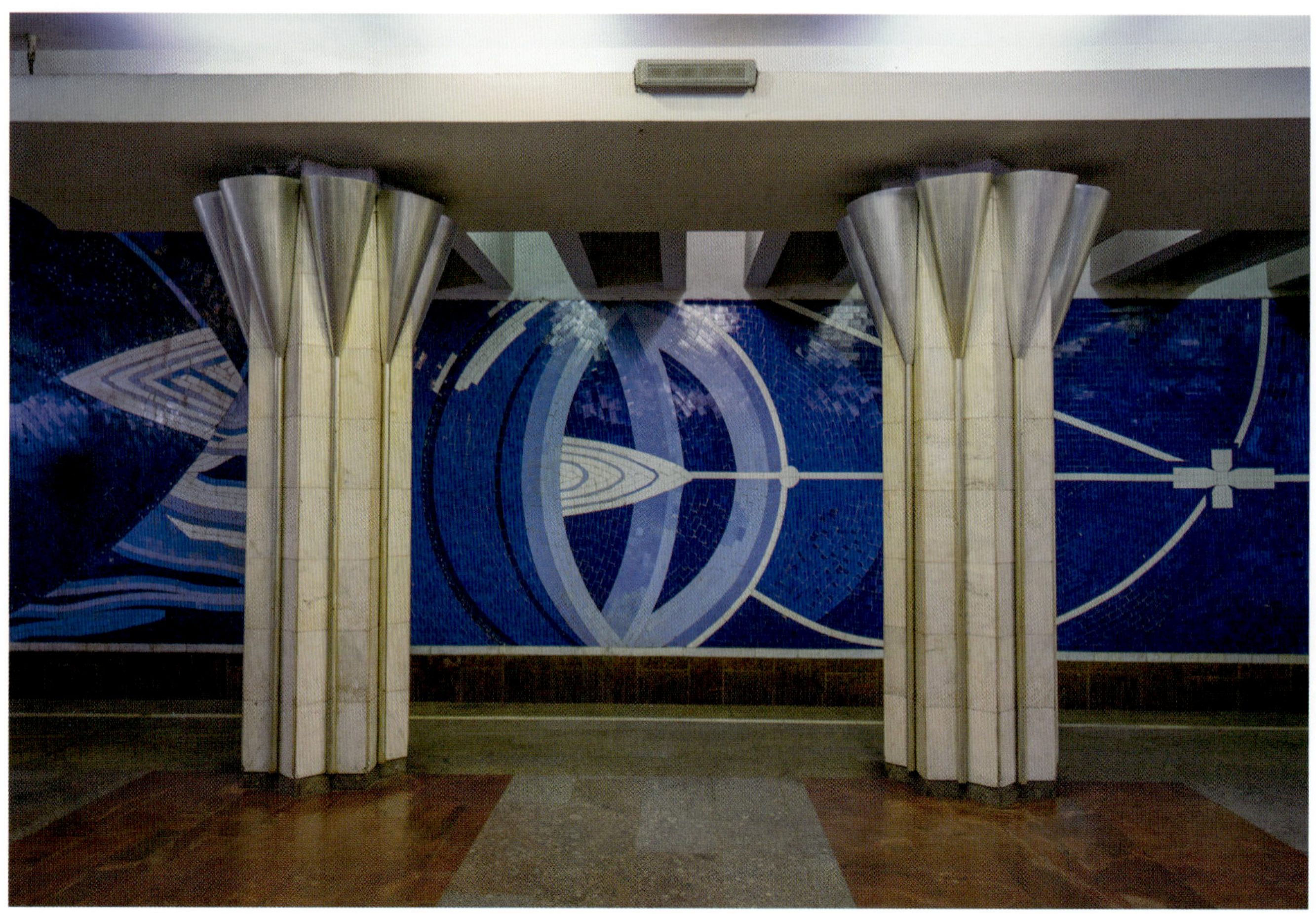

50   Gagarinskaya, SAMARA

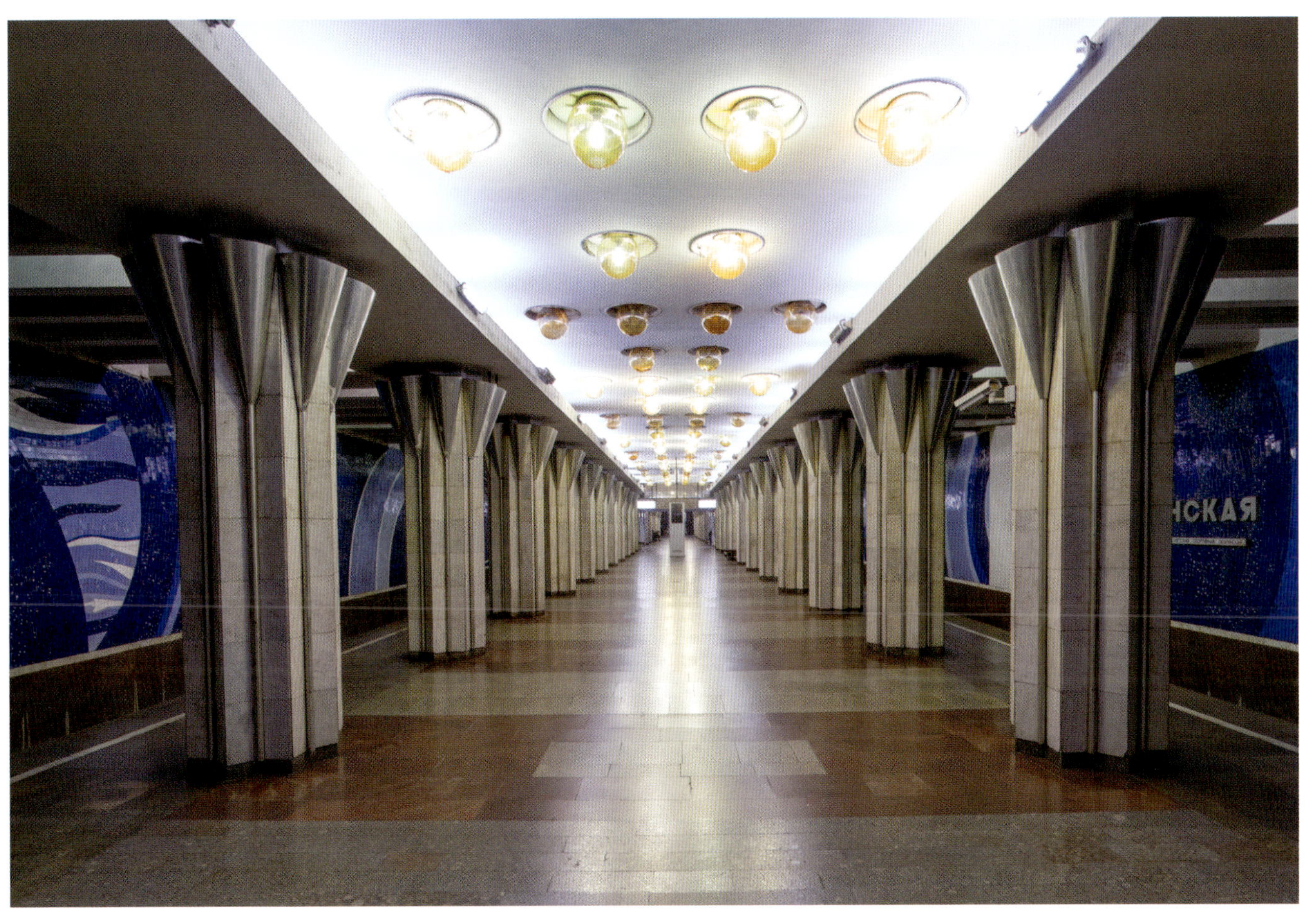

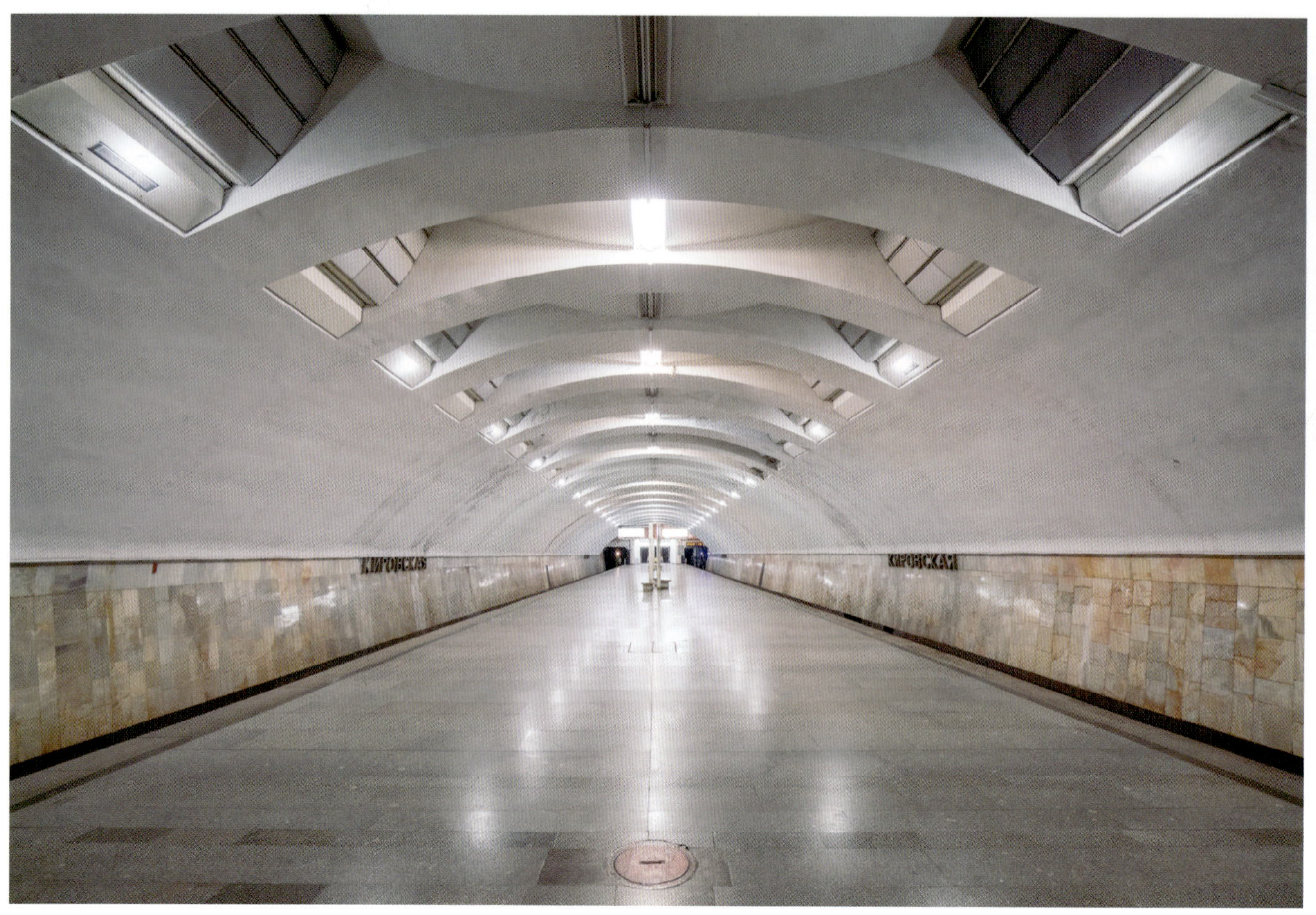

52   Kirovskaya, SAMARA

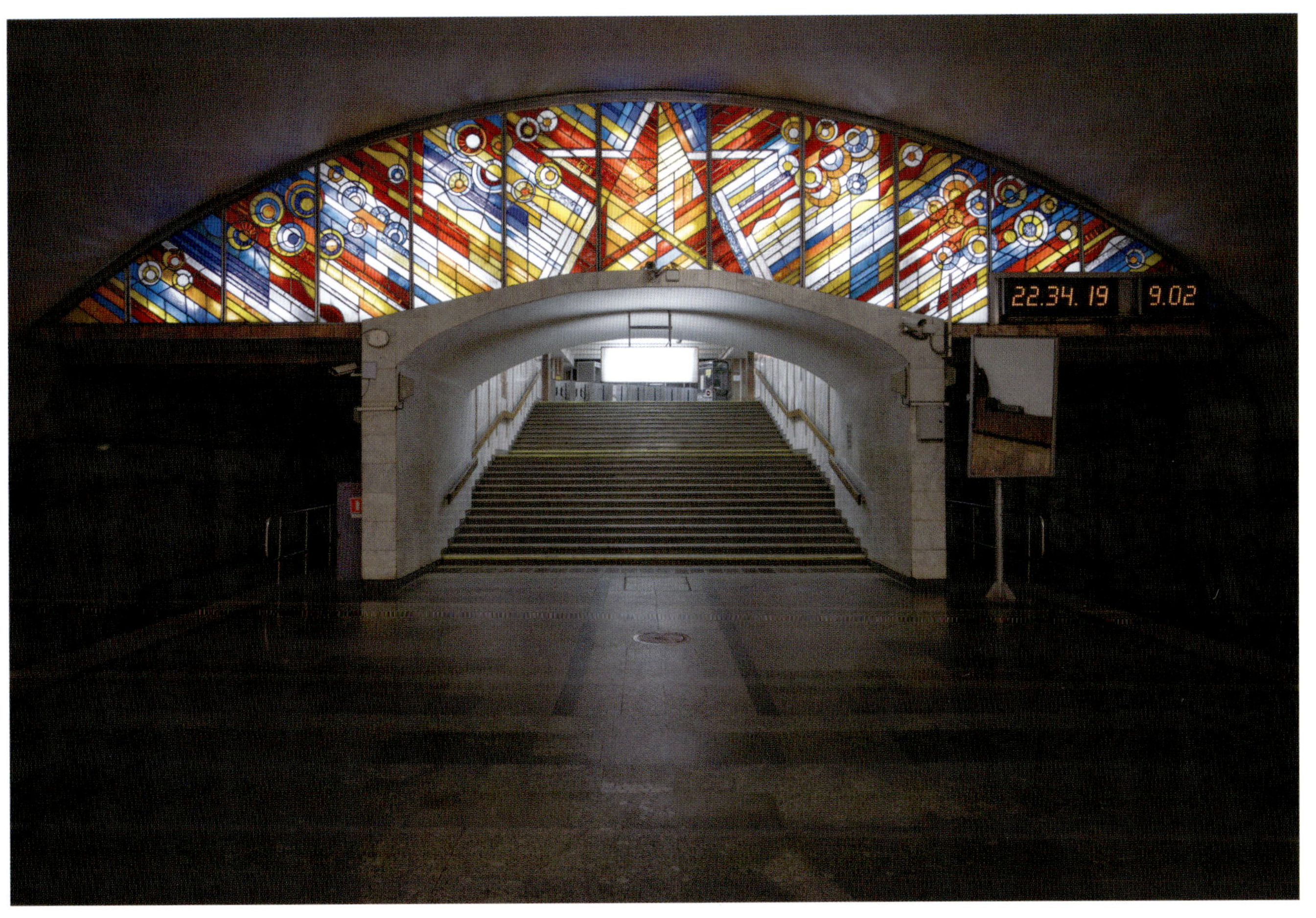

Pobeda, SAMARA   53

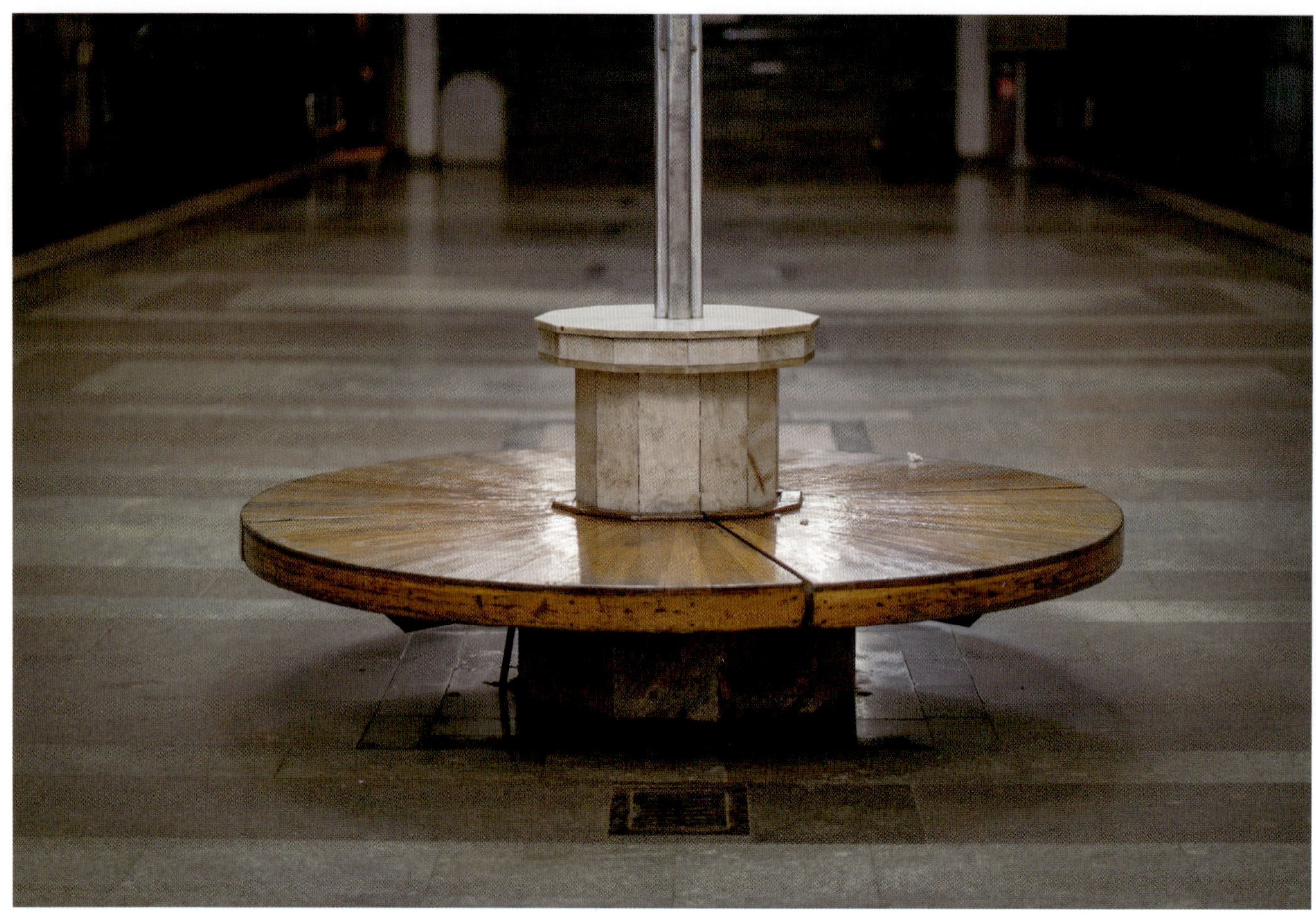

54   Pobeda, SAMARA

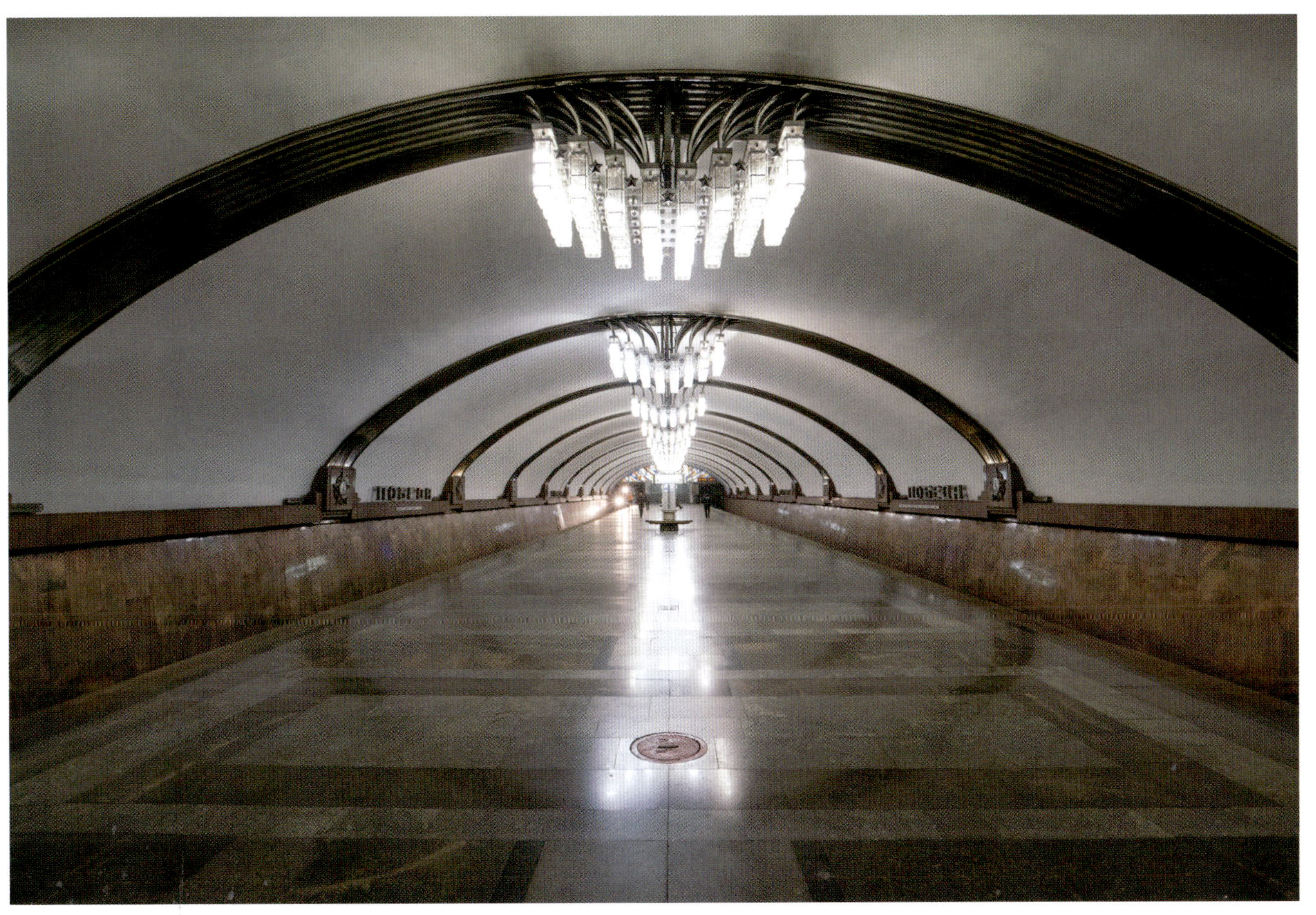

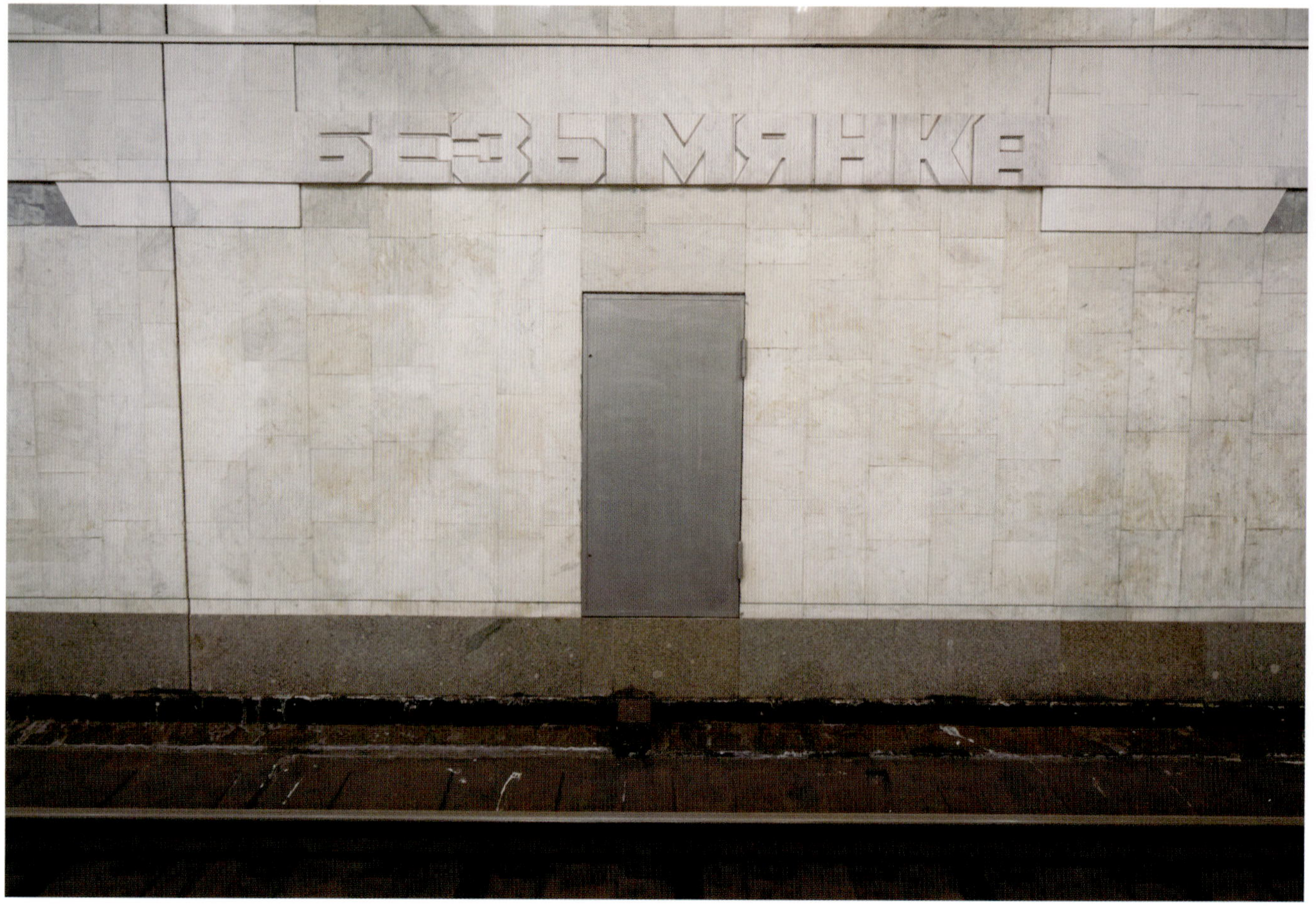

56   Bezymyanka, SAMARA

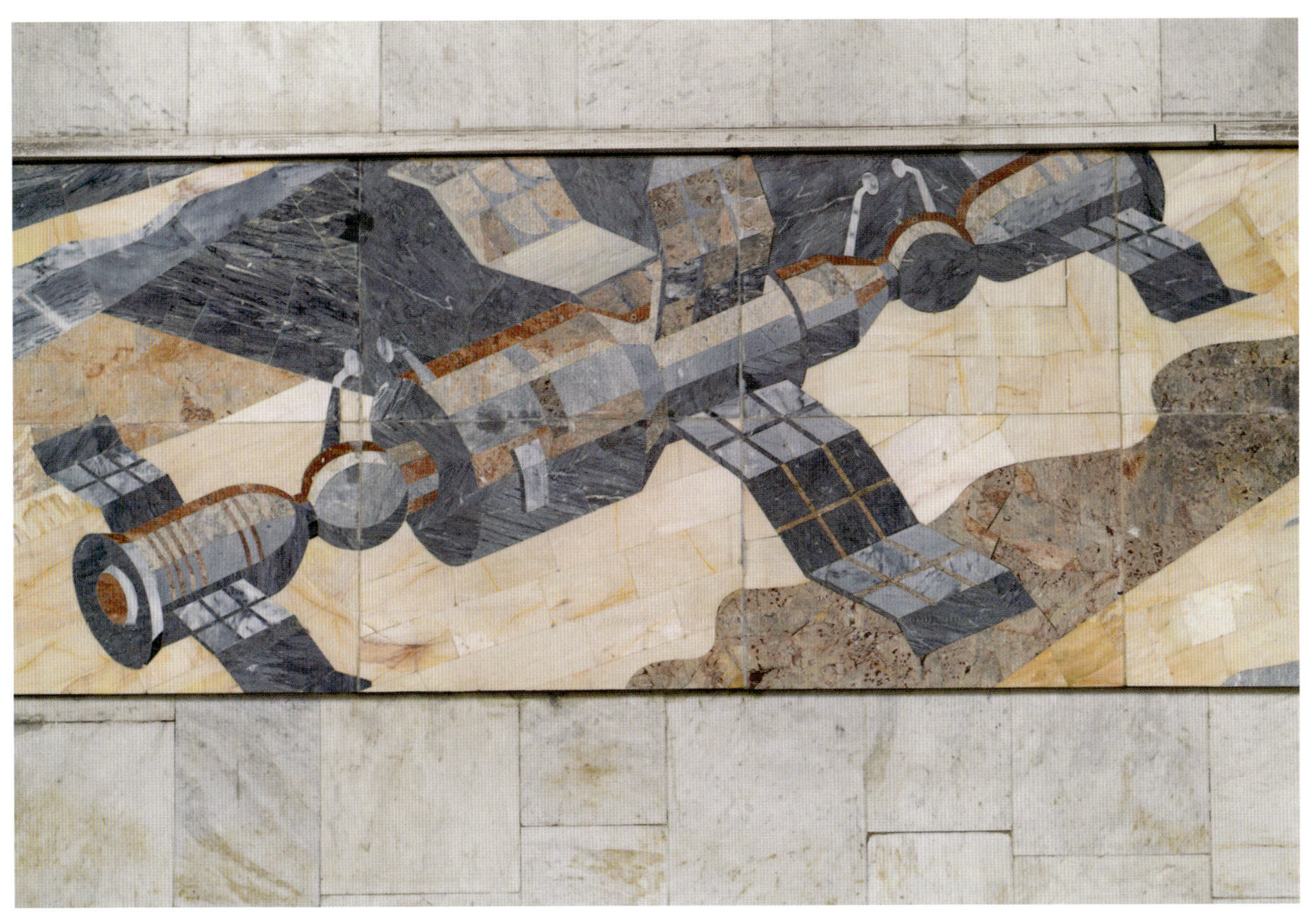

overleaf: Sportivnaya, SAMARA

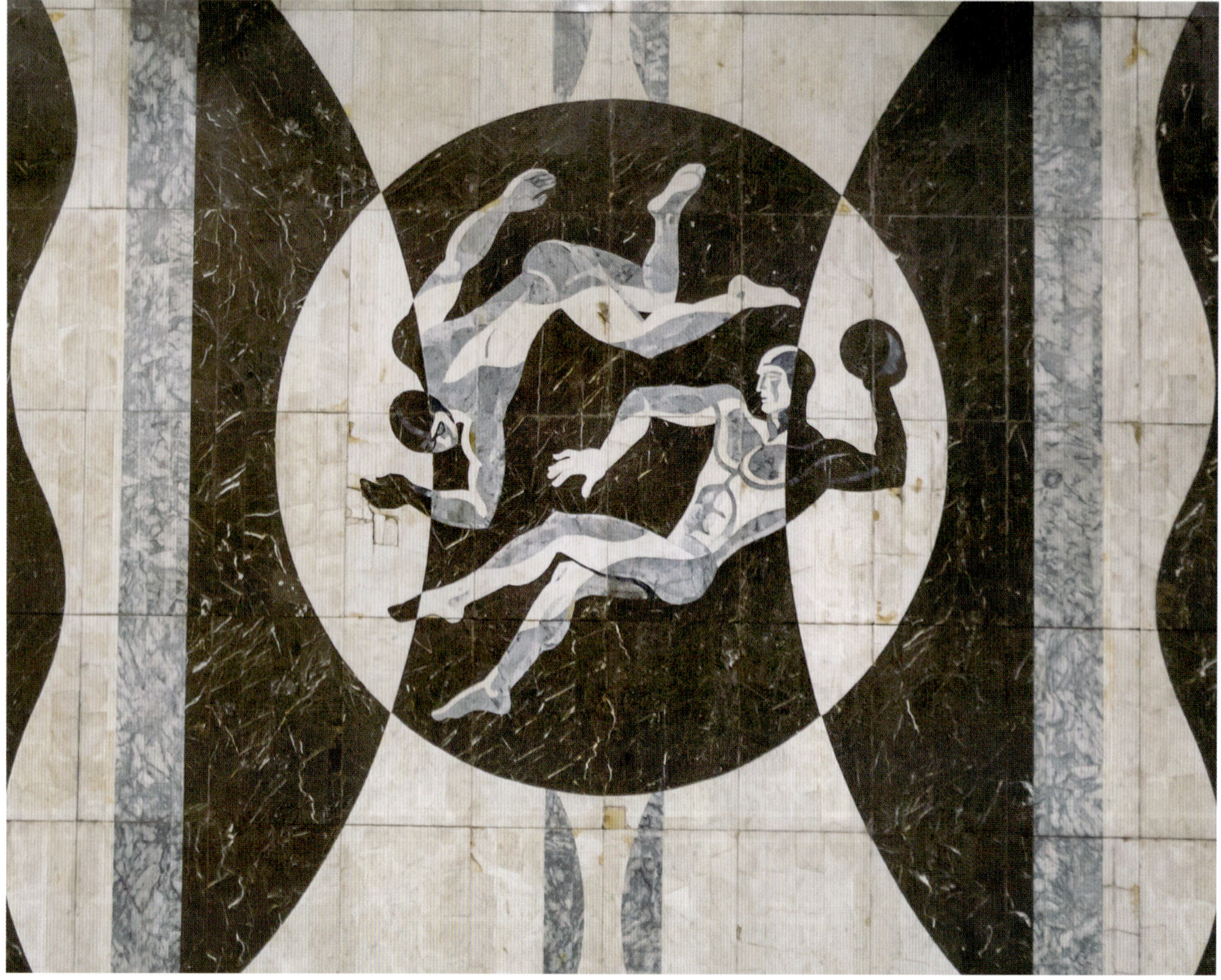

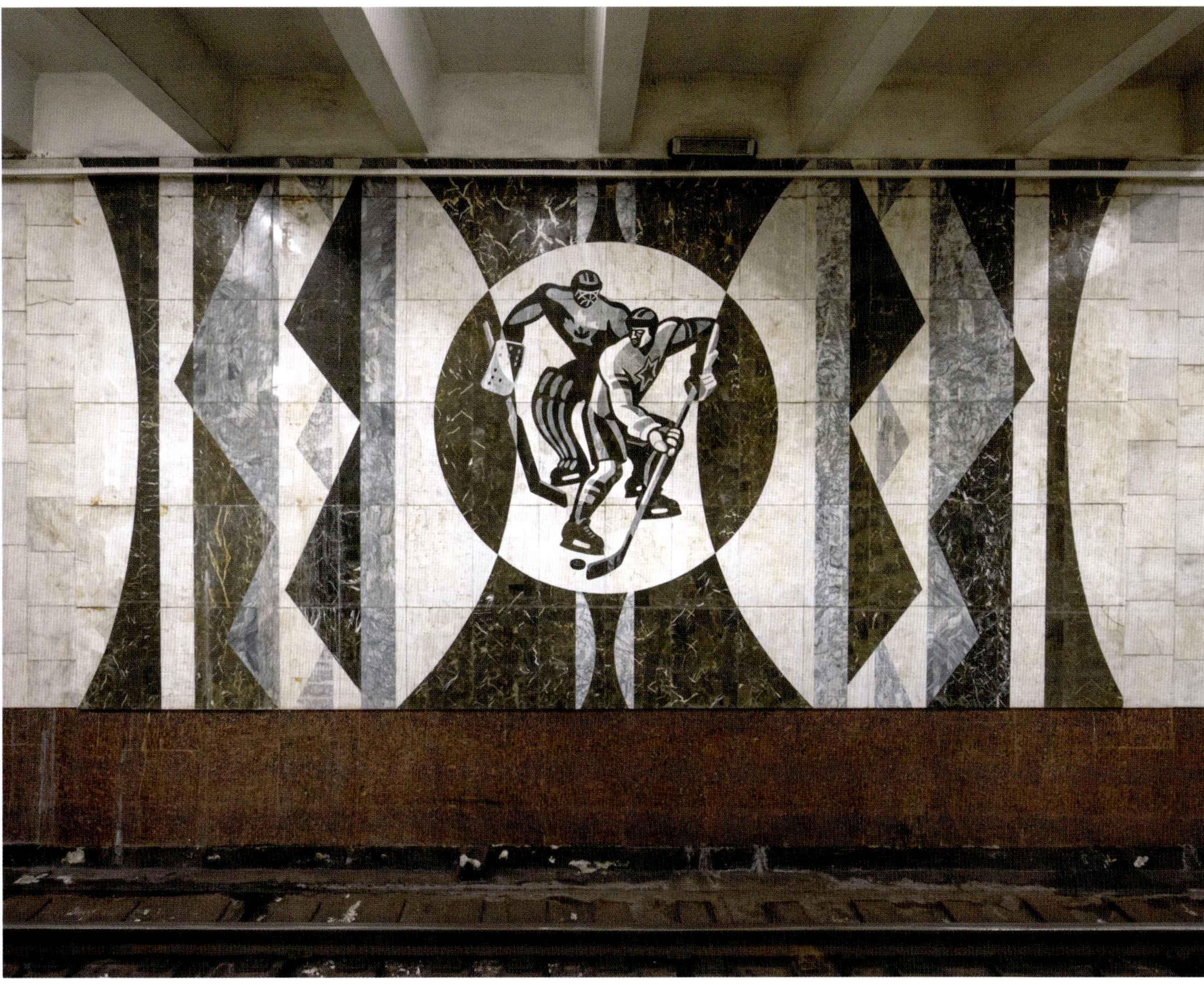

**НОВОСИБИРСК
РОССИЯ**

**NOVOSIBIRSK
RUSSIA**

OPENED 1986

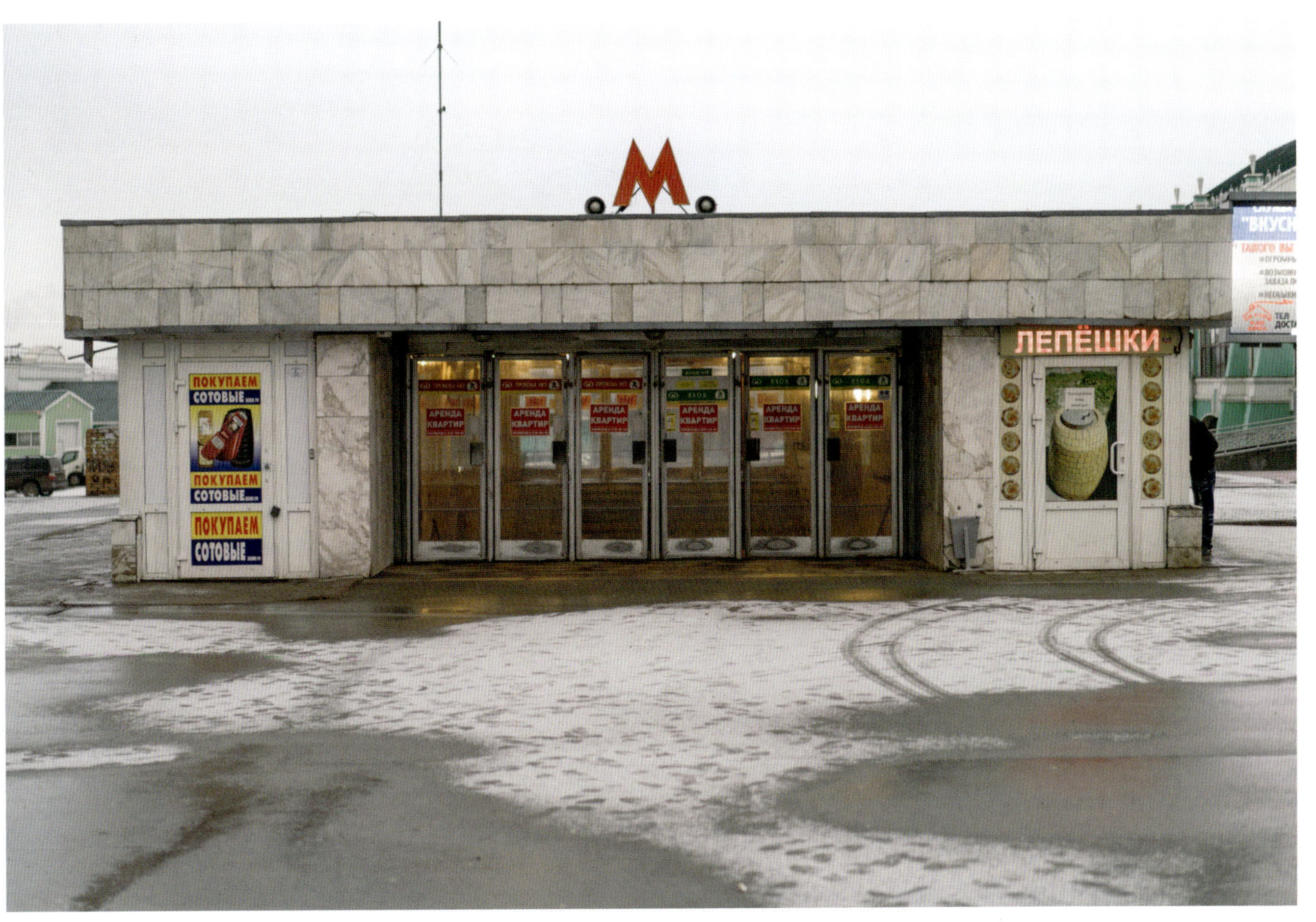
ПОКУПАЕМ
СОТОВЫЕ
ПОКУПАЕМ
СОТОВЫЕ
АРЕНДА
КВАРТИР
ЛЕПЁШКИ
"ВКУСН
ТАКОГО ВЫ

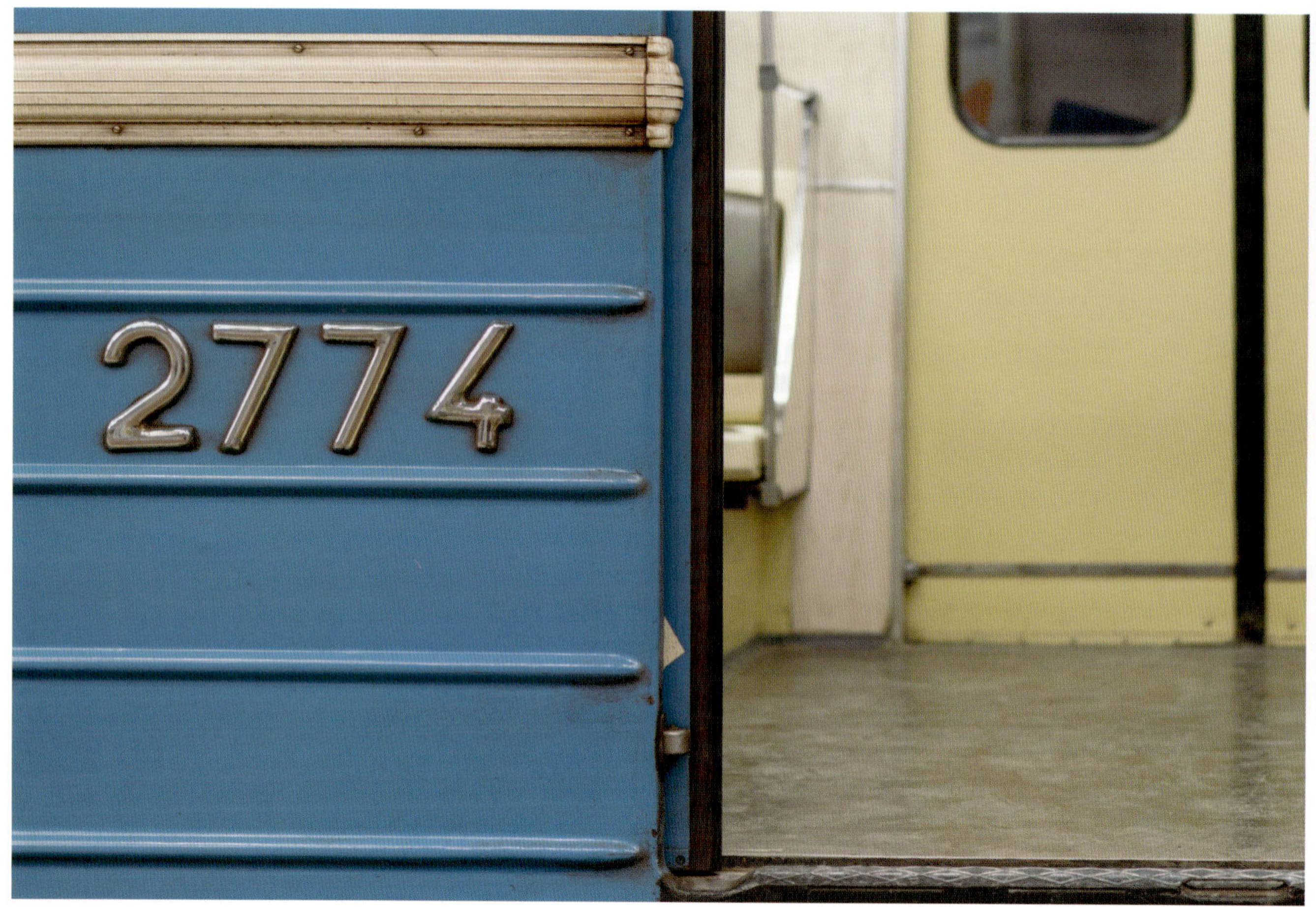

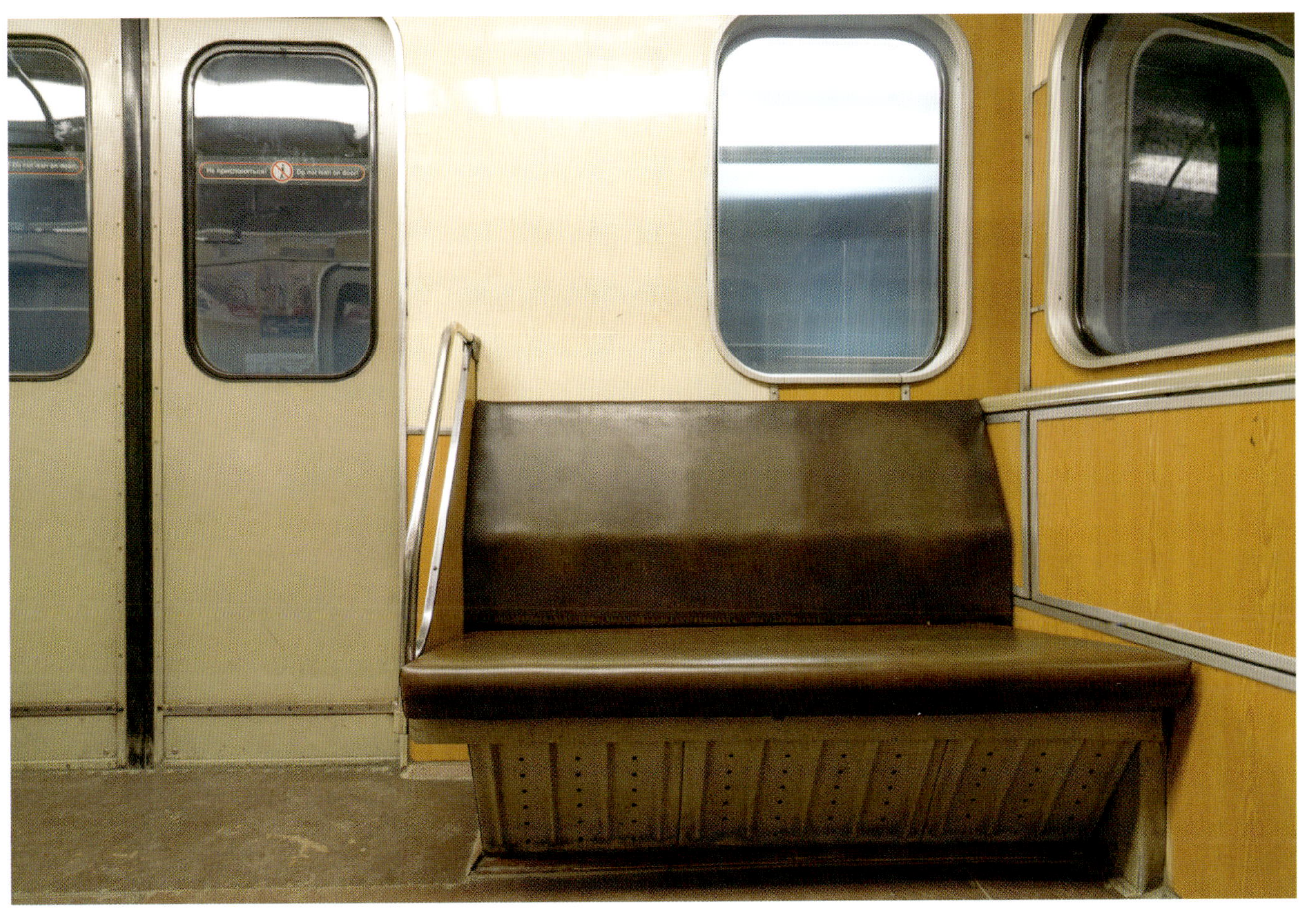

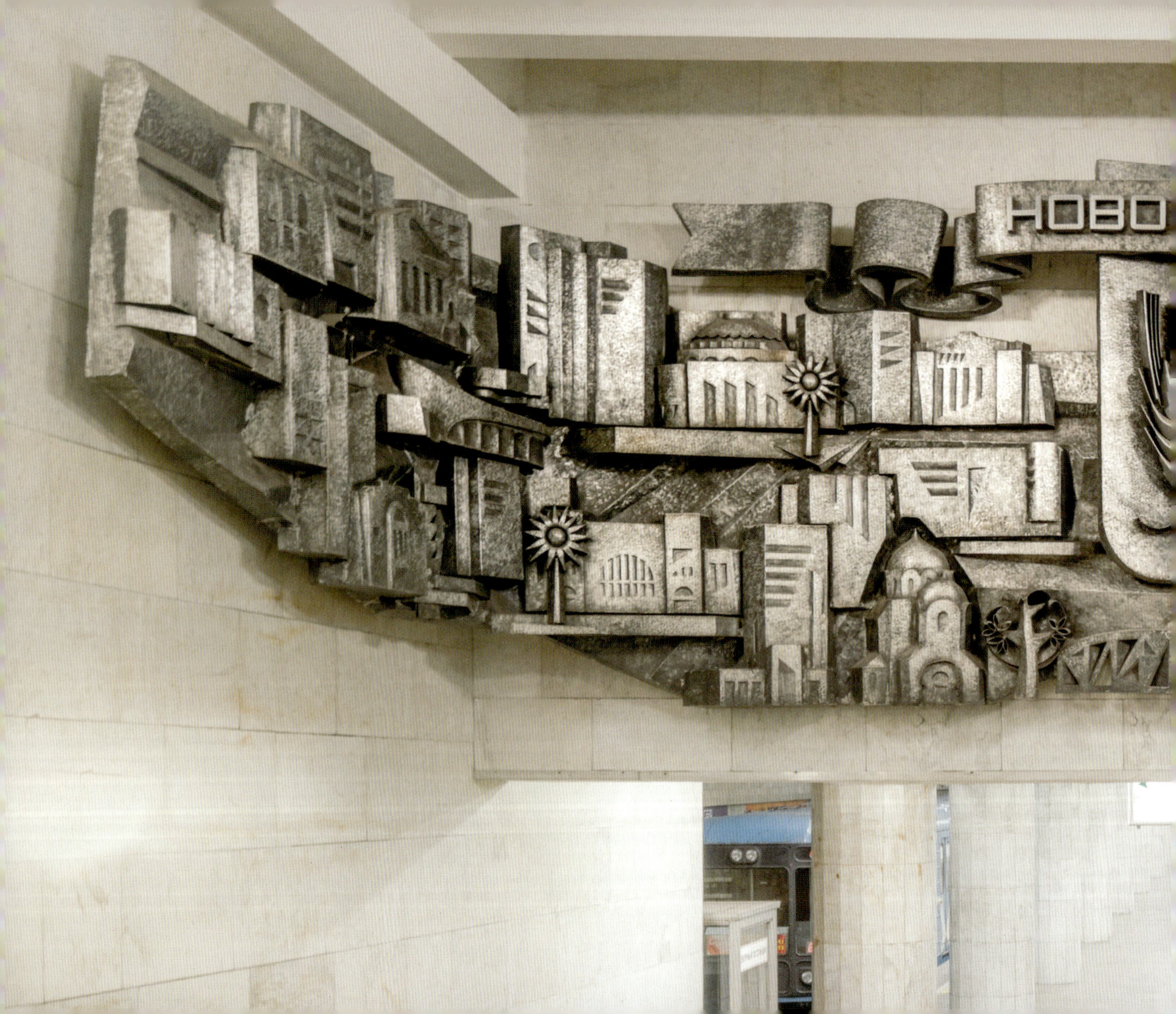

НОВО

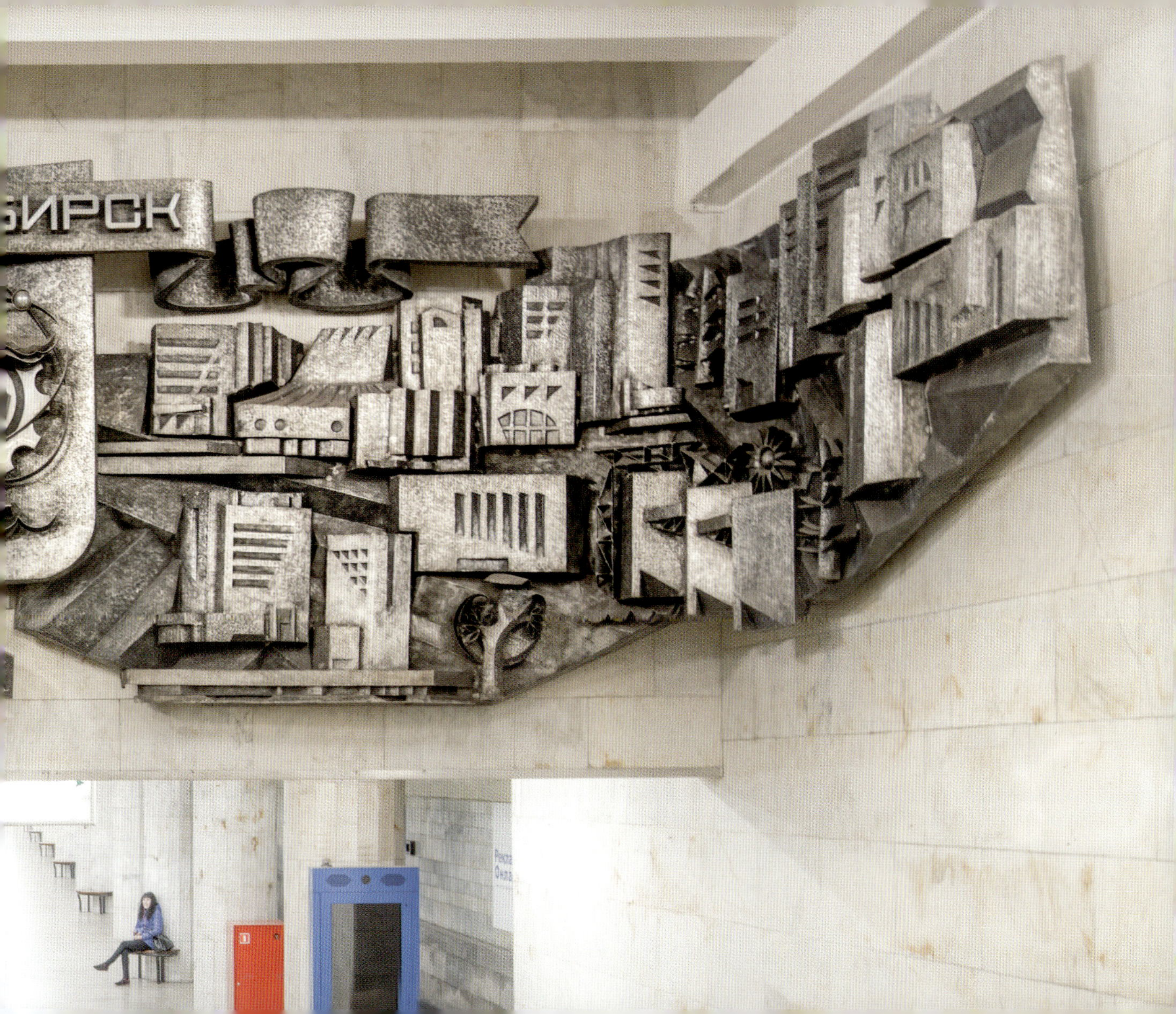
БИРСК

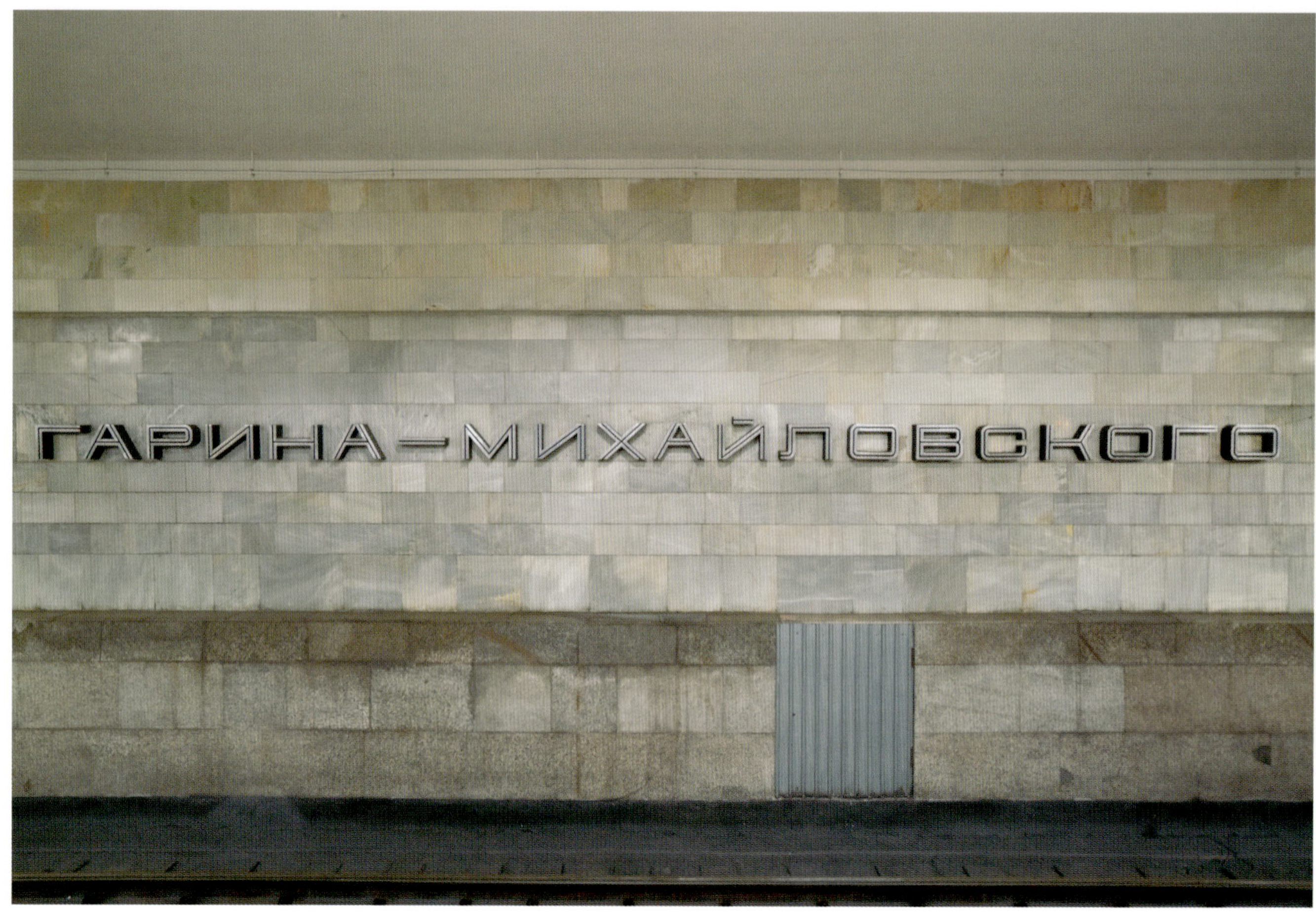

 Ploshchad Garina-Mikhaylovskogo, NOVOSIBIRSK

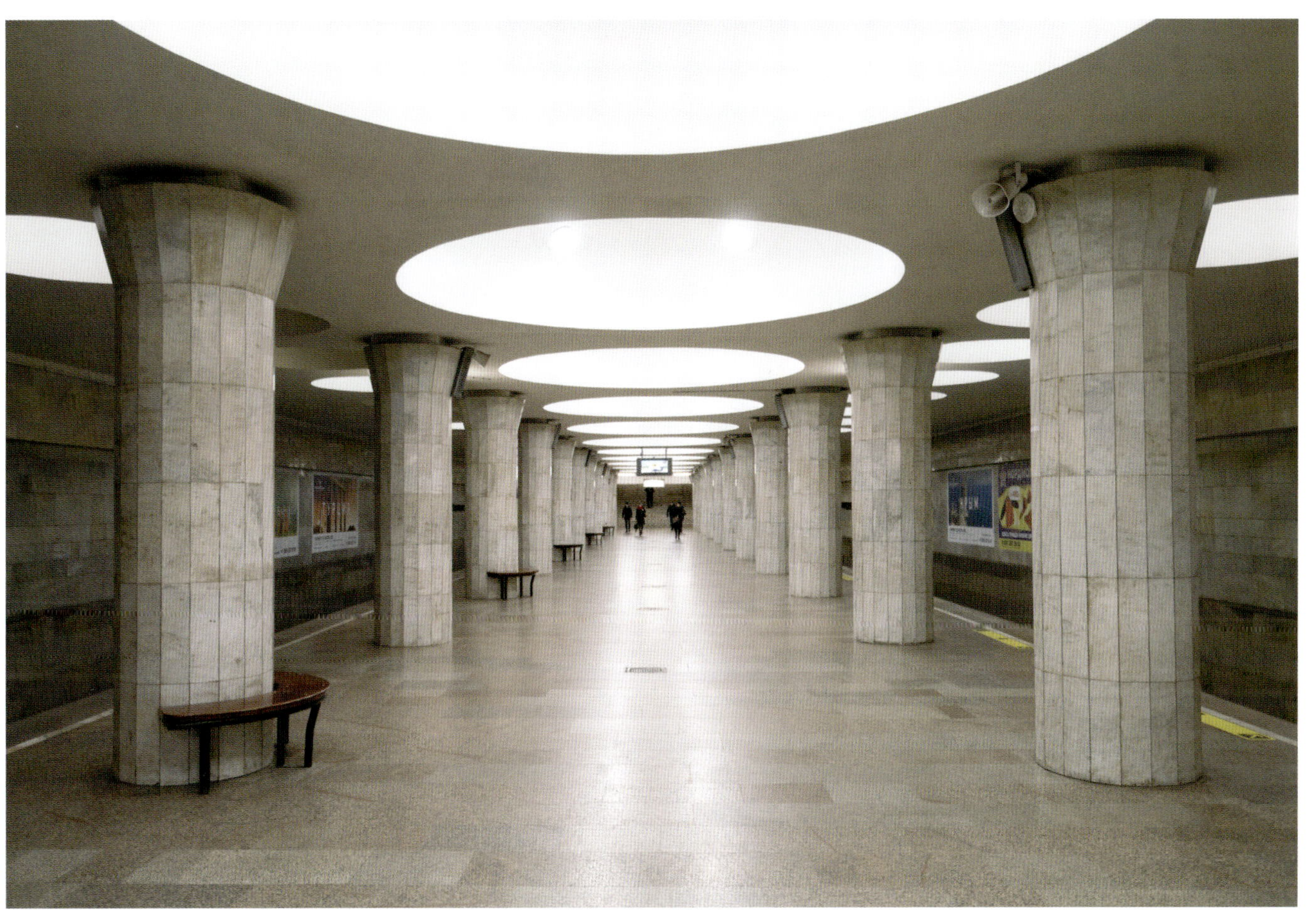

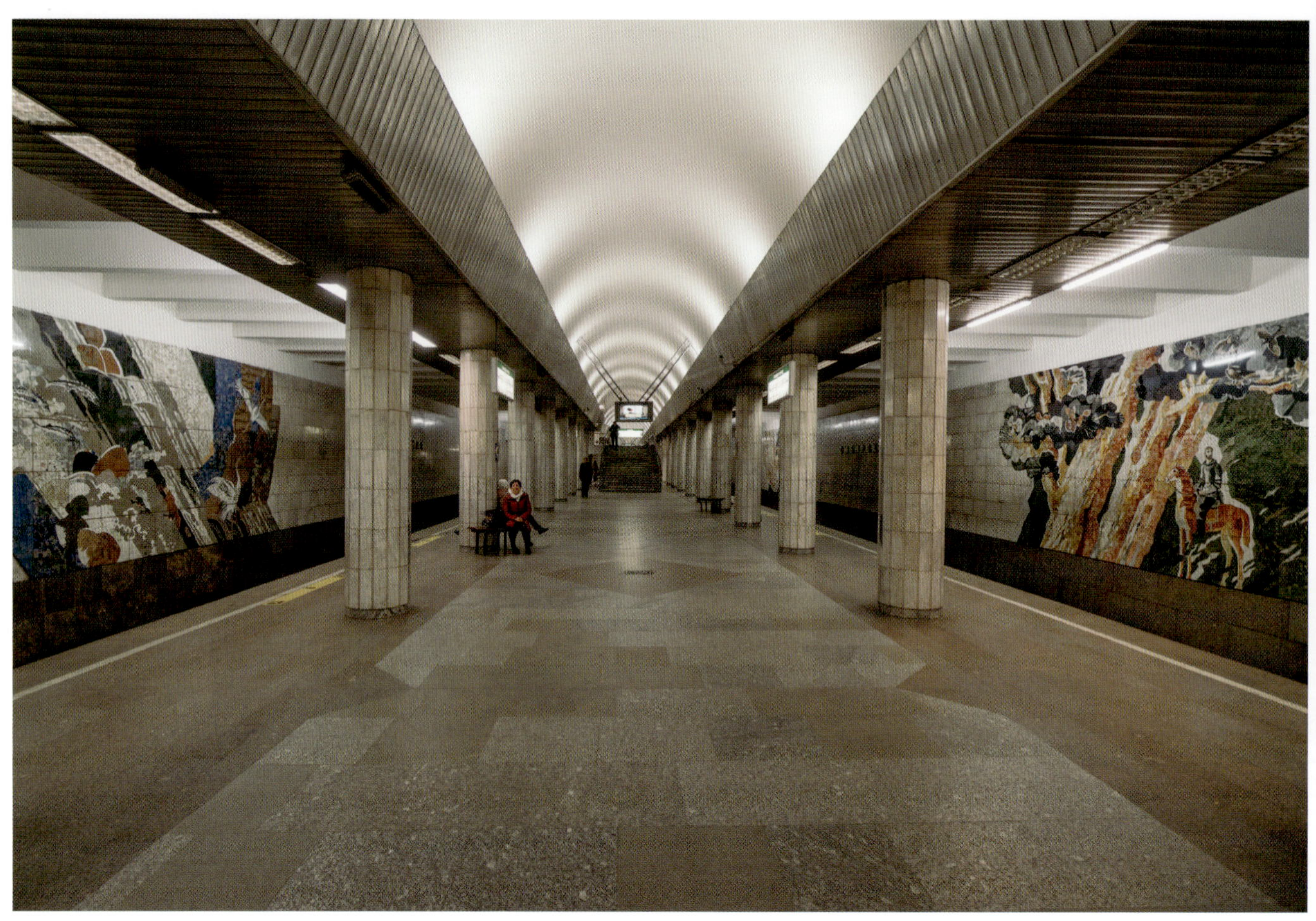

    Sibirskaya, NOVOSIBIRSK

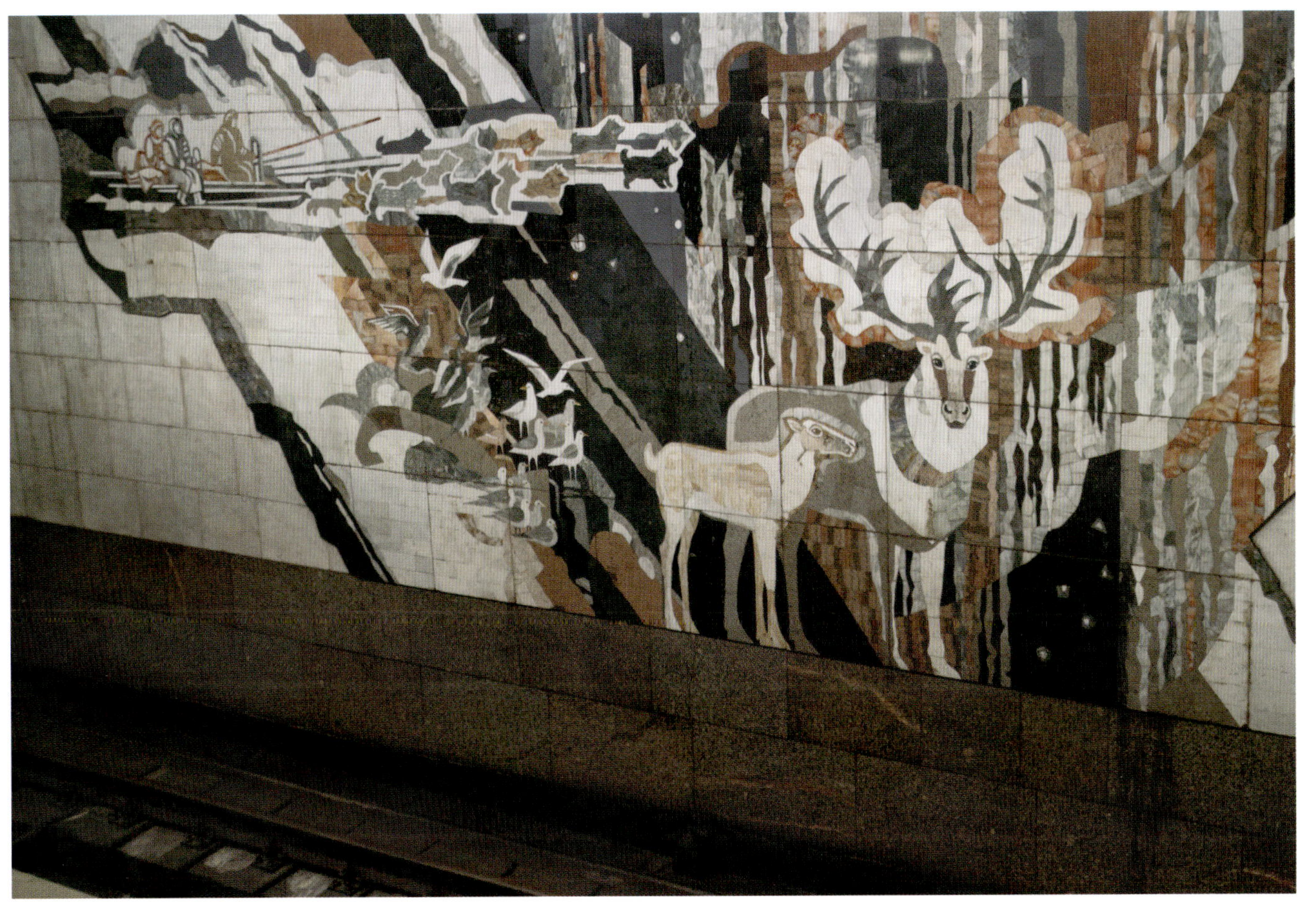

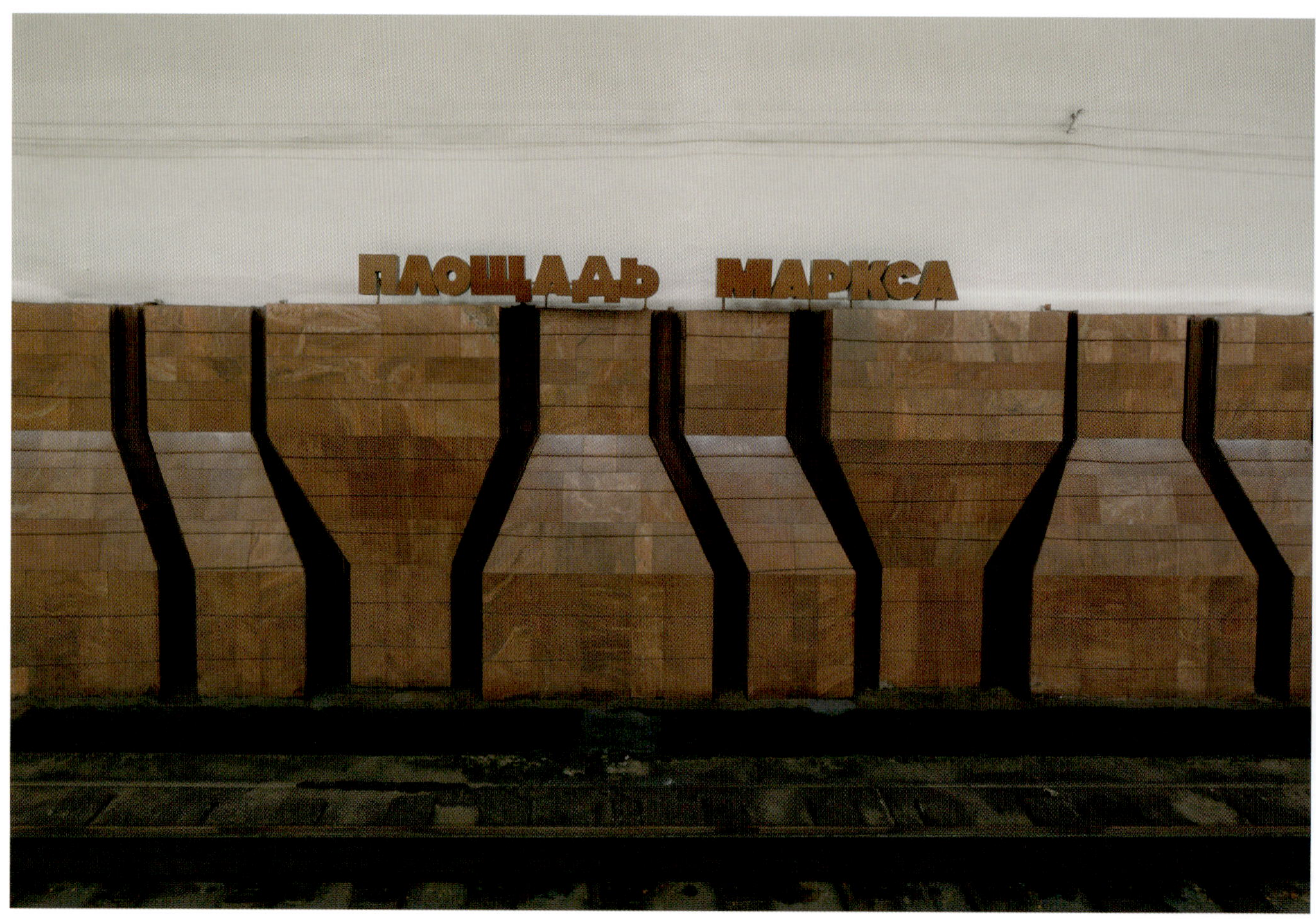

Ploschad Marksa, NOVOSIBIRSK

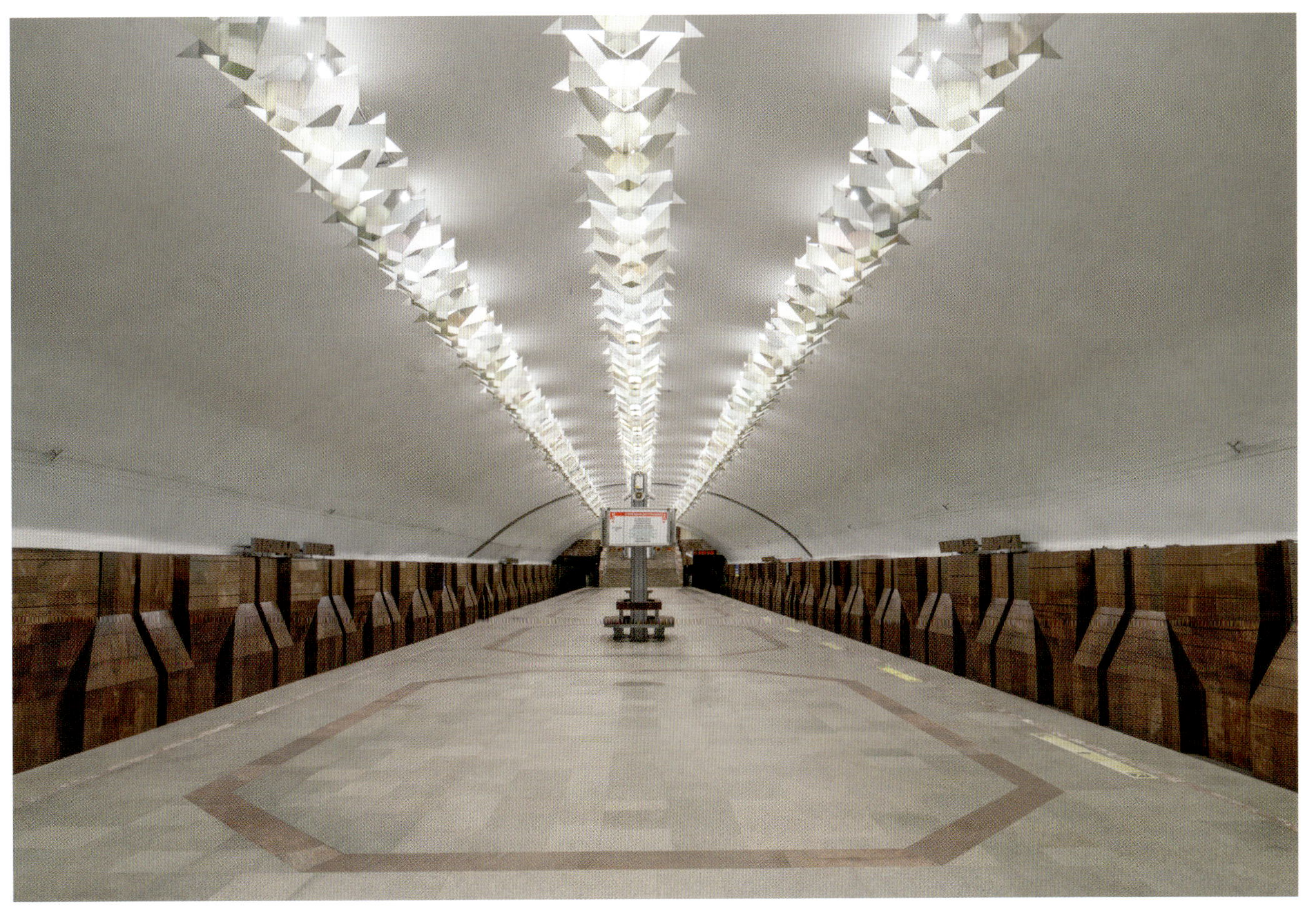

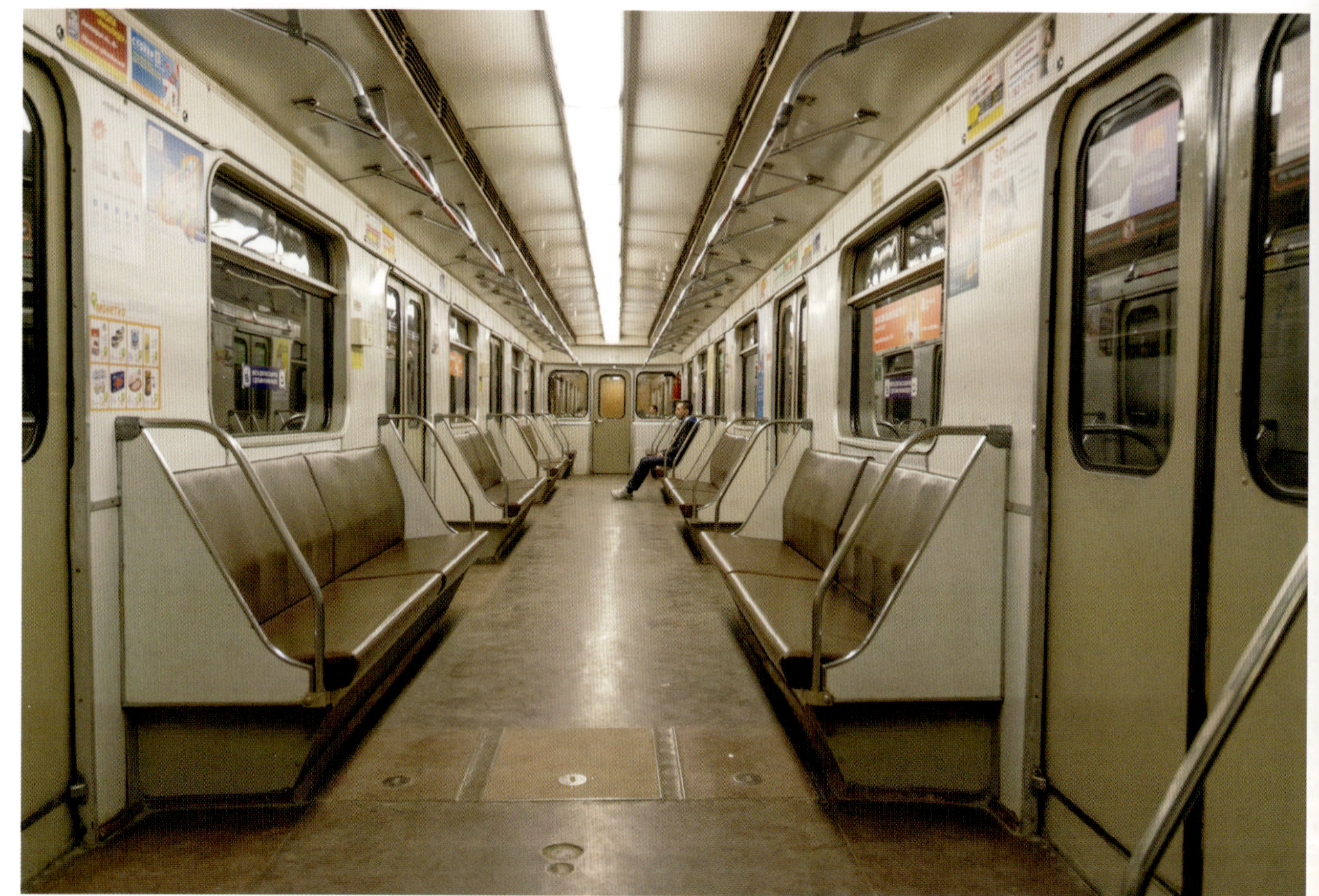

Krasny Prospekt, NOVOSIBIRSK

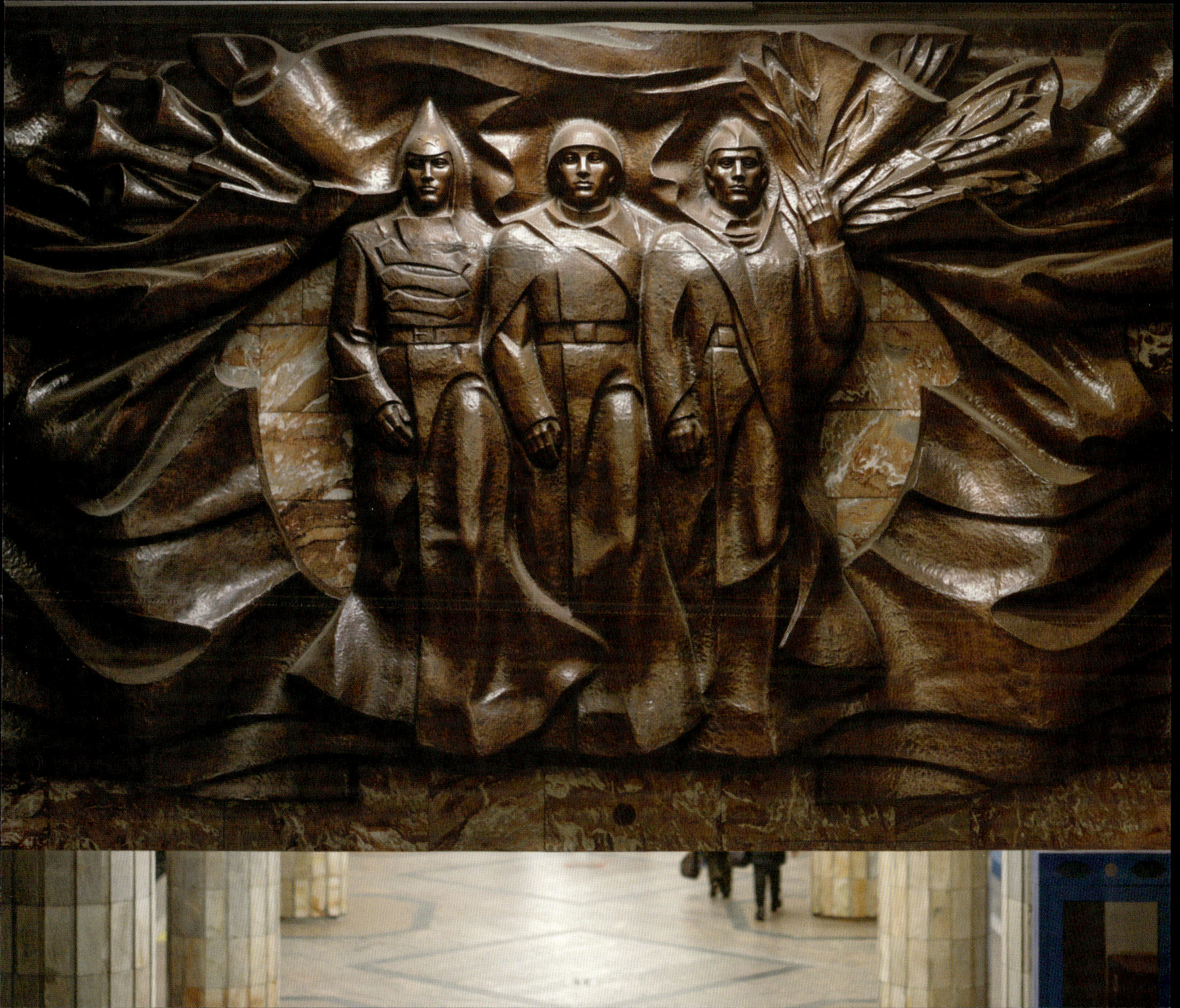

**КРИВОЙ РОГ
УКРАИНА**

**KRYVYI RIH
UKRAINE**

OPENED 1986

    Budynok Rad, KRYVYI RIH

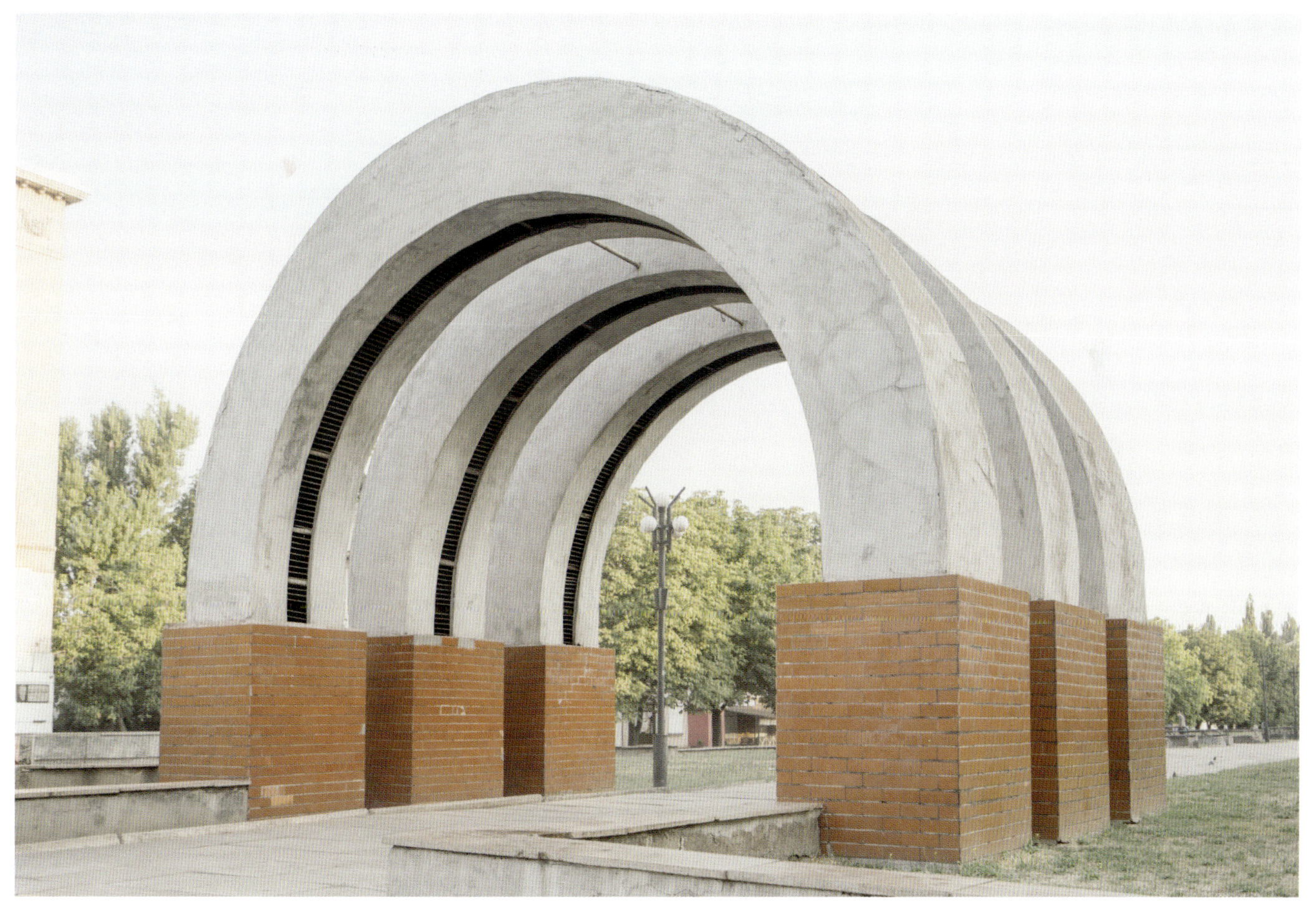

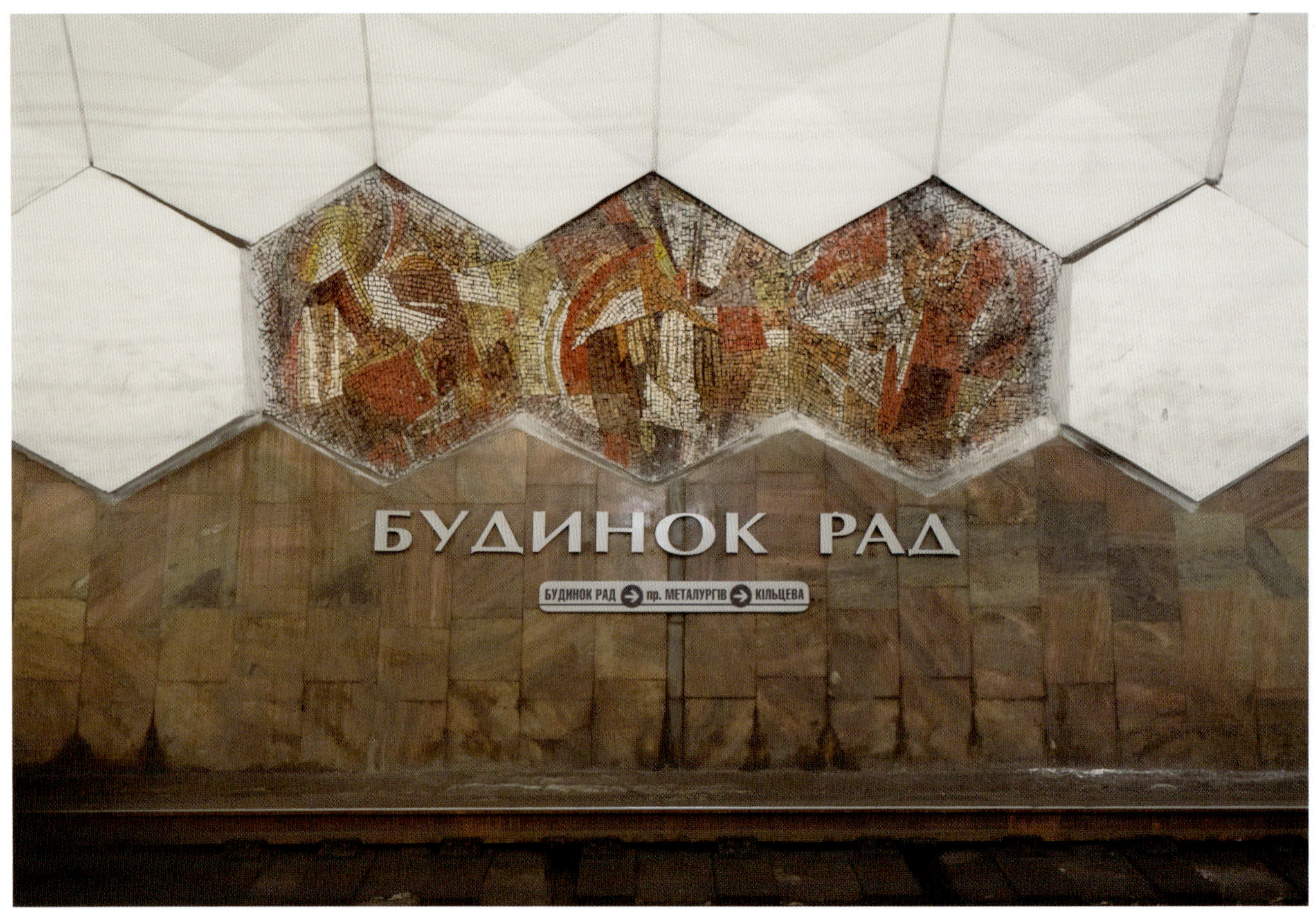

76   Budynok Rad, KRYVYI RIH

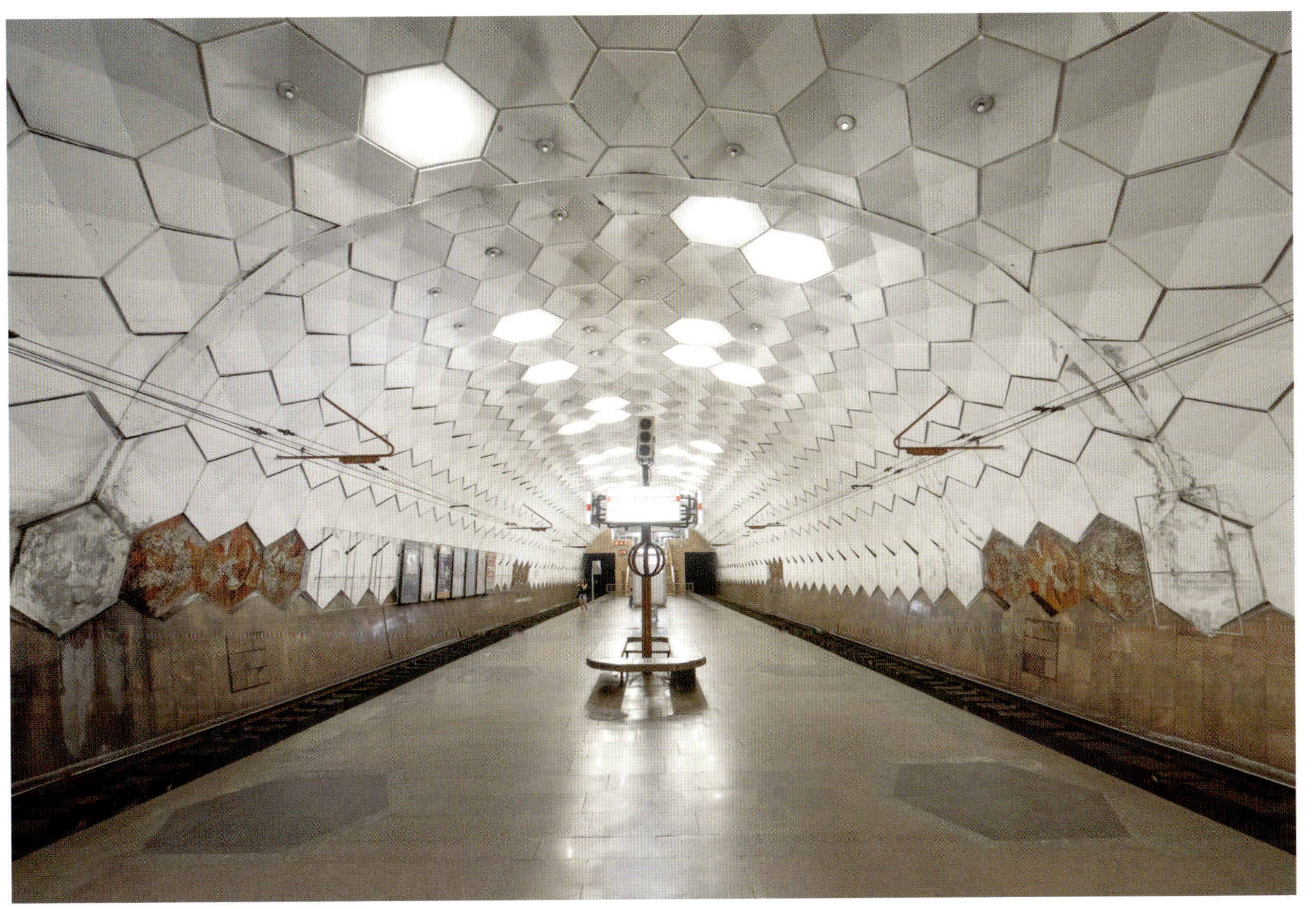

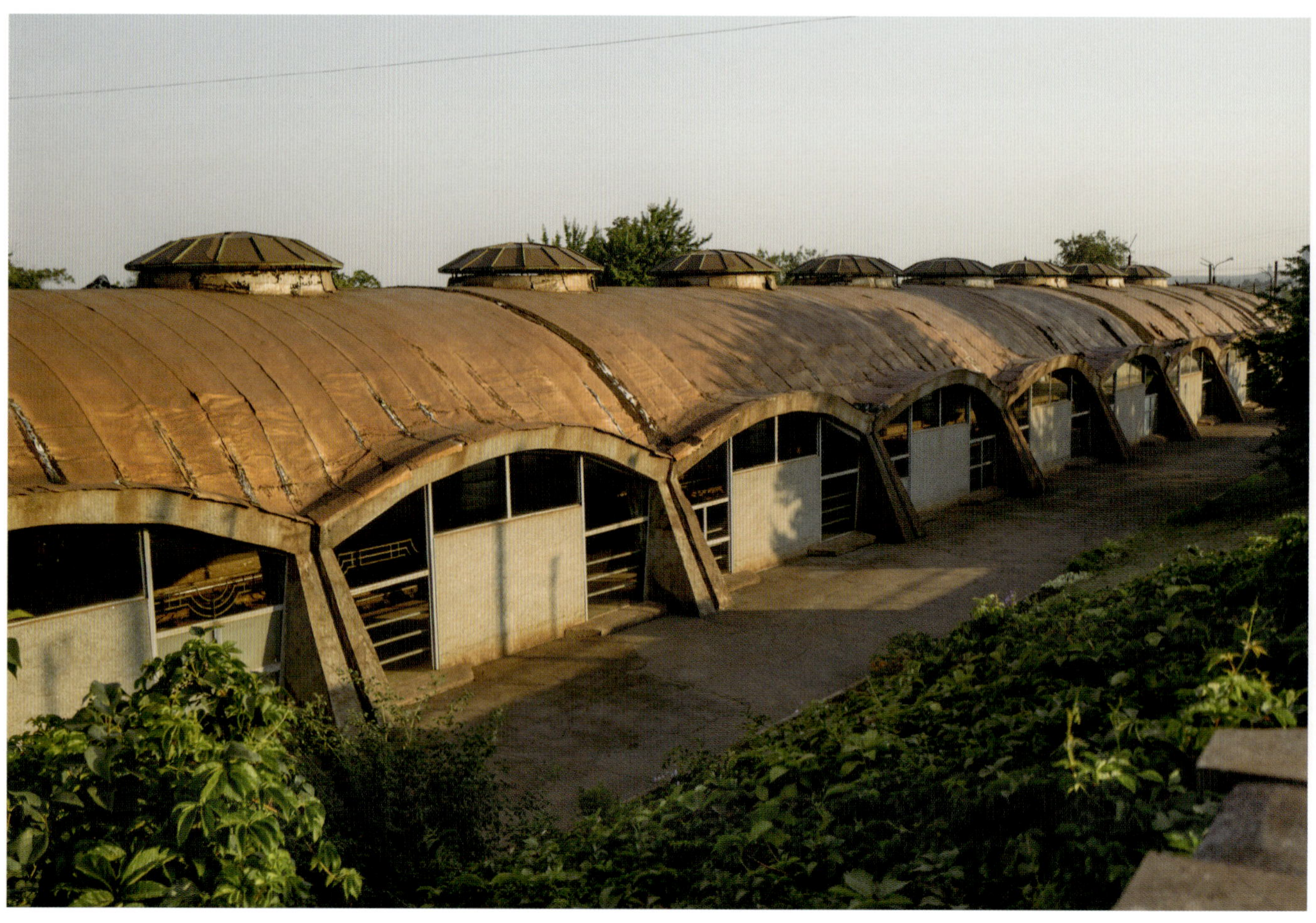

　Mudryona, KRYVYI RIH

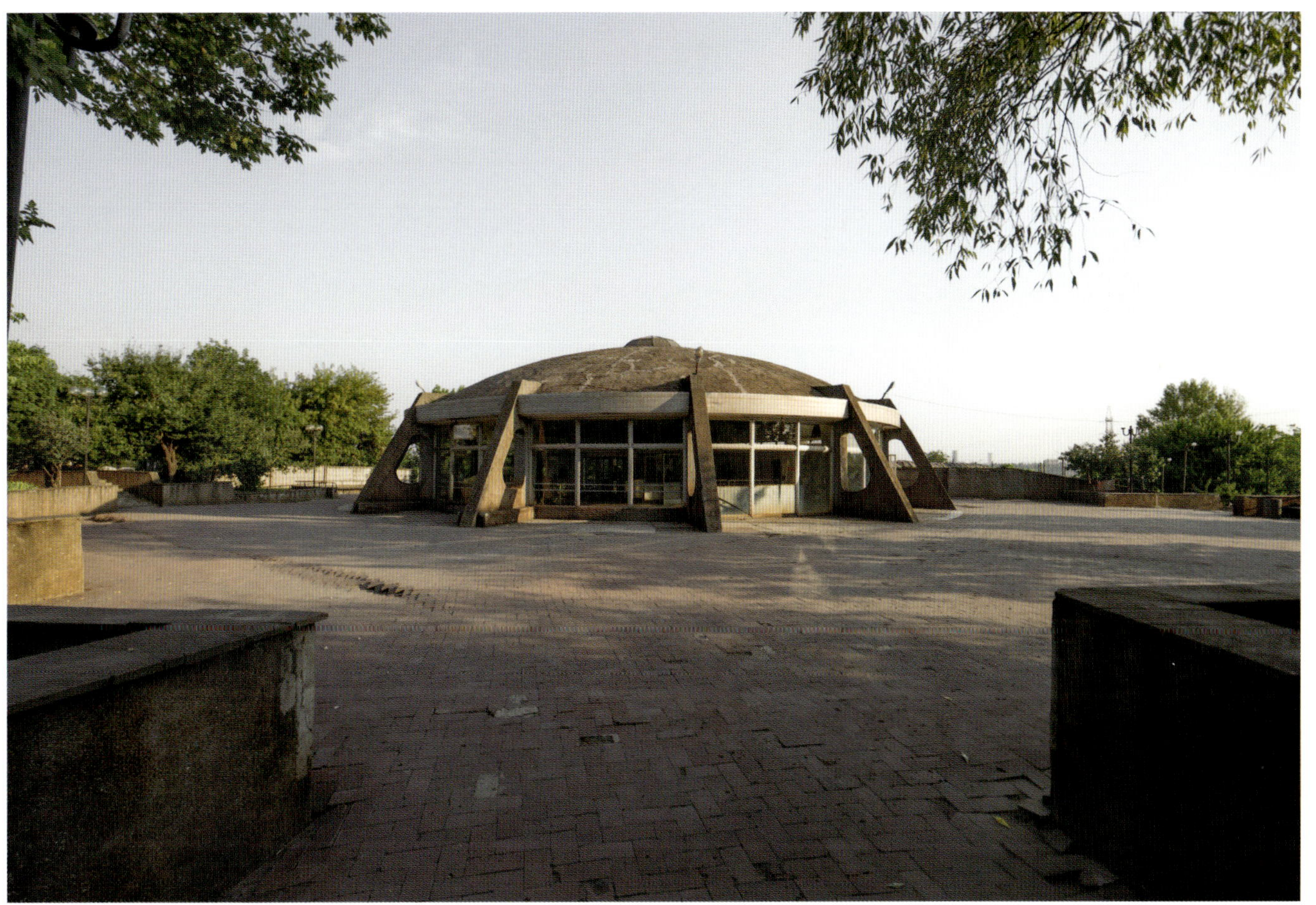

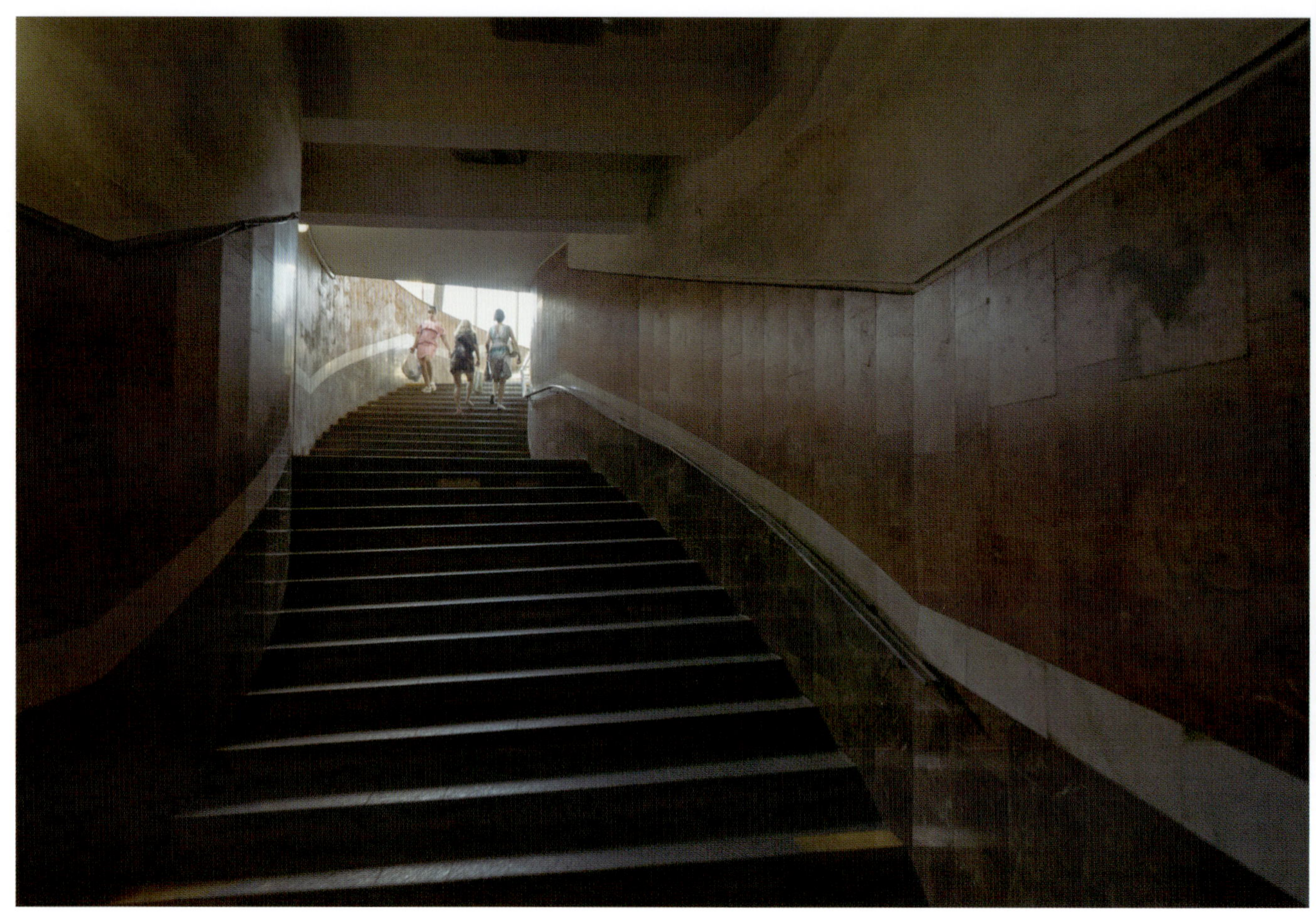

80 Vechirniy Bulvar, KRYVYI RIH

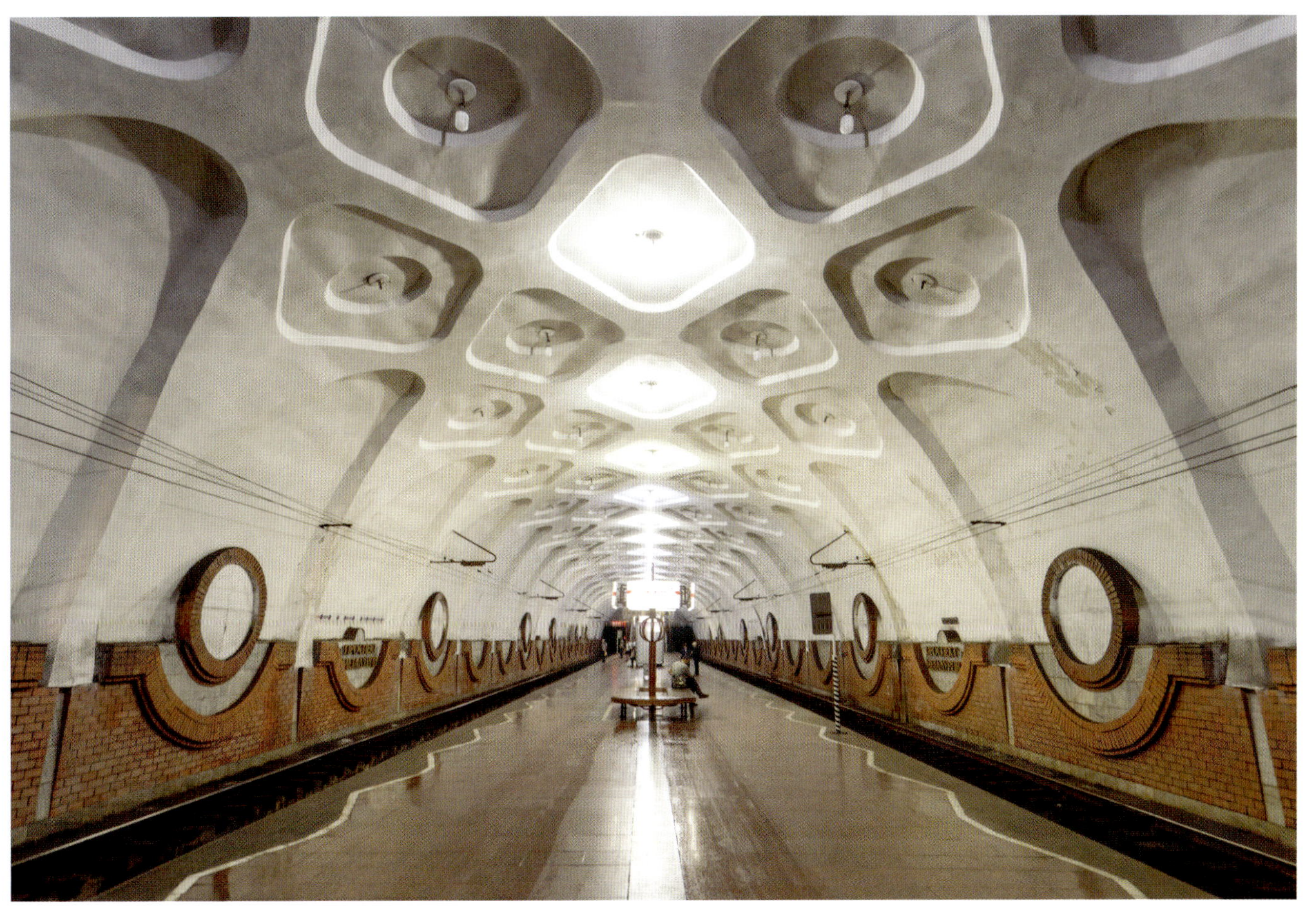

Prospekt Metalurhiv, KRYVYI RIH 81

**НИЖНИЙ НОВГОРОД
РОССИЯ**

**NIZHNY NOVGOROD
RUSSIA**

OPENED 1985

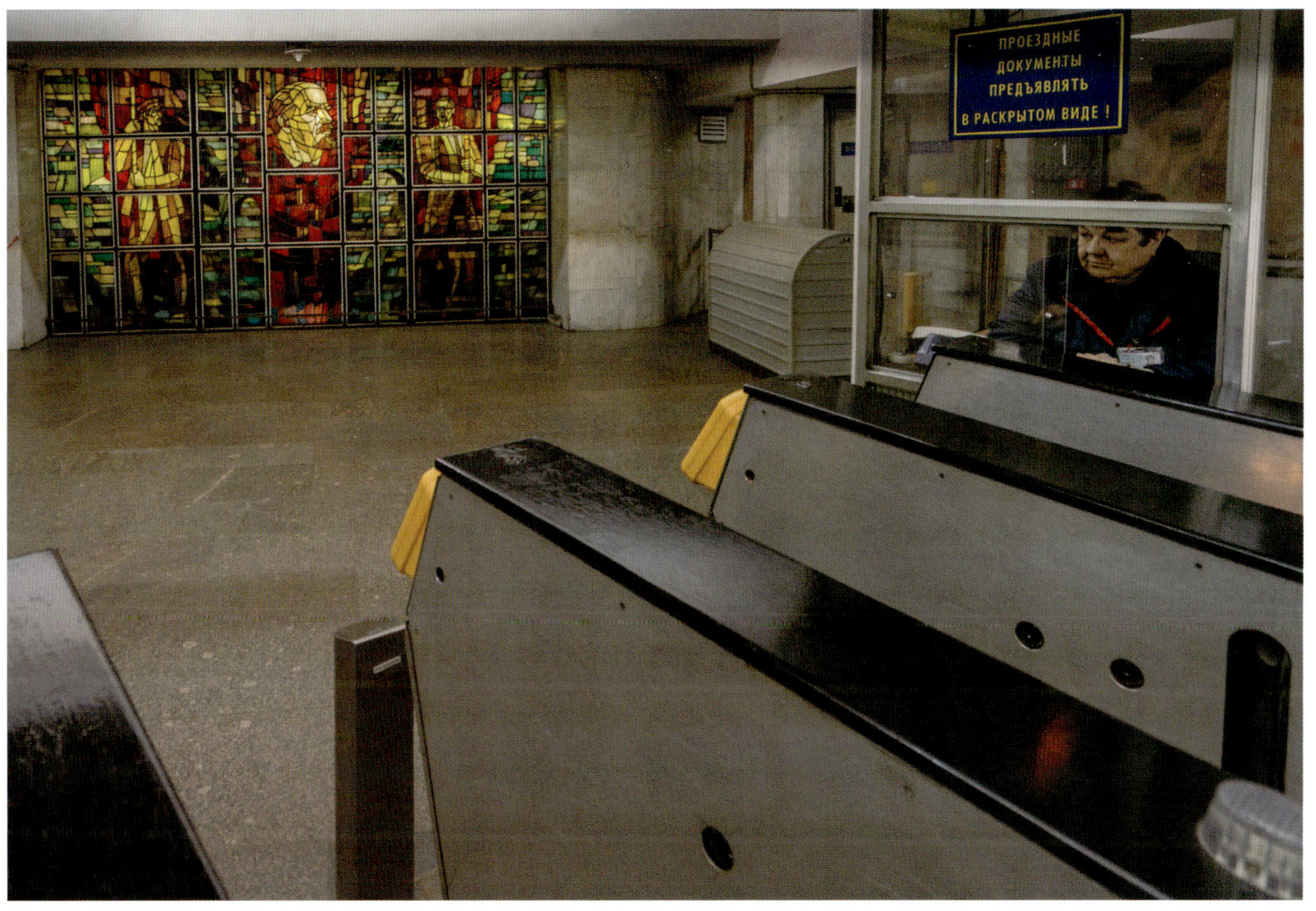

ПРОЕЗДНЫЕ
ДОКУМЕНТЫ
ПРЕДЪЯВЛЯТЬ
В РАСКРЫТОМ ВИДЕ !

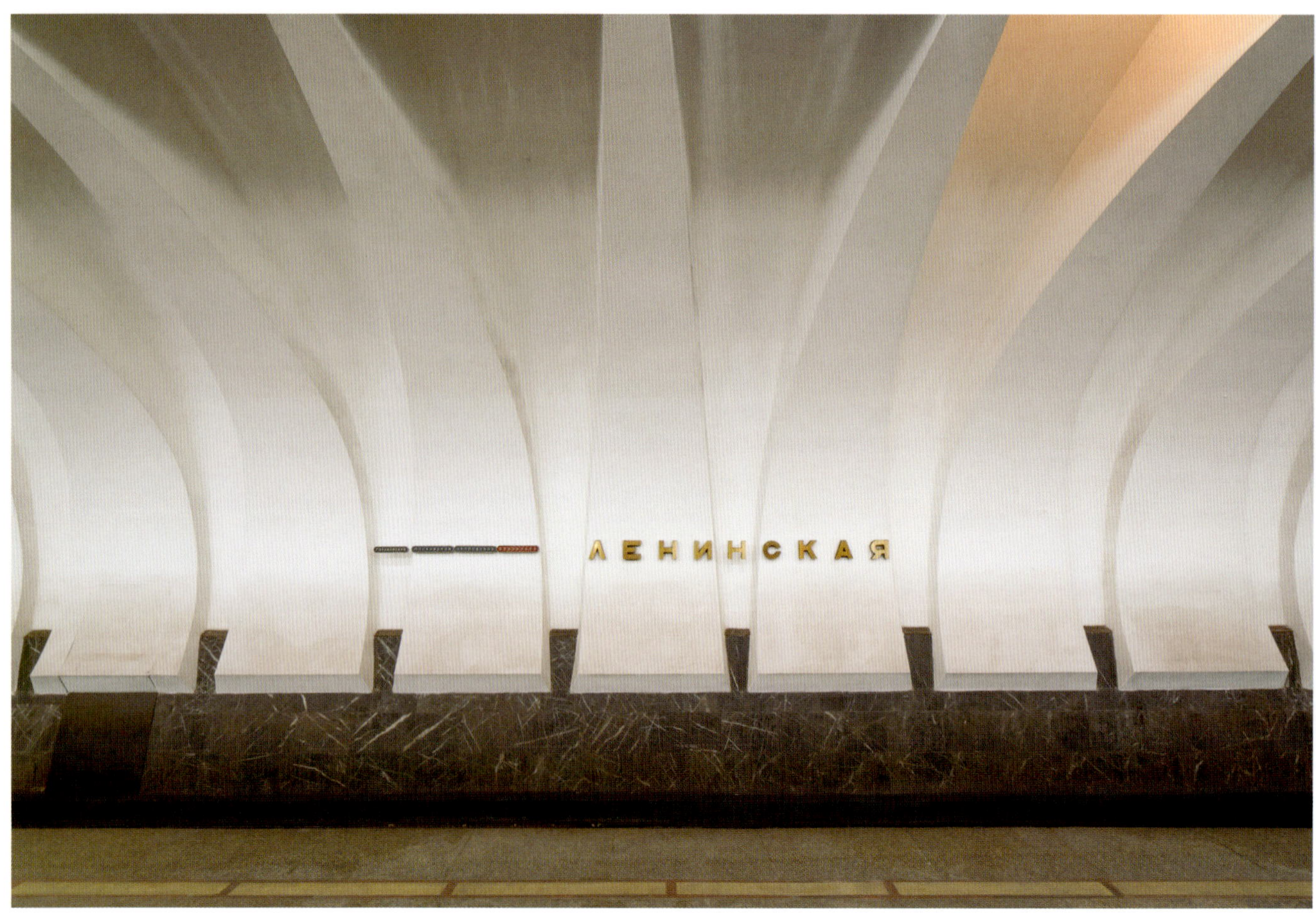

84   Leninskaya, NIZHNY NOVGOROD

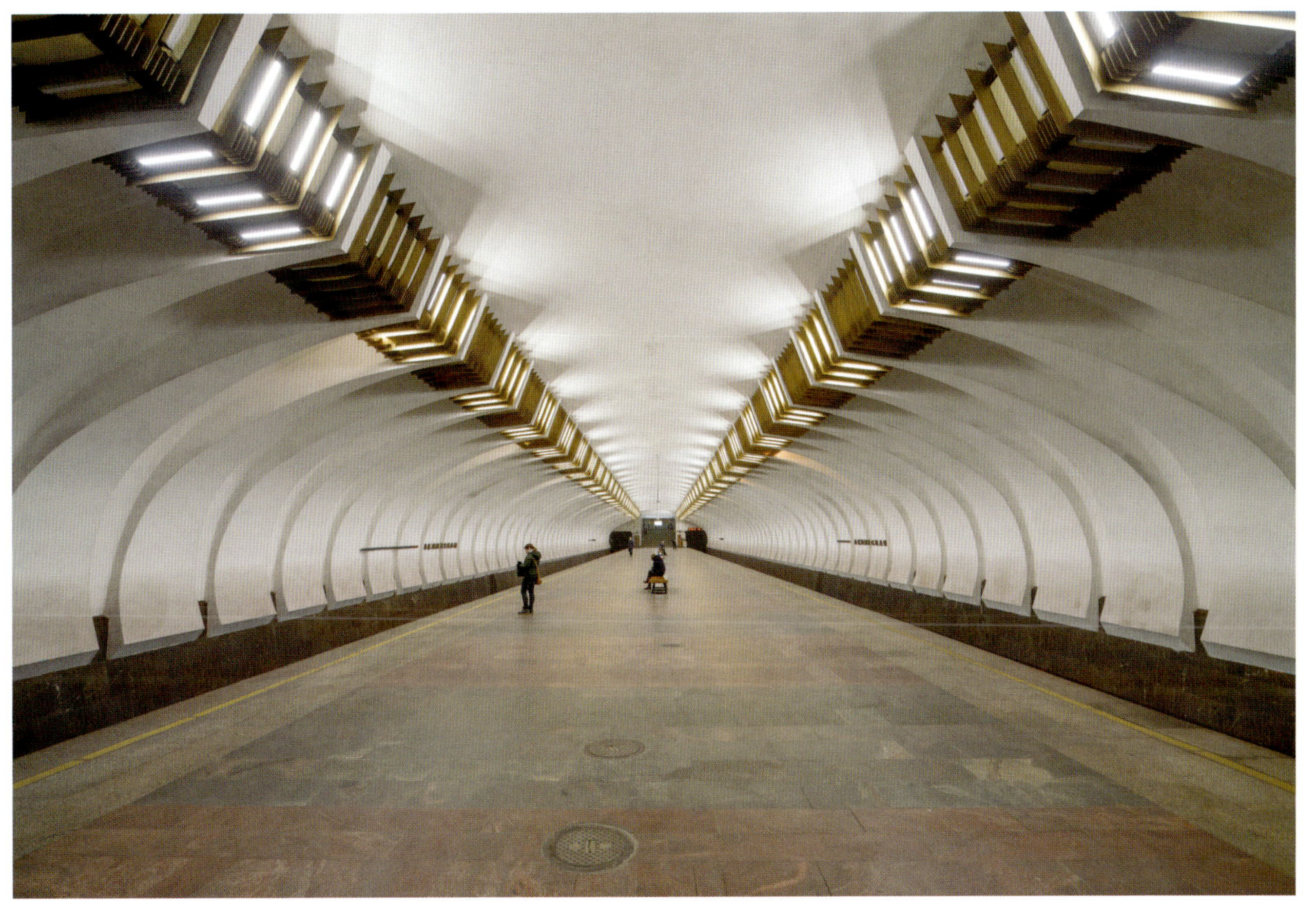

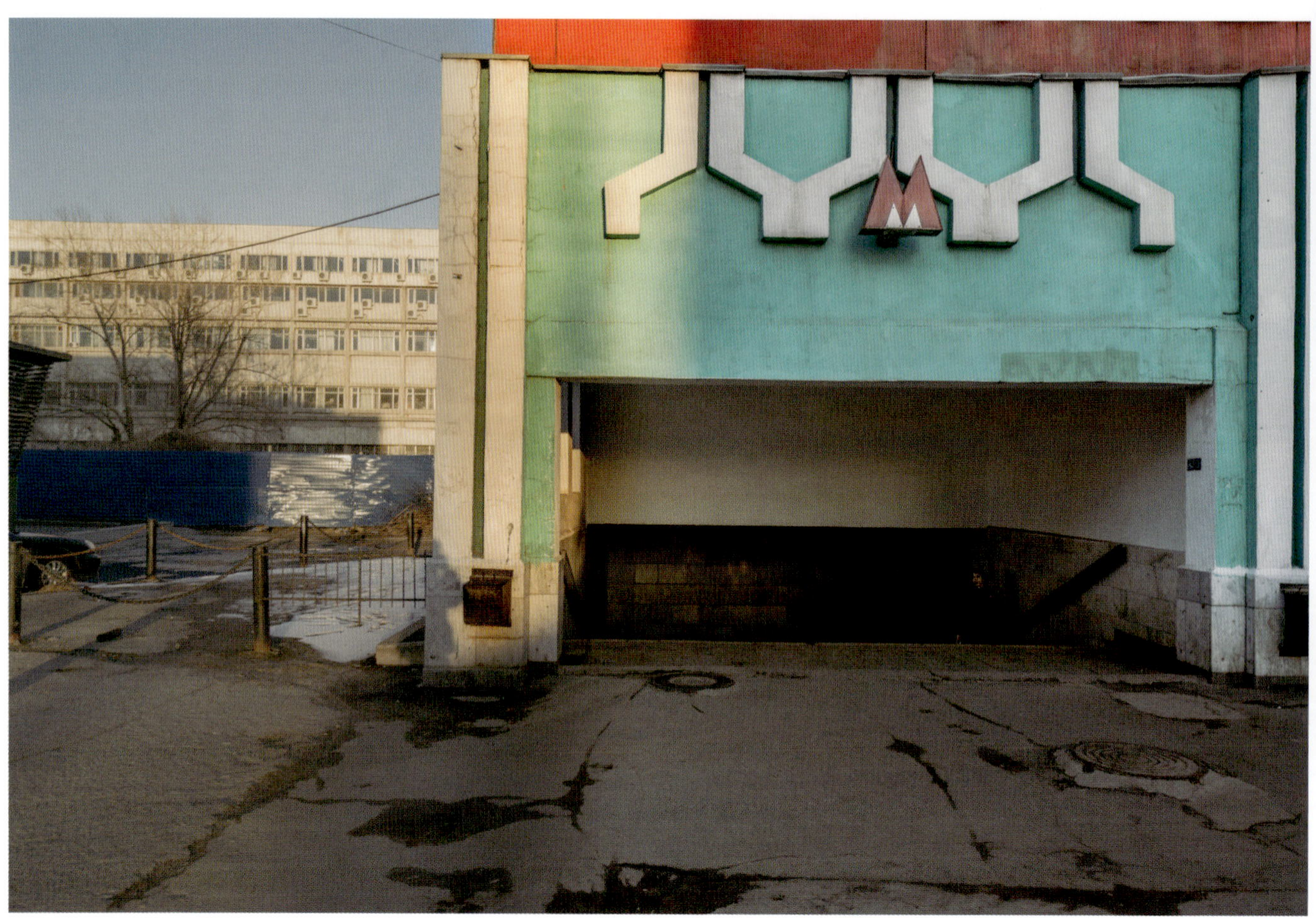

86   Leninskaya, NIZHNY NOVGOROD

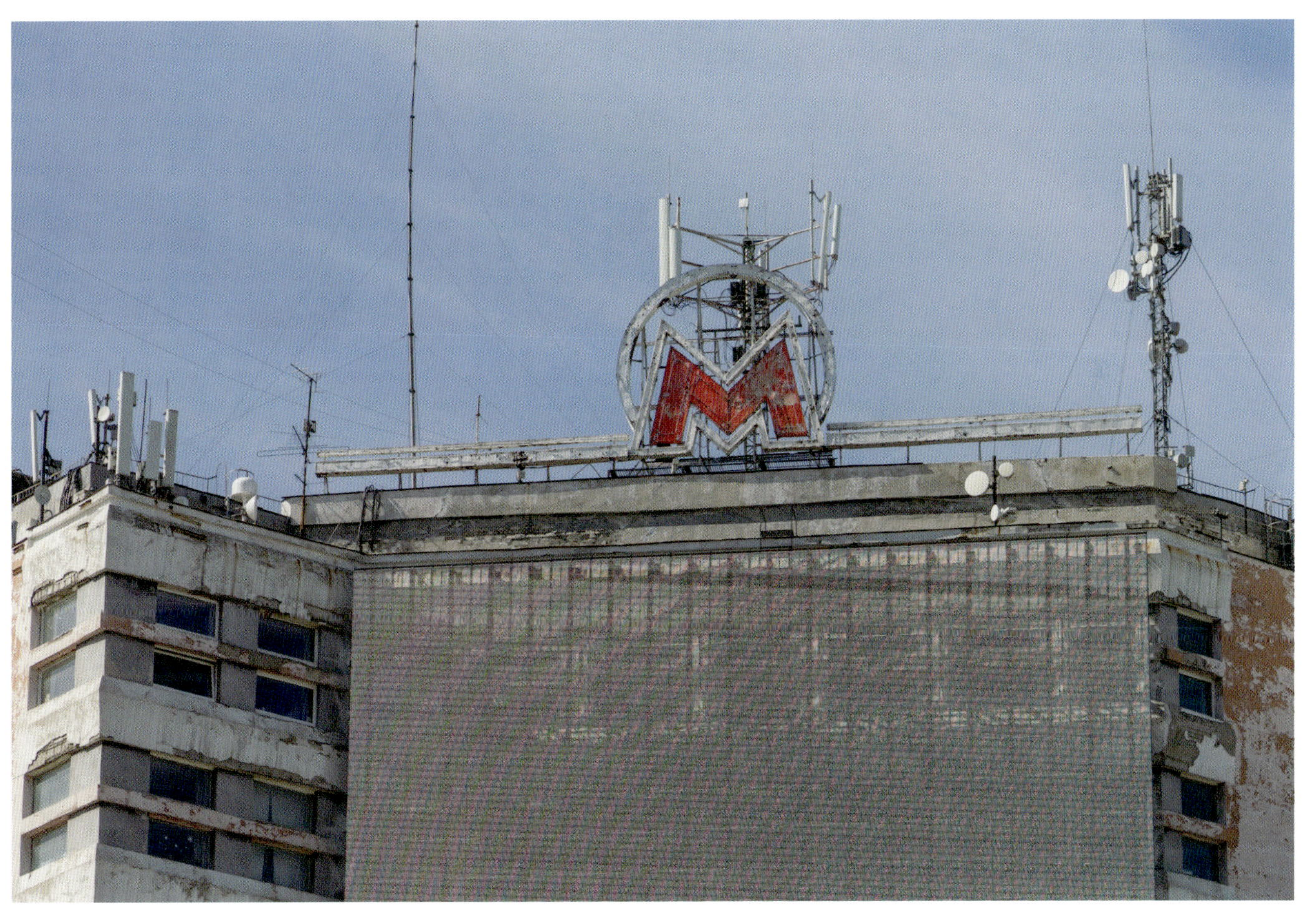

Moskovskaya, NIZHNY NOVGOROD   87

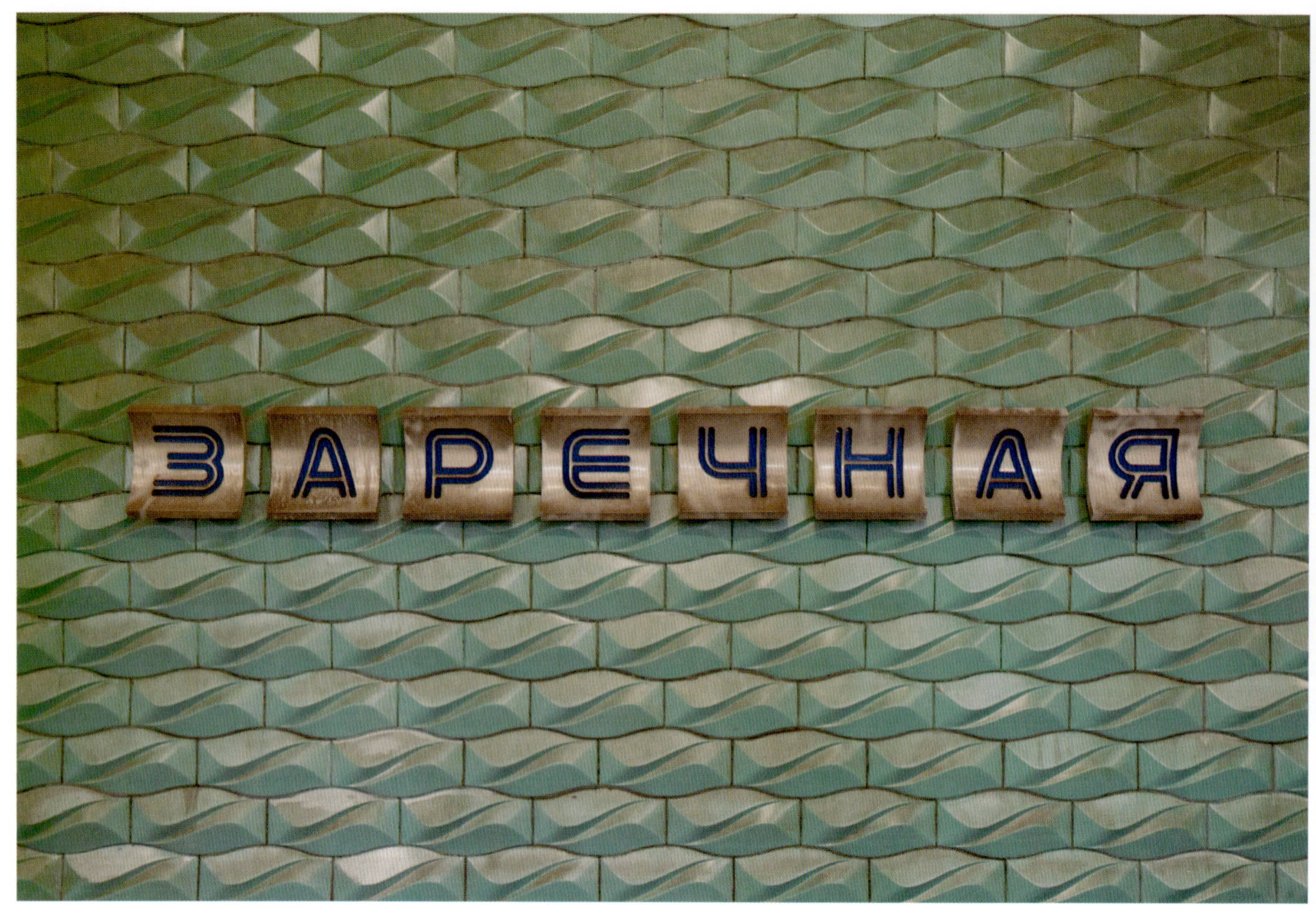

Zarechnaya, NIZHNY NOVGOROD

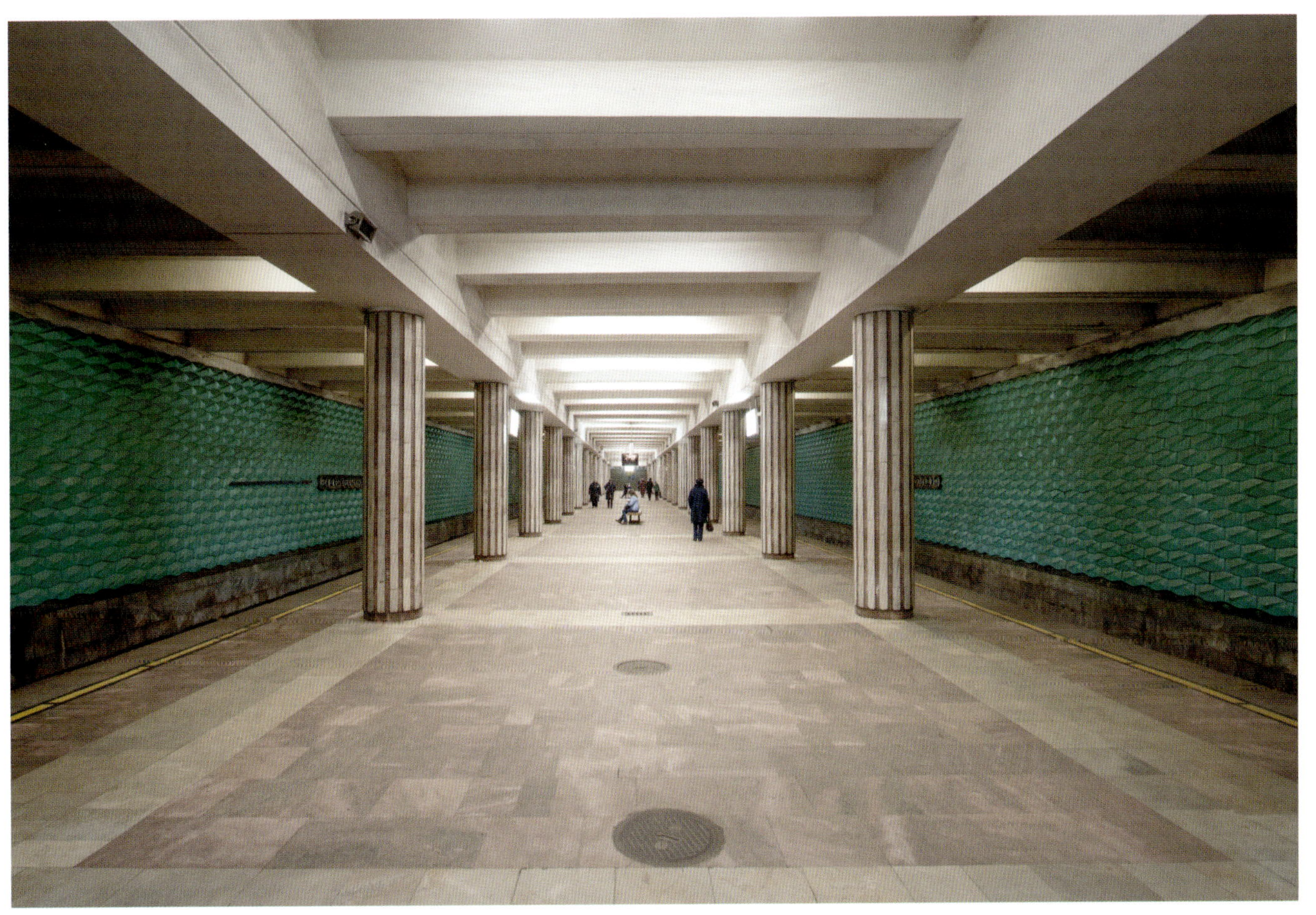

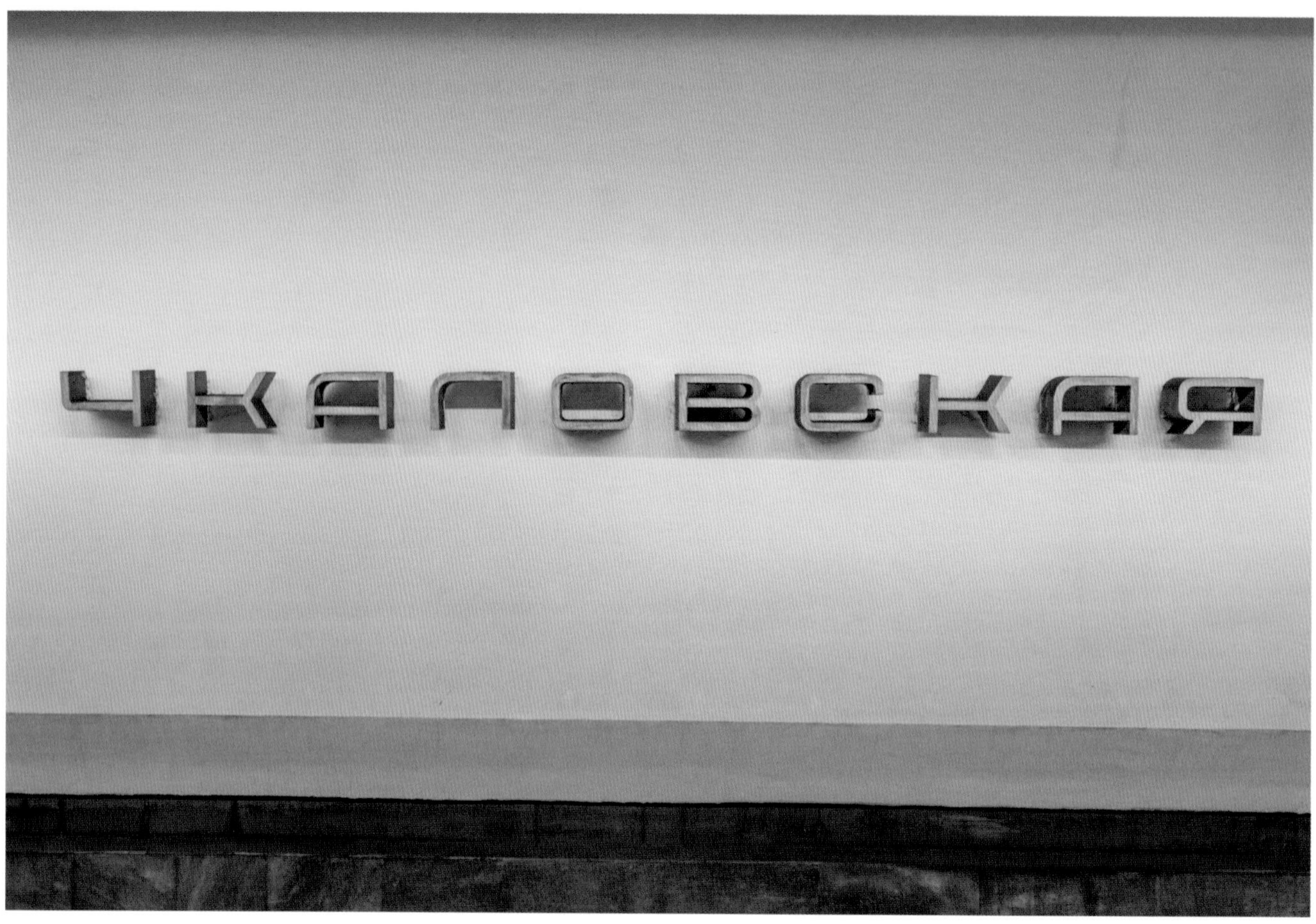

90   Chkalovskaya, NIZHNY NOVGOROD

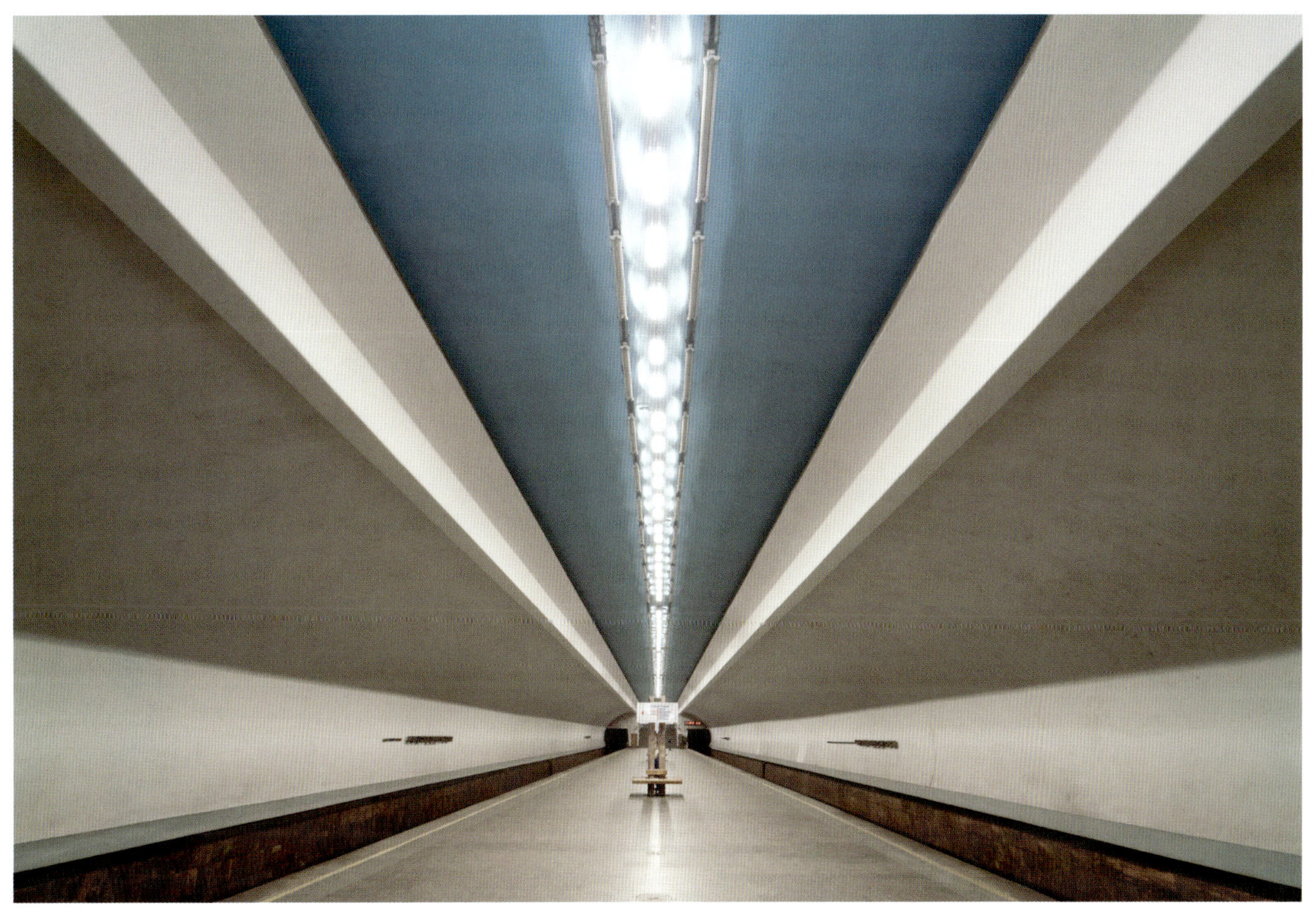

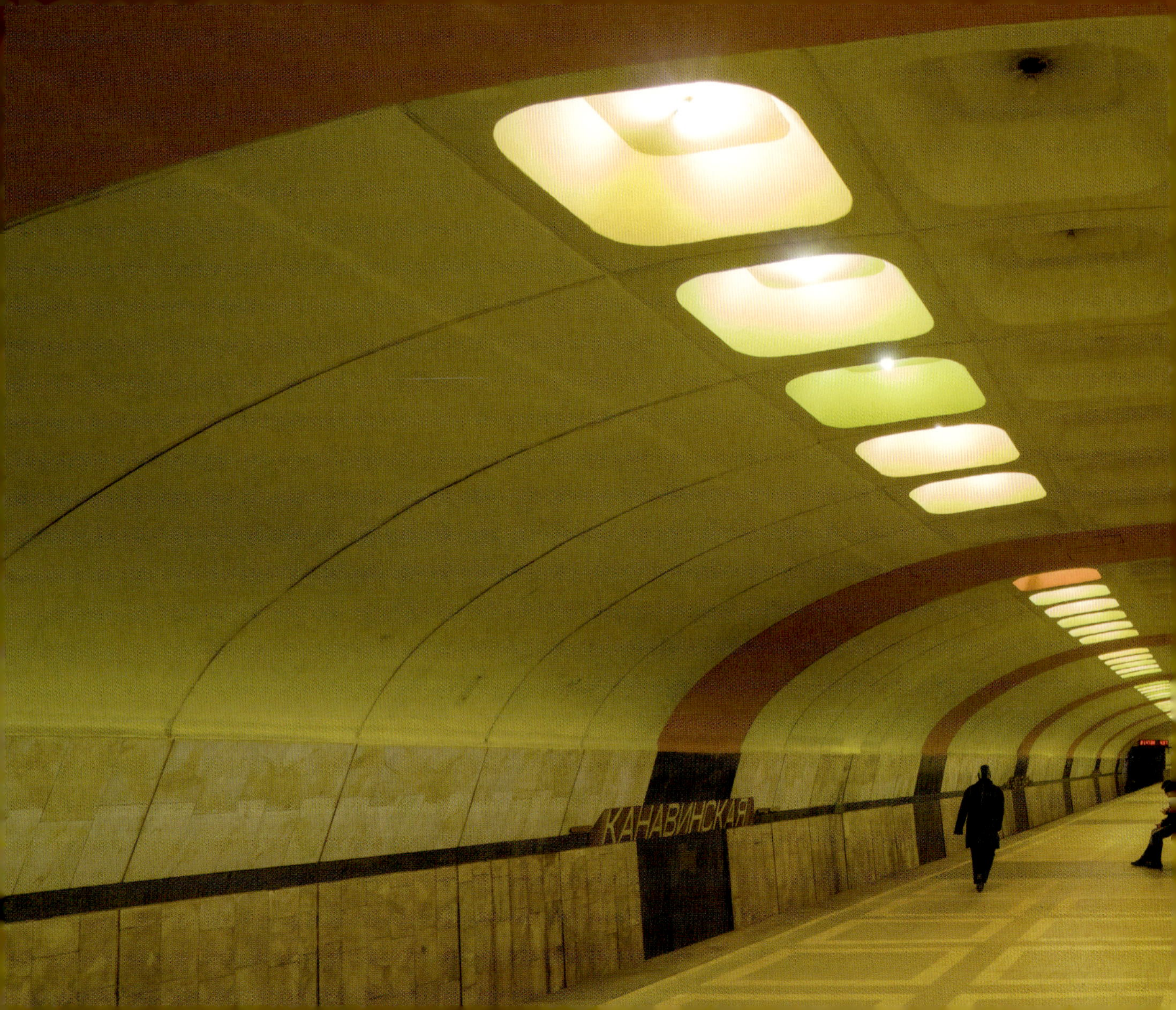
КАНАВИНСКАЯ

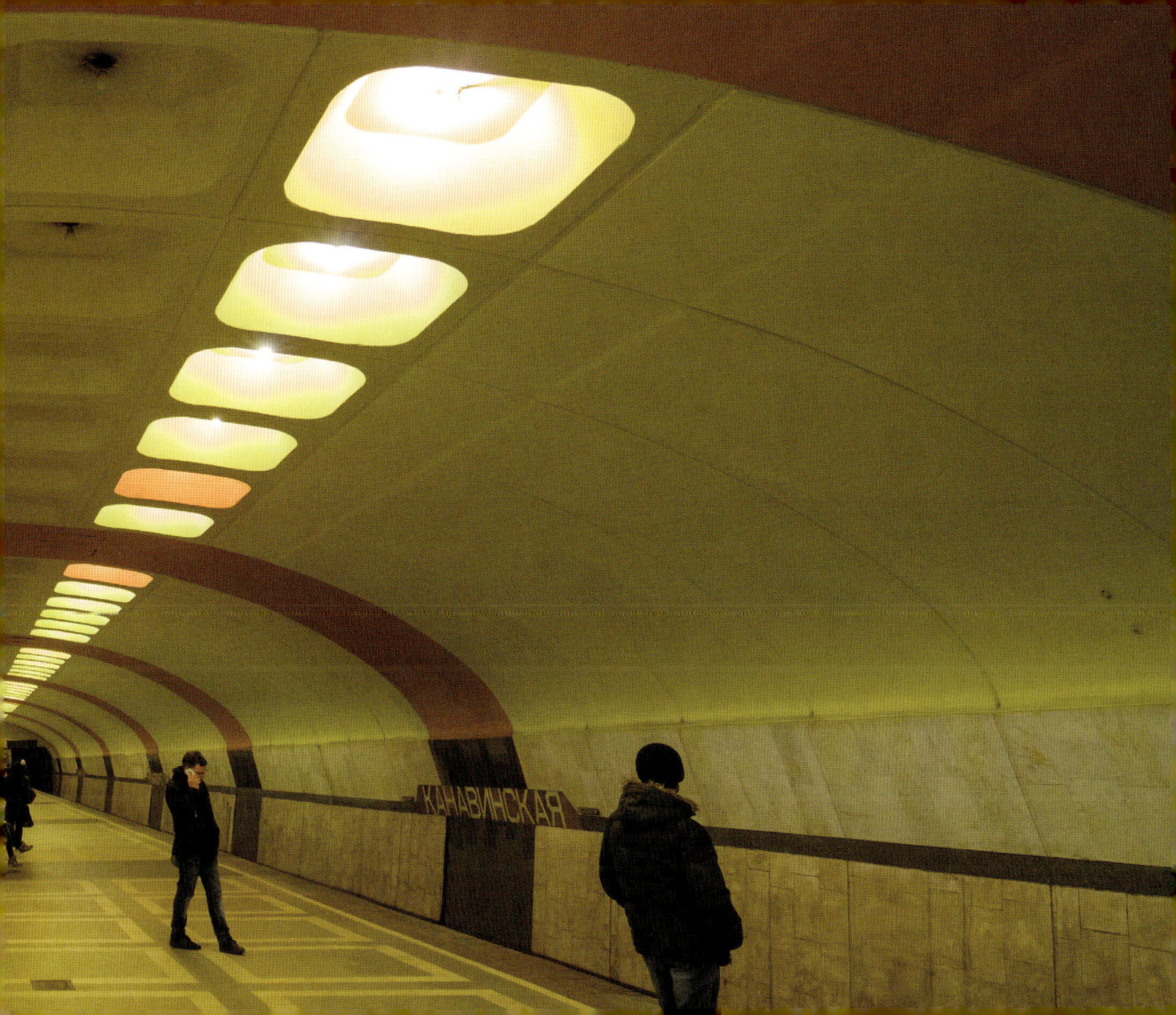

КАНАВИНСКАЯ

МИНСК
БЕЛАРУСЬ

MINSK
BELARUS

OPENED 1984

   Plošča Lenina, MINSK

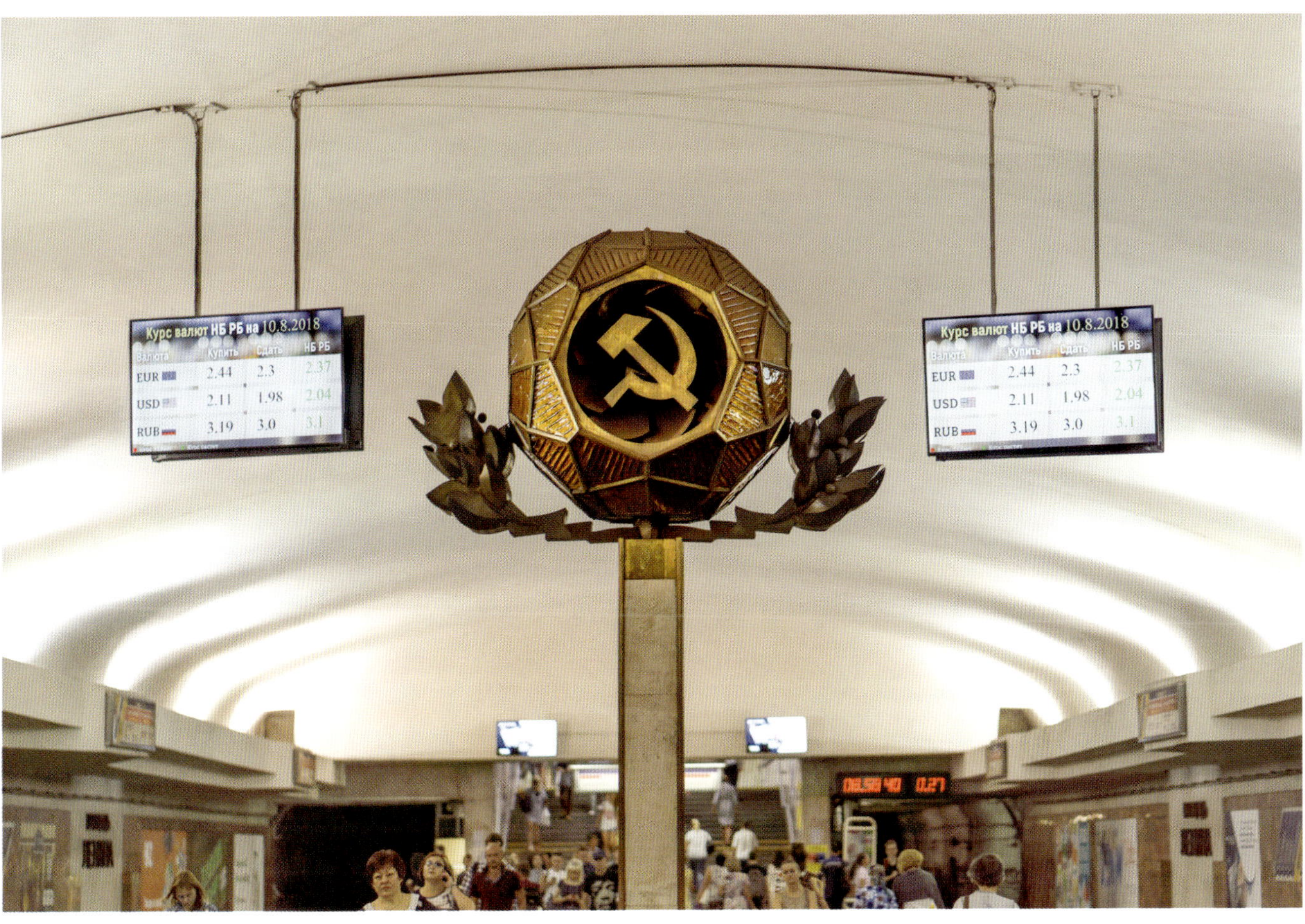

Курс валют НБ РБ на 10.8.2018
Валюта Купить Сдать НБ РБ
EUR 2.44 2.3 2.37
USD 2.11 1.98 2.04
RUB 3.19 3.0 3.1

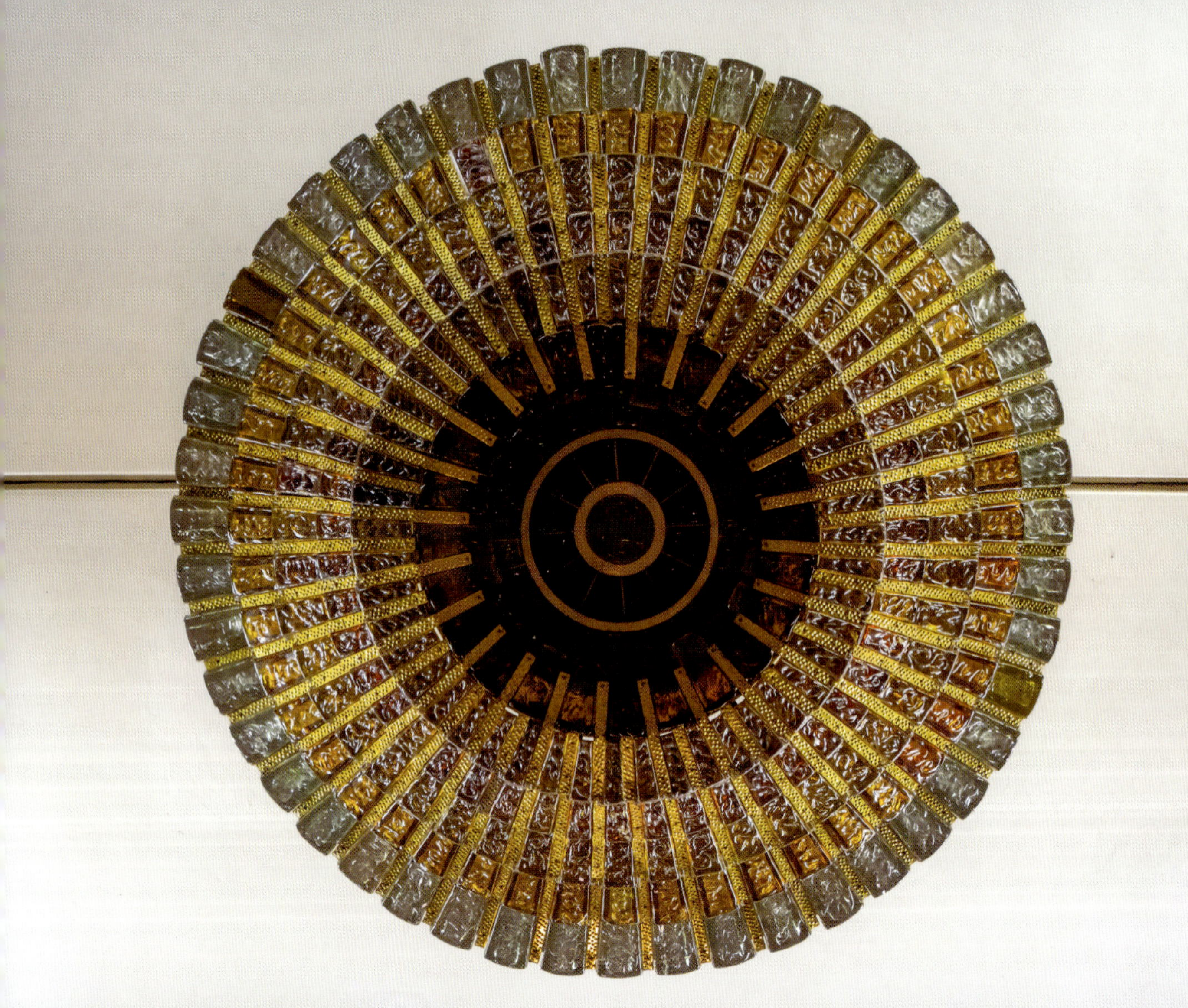

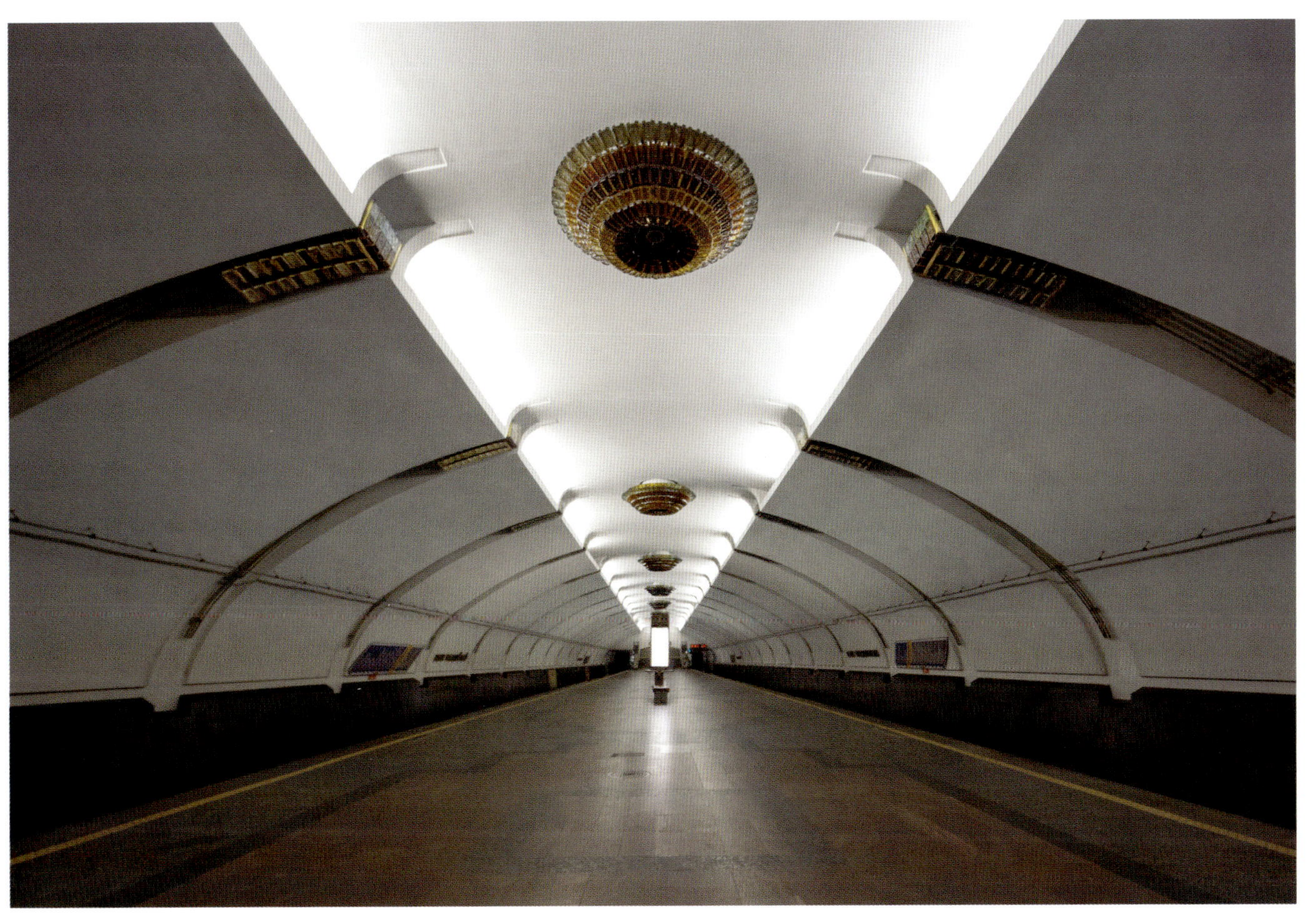

Park Čaliuskincaŭ, MINSK

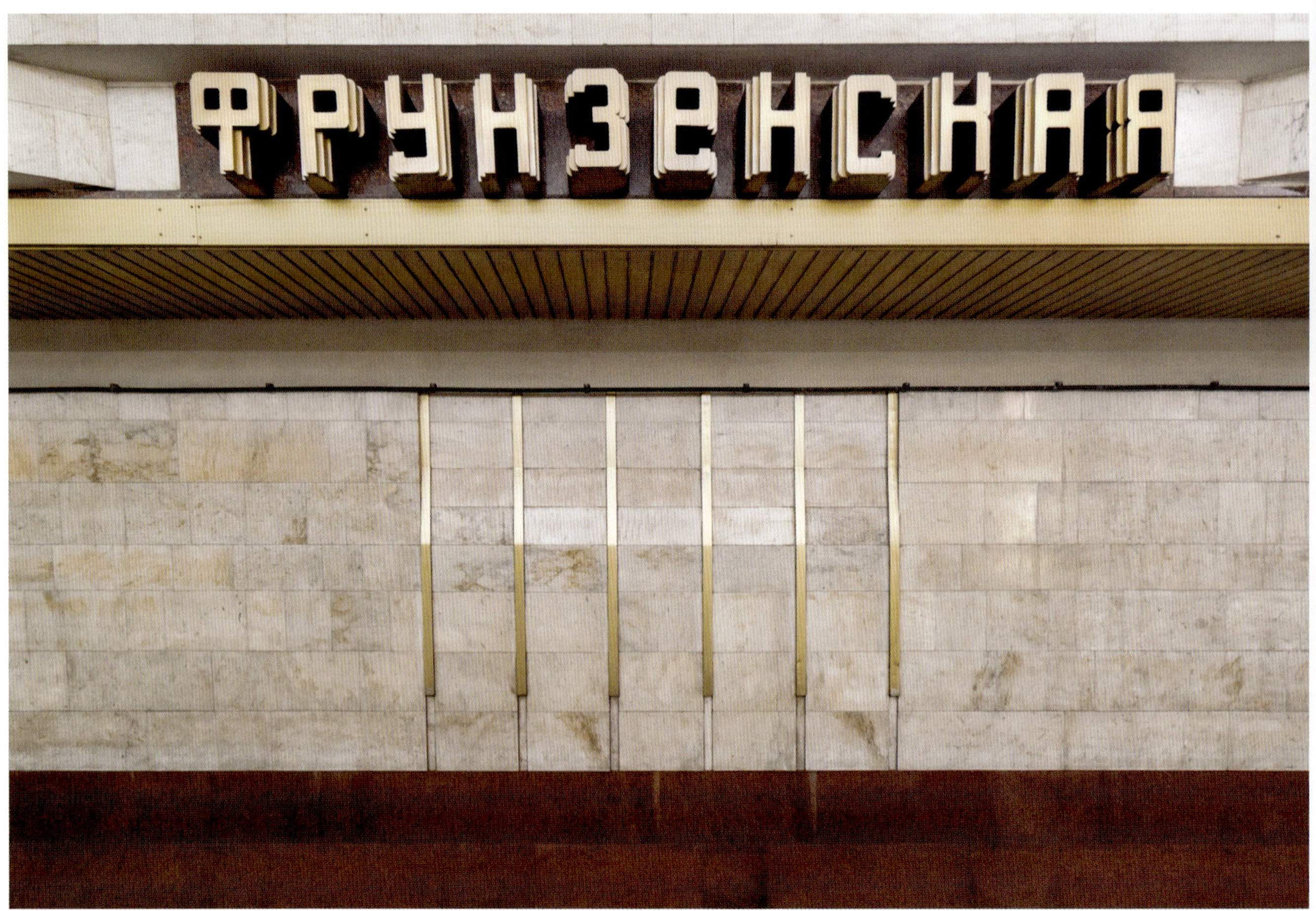

ФРУНЗЕНСКАЯ

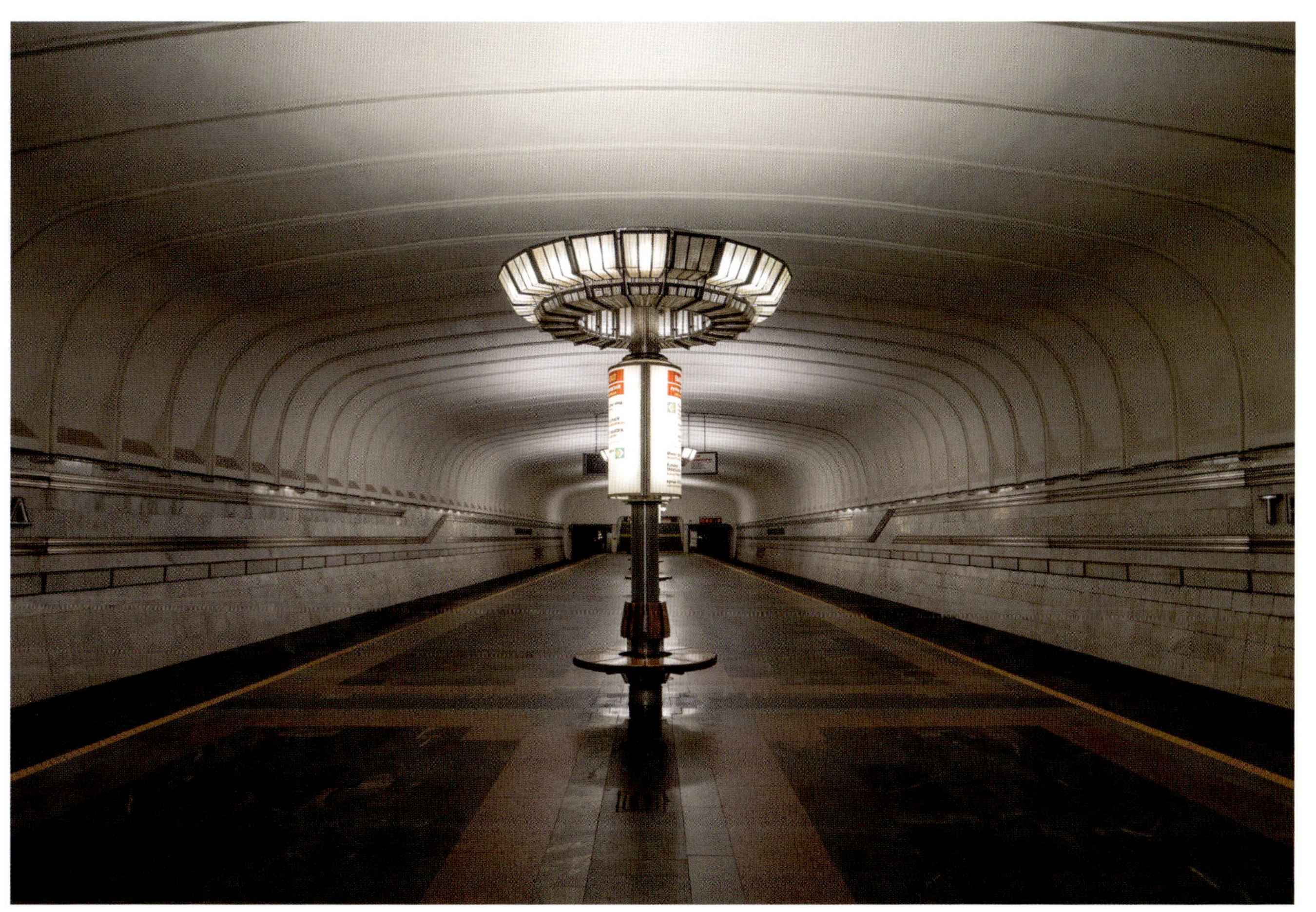

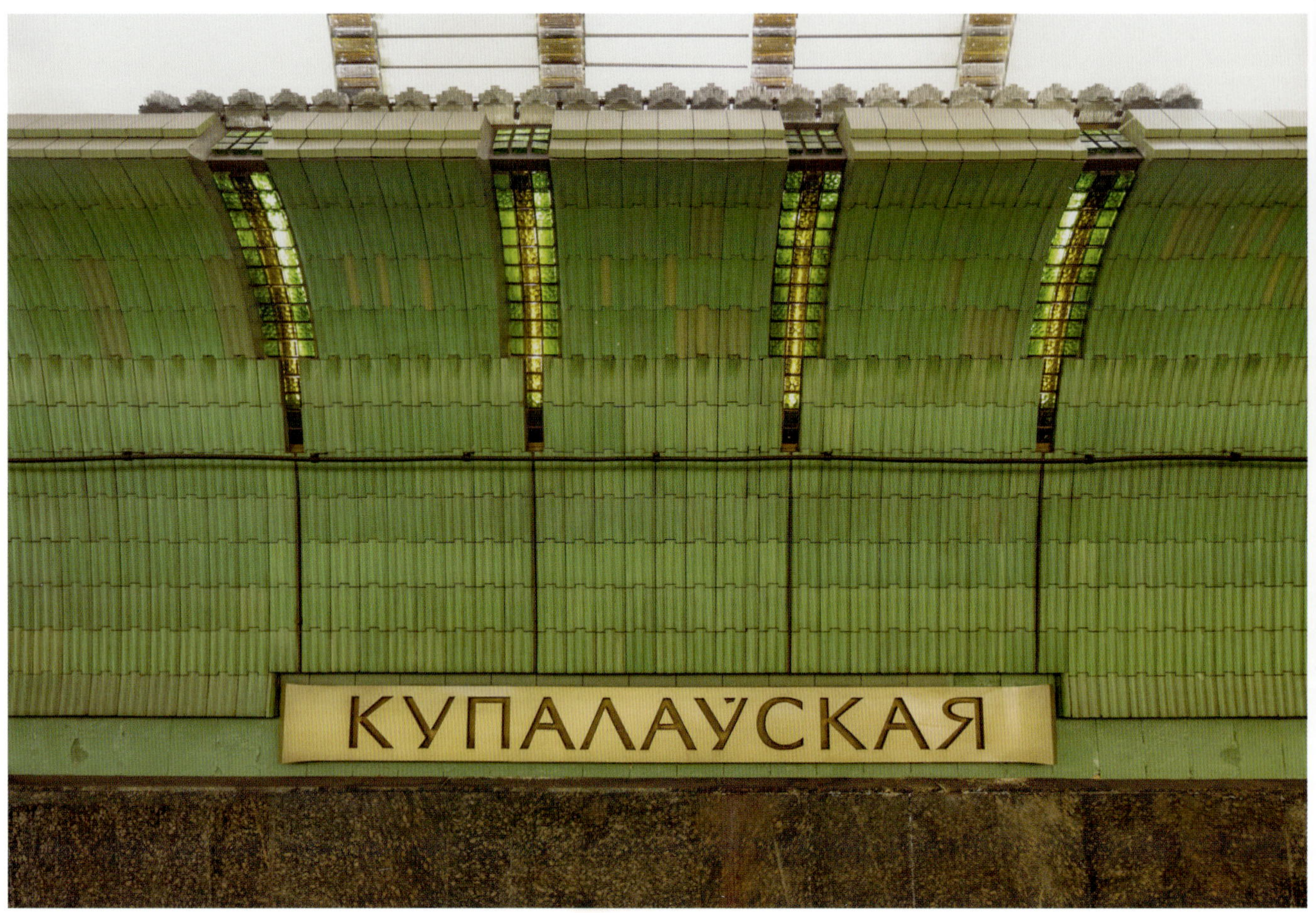

КУПАЛАЎСКАЯ

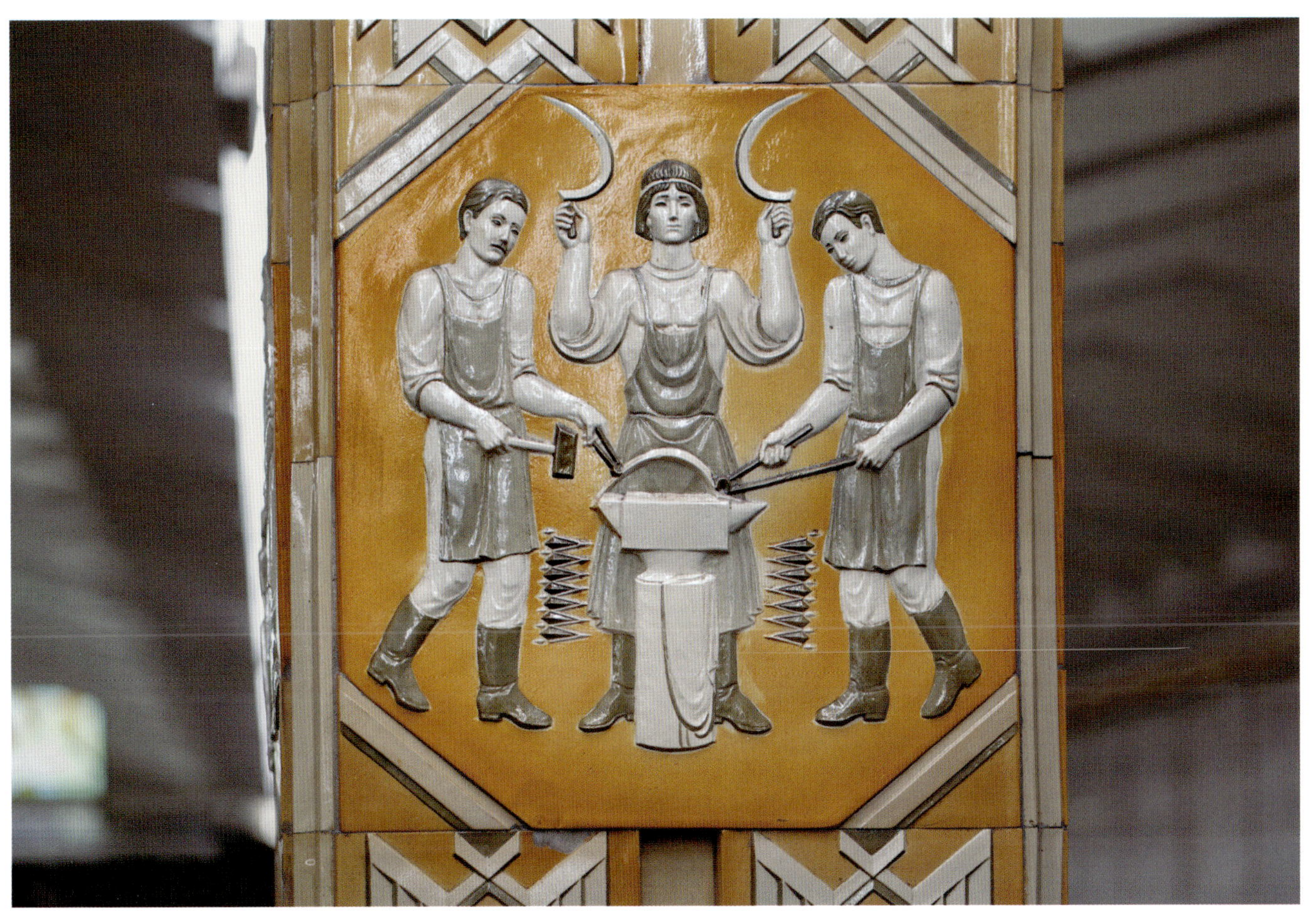

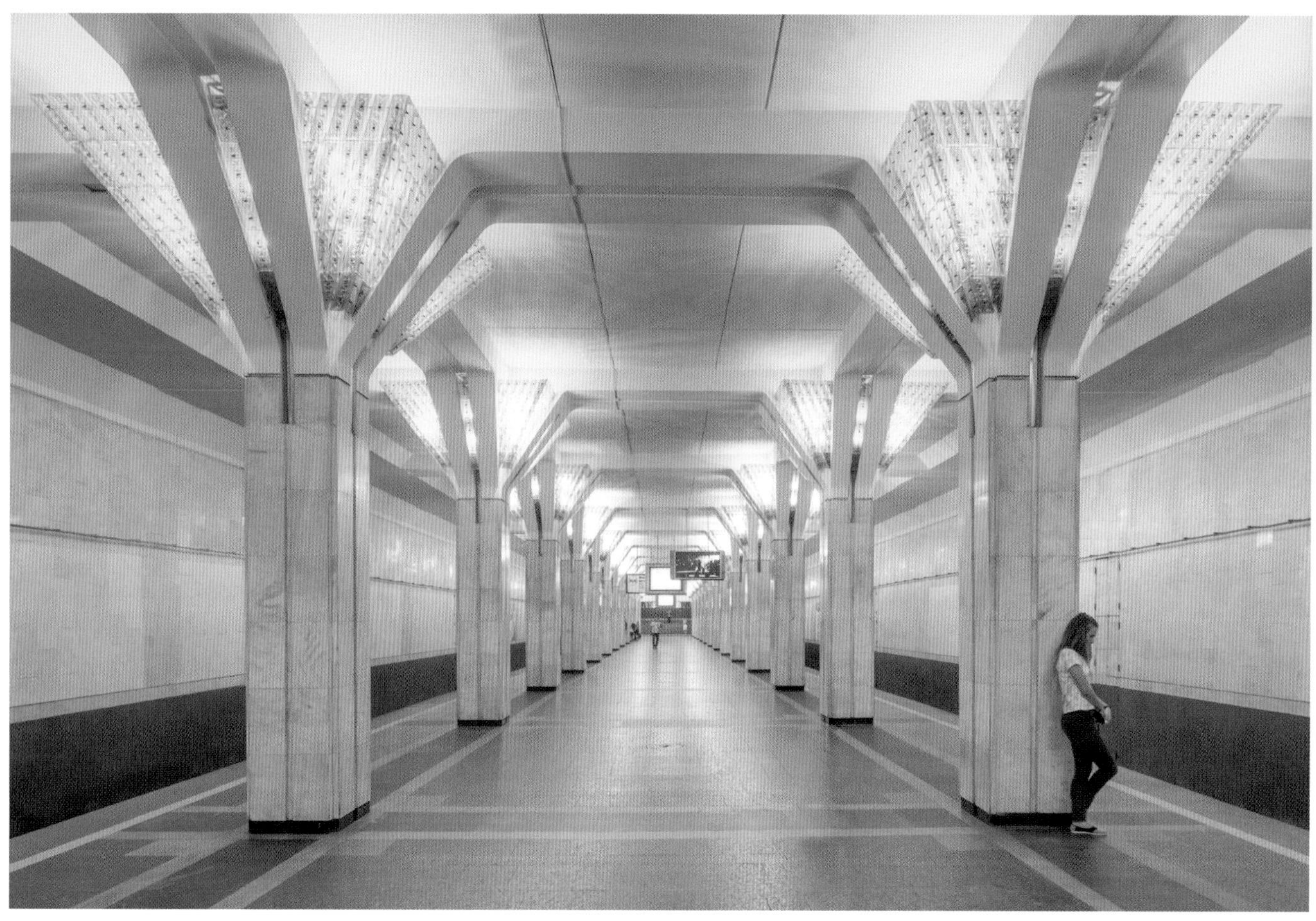

102   Plošča Pieramohi, MINSK

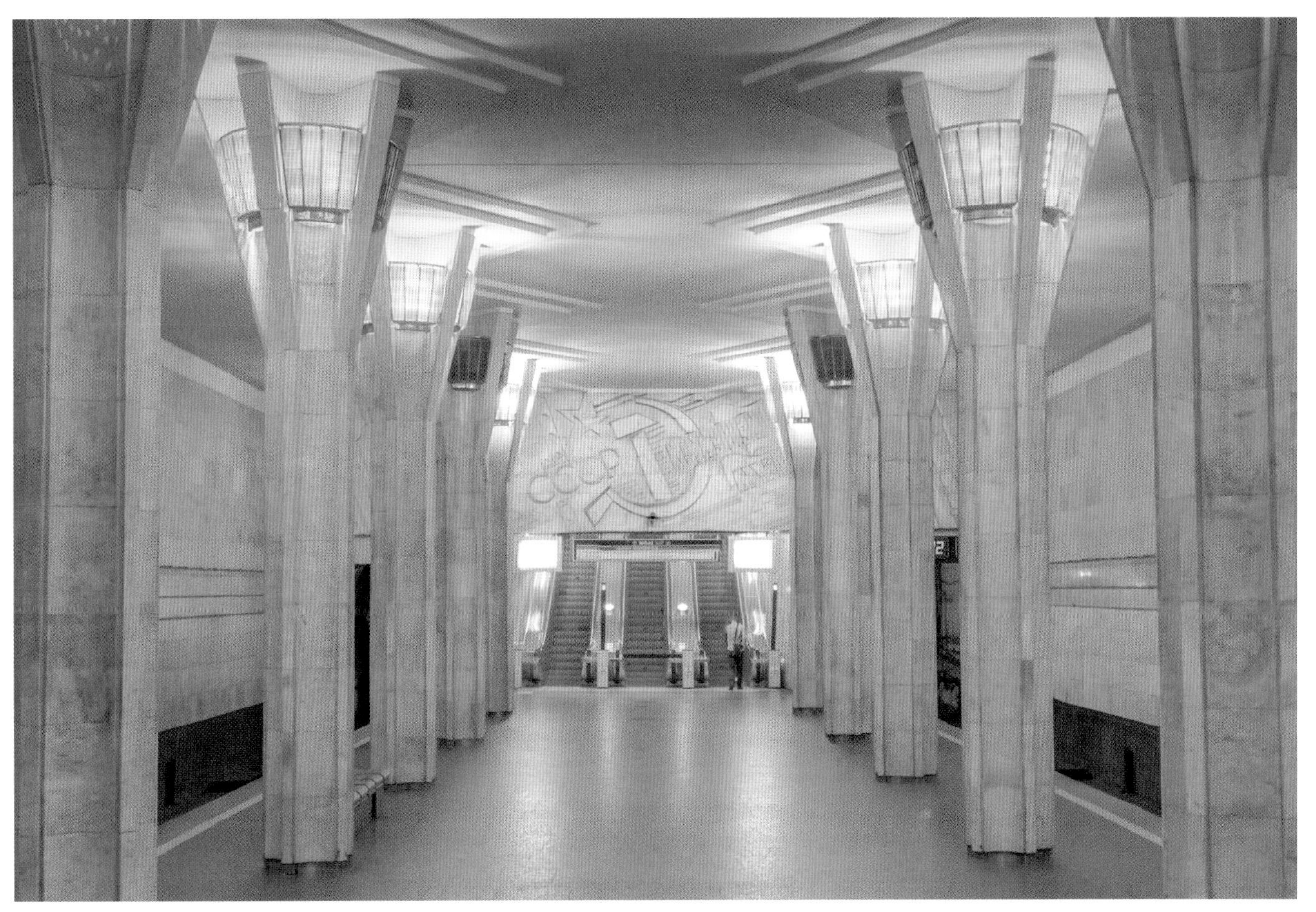

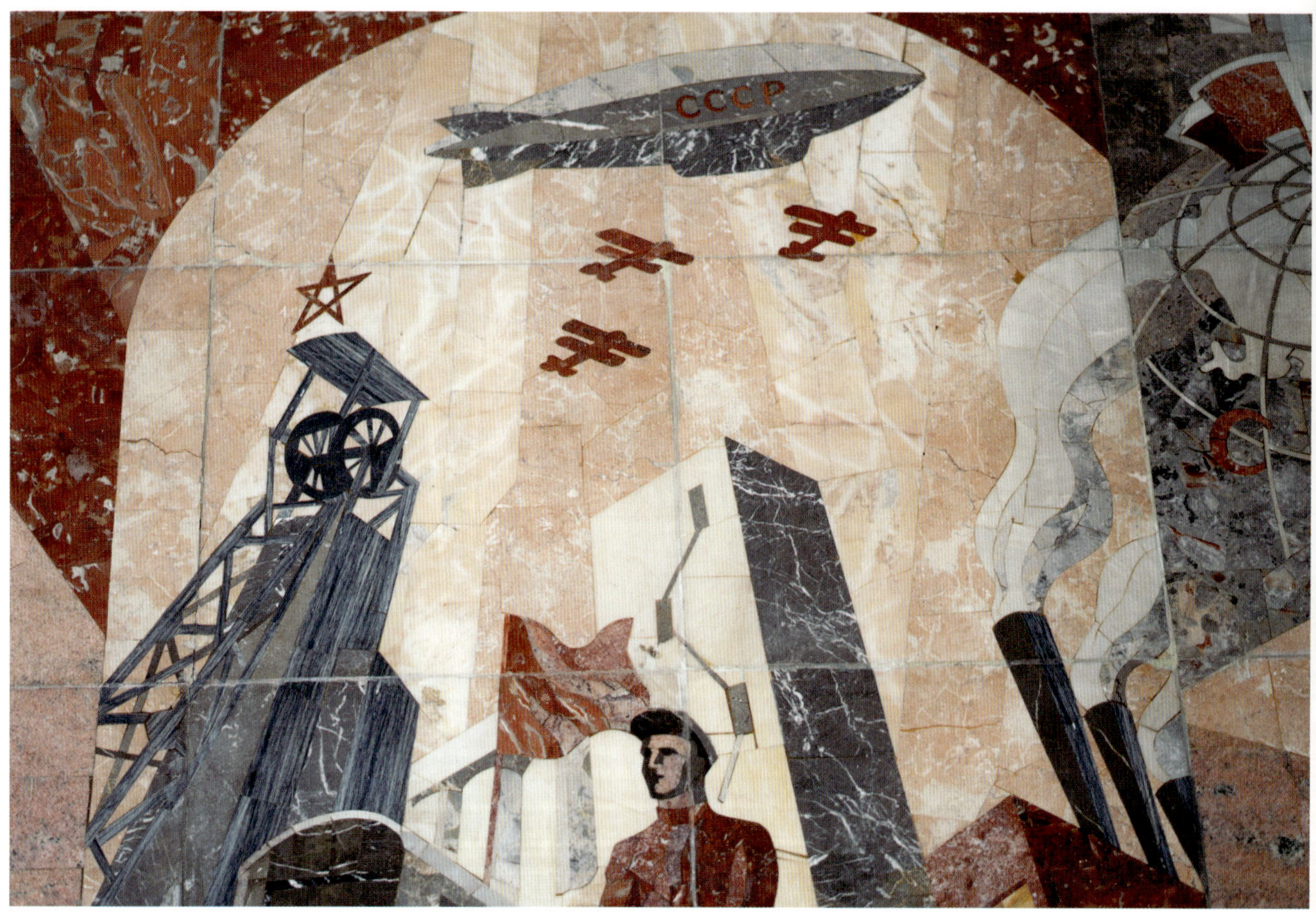

104   Kastryčnickaja, MINSK

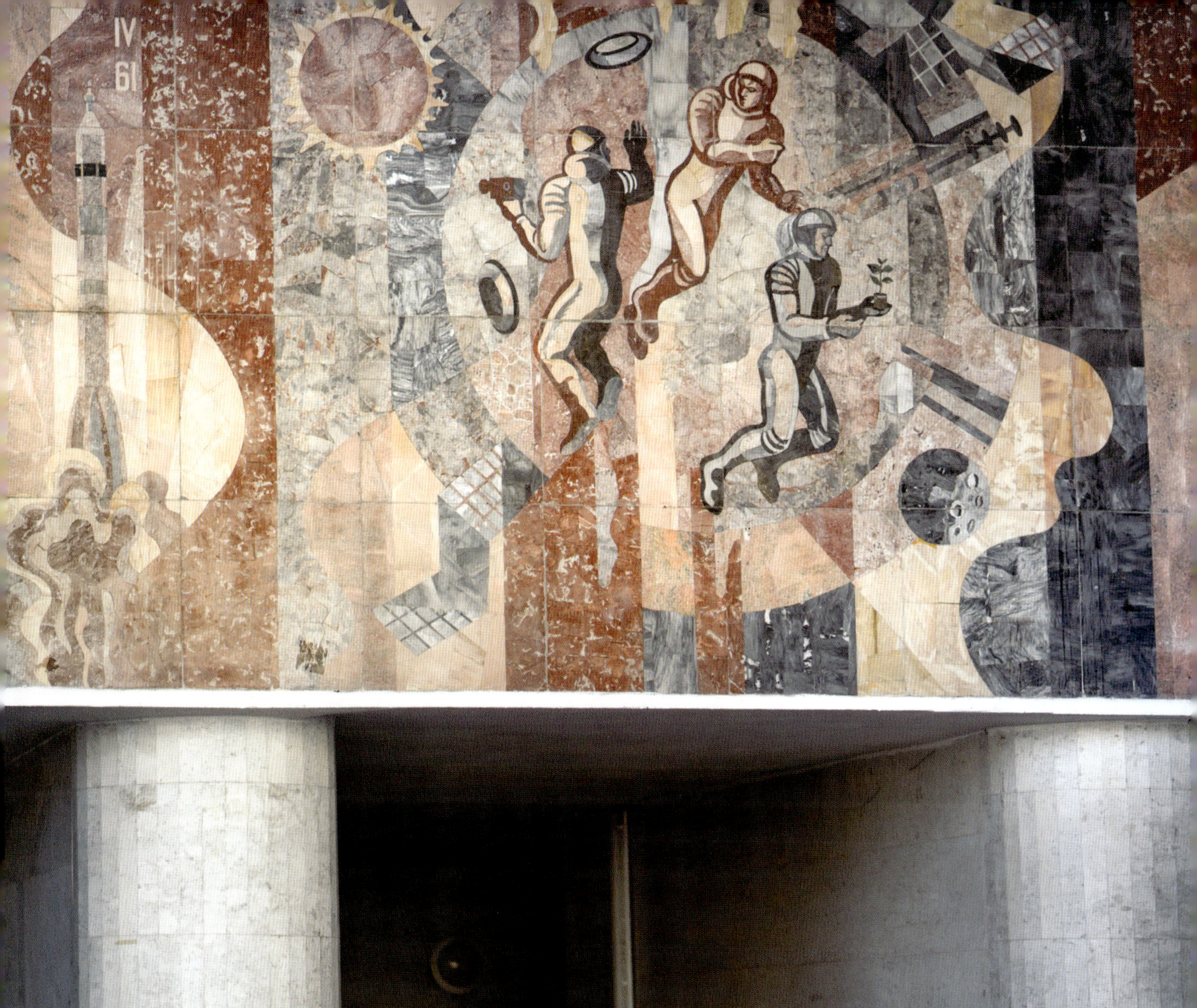

IV
61

**ЕРЕВАН
АРМЕНИЯ**

**YEREVAN
ARMENIA**

OPENED 1981

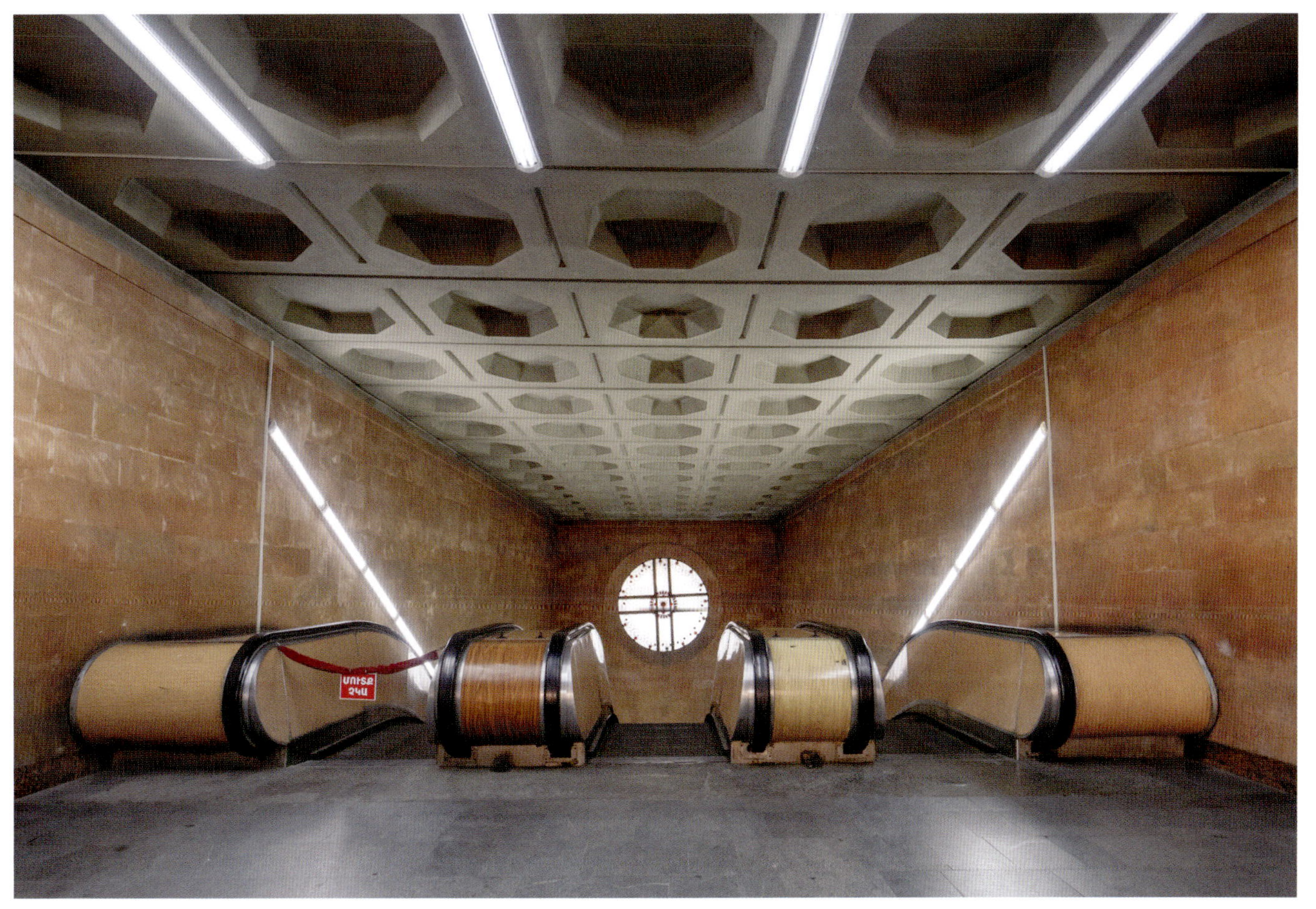

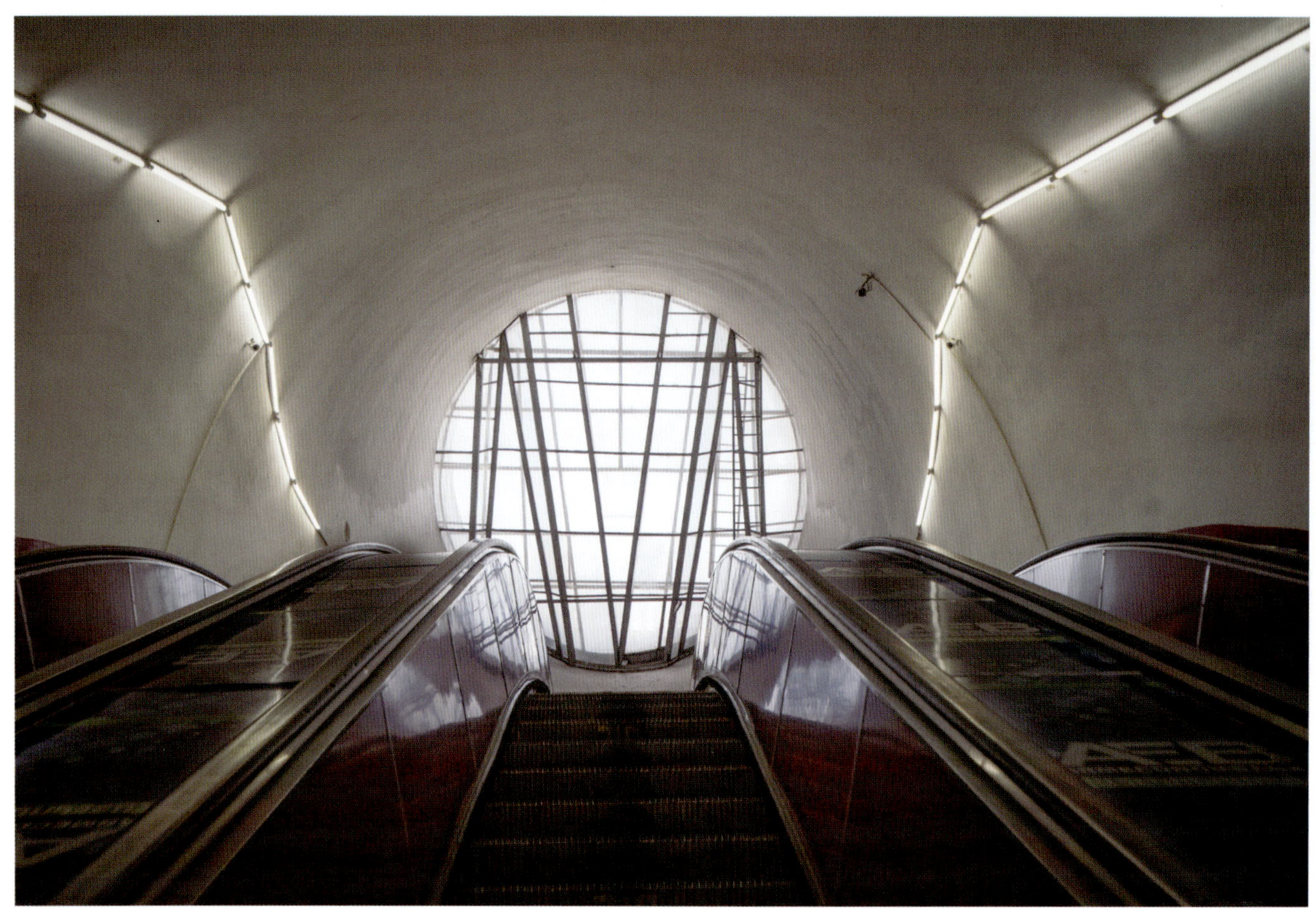

108   Yeritasardakan, YEREVAN

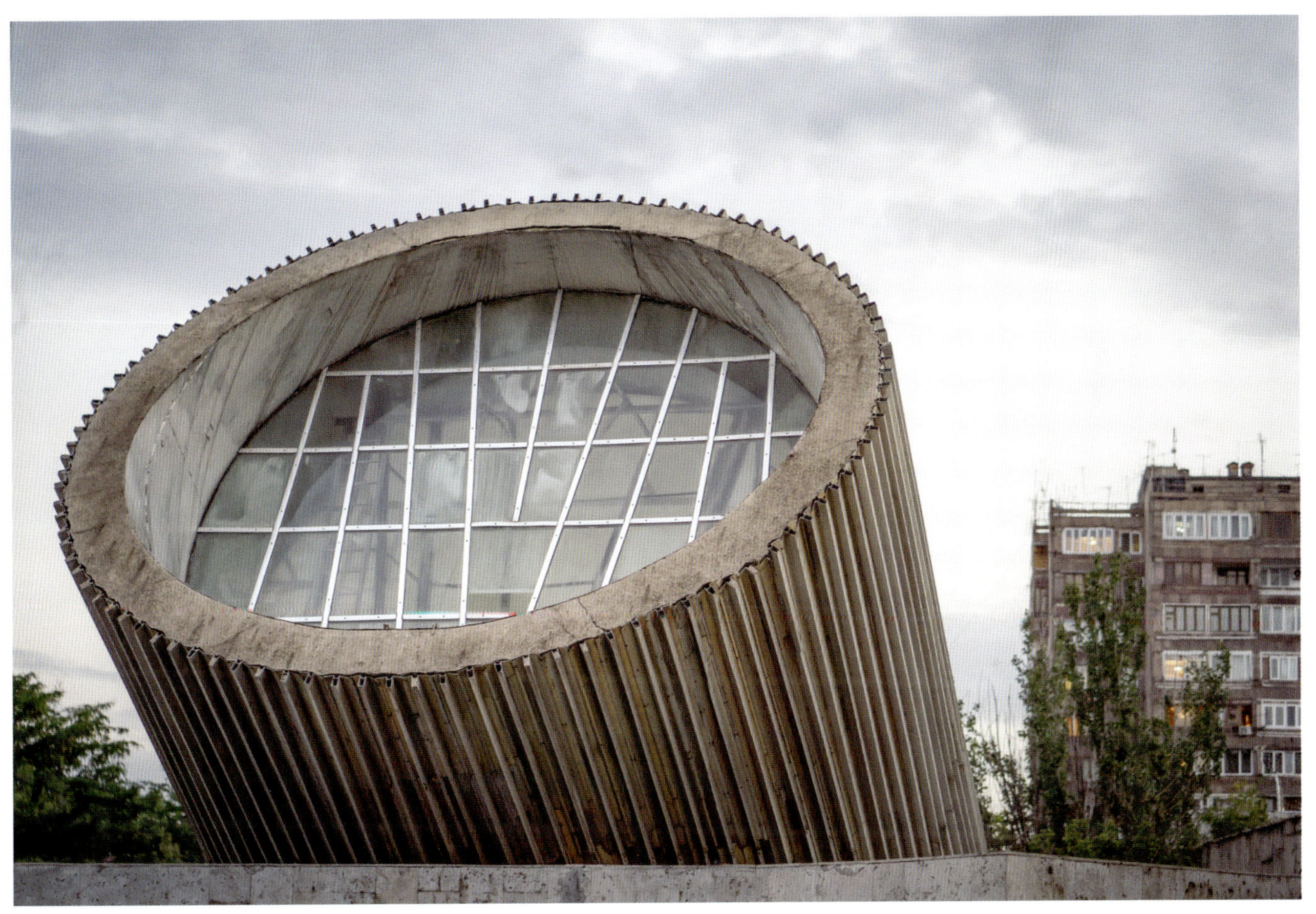

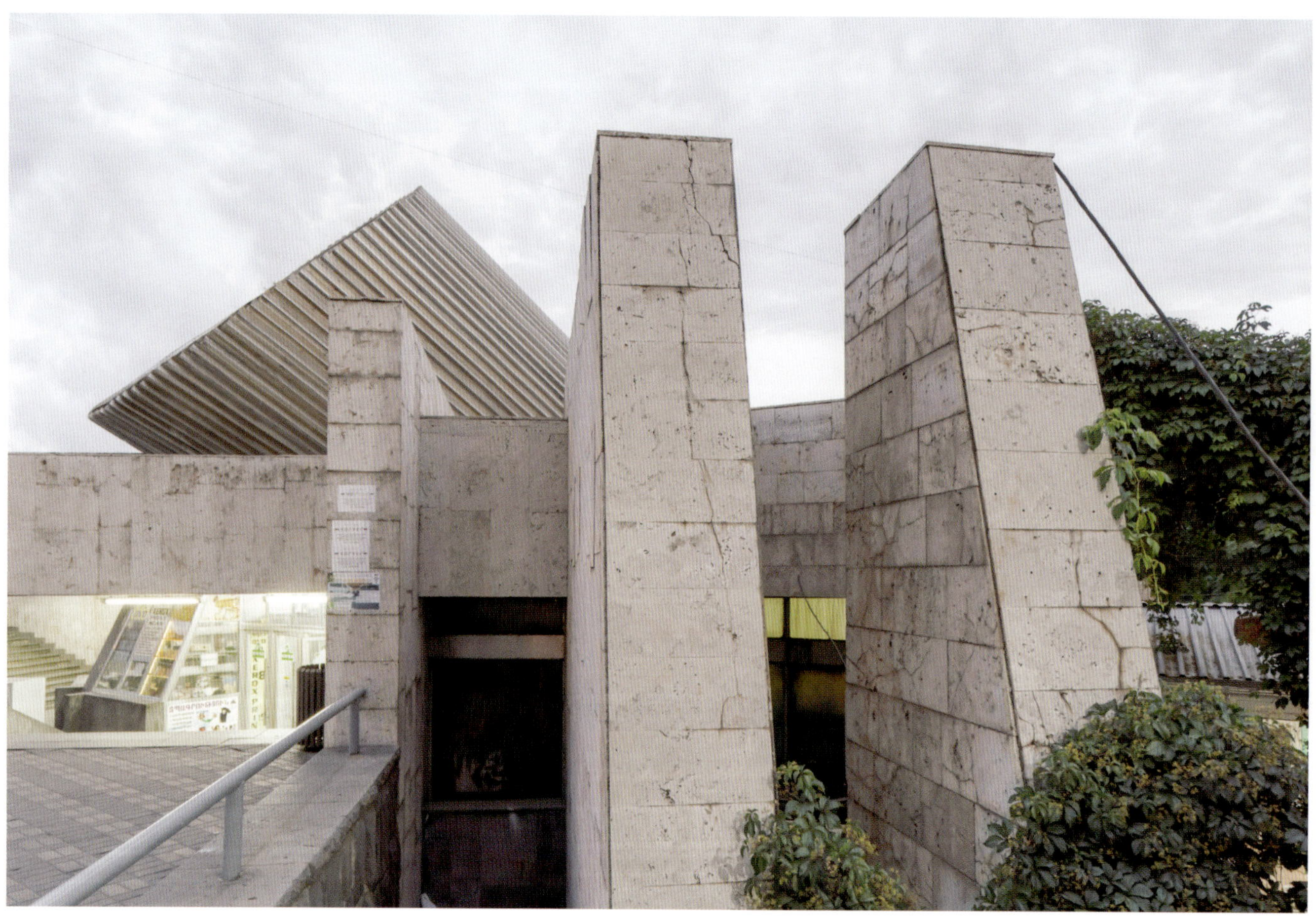

110   Yeritasardakan, YEREVAN

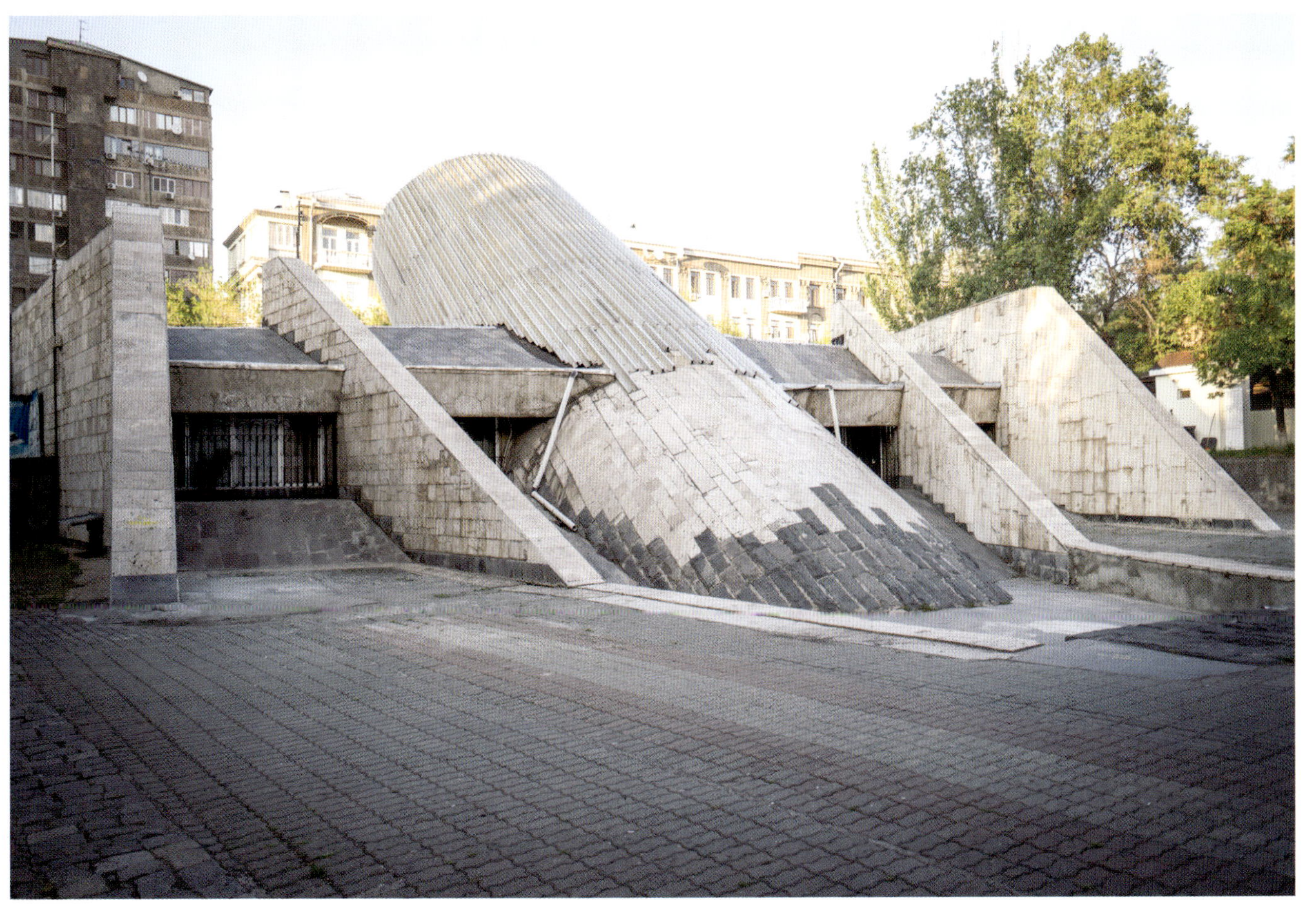

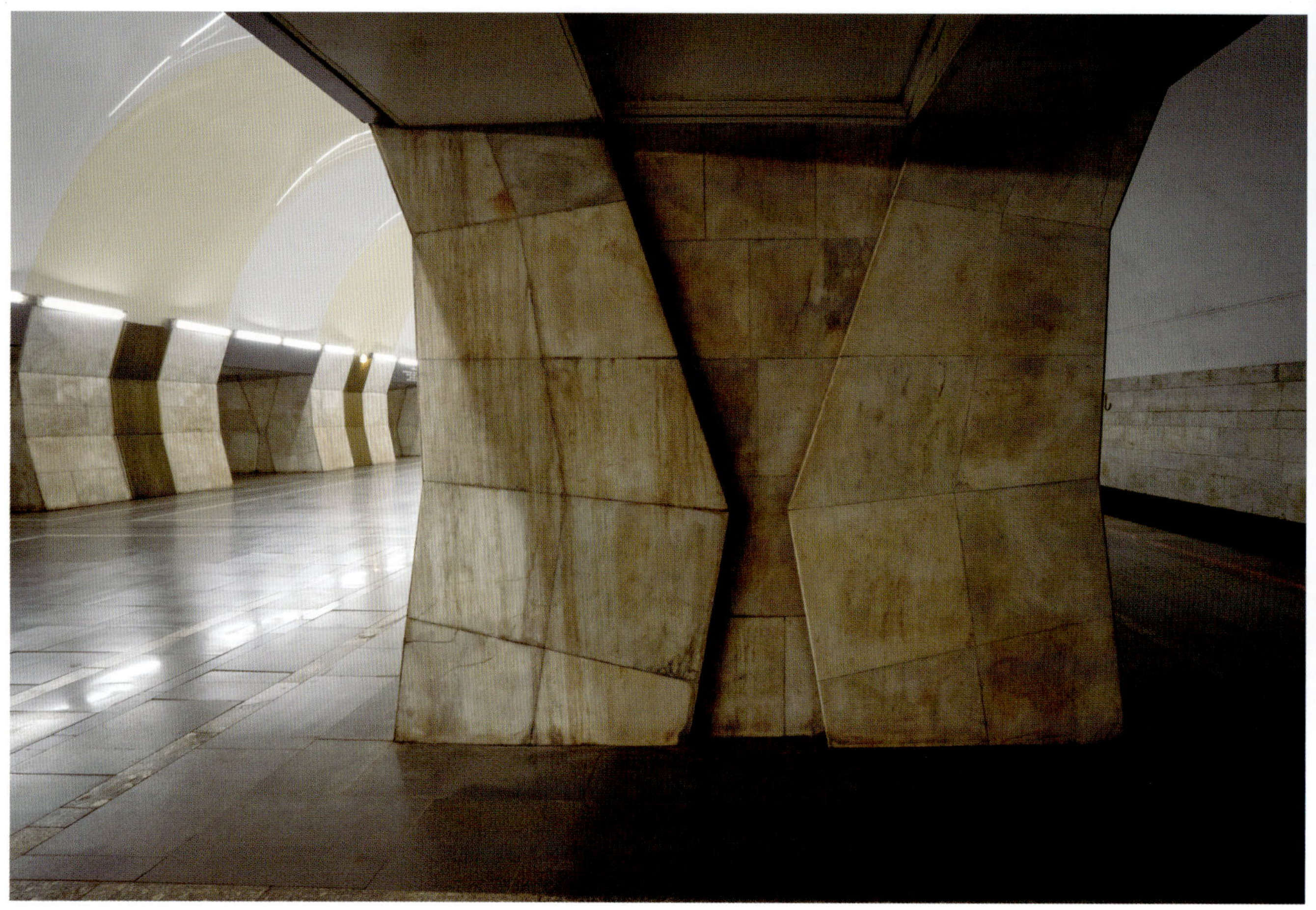

112   Yeritasardakan, YEREVAN

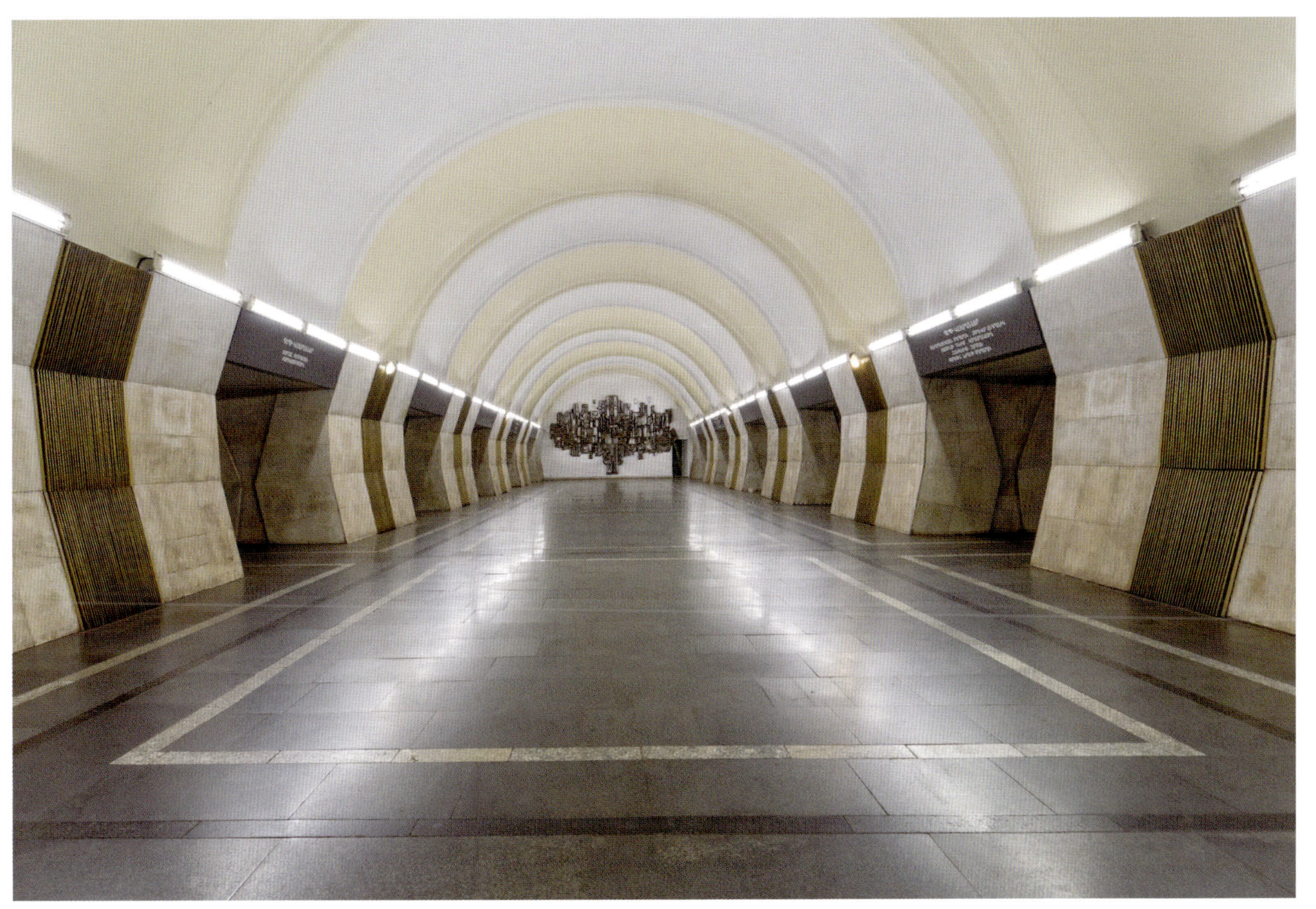

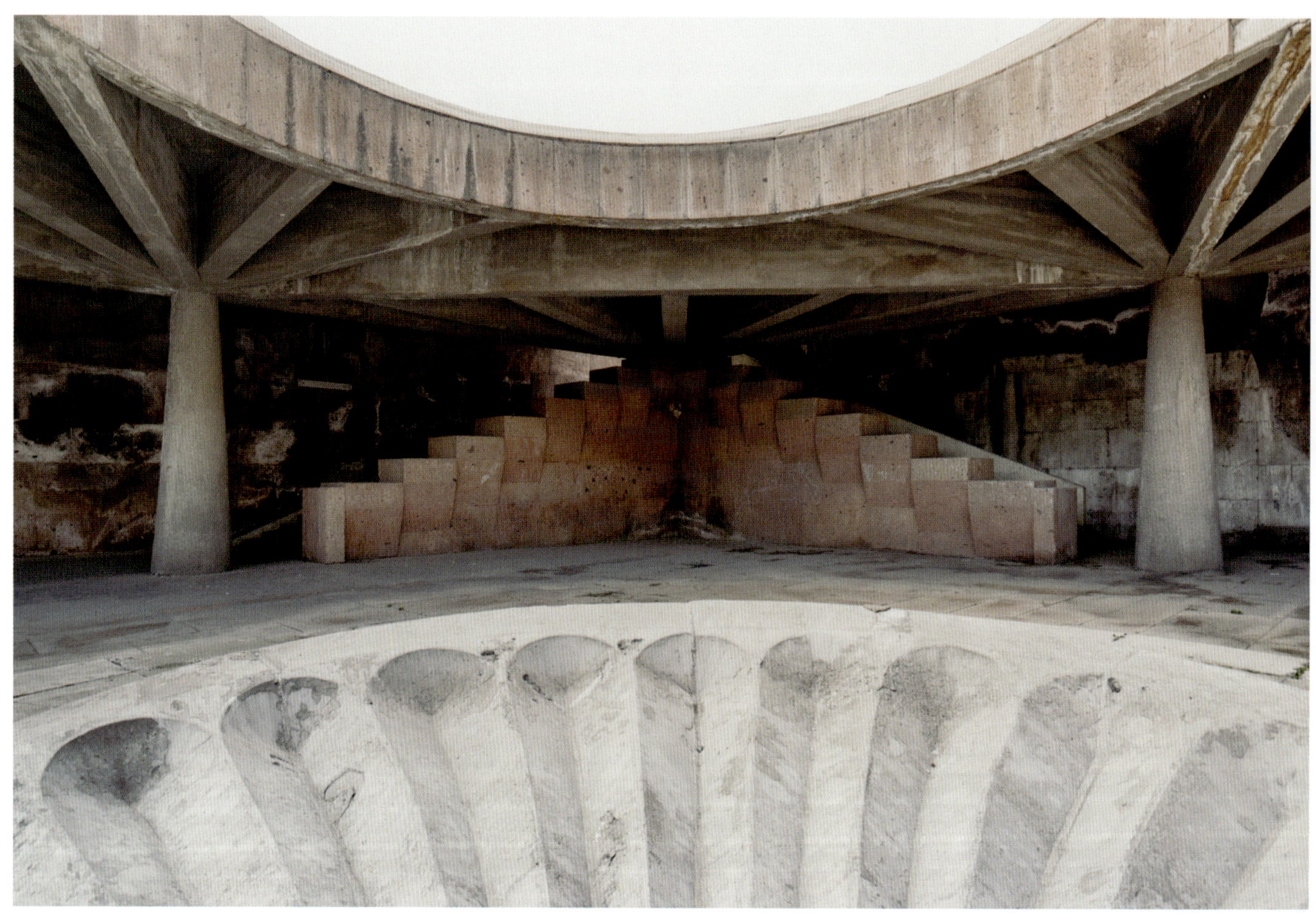

114　　Republic Square, YEREVAN

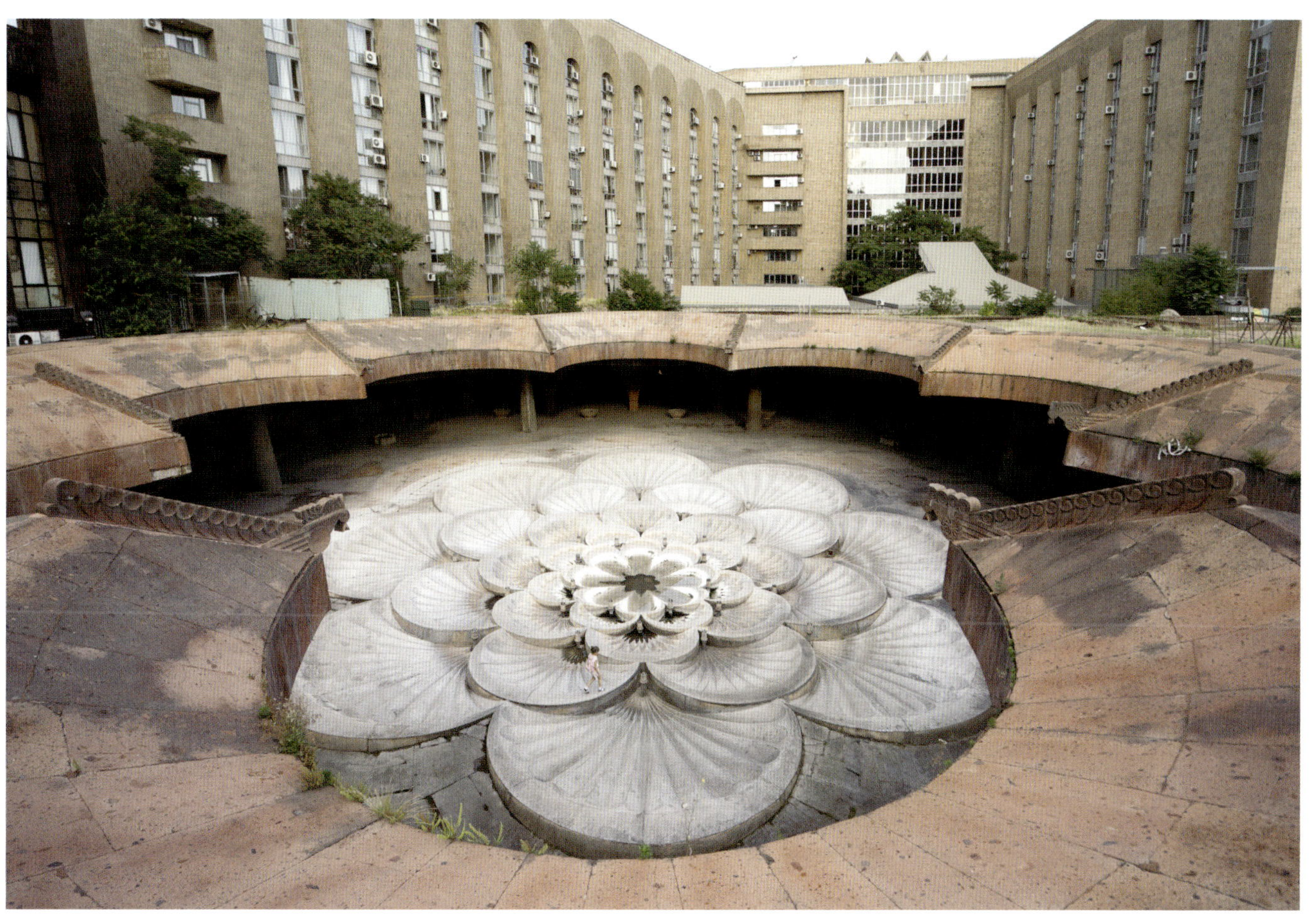

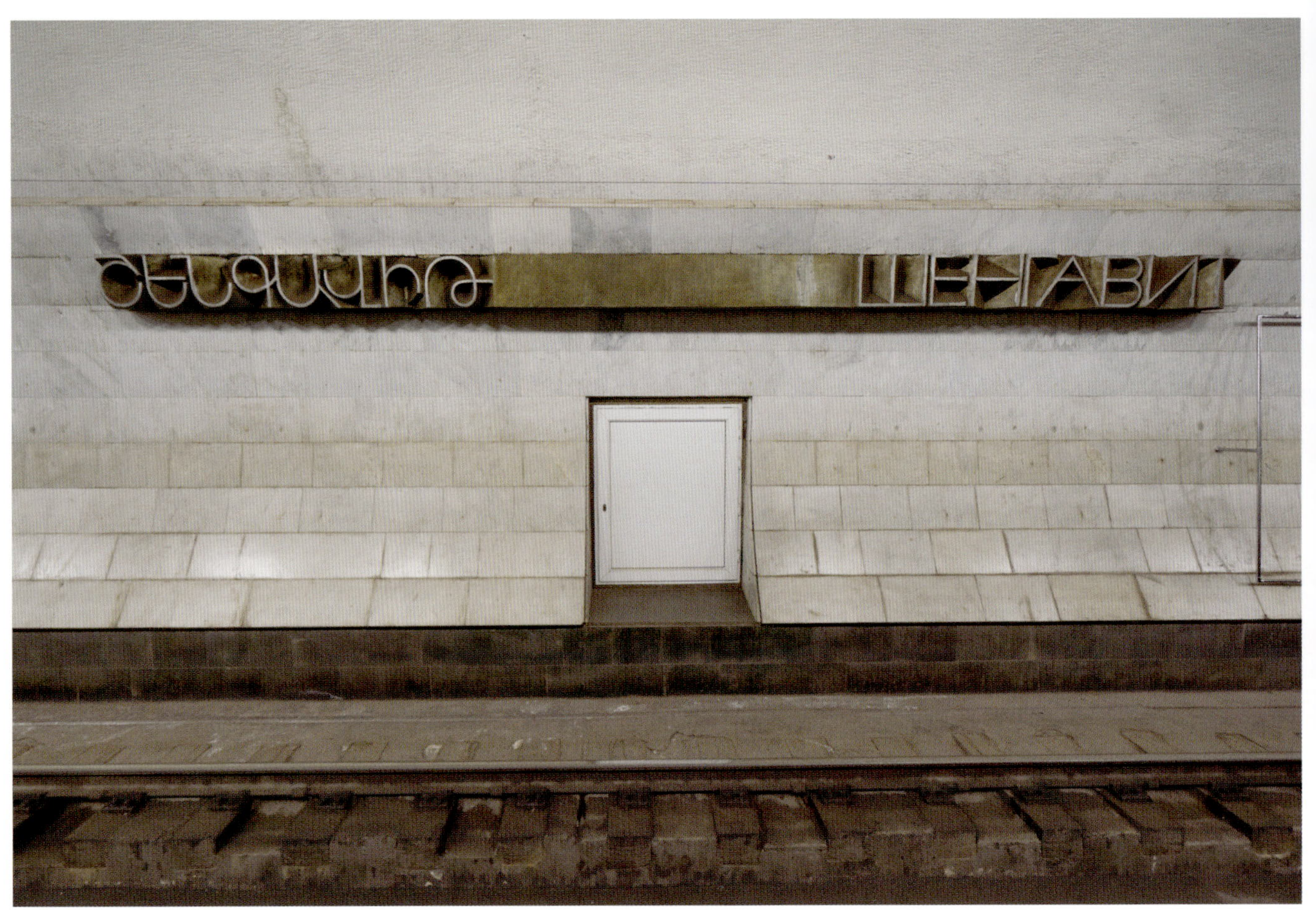

116   Shengavit, YEREVAN

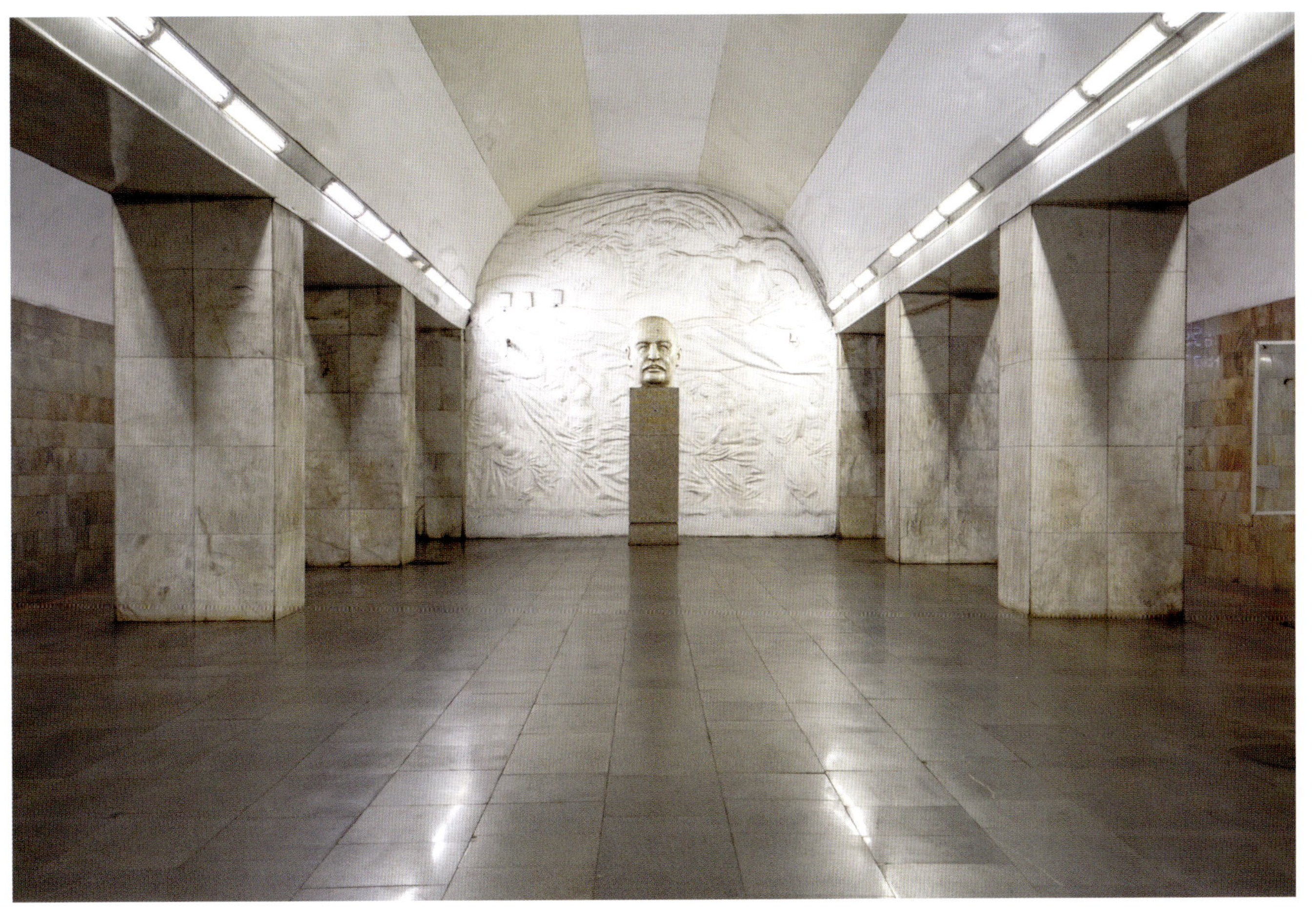

Marshal Baghramyan, YEREVAN   117

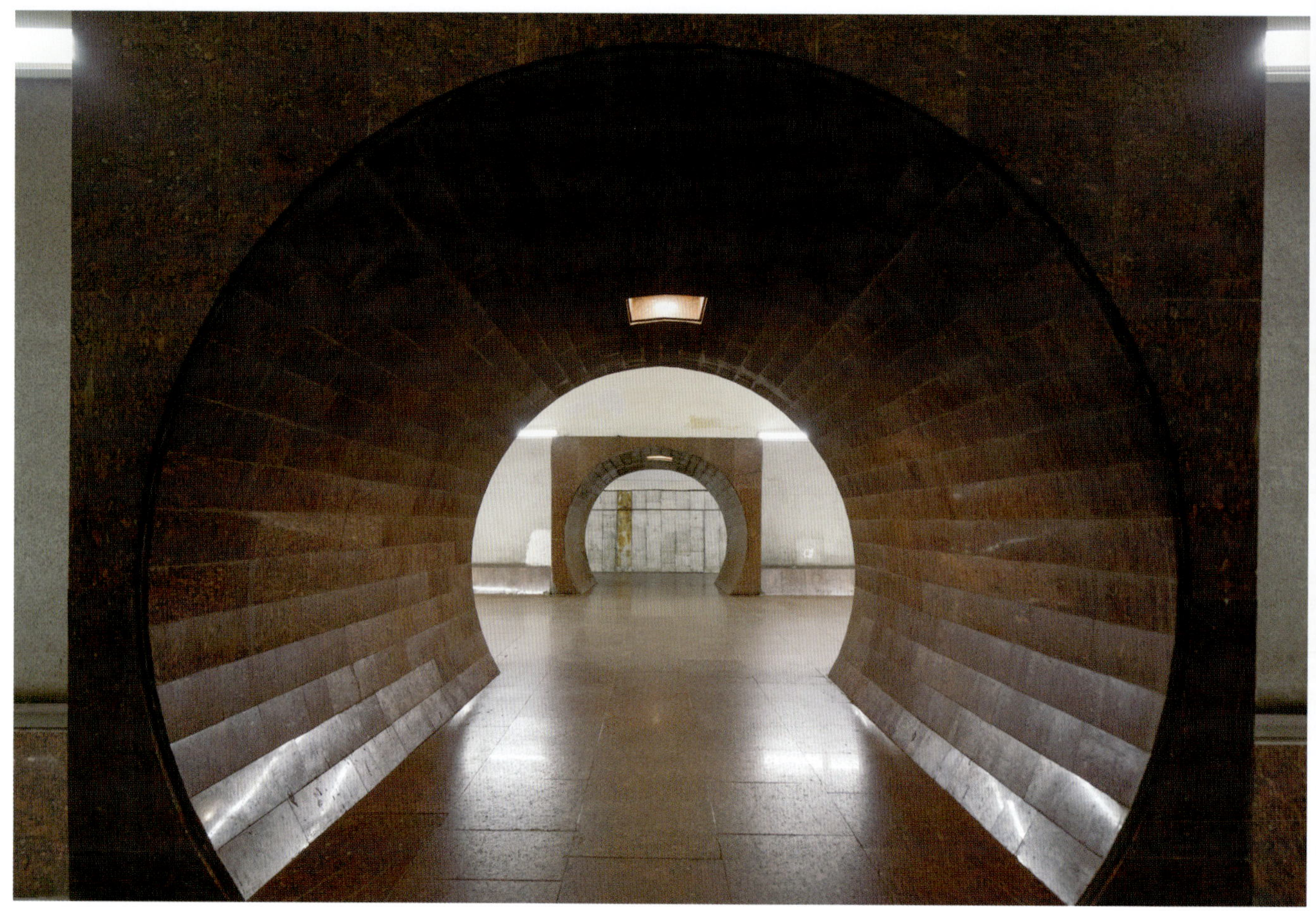

118   General Andranik, YEREVAN

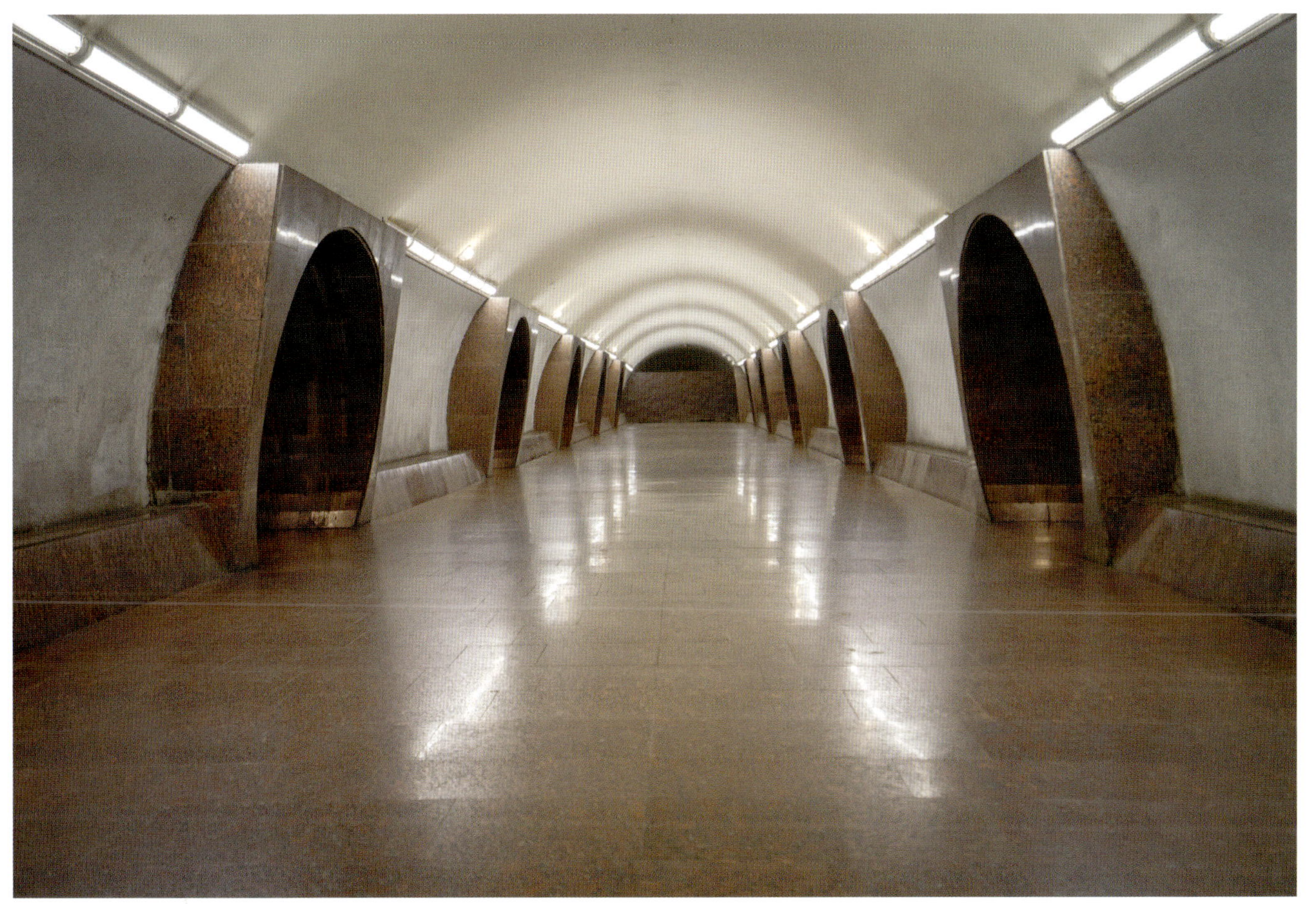

ТАШКЕНТ УЗБЕКИСТАН

TASHKENT UZBEKISTAN

OPENED 1977

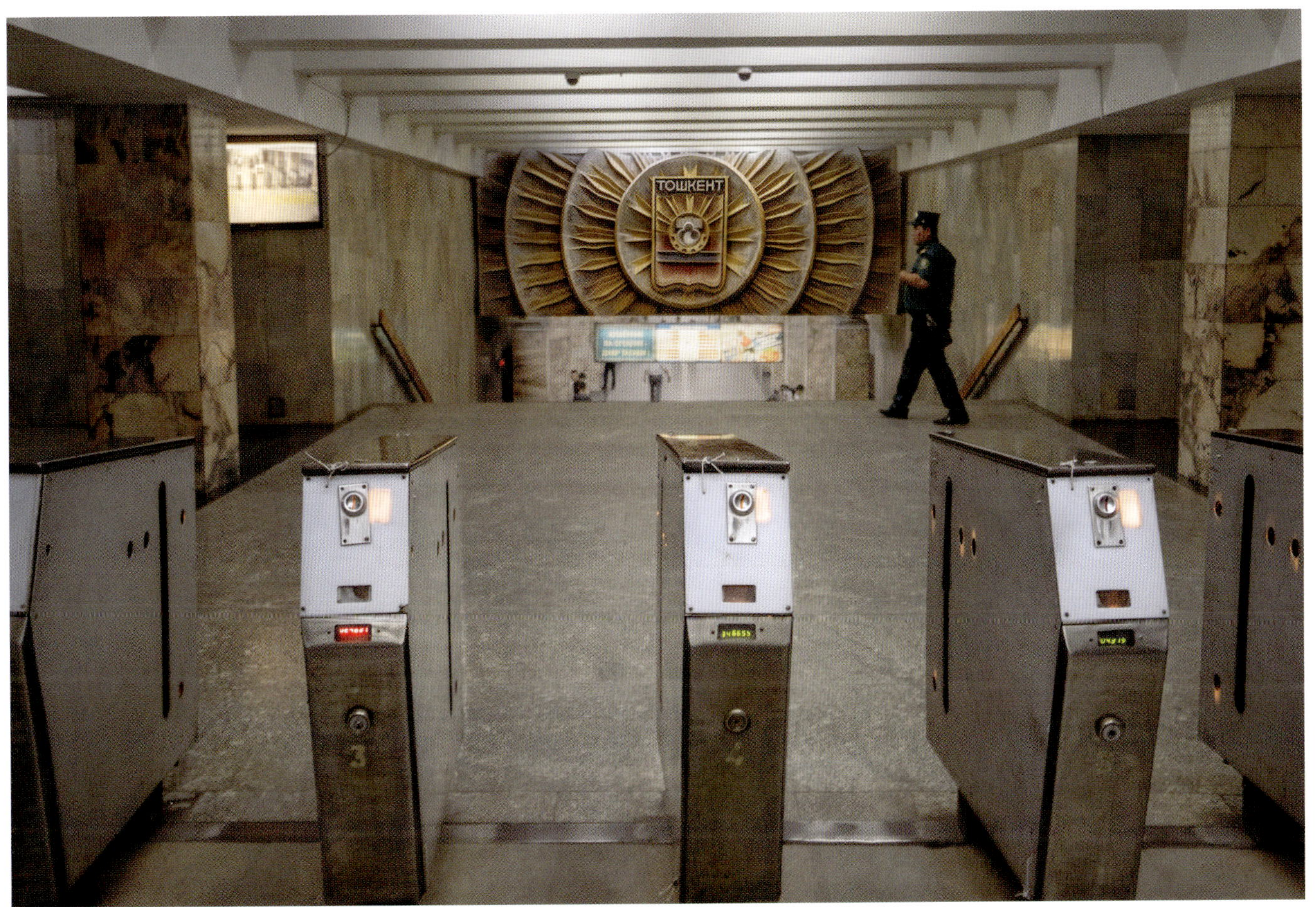
ТОШКЕНТ

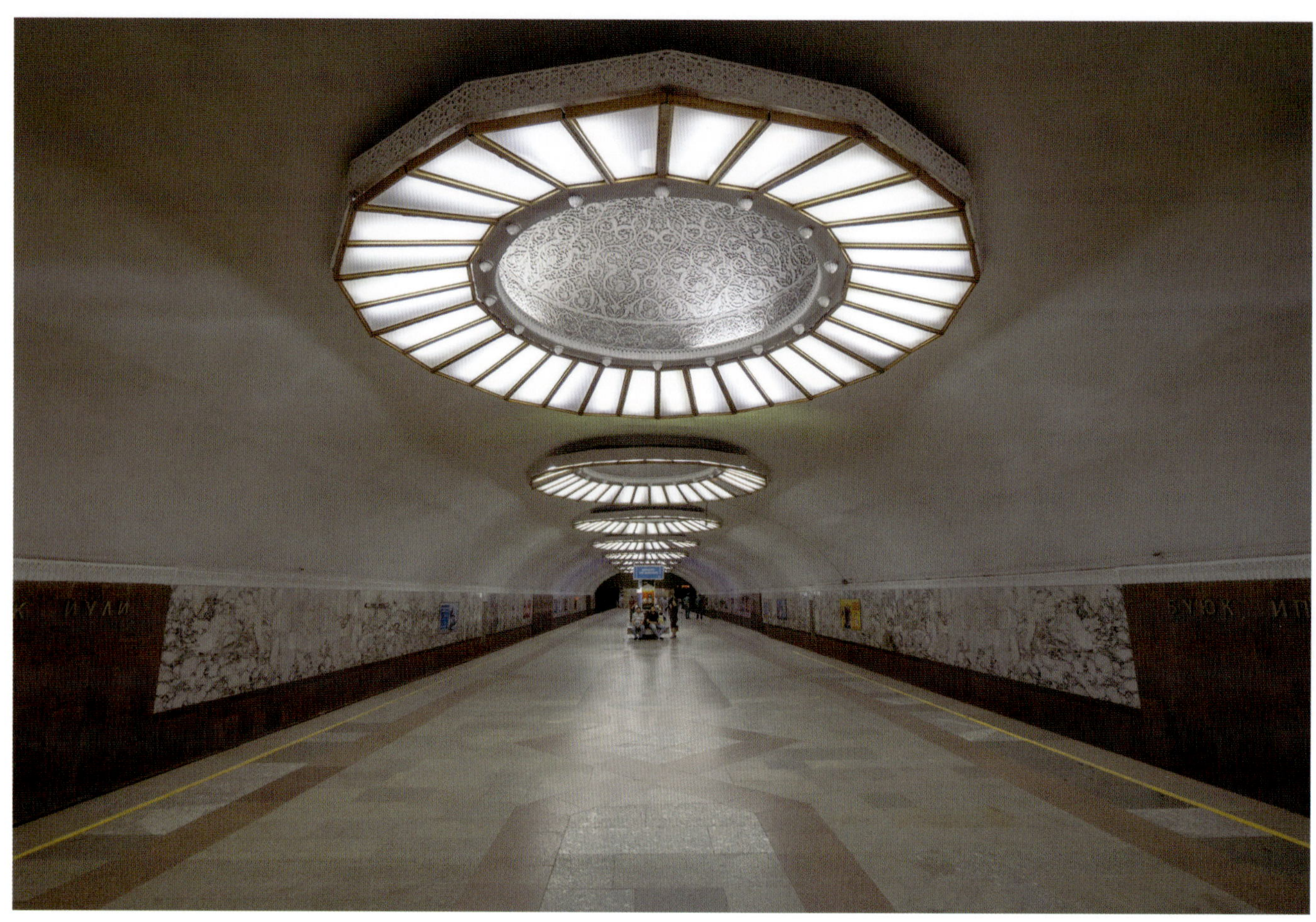

122   Buyuk Ipak Yuli, TASHKENT

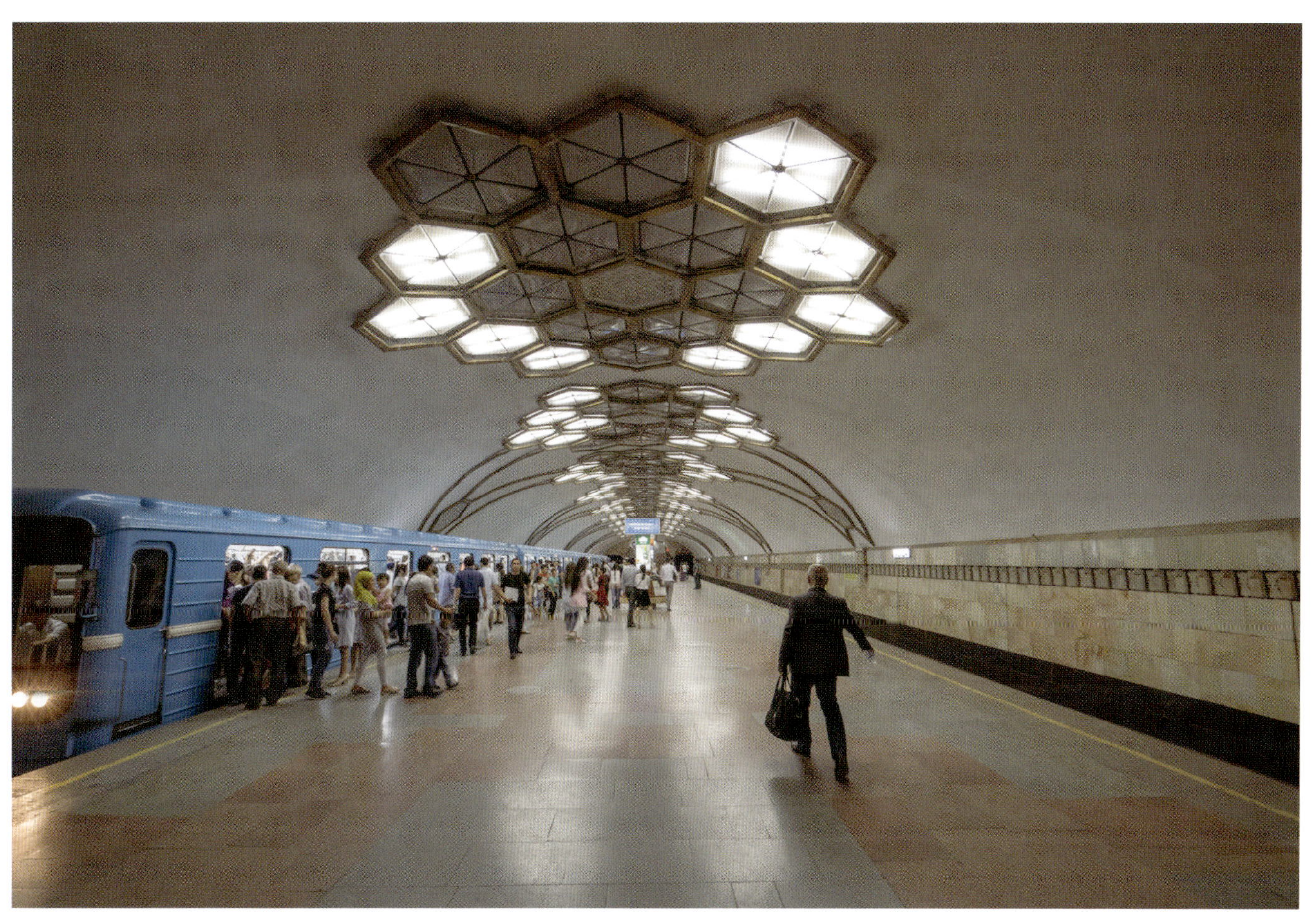

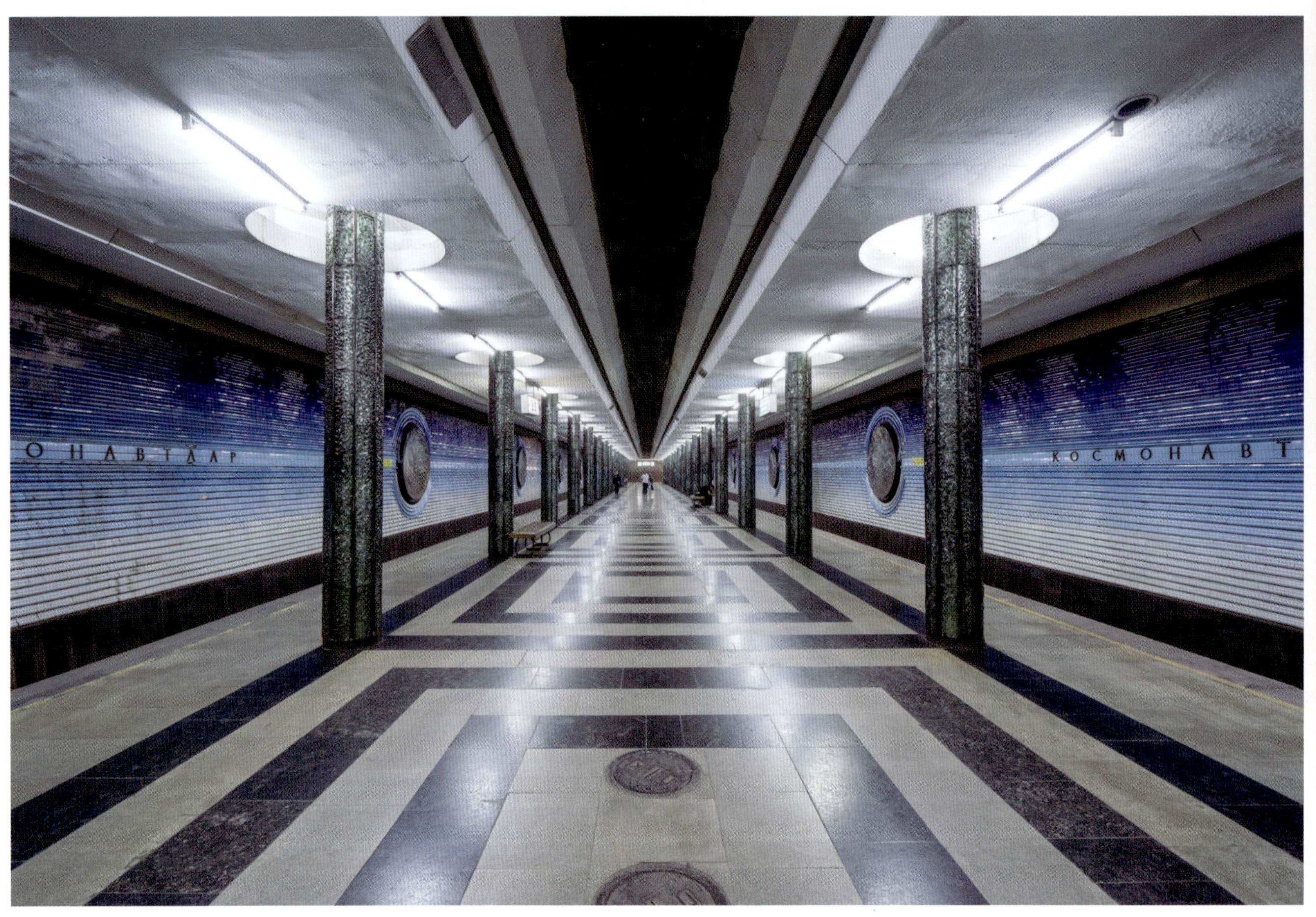

124   Kosmonavtlar, TASHKENT

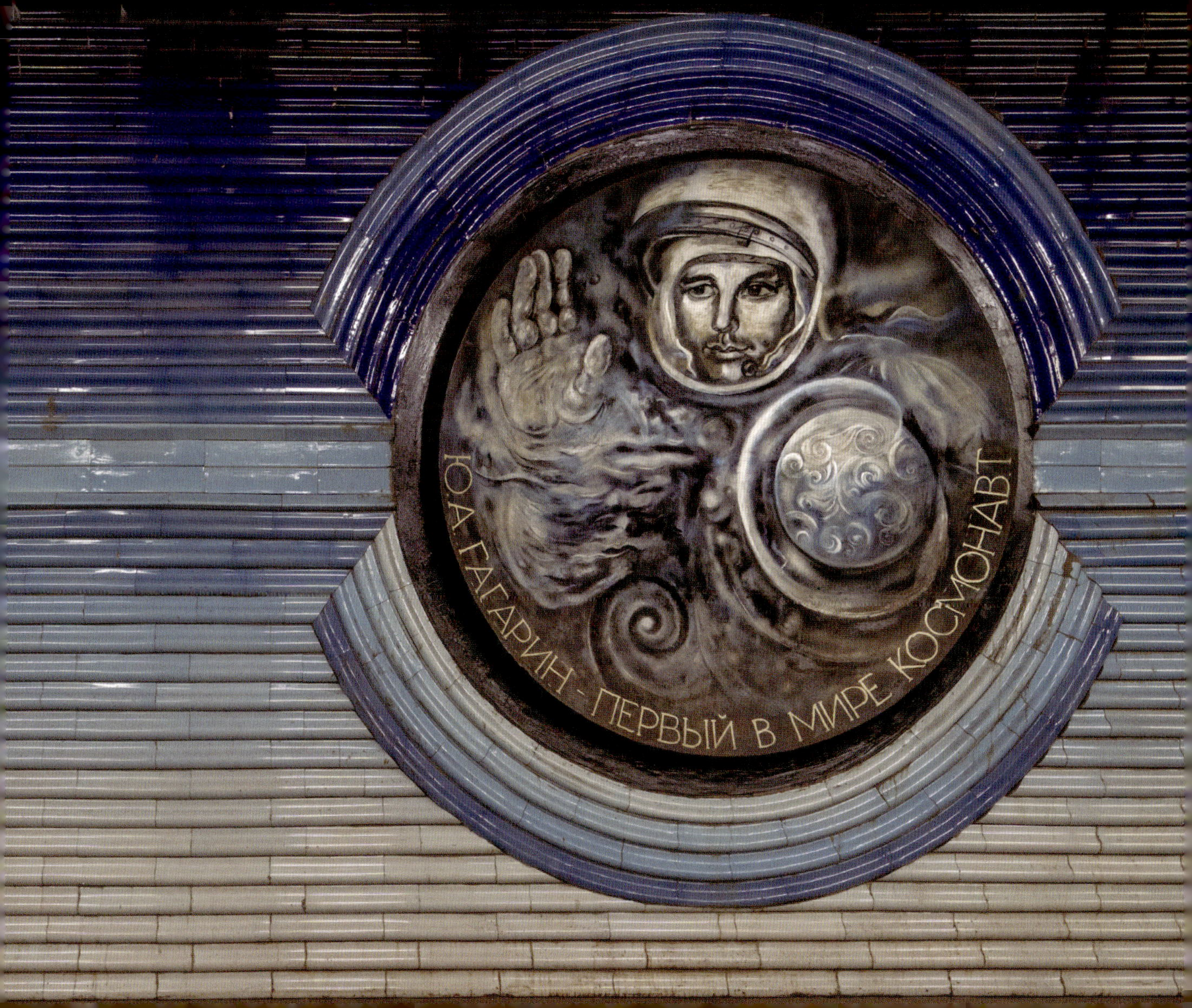

Ю.А ГАГАРИН - ПЕРВЫЙ В МИРЕ КОСМОНАВТ

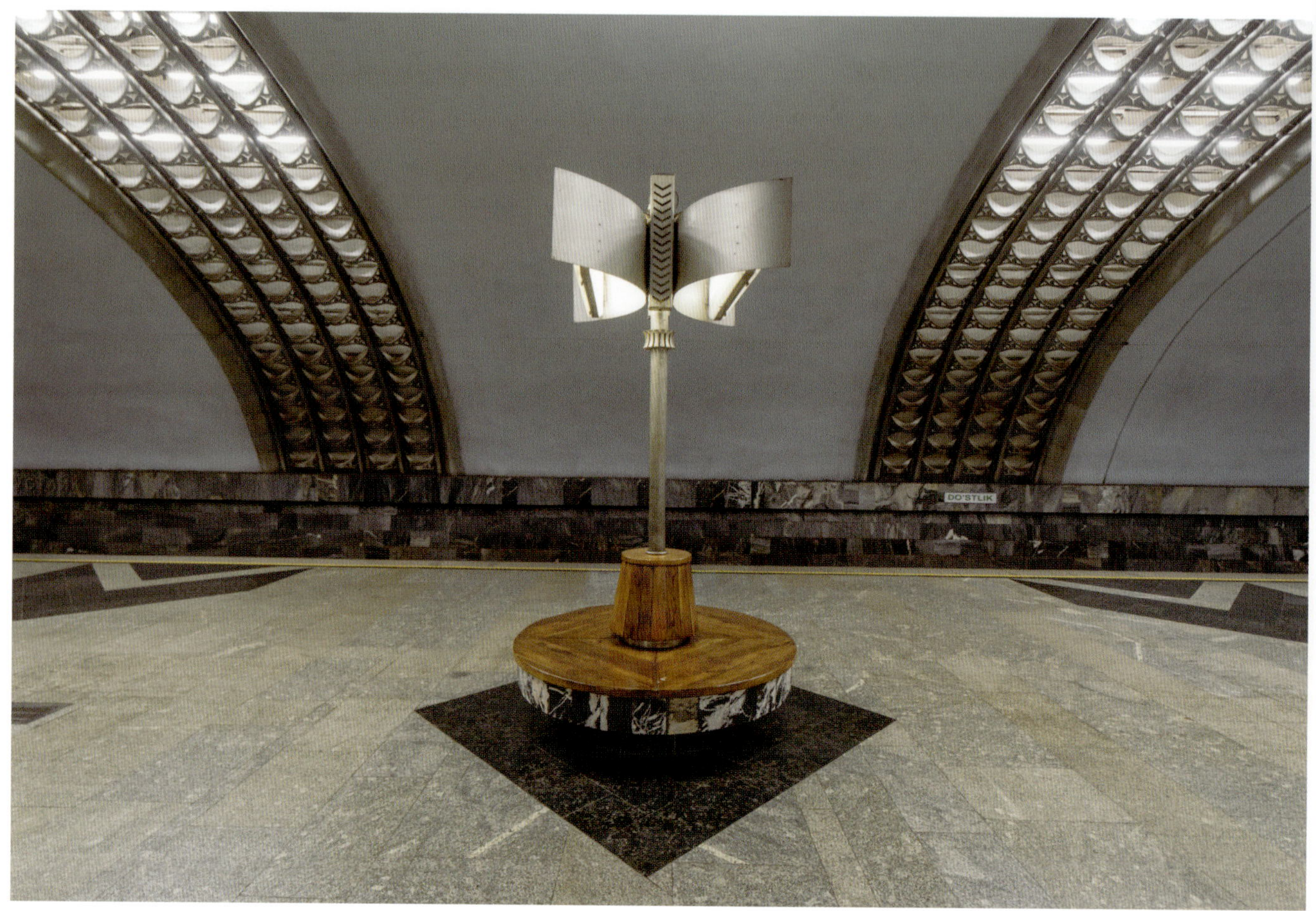

126   Dustlik, TASHKENT

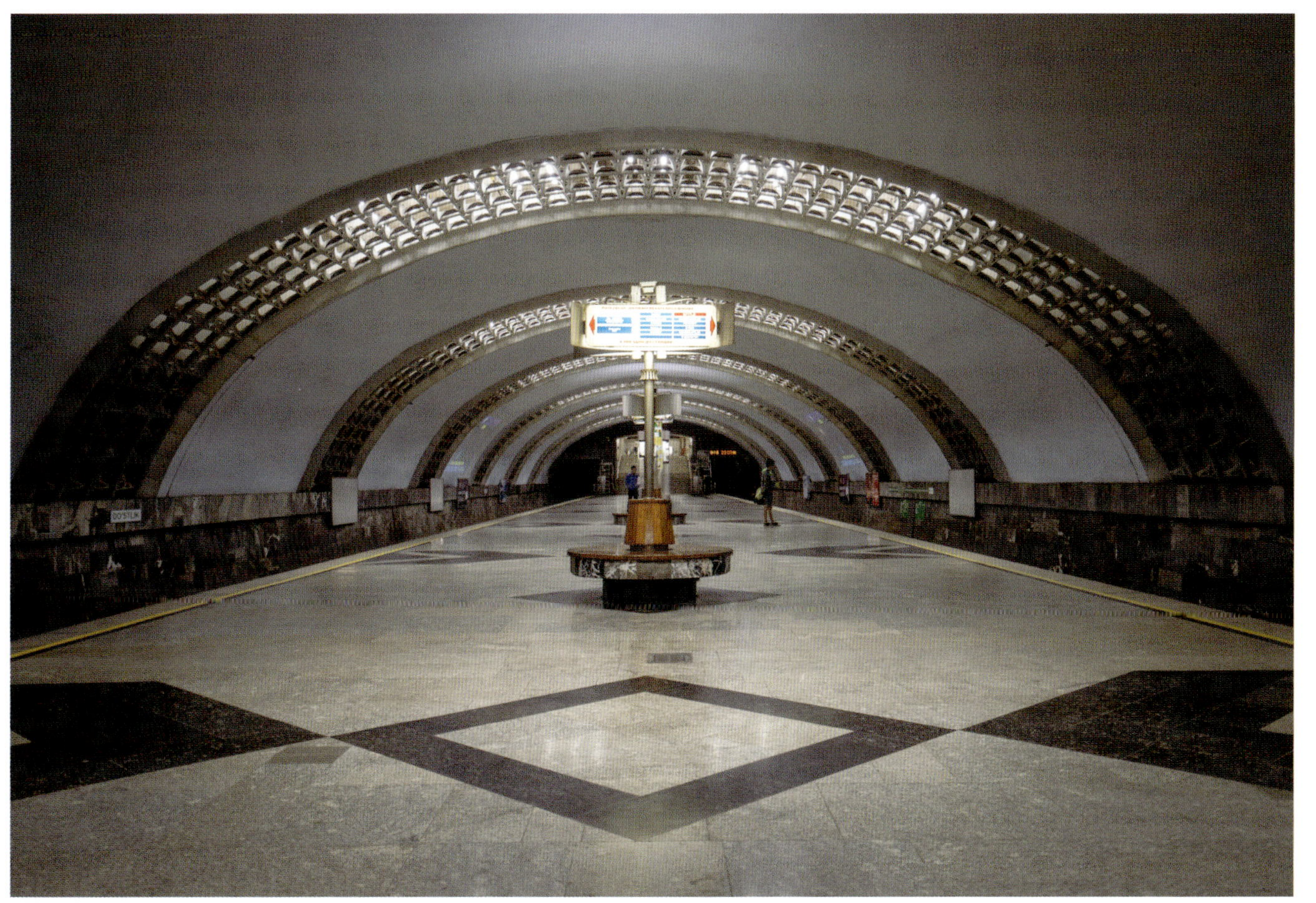

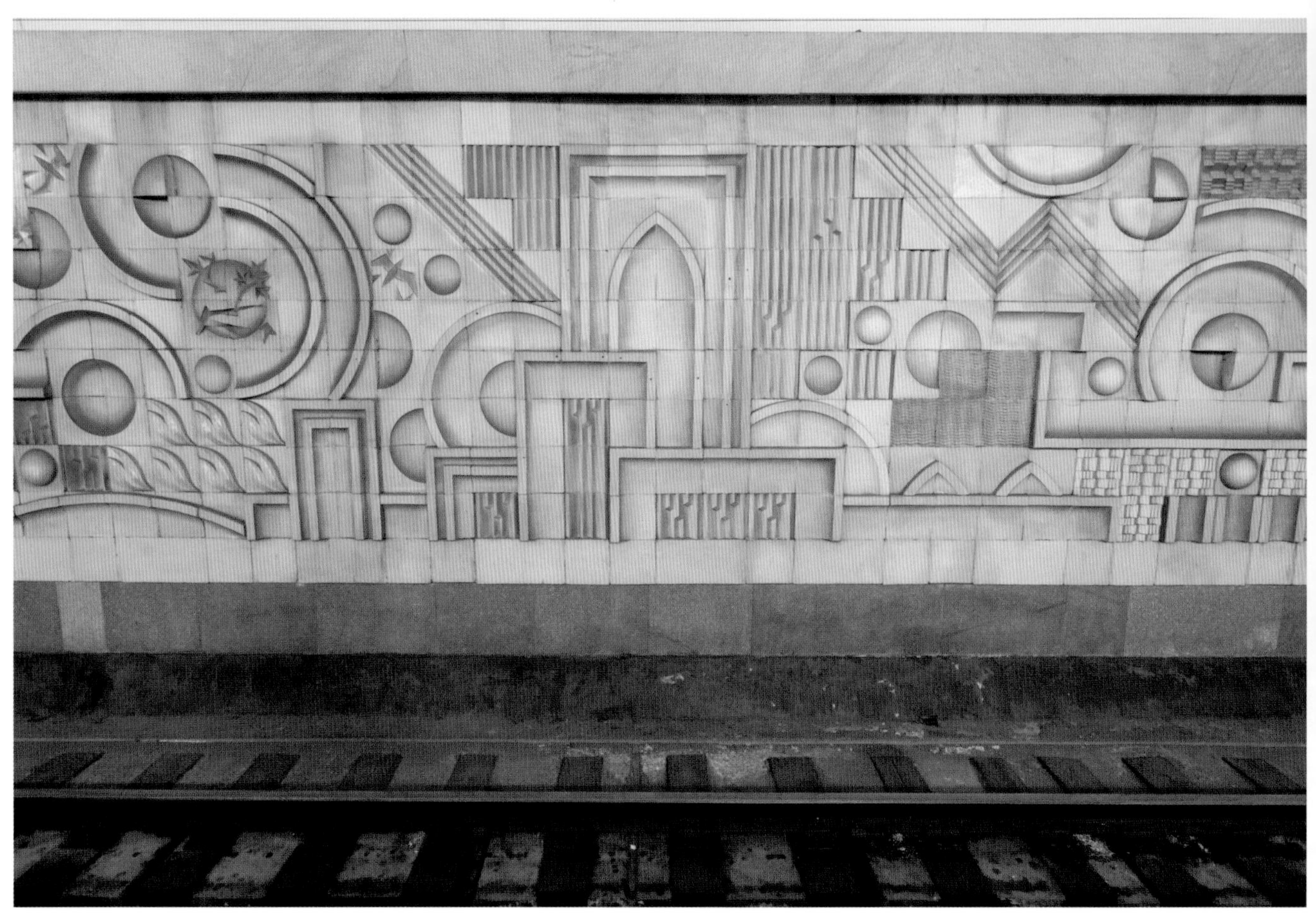

128   Tinchlik, TASHKENT

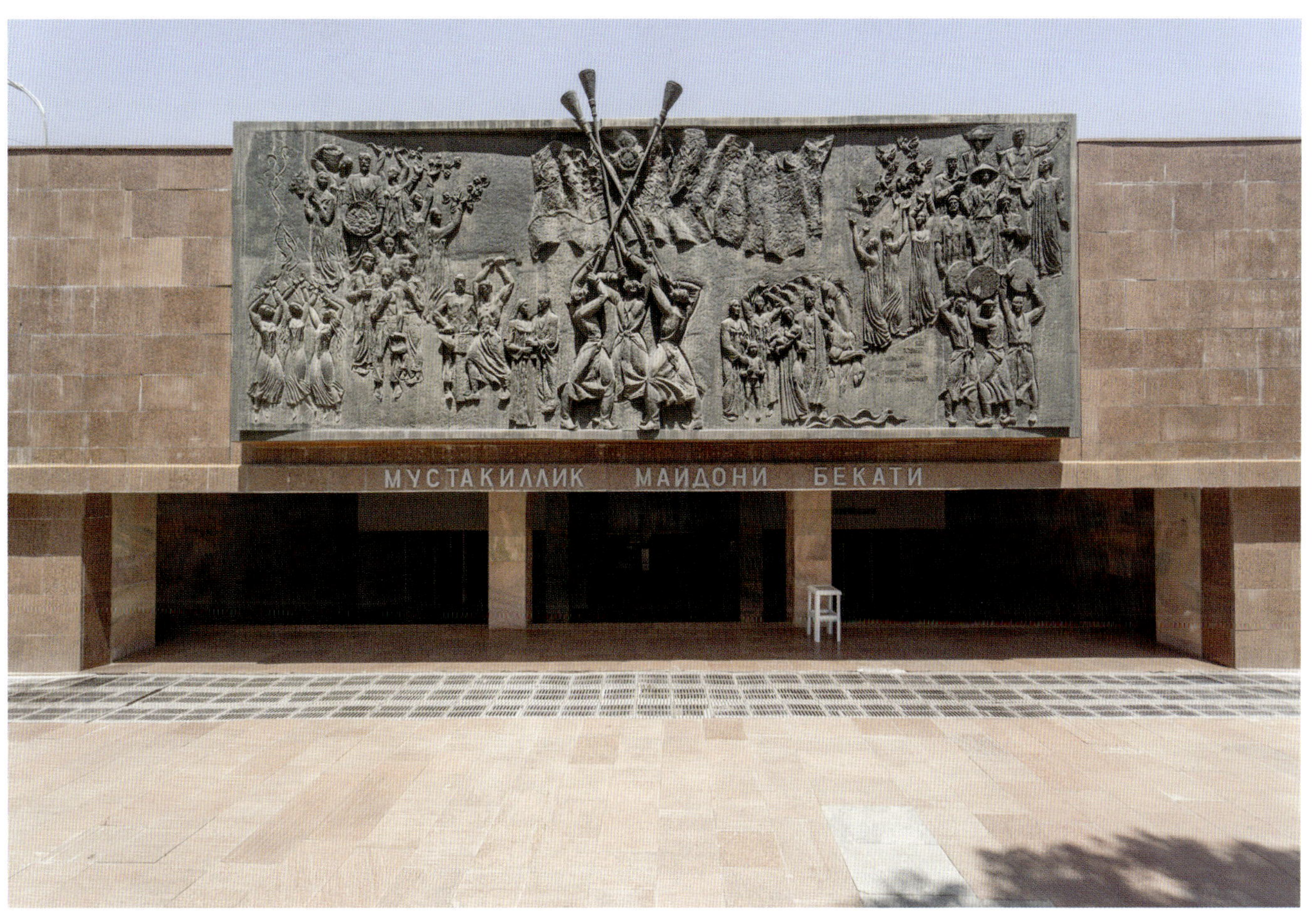

Mustaqilliq Maydoni, TASHKENT   129

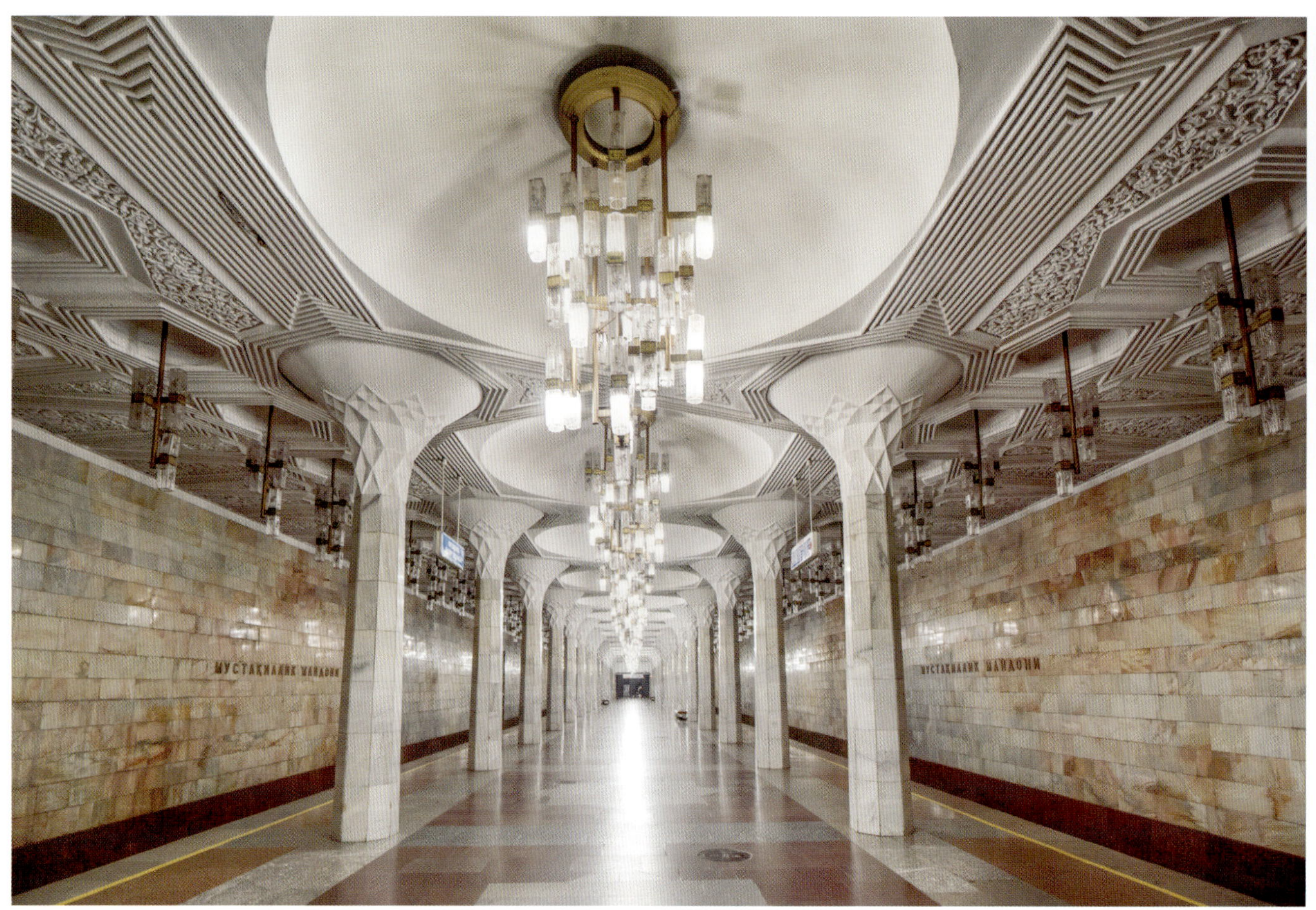

130   Mustaqilliq Maydoni, TASHKENT

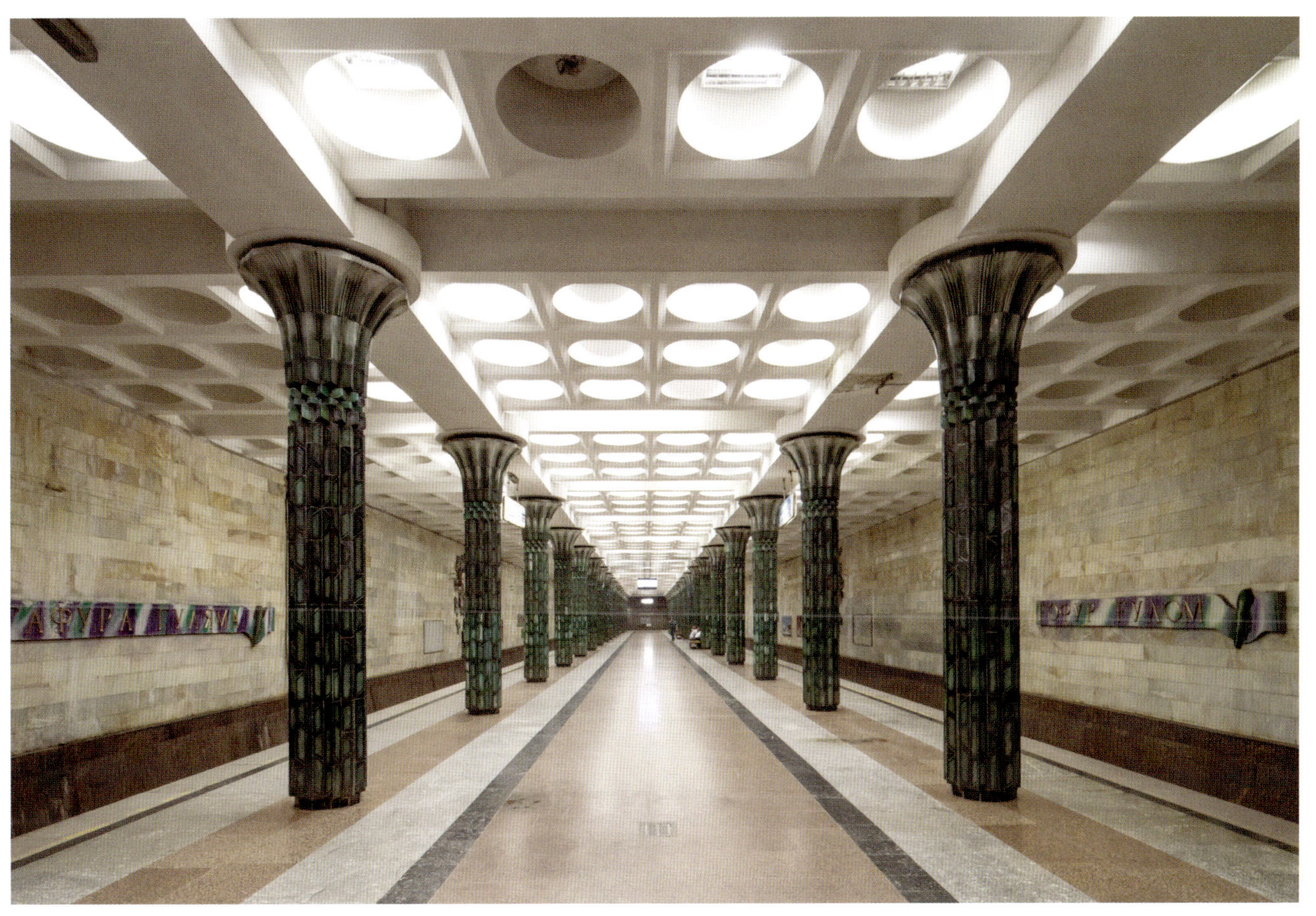

G'afur G'ulom, TASHKENT   131

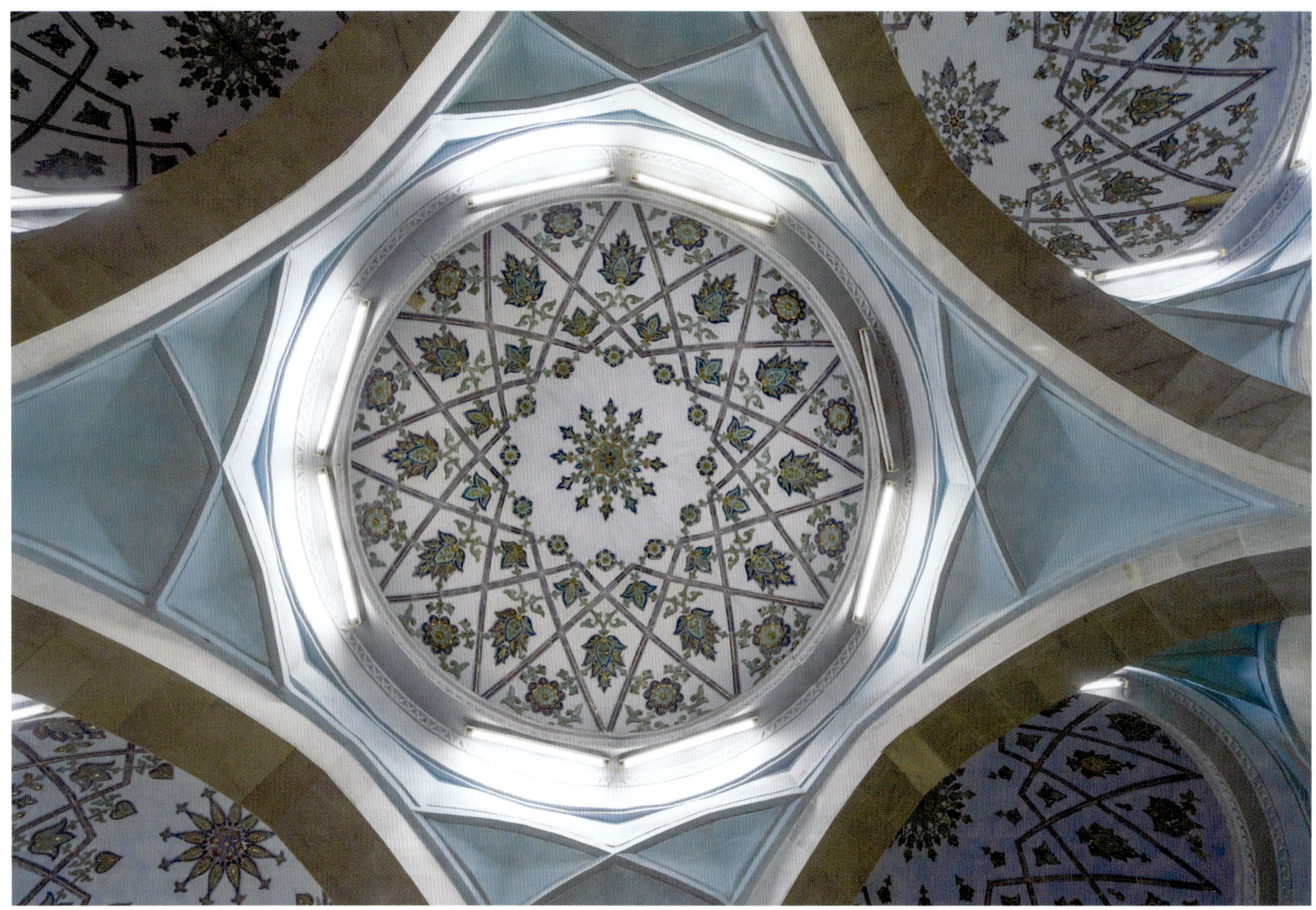

132　Alisher Navoi, TASHKENT

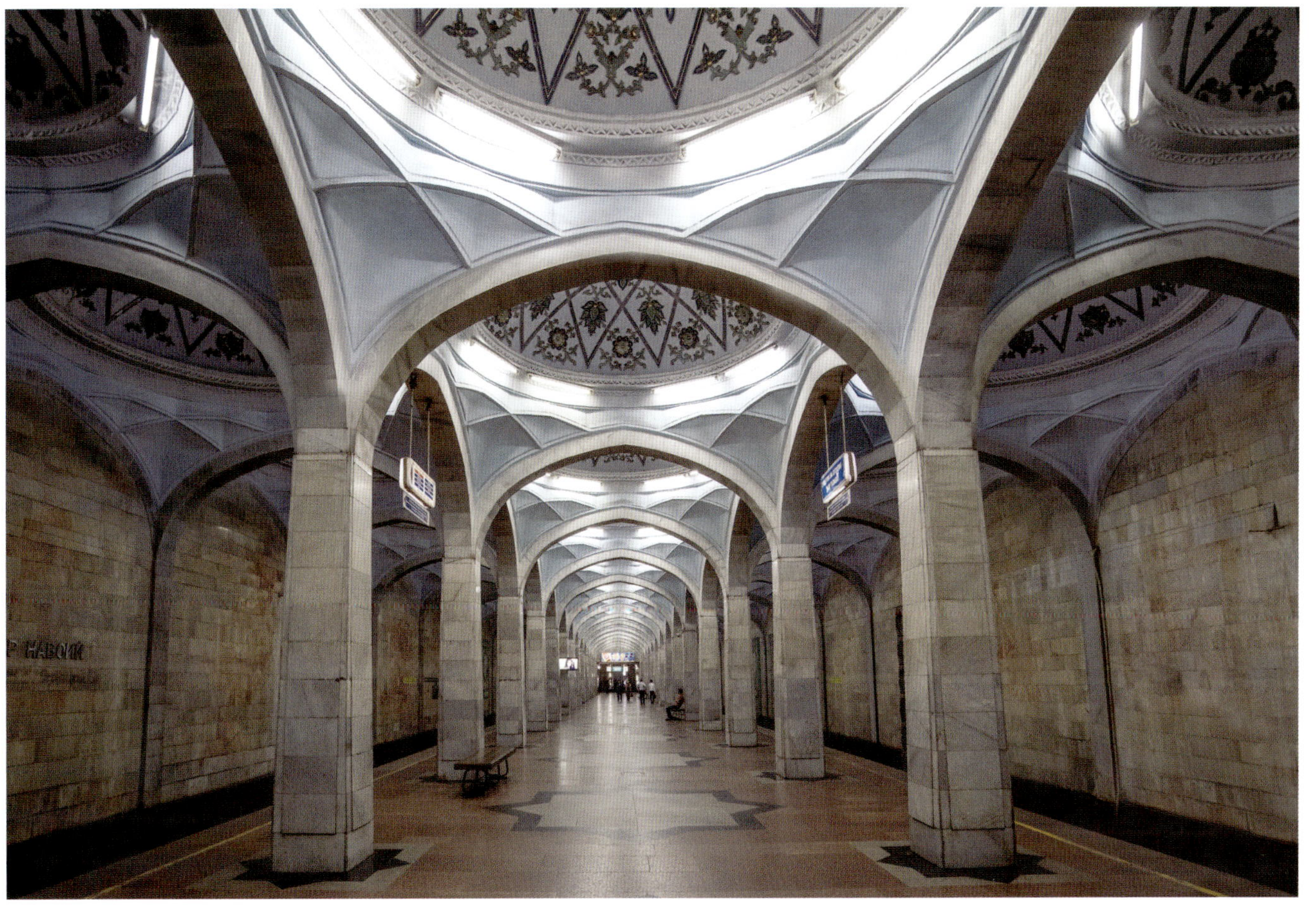

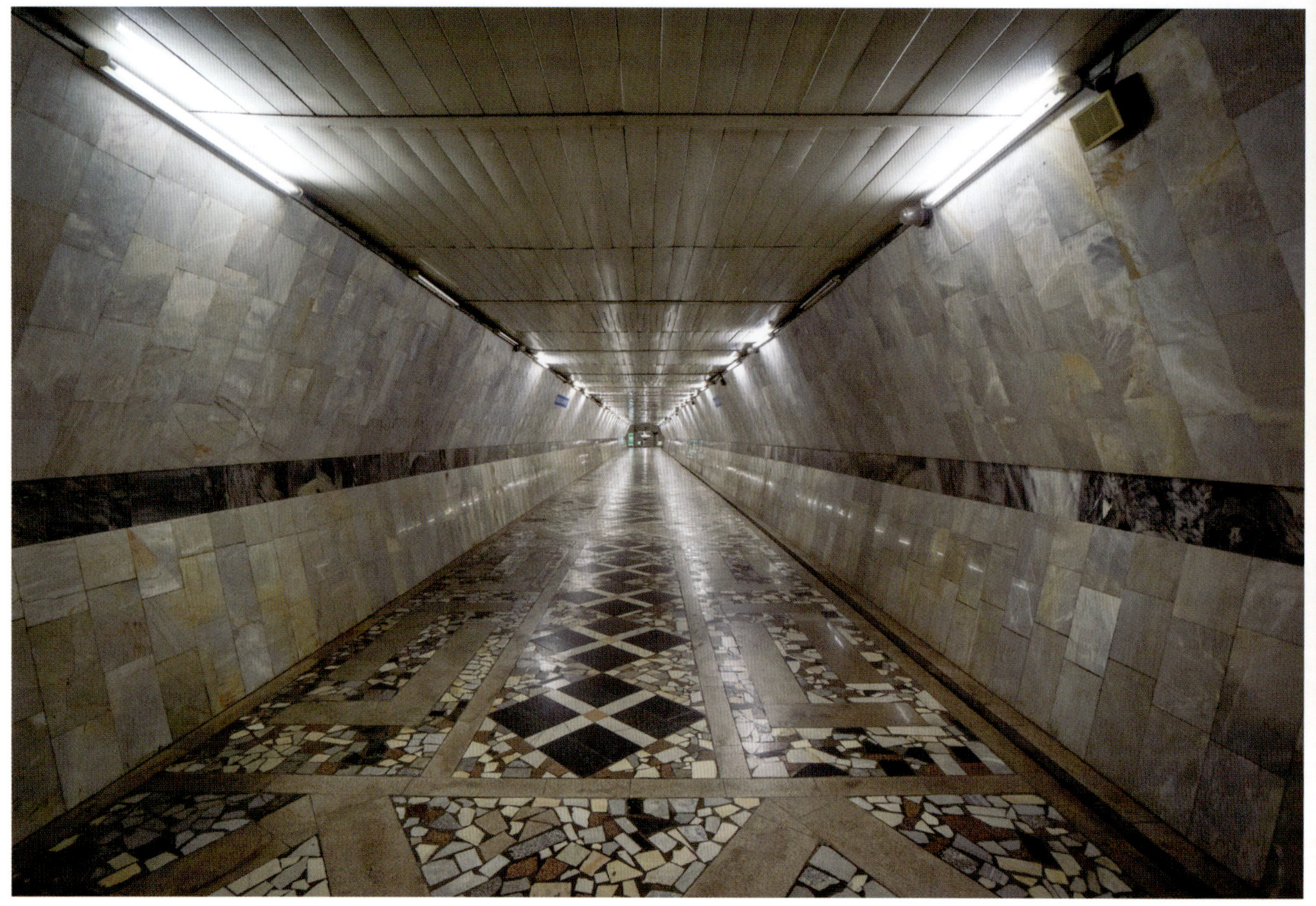

    Ynus Rajabiy, TASHKENT

Olmazor, TASHKENT

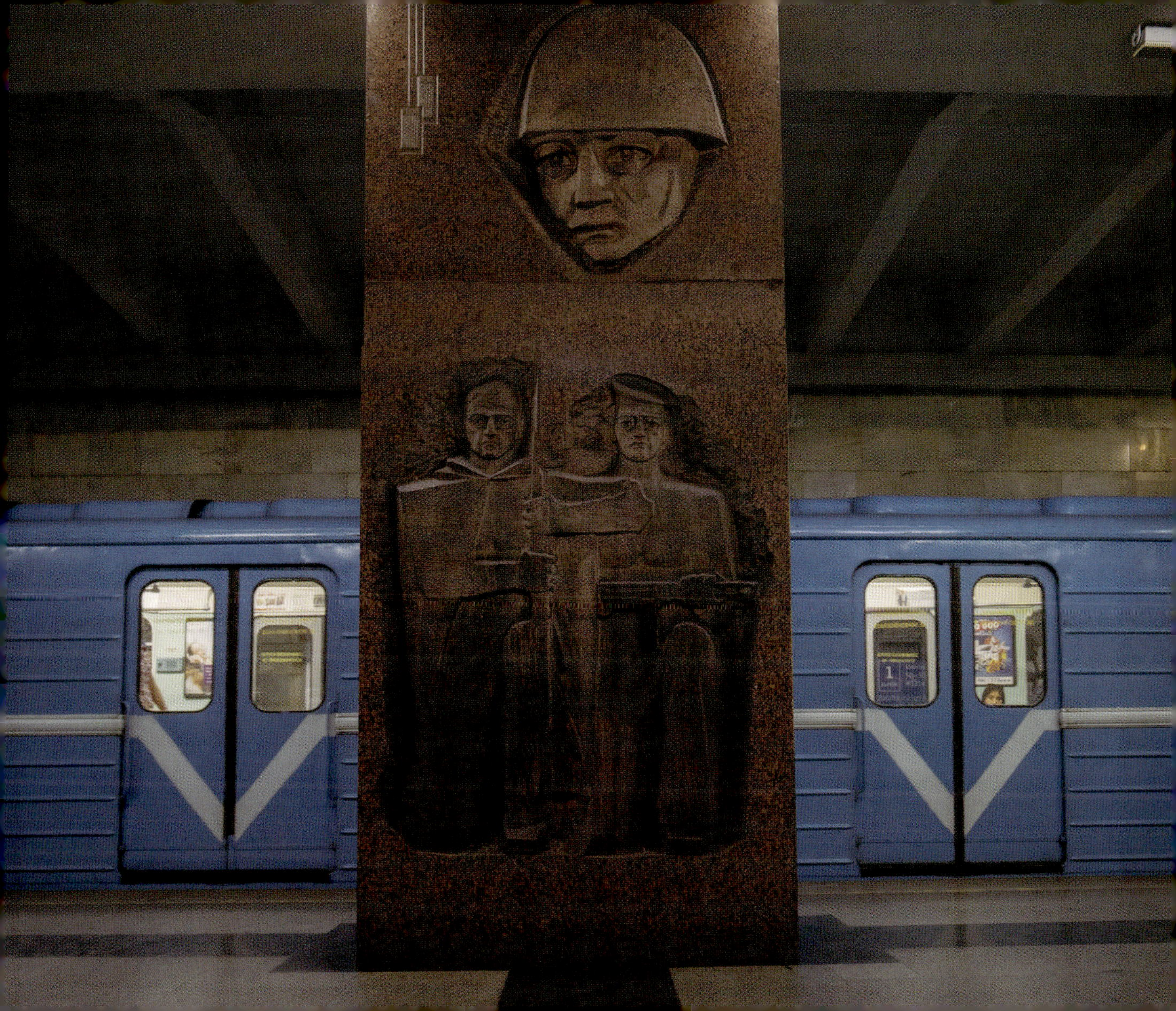

**ХАРЬКОВ   KHARKIV
УКРАИНА   UKRAINE**

OPENED 1975

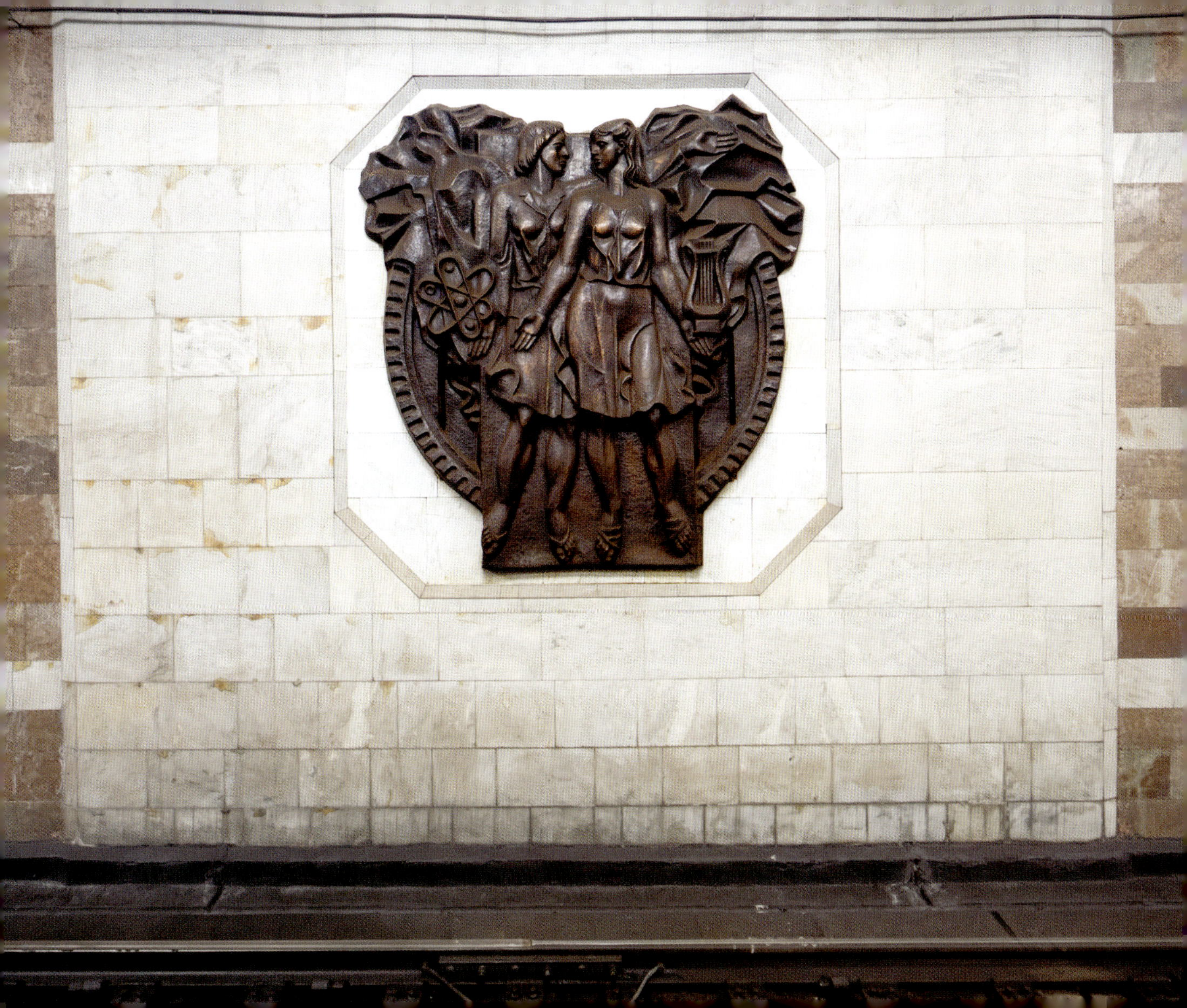

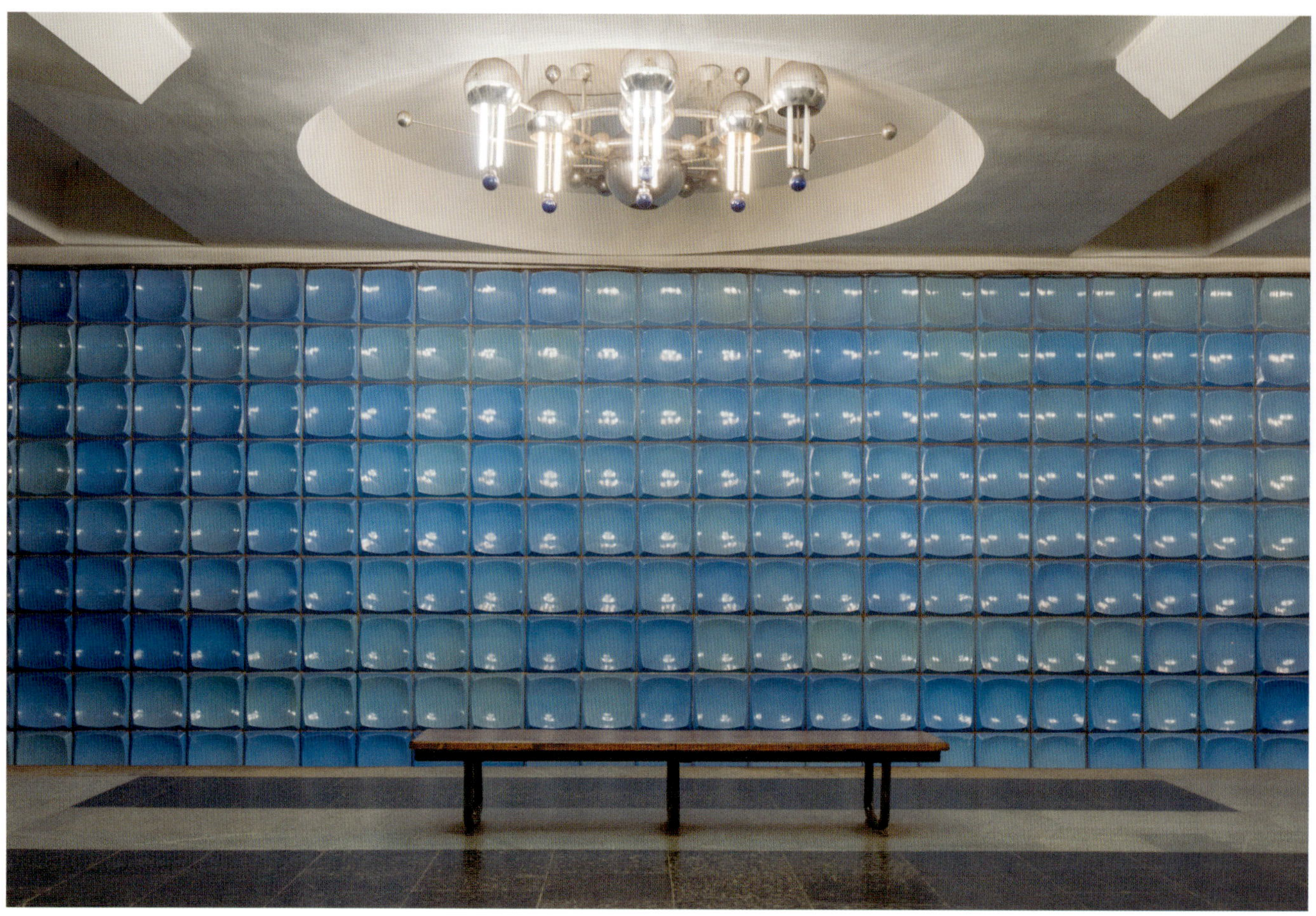

138 Akademika Barabashova, KHARKIV

overleaf left: Moskovskyi Prospekt, KHARKIV

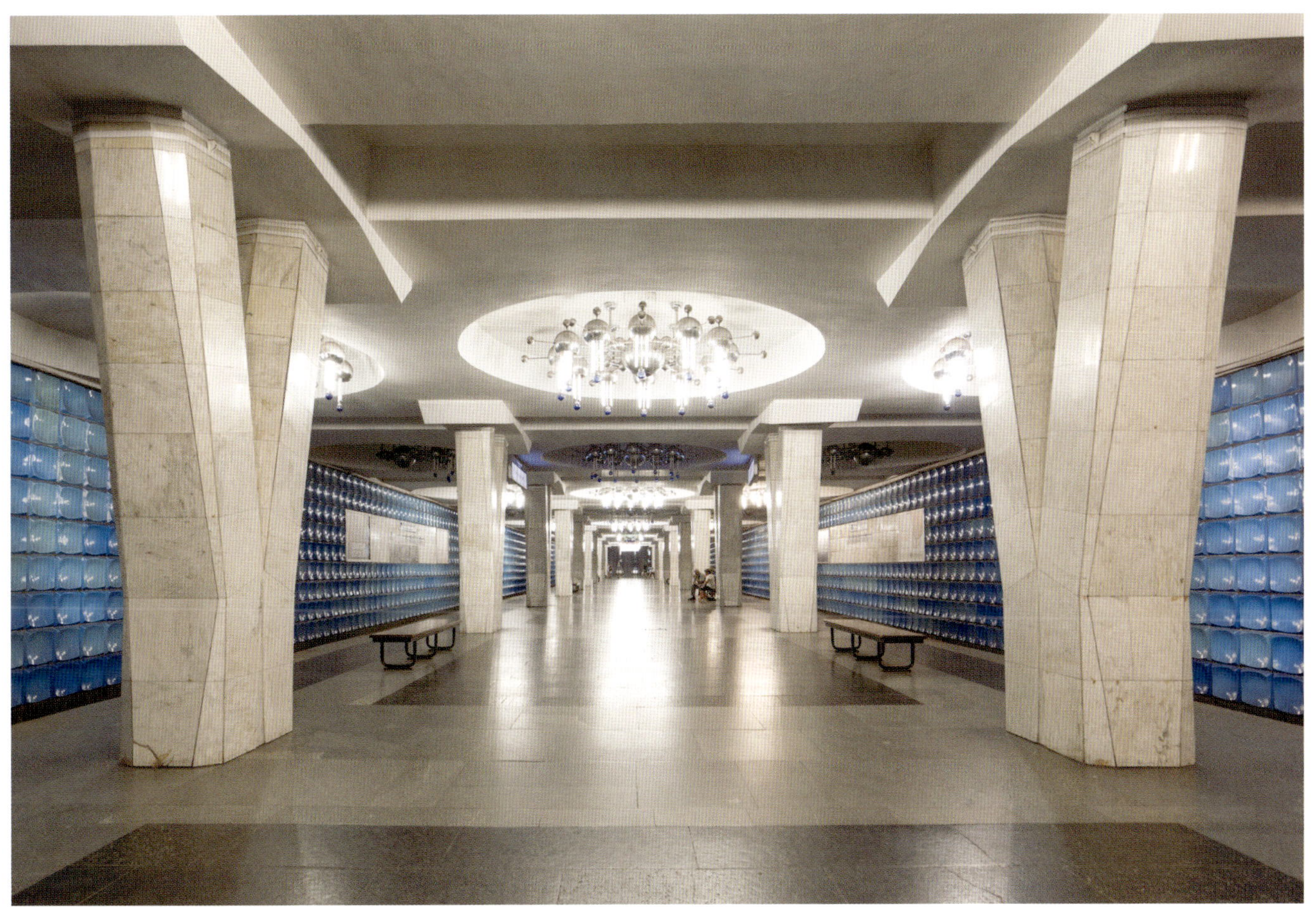

overleaf right: Imeni O.S. Maselskoho, KHARKIV

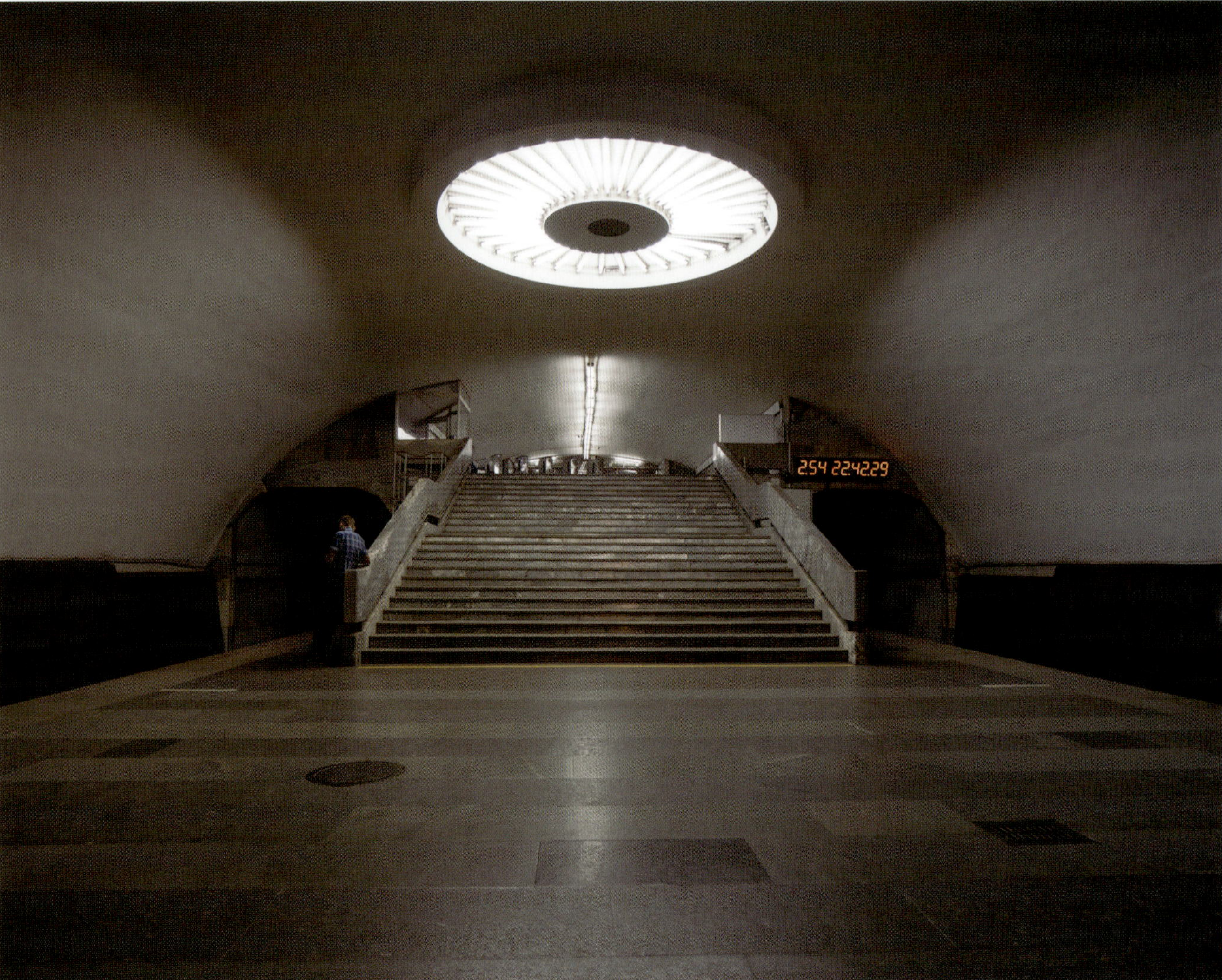

2:54 22:42.29

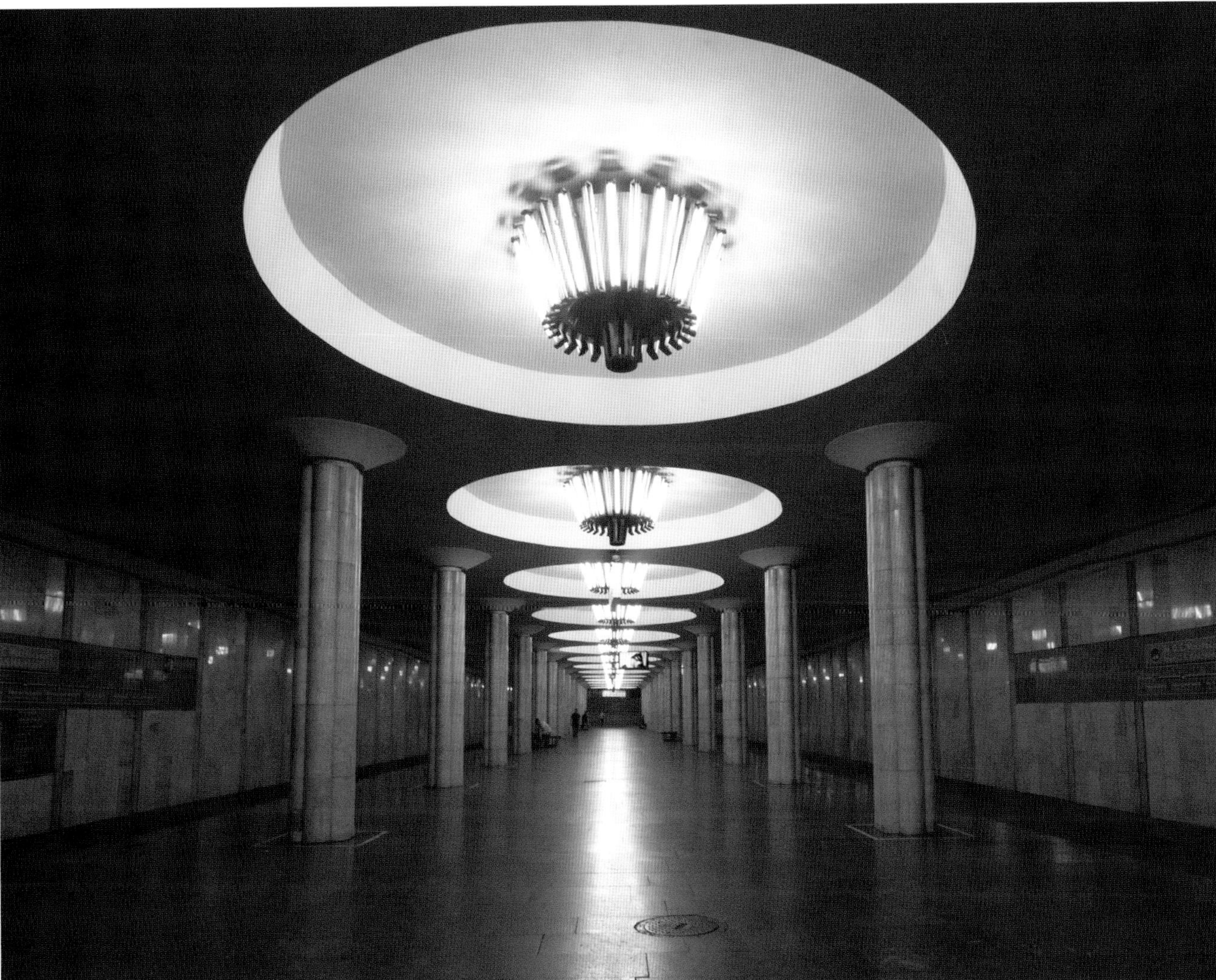

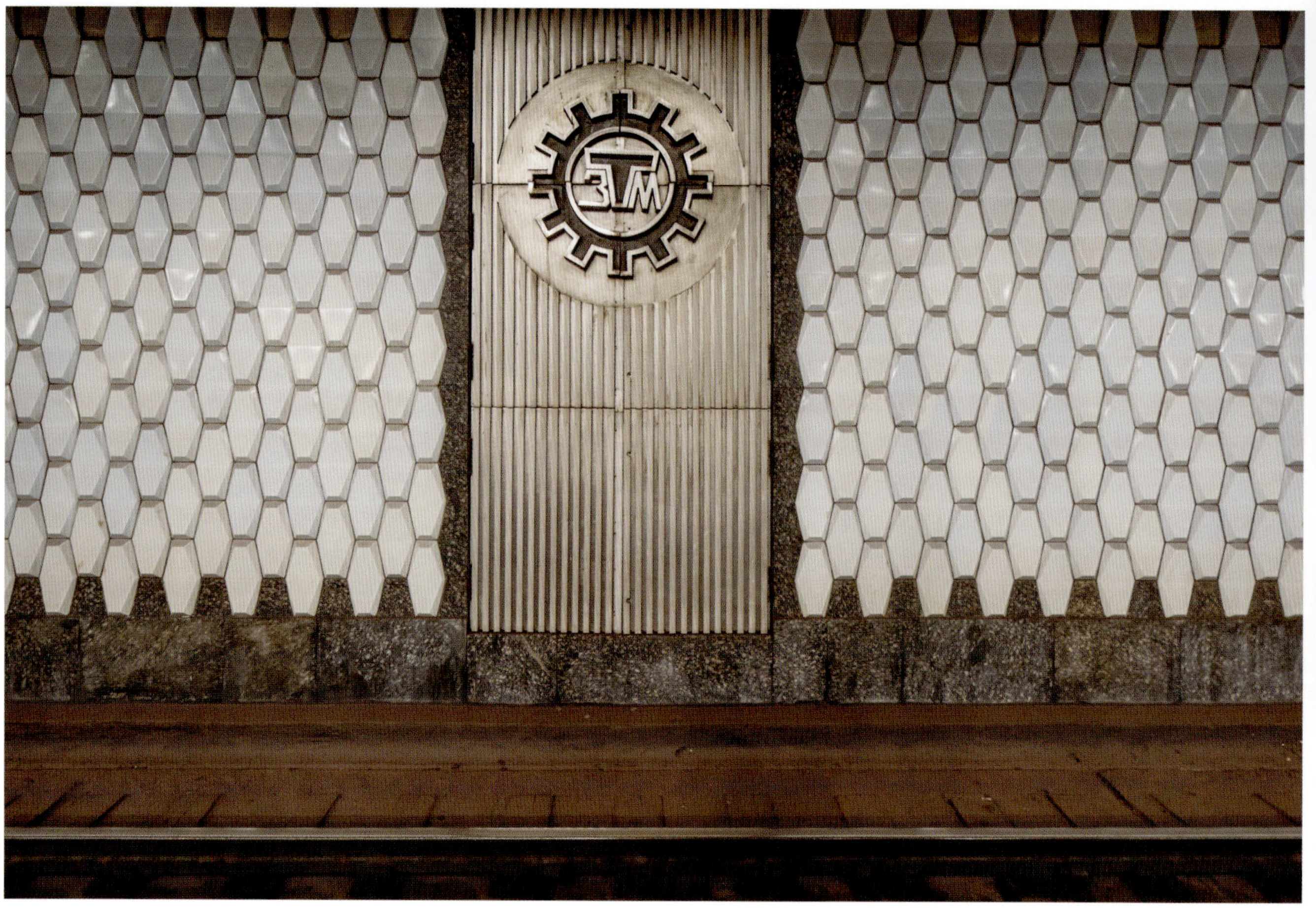

142   Zavod Imeni Malysheva, KHARKIV

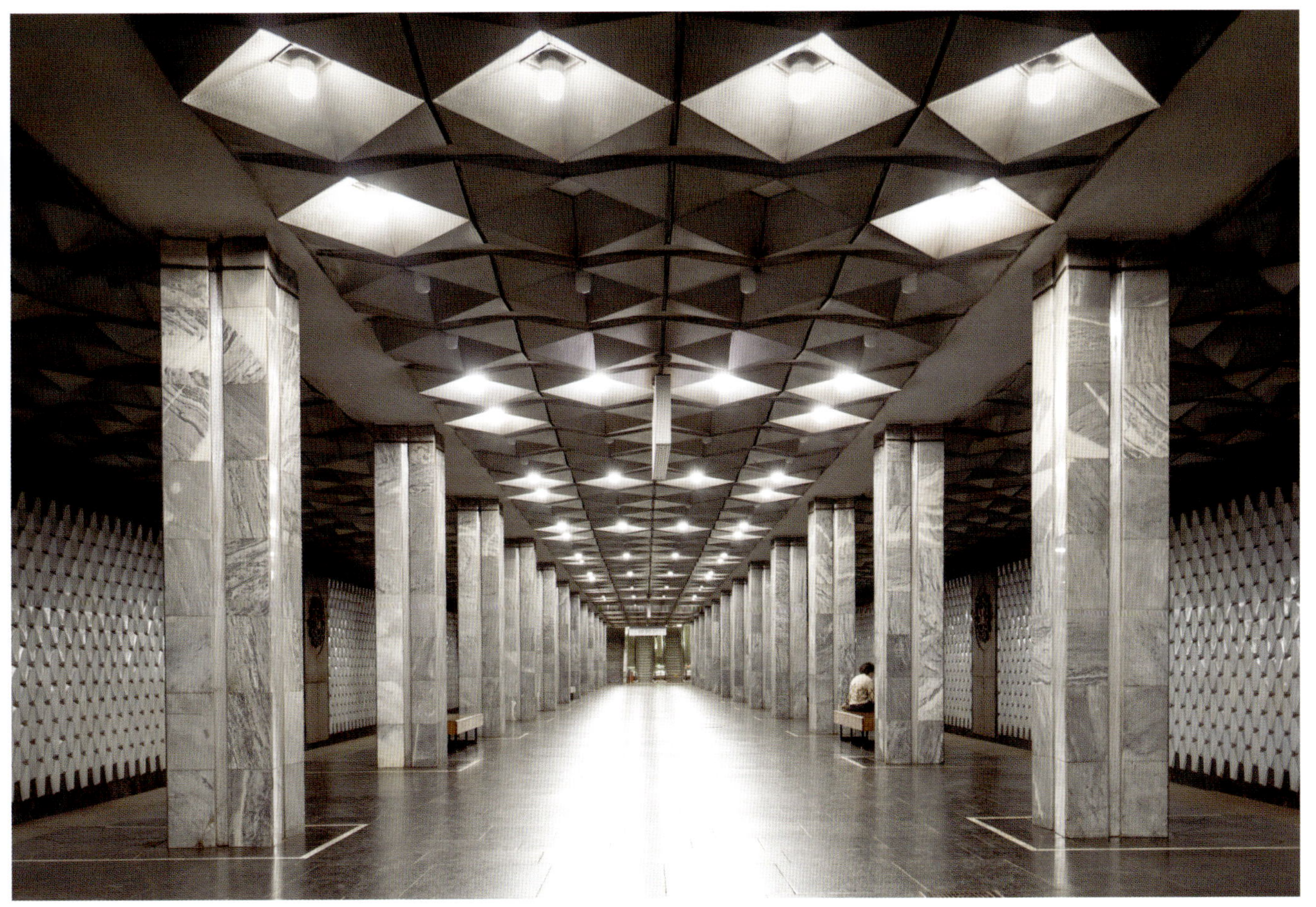

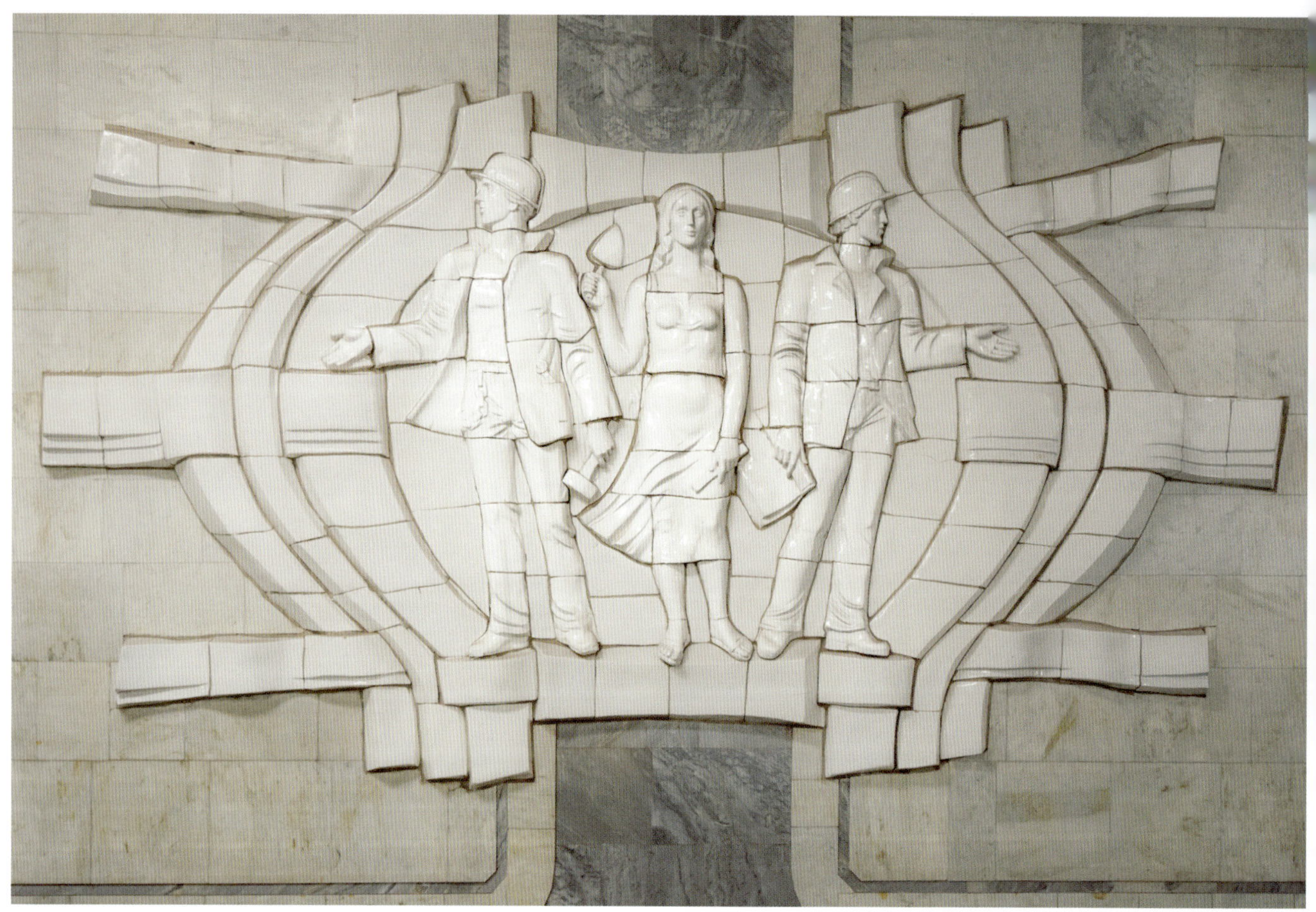

144 Studentska, KHARKIV

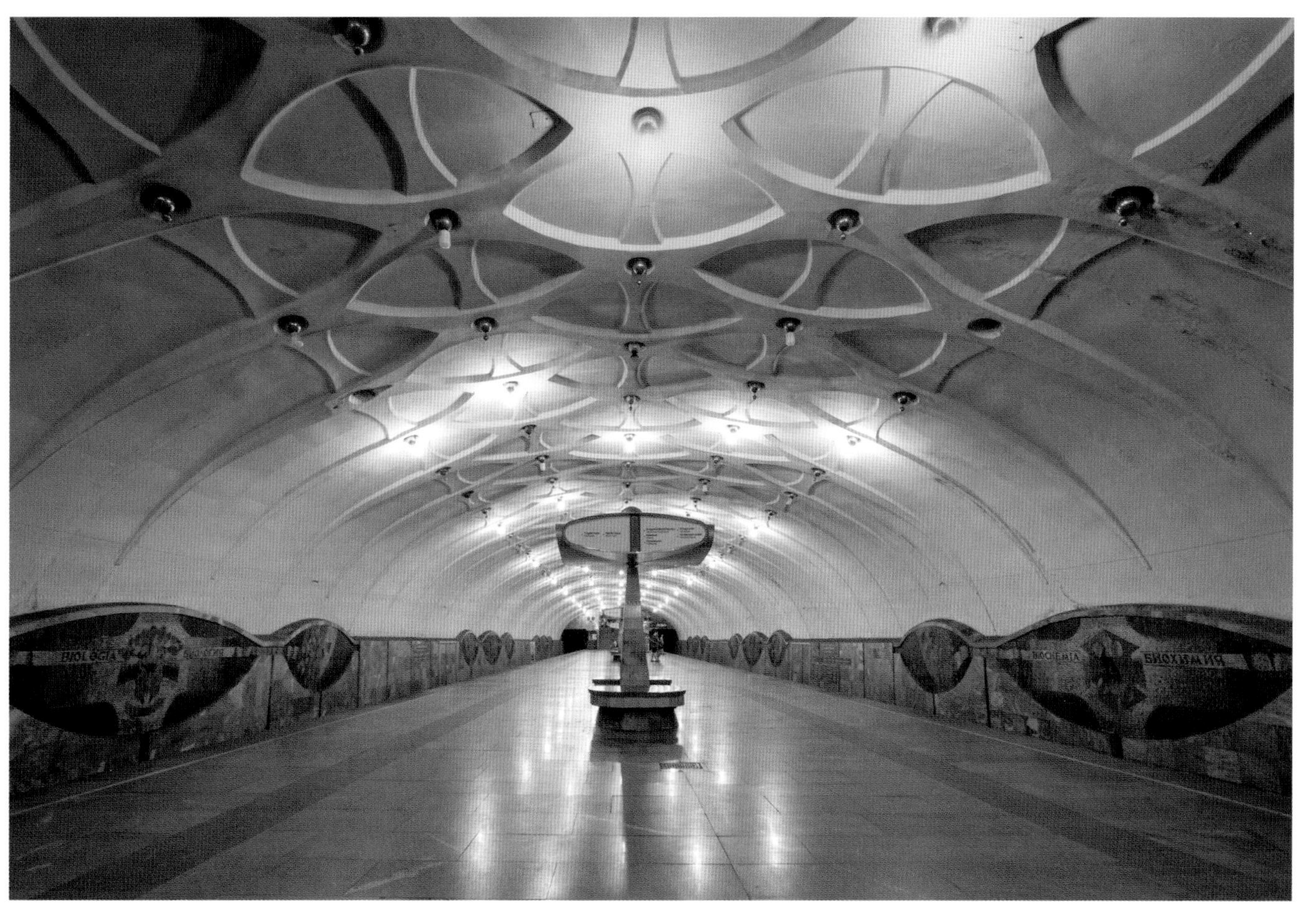

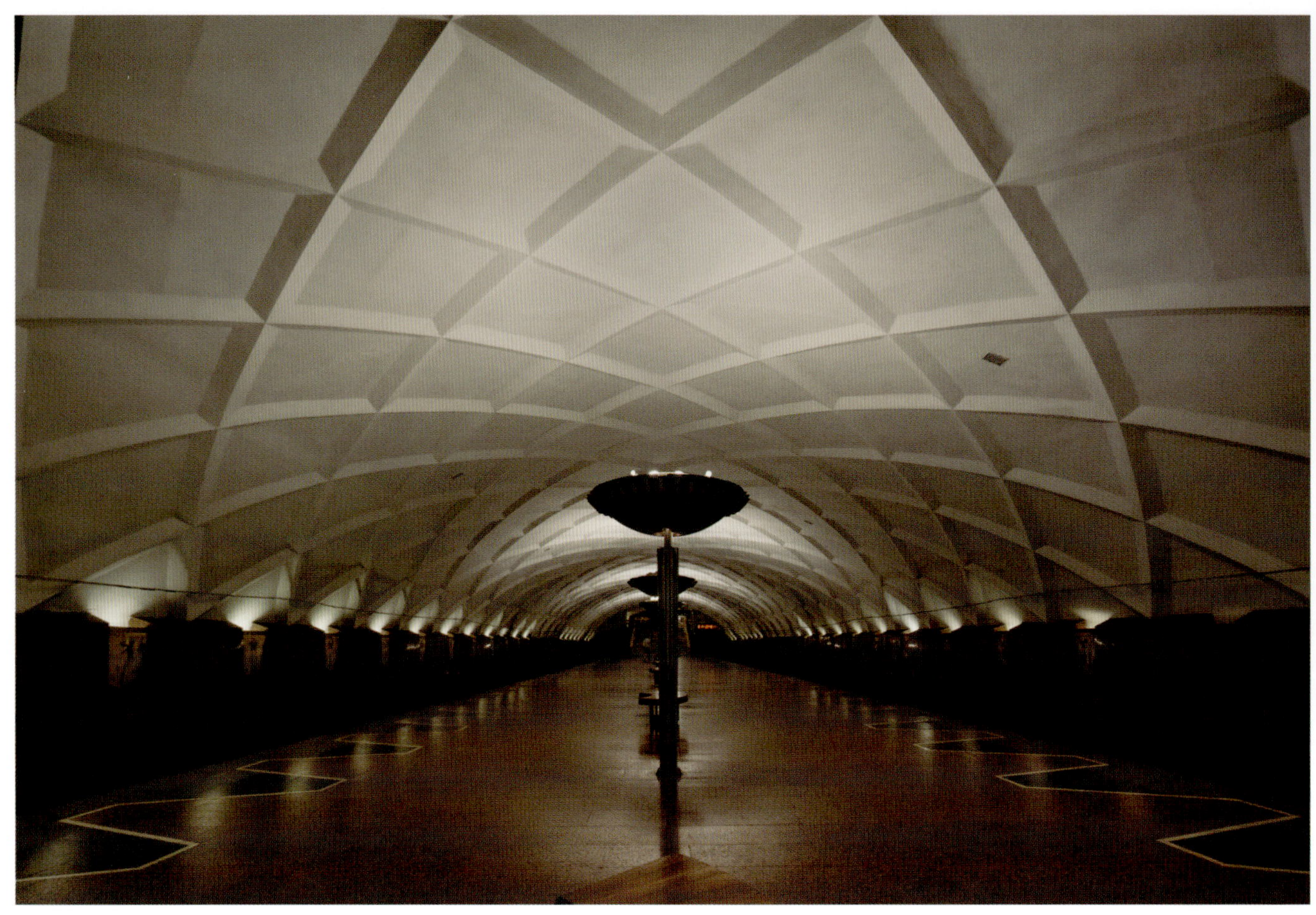

146   Armiyska, KHARKIV

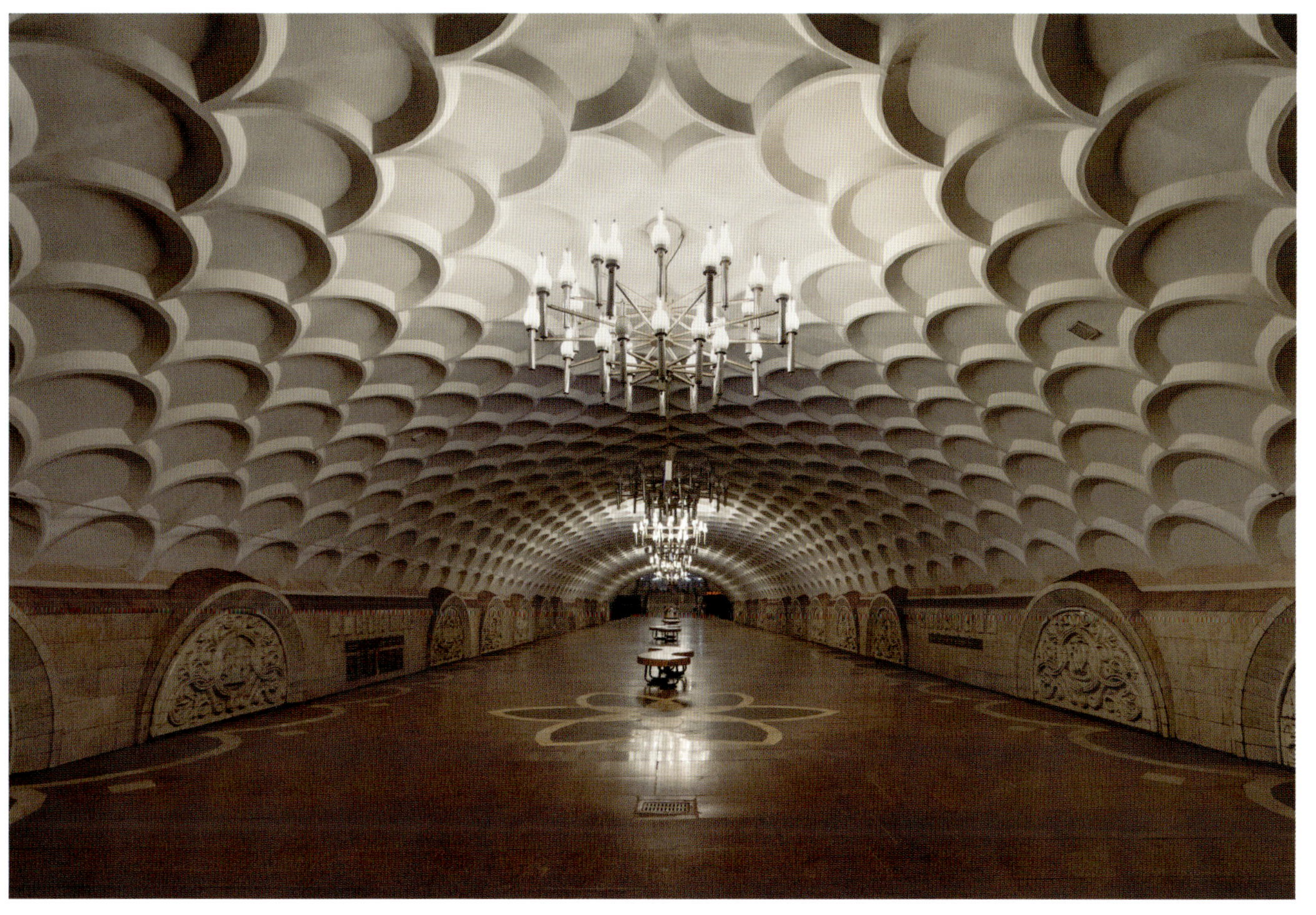

Kyivska, KHARKIV   147

**БАКУ
АЗЕРБАЙДЖАН**

**BAKU
AZERBAIJAN**

OPENED 1967

    Ulduz, BAKU

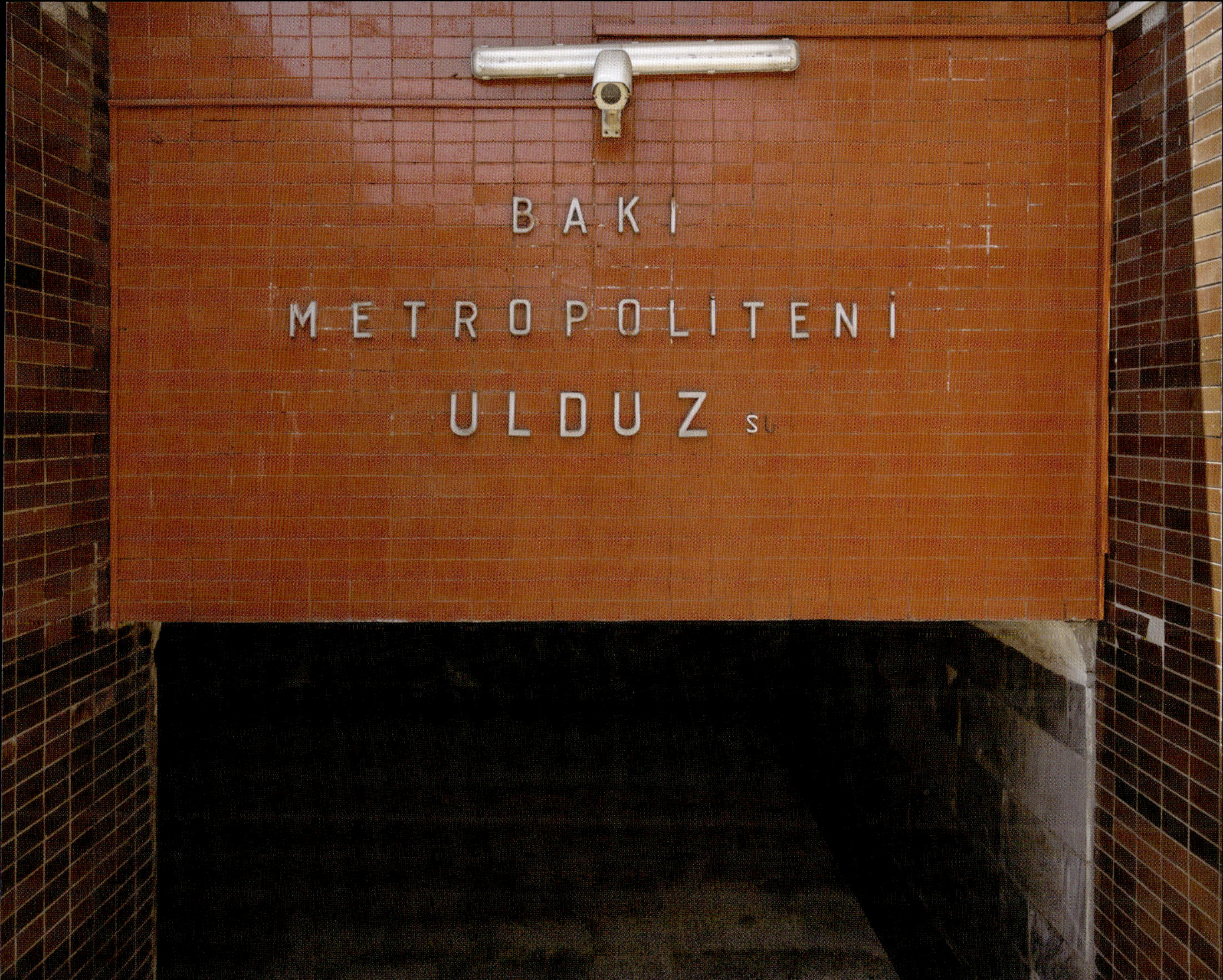
BAKI
METROPOLİTENİ
ULDUZ su

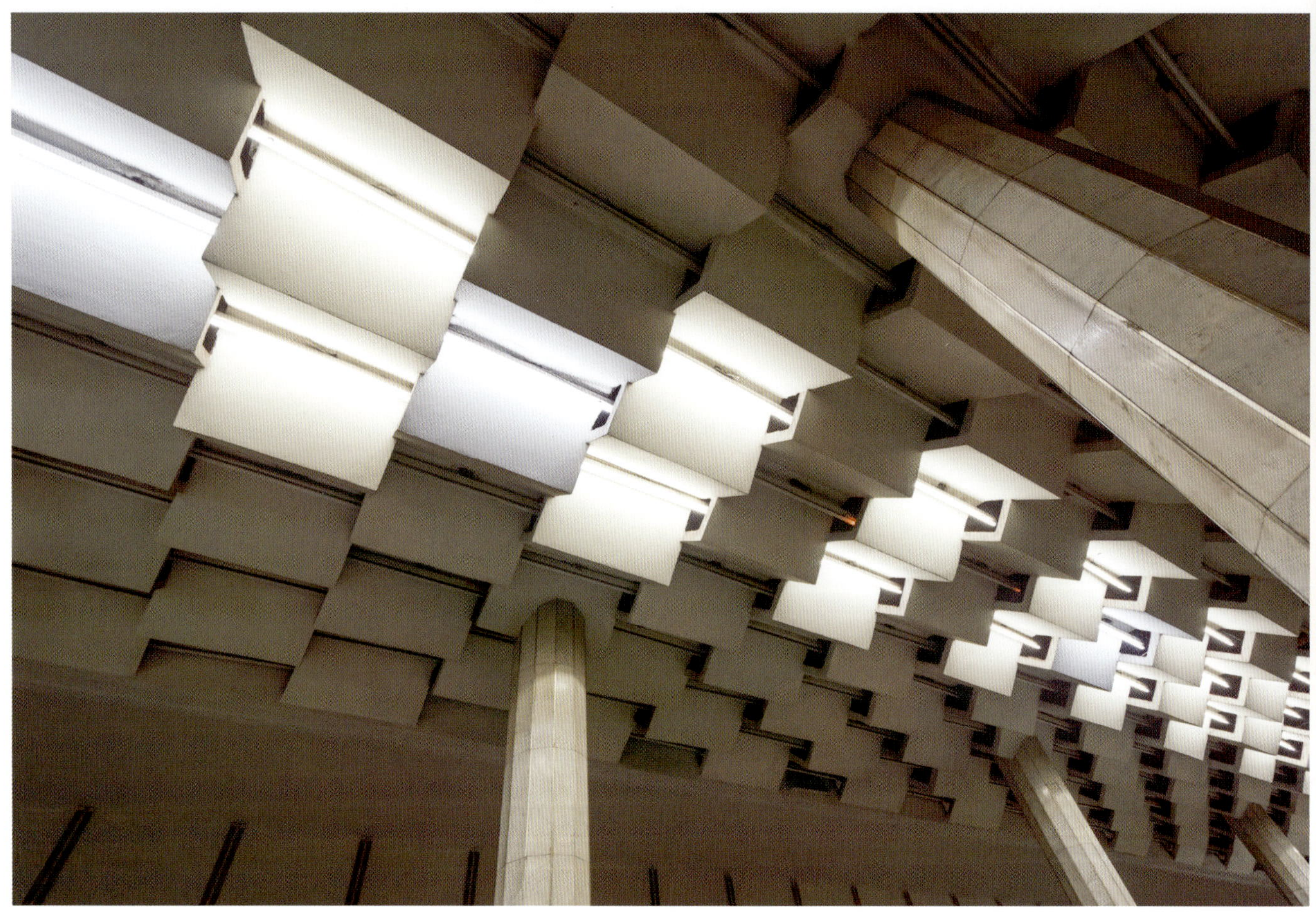

150   Ulduz, BAKU

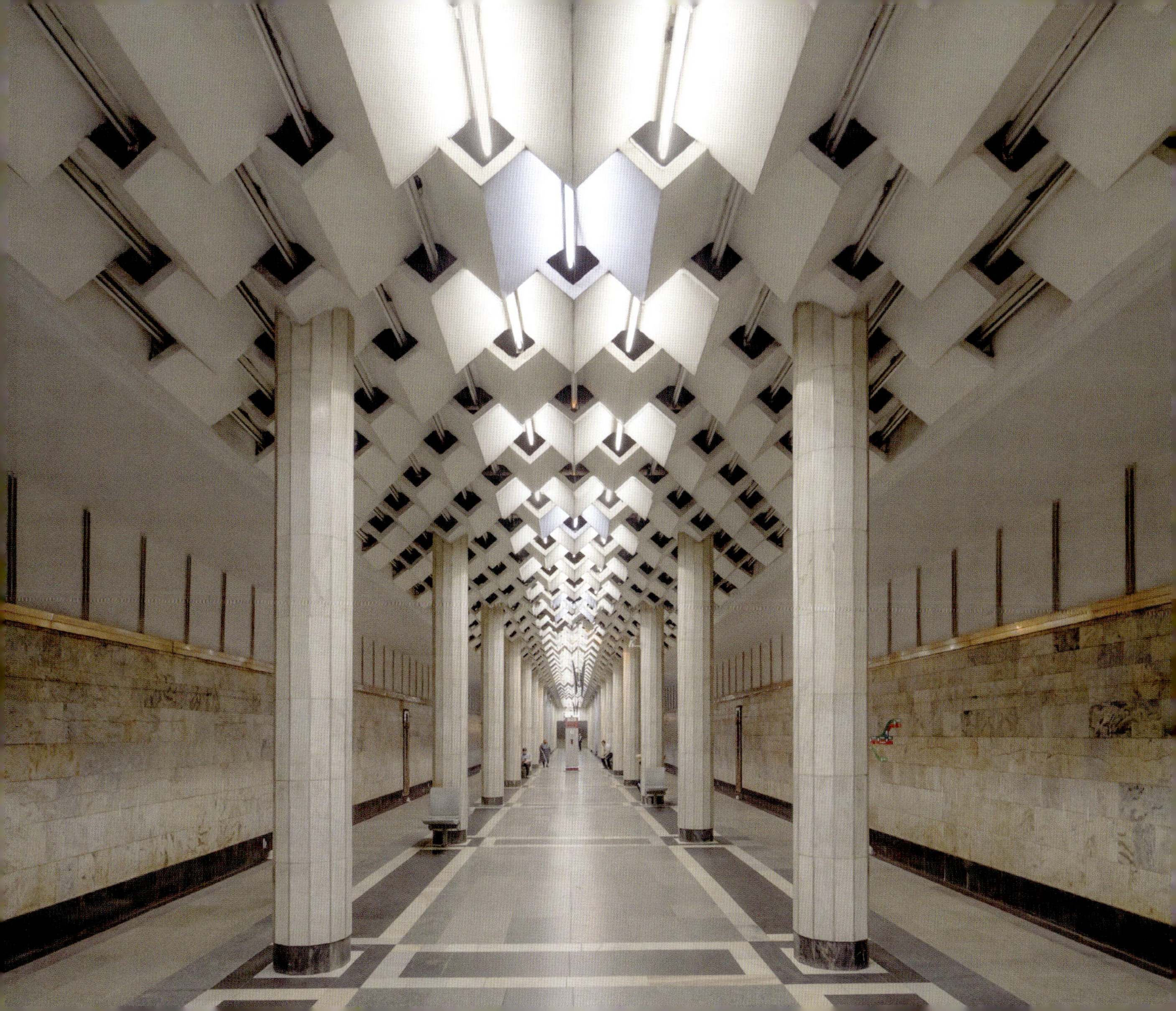

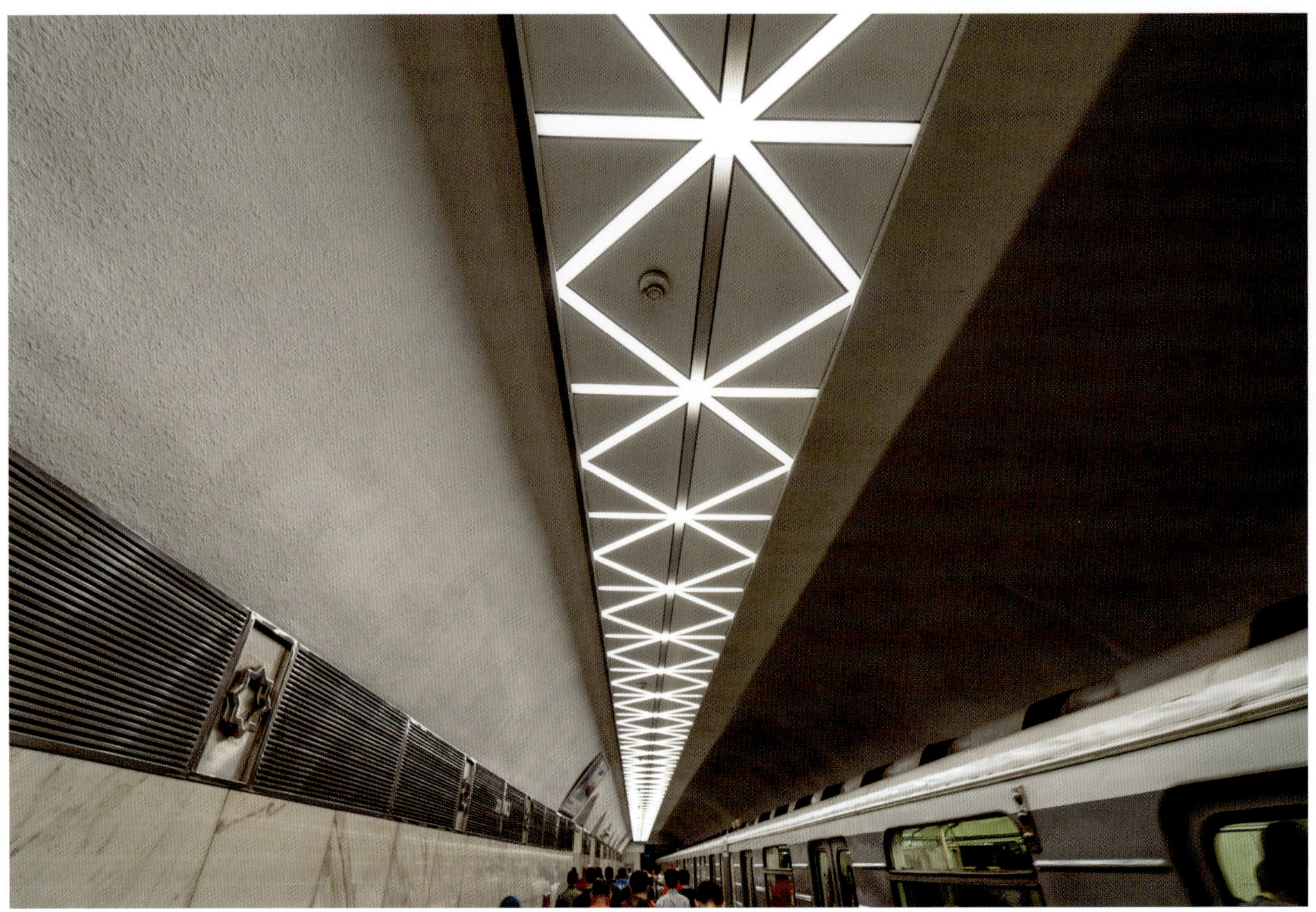

152   28 May, BAKU

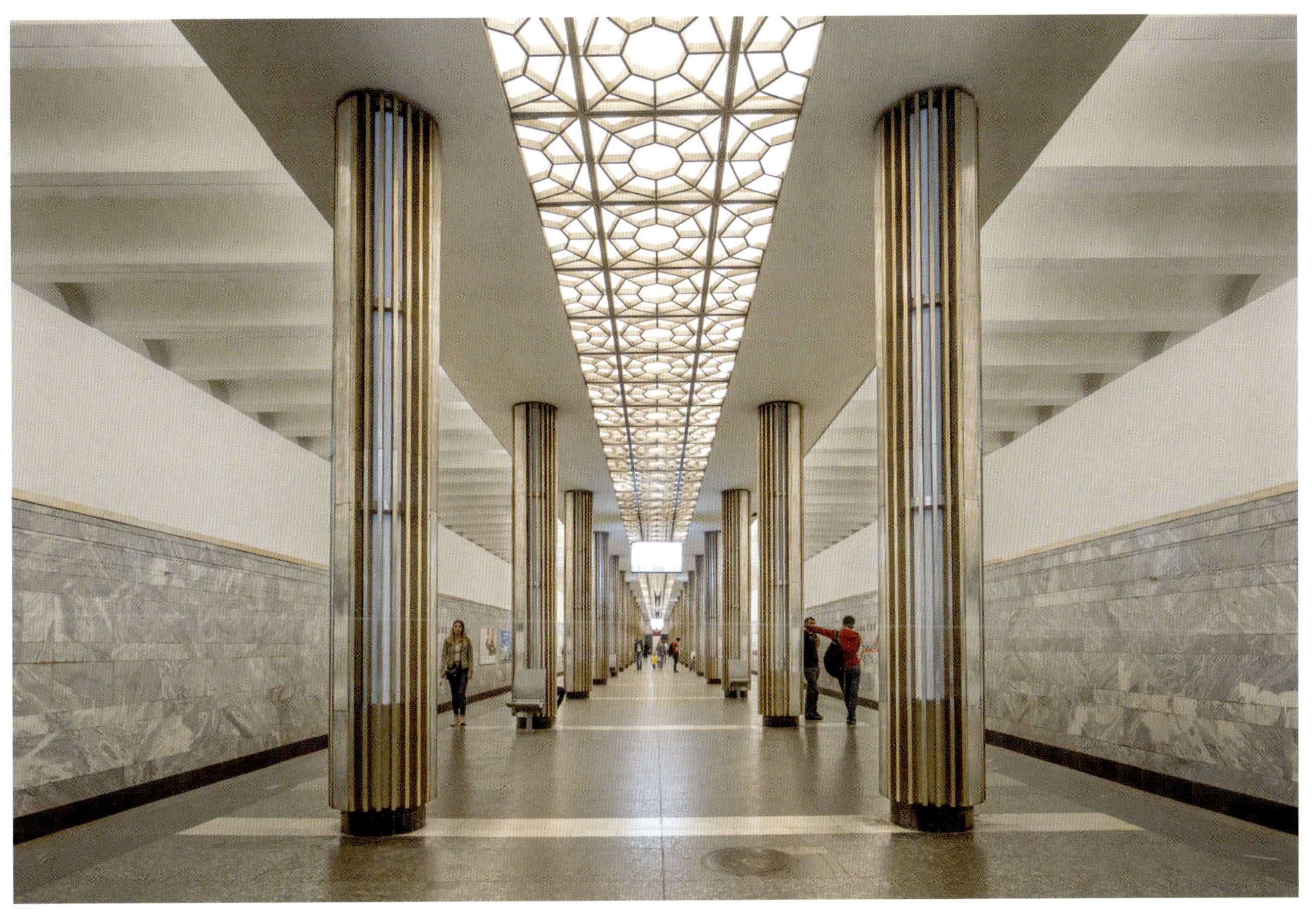

Gara Garayev, BAKU

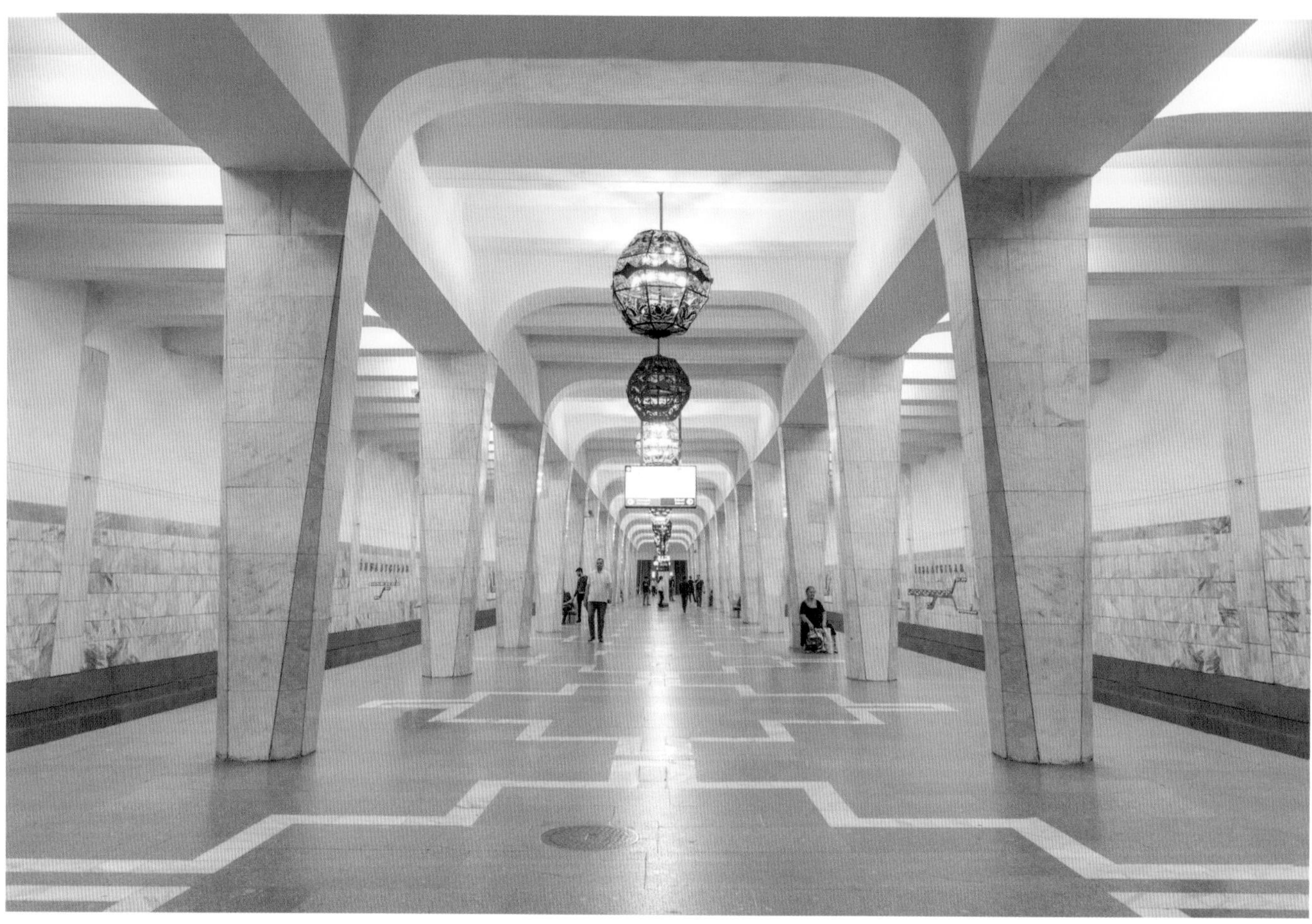

154 Inshaatchilar, BAKU

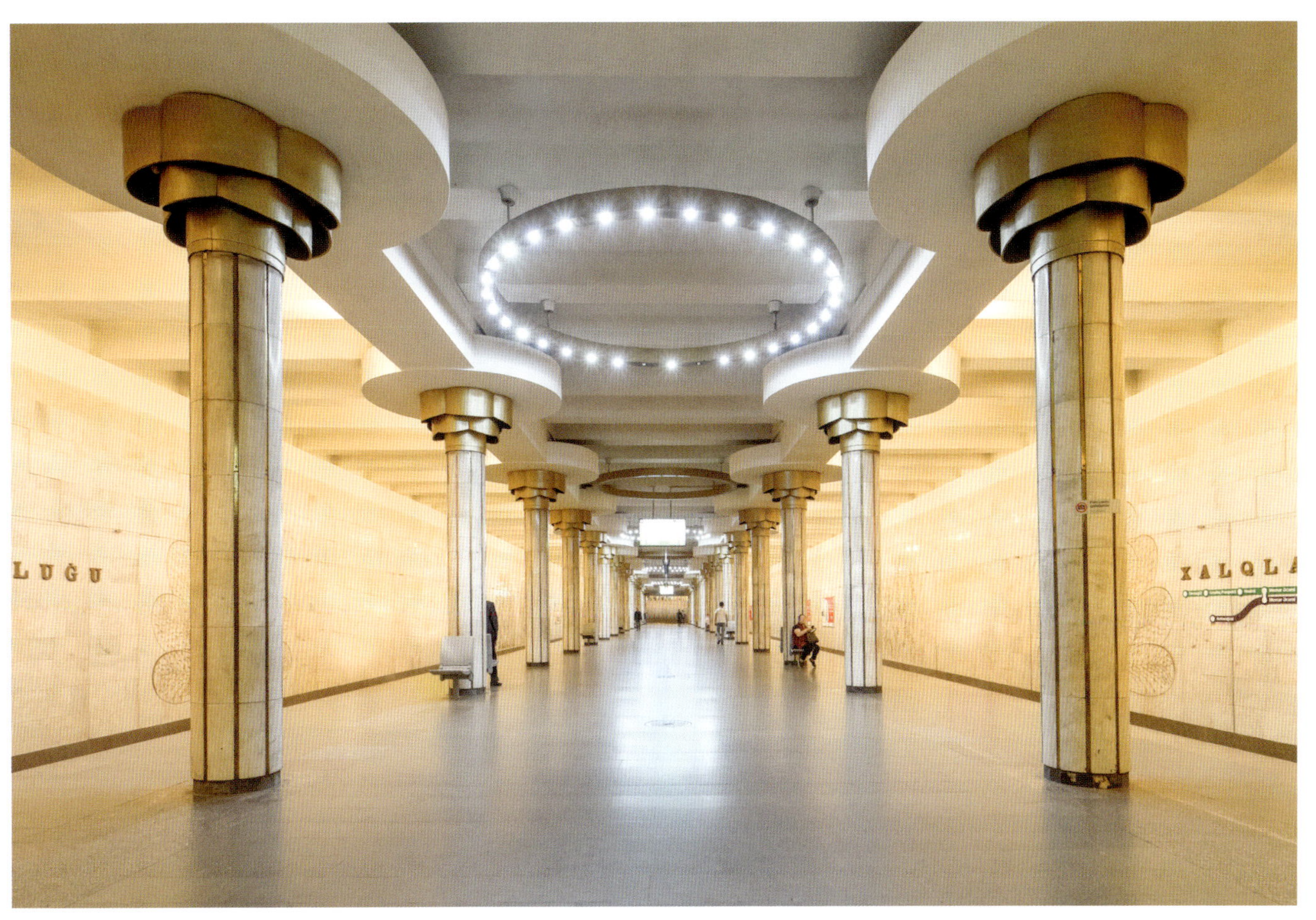
LUĞU
XALQLA

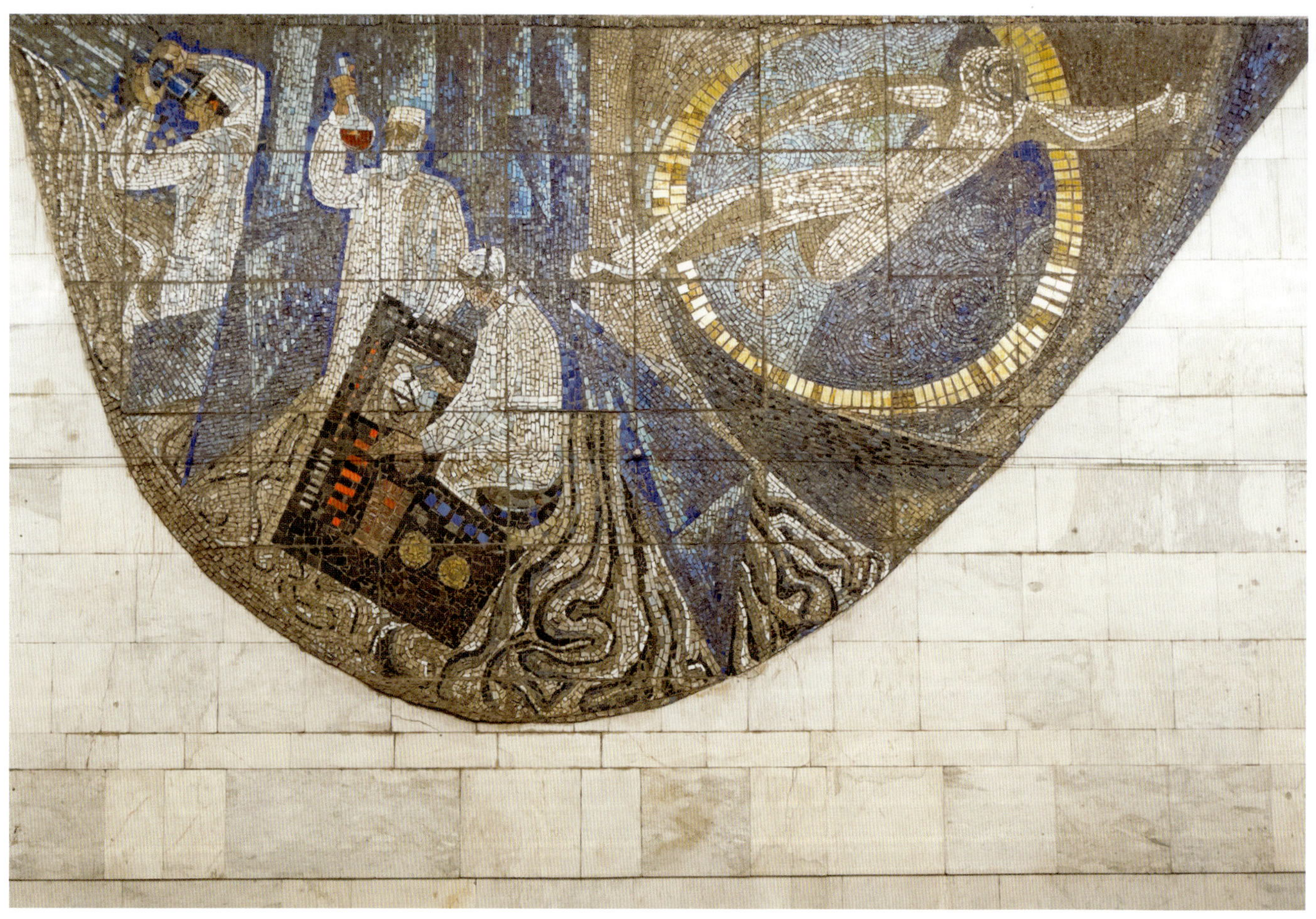

156   Neftchilar, BAKU

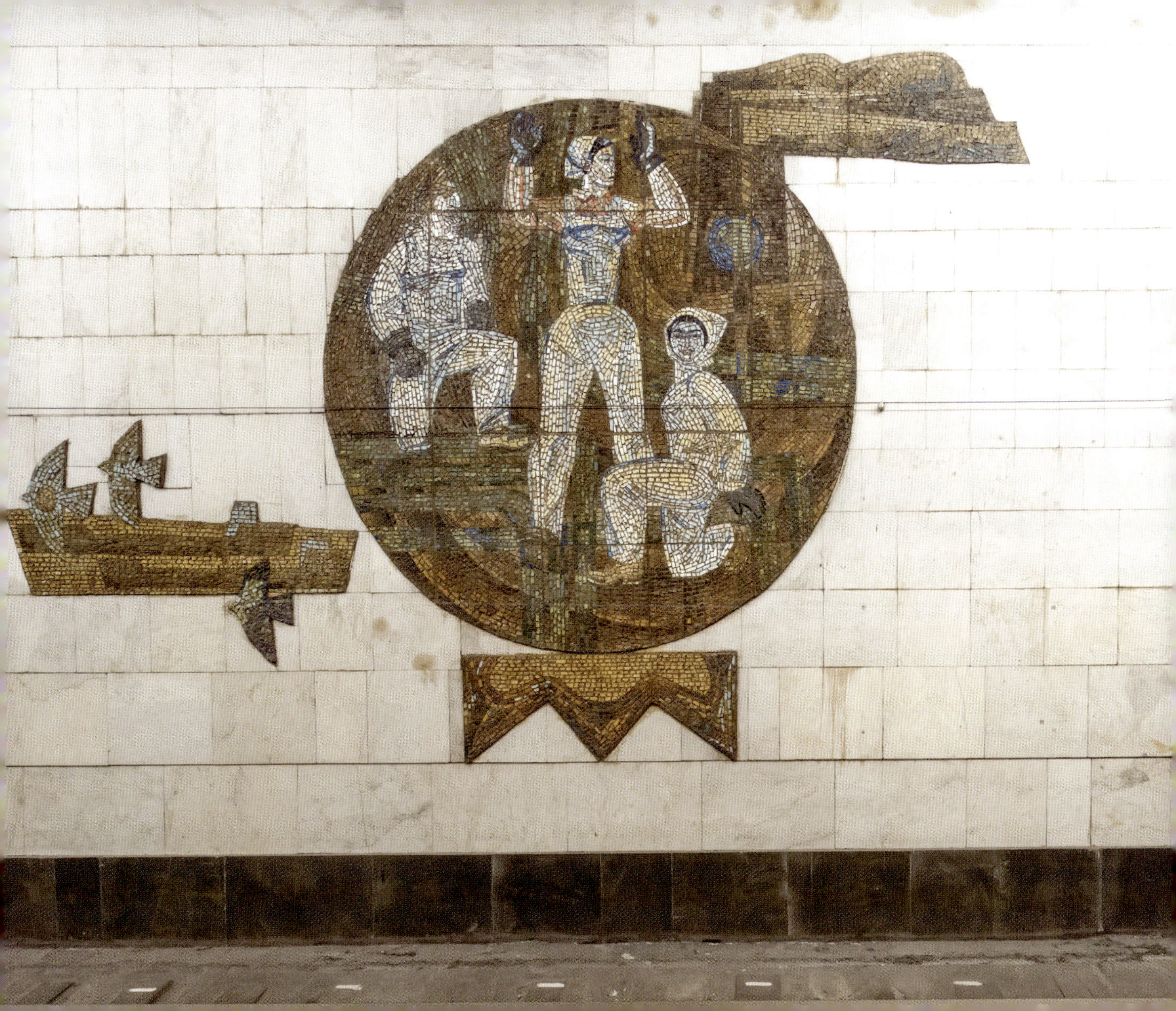

**ТБИЛИСИ
ГРУЗИЯ**

**TBILISI
GEORGIA**

OPENED 1966

 Technical University, TBILISI

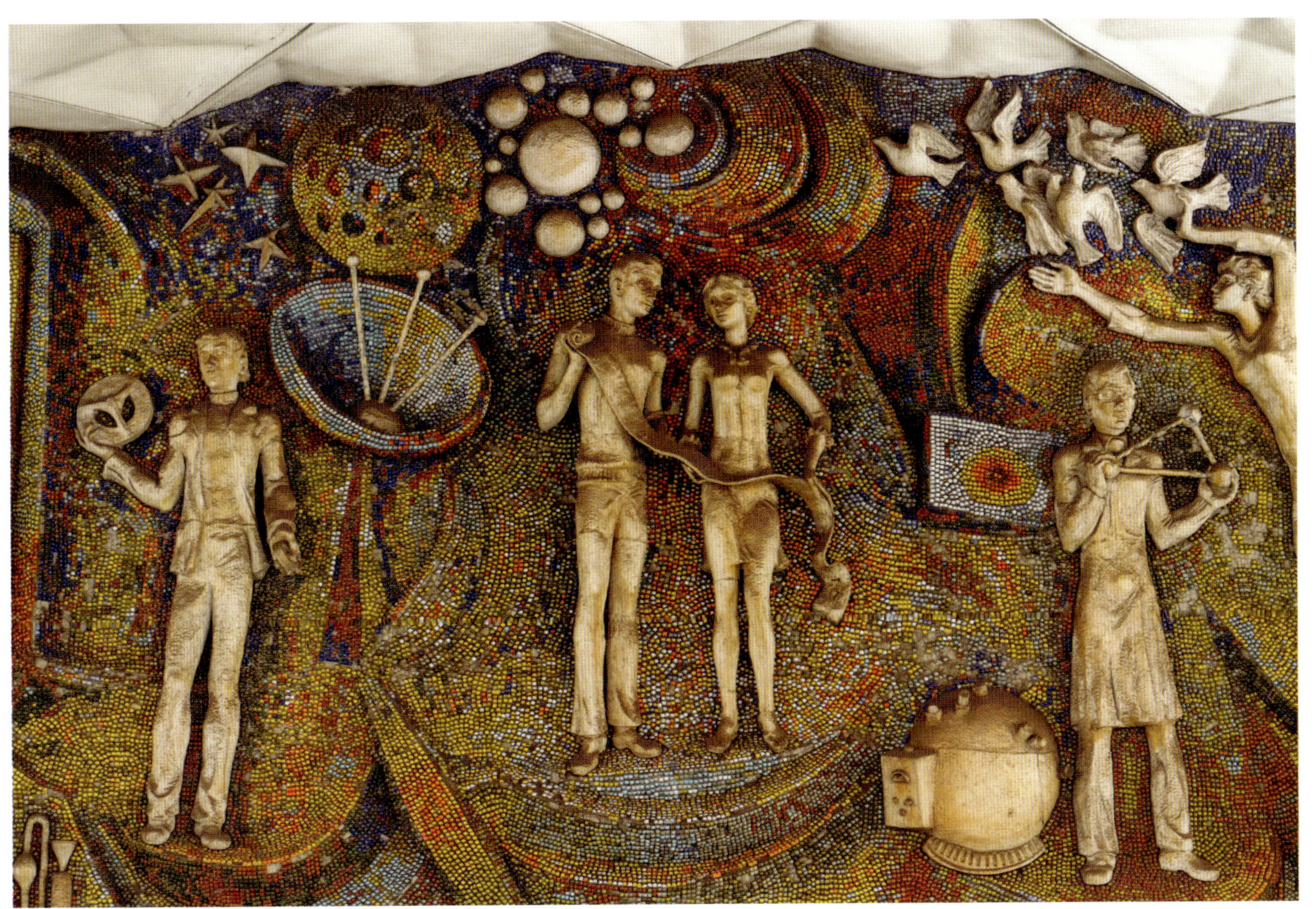

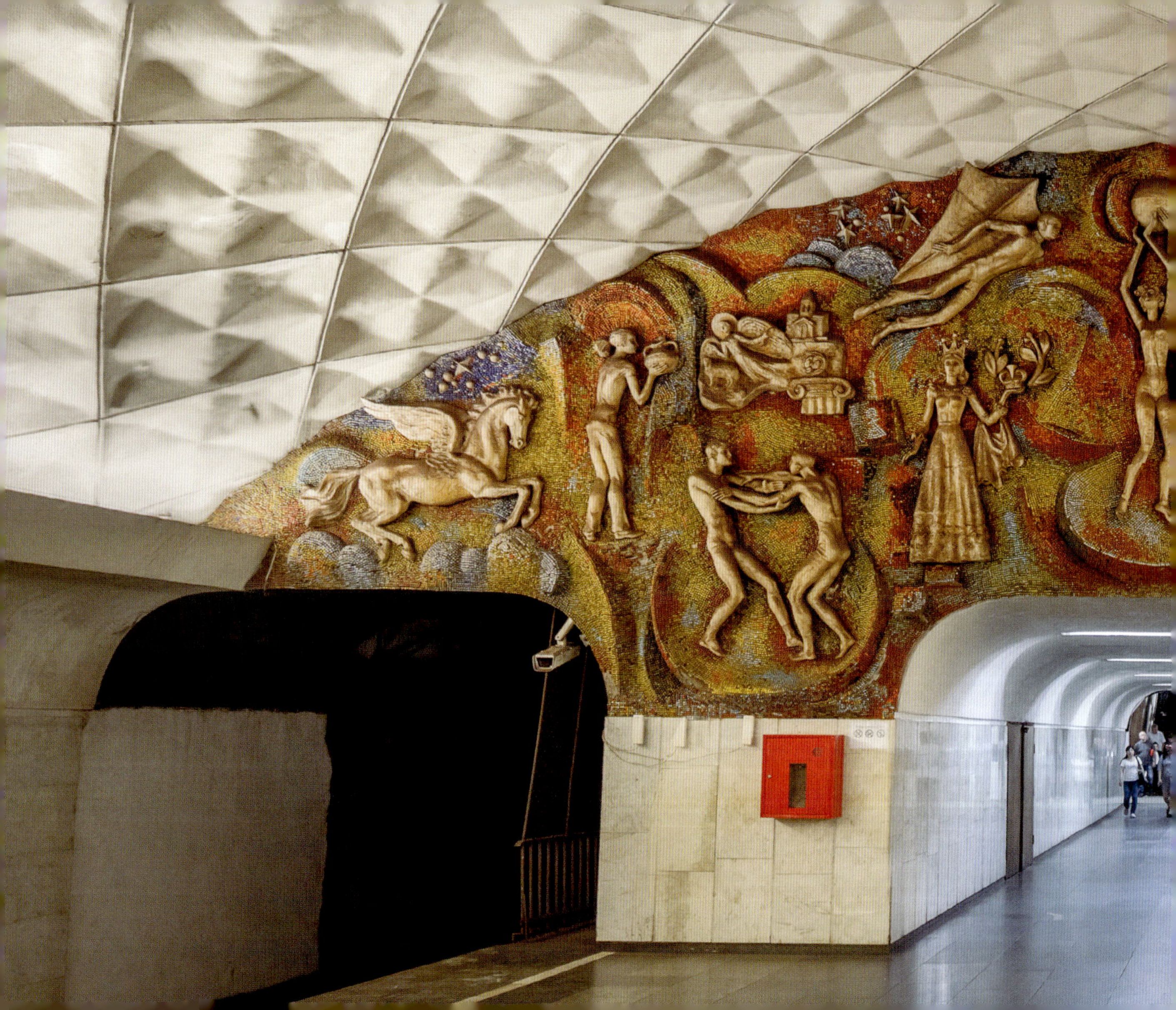

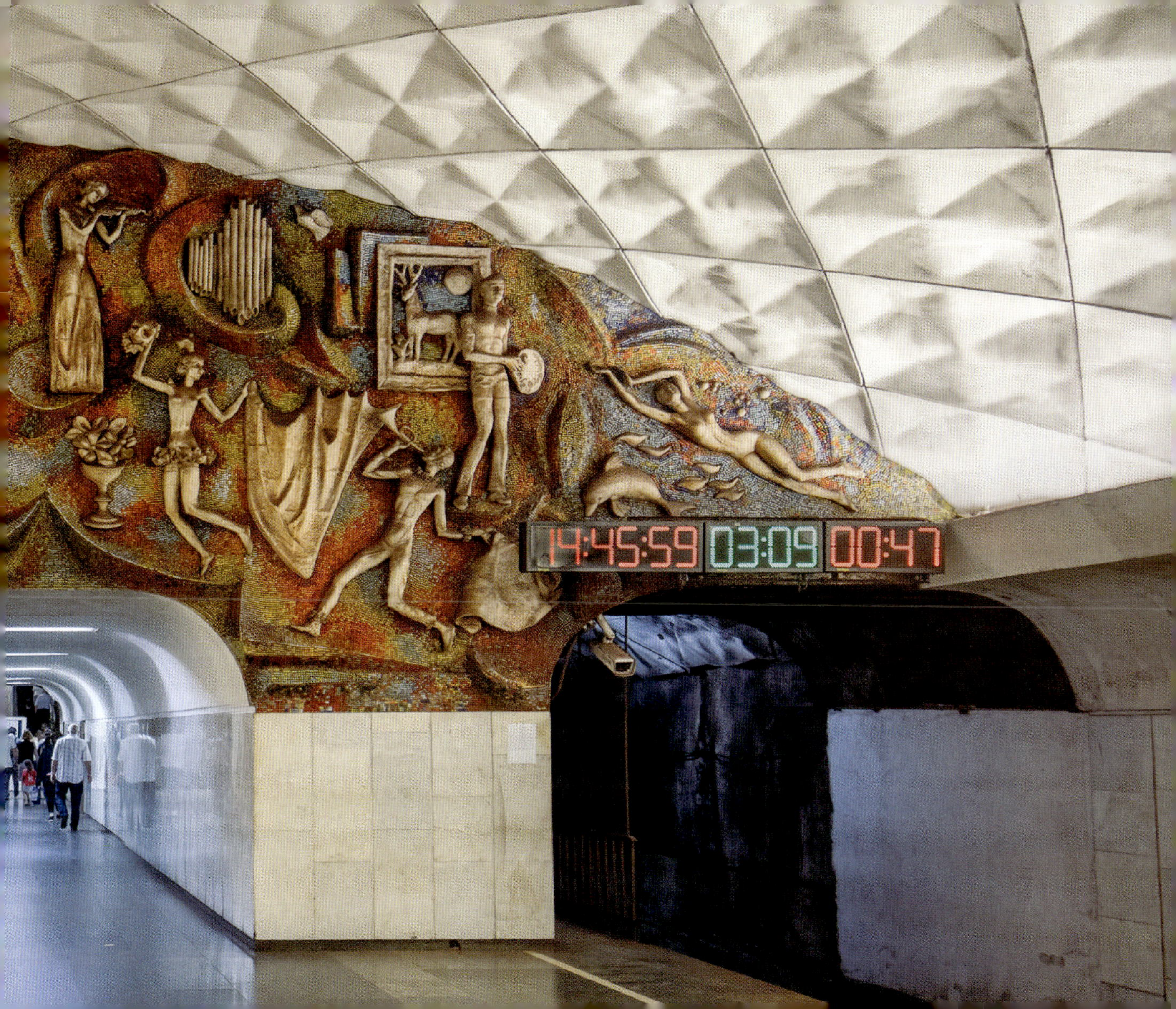

14:45:59 03:09 00:47

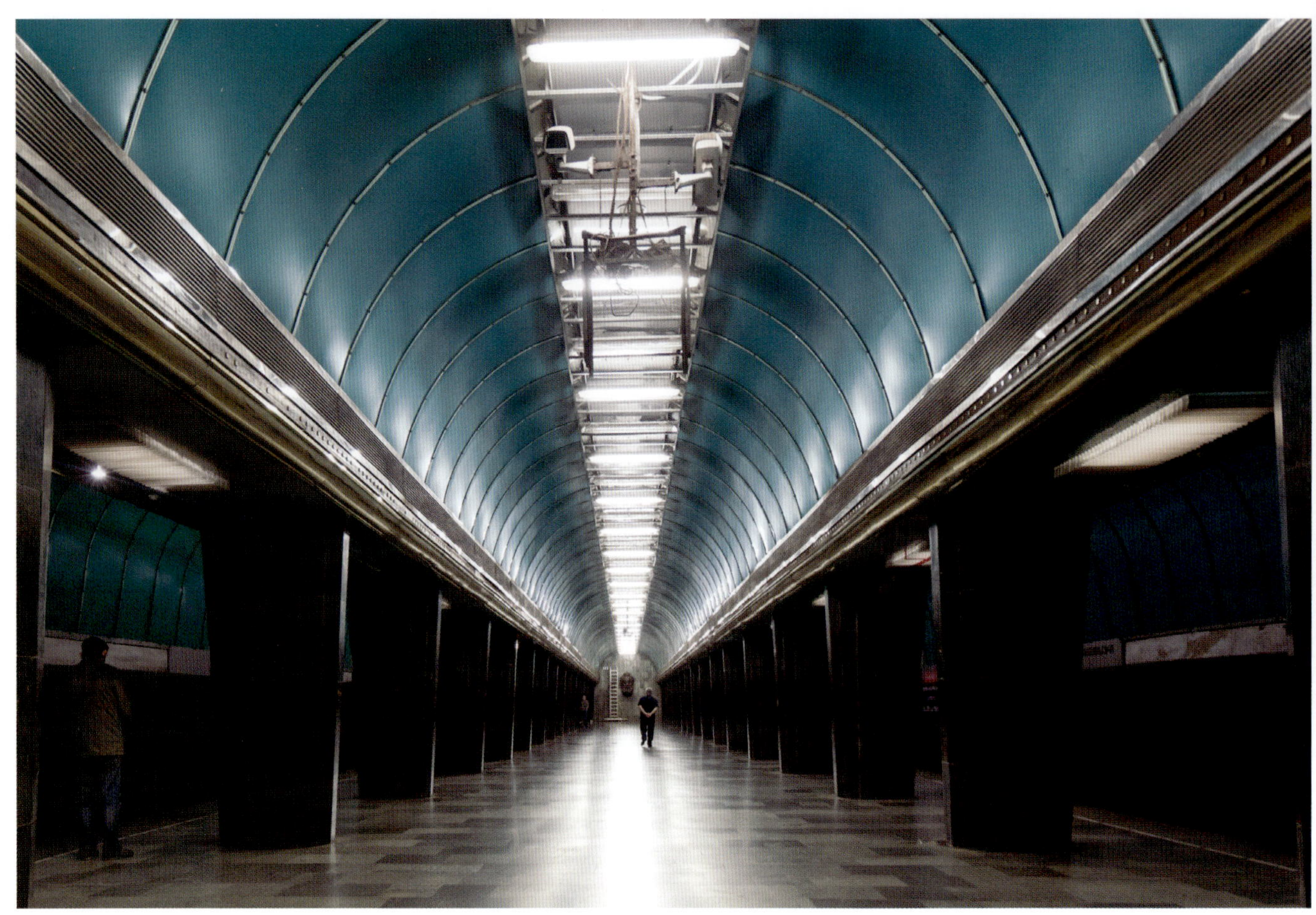

162   Tsereteli, TBILISI

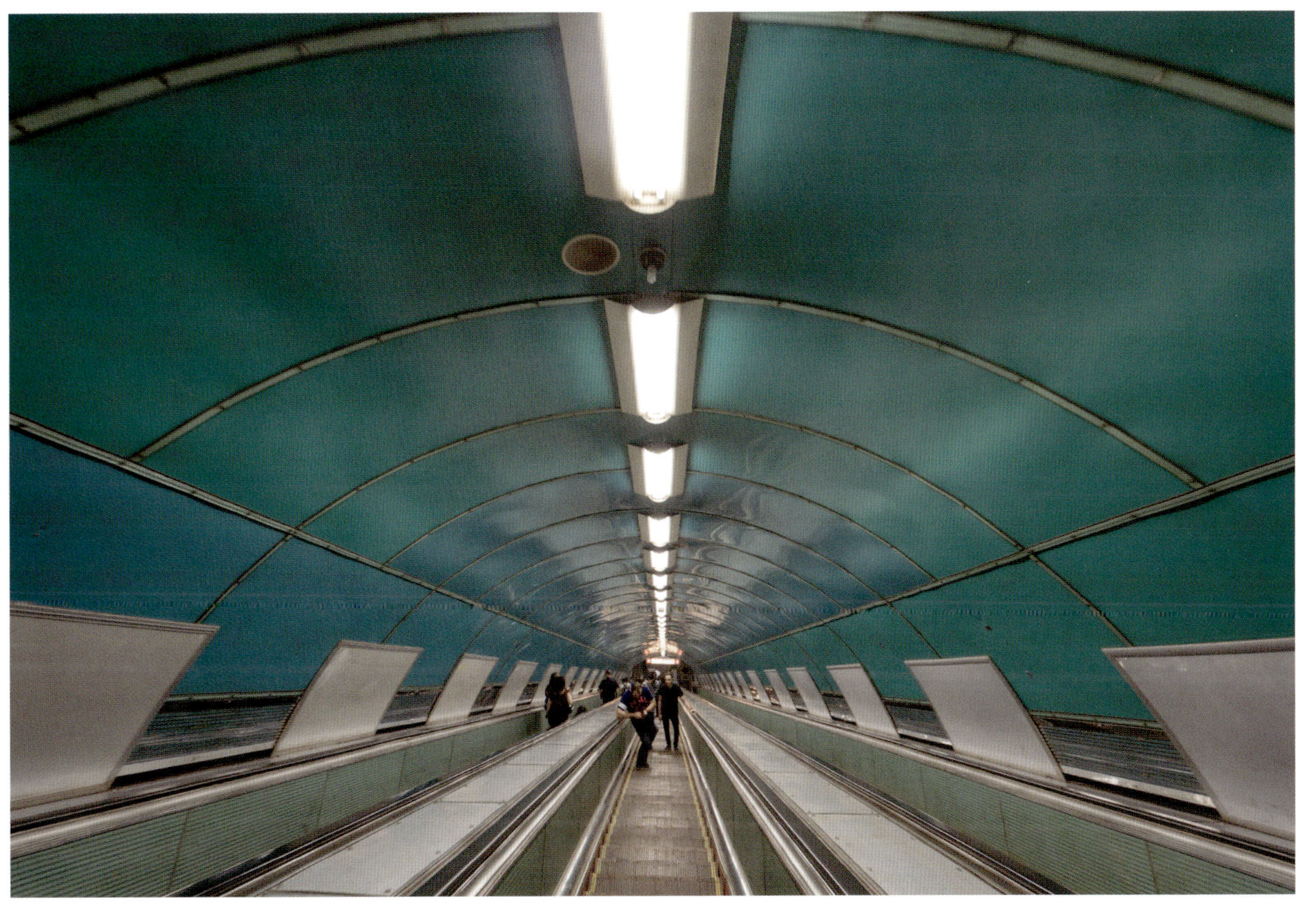

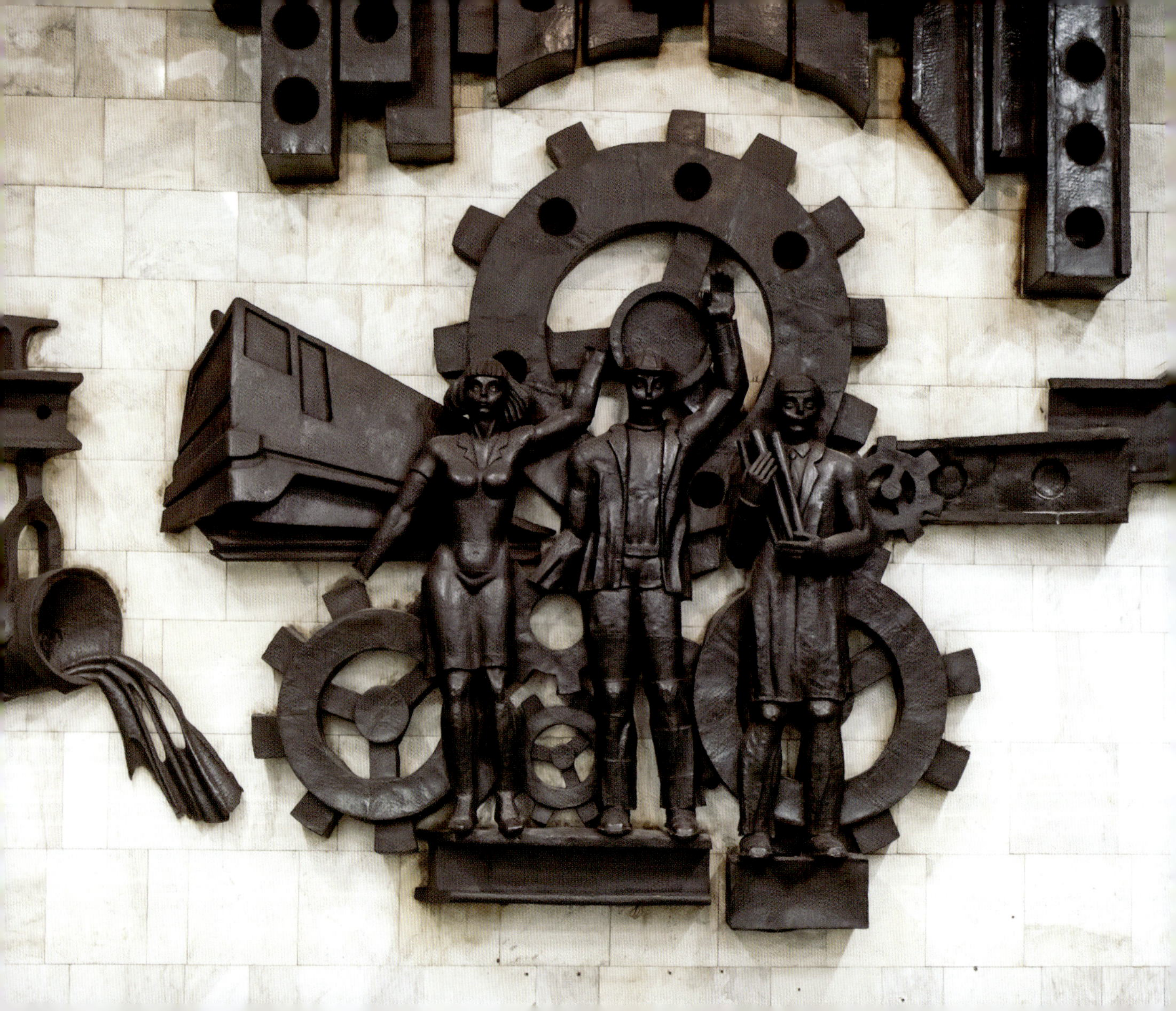

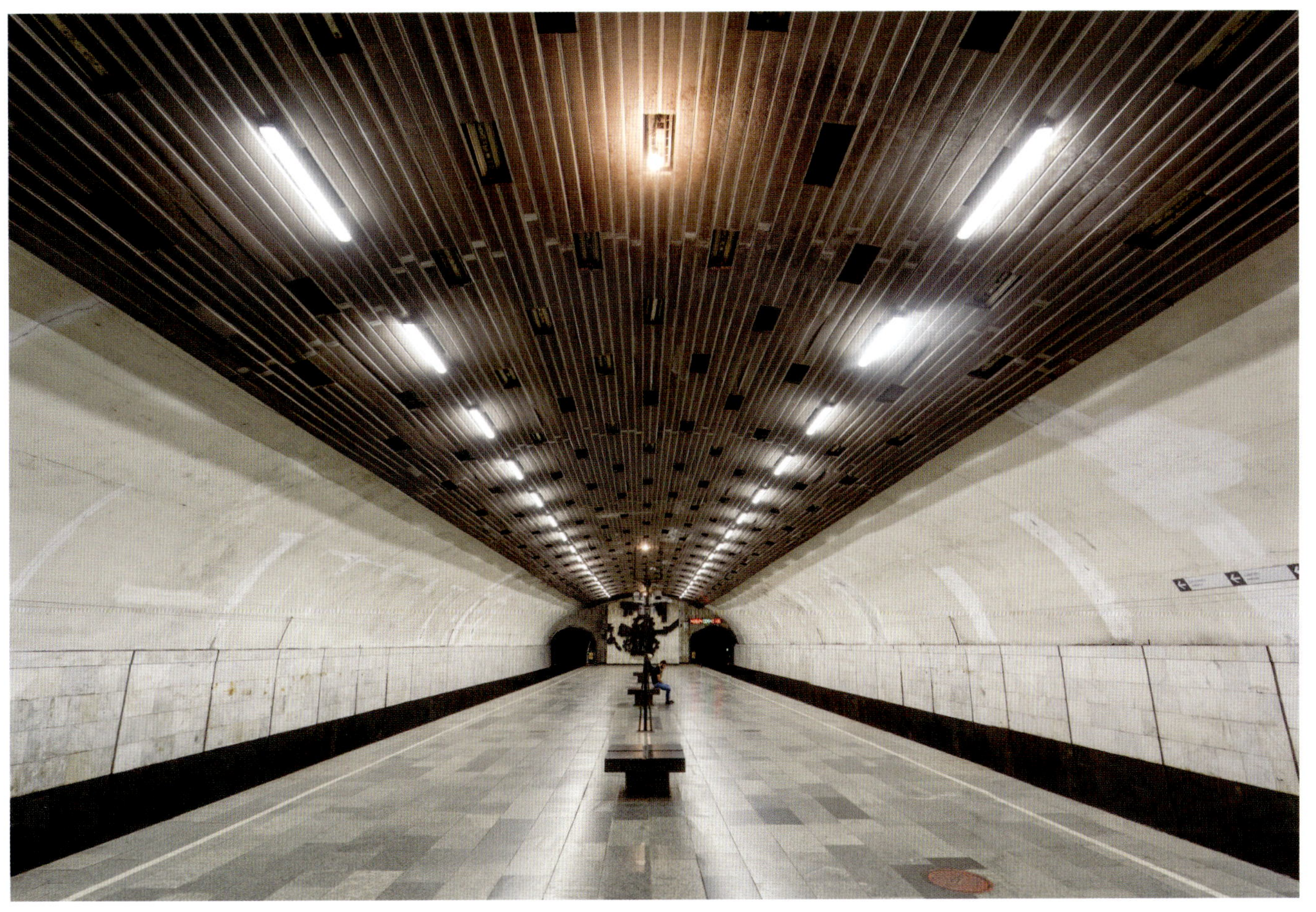

Ghrmaghele, TBILISI 165

**КИЕВ
УКРАИНА**

**KYIV
UKRAINE**

OPENED 1960

    Hidropark, KYIV

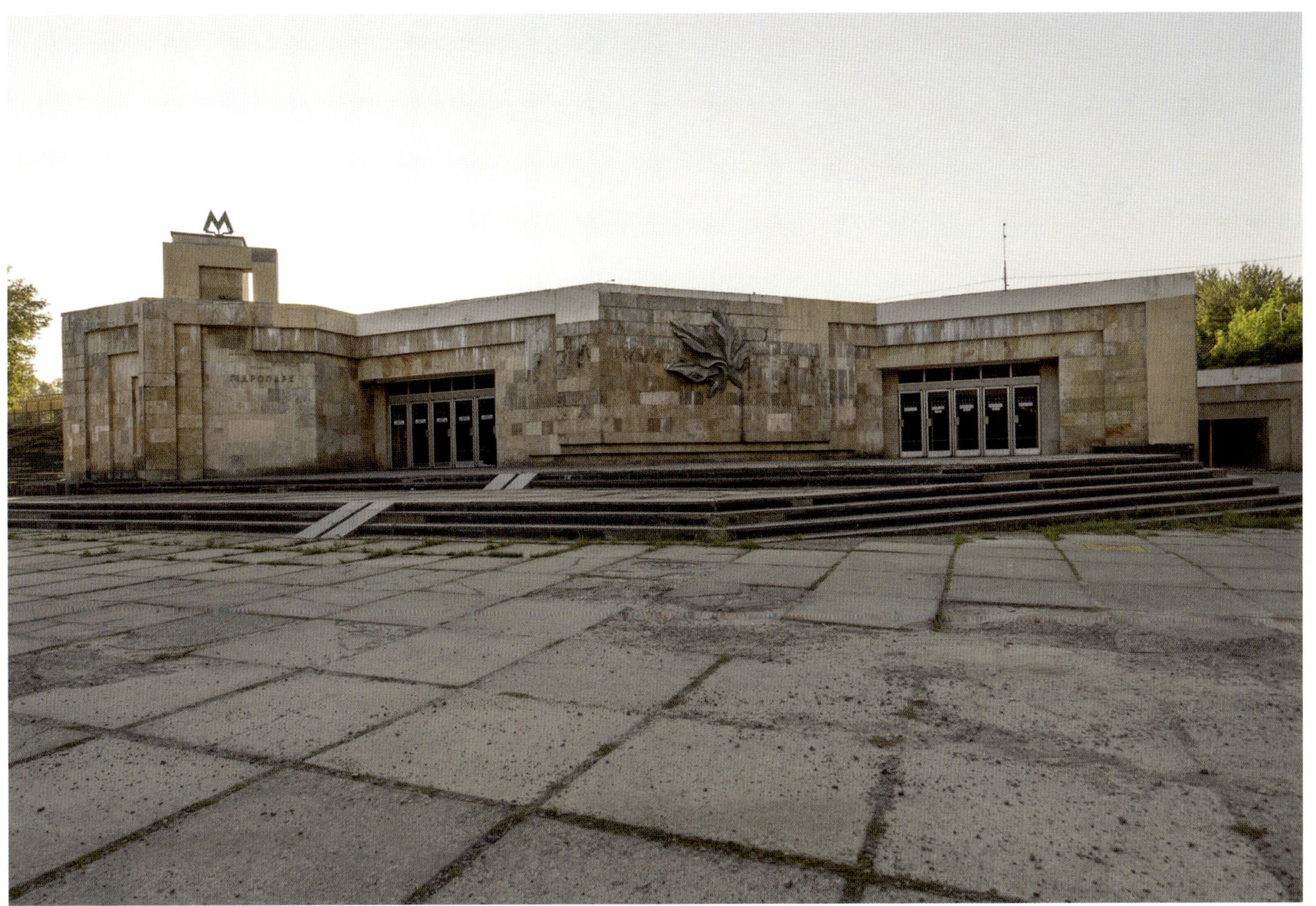

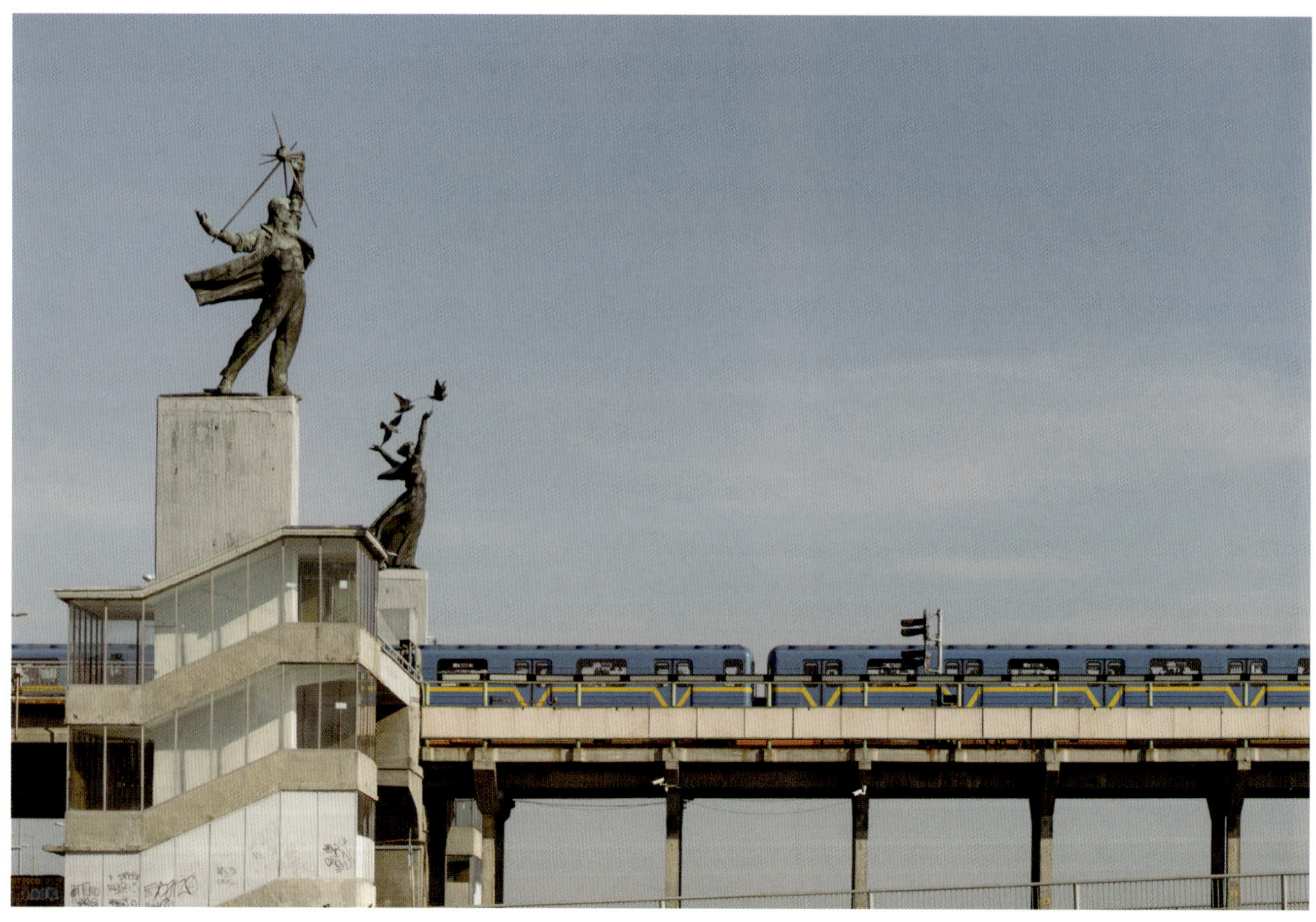

168　Dnipro, KYIV

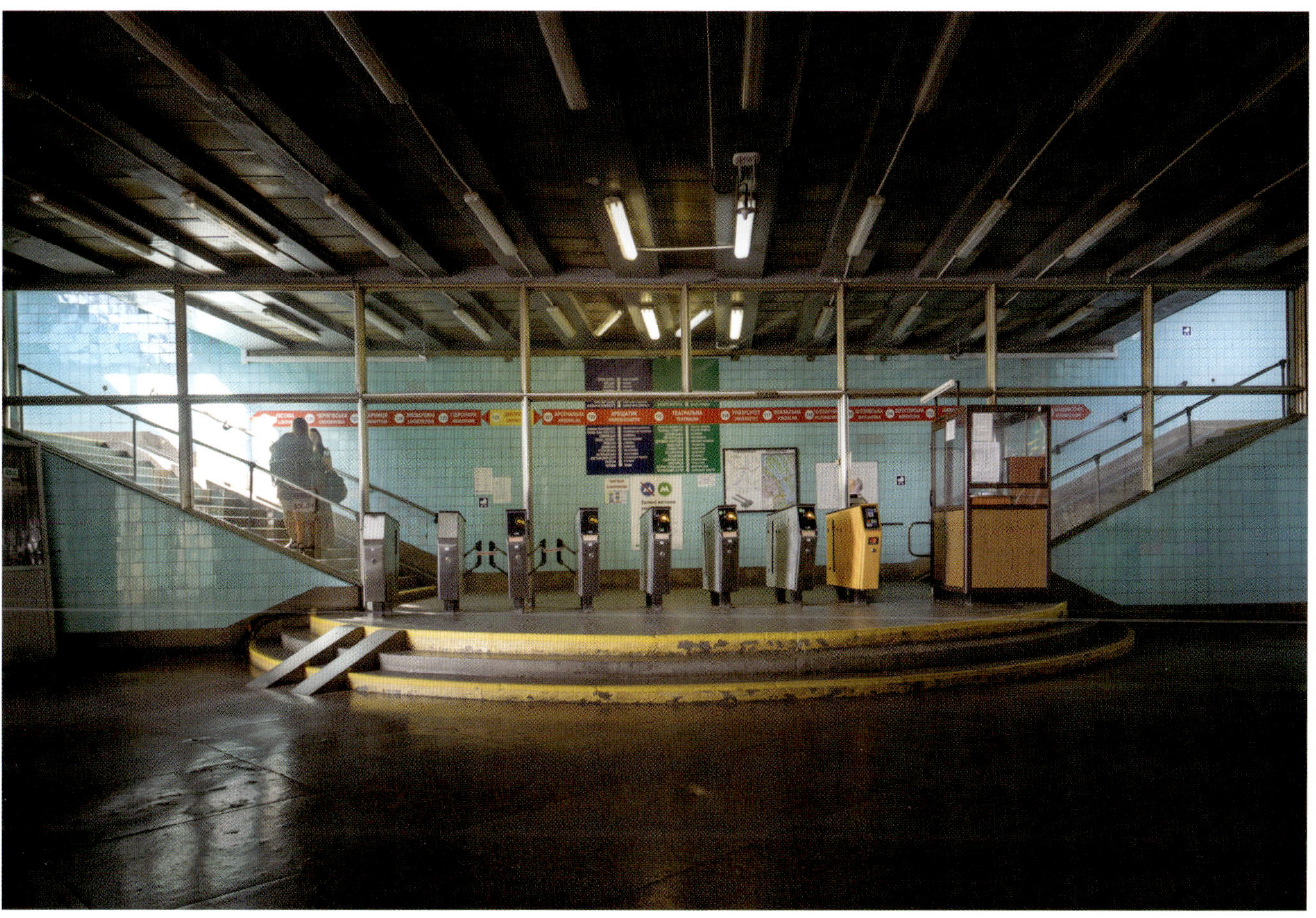

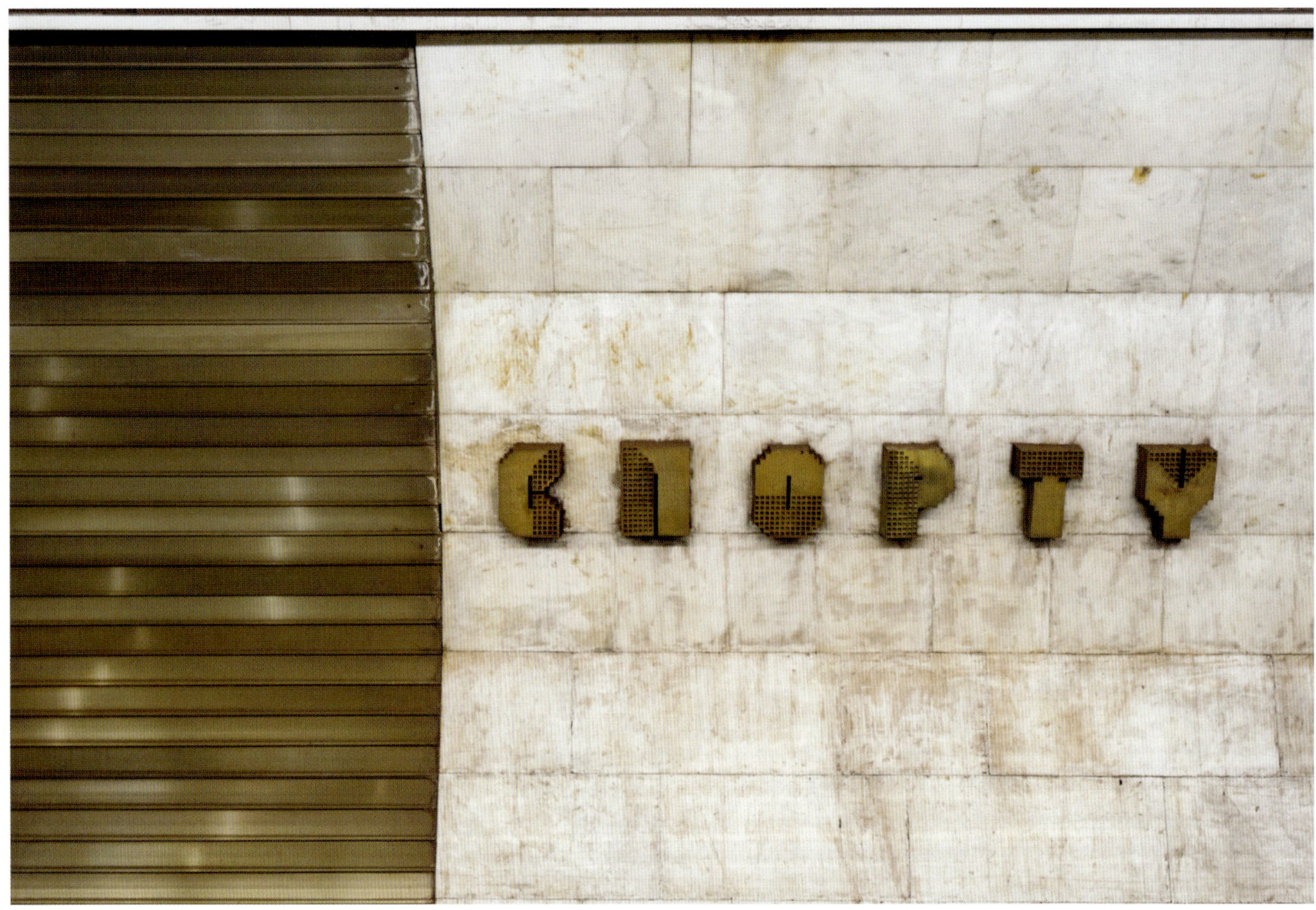

 Palats Sportu, KYIV

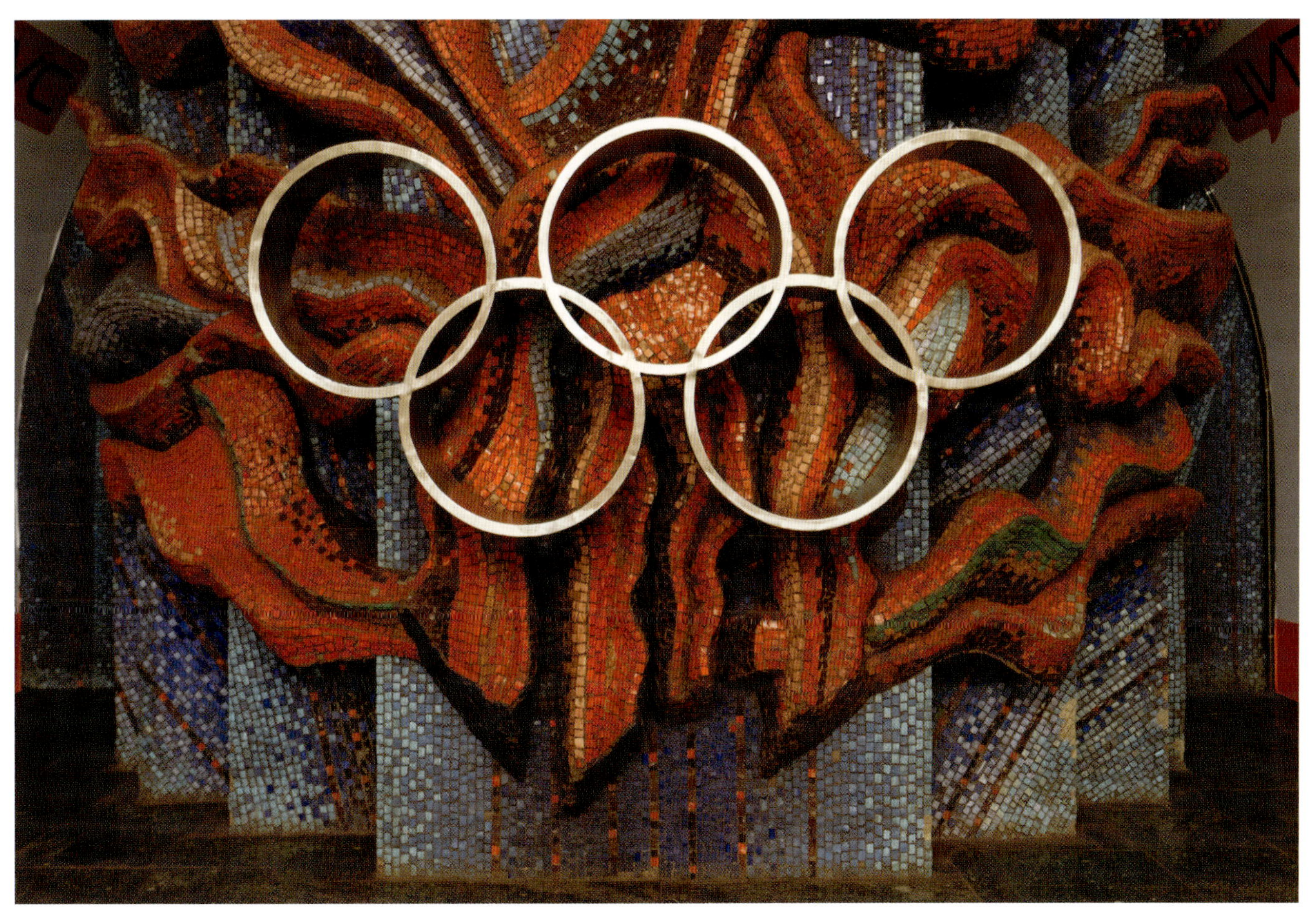

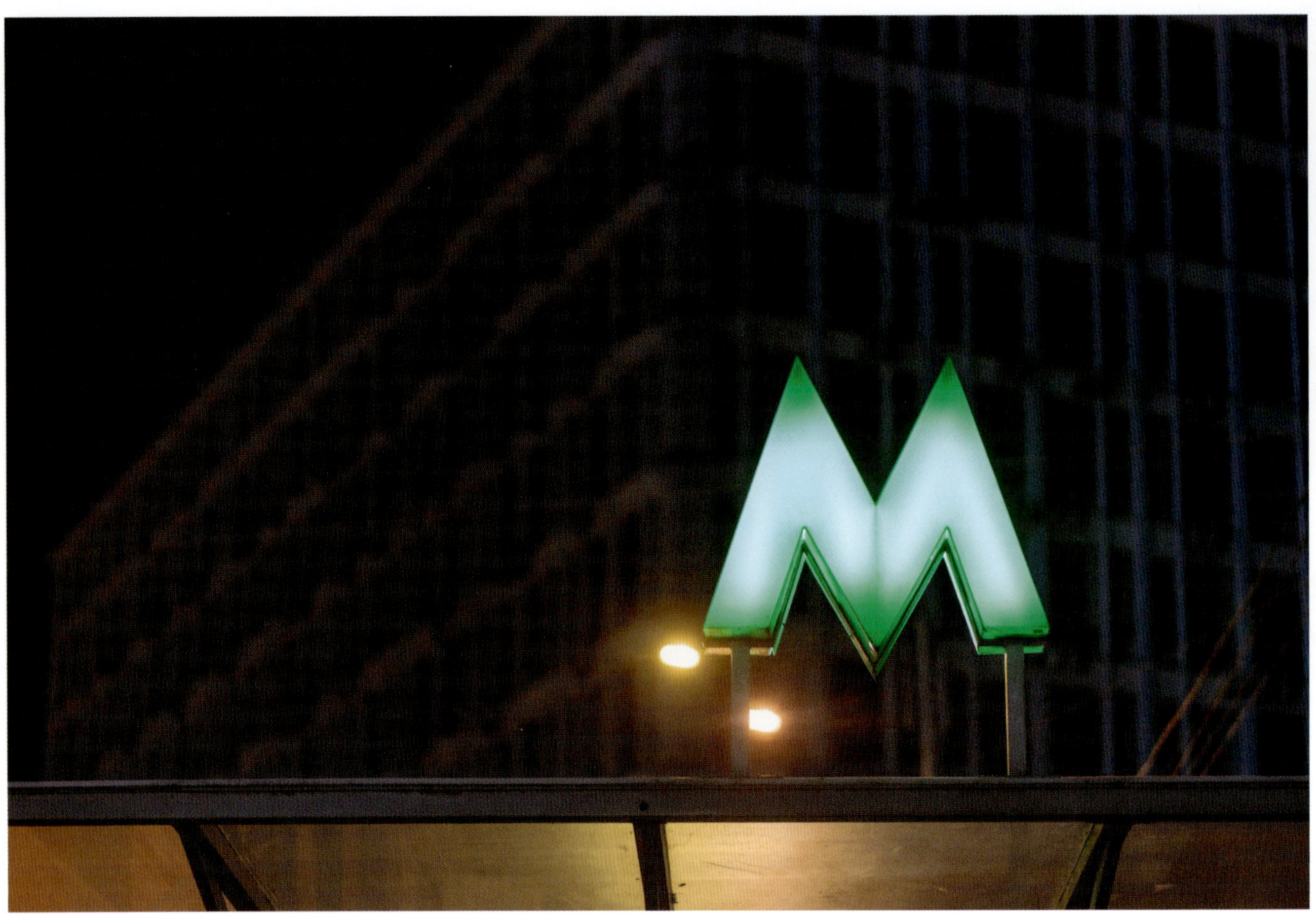

    Palats Sportu, KYIV

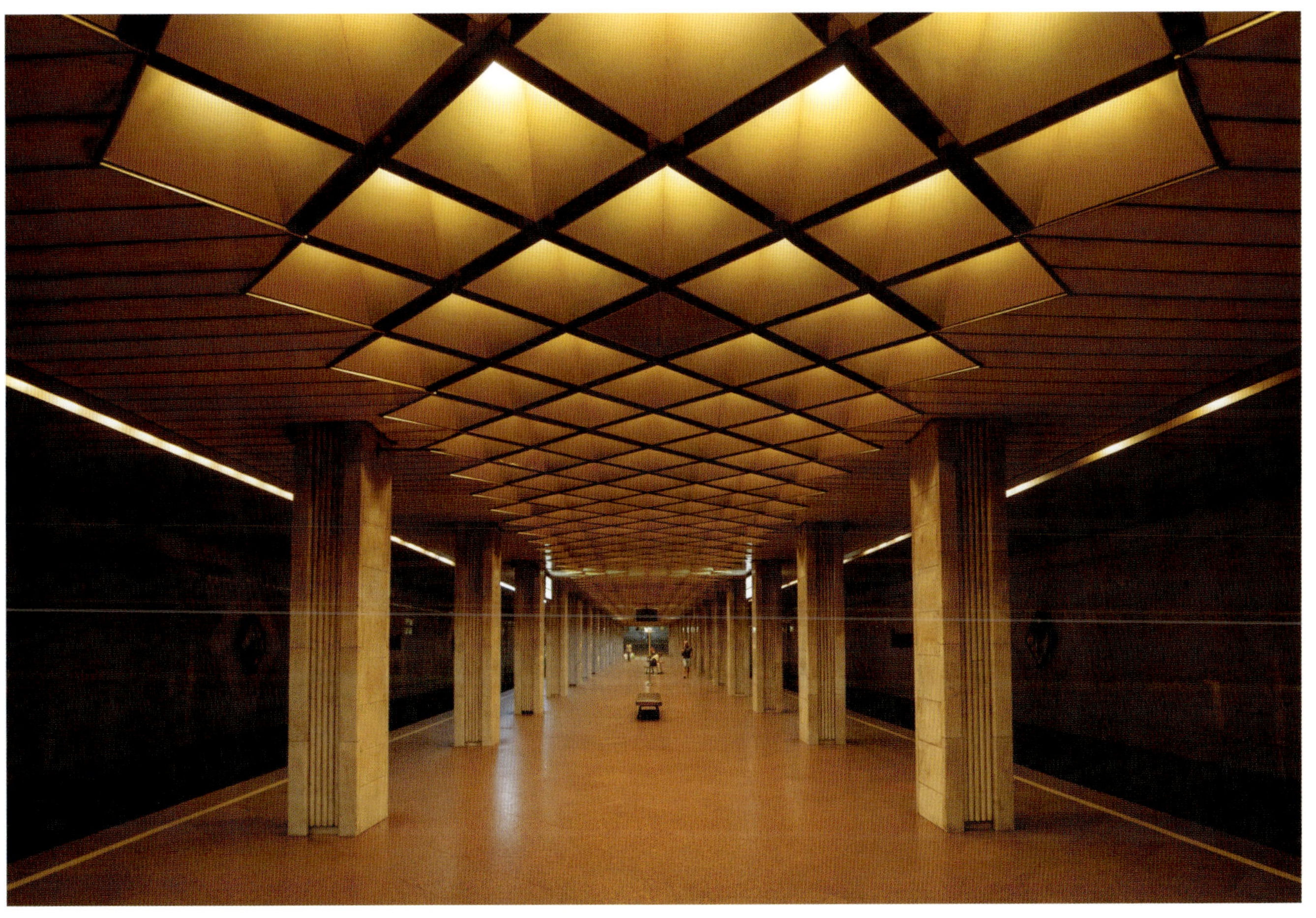

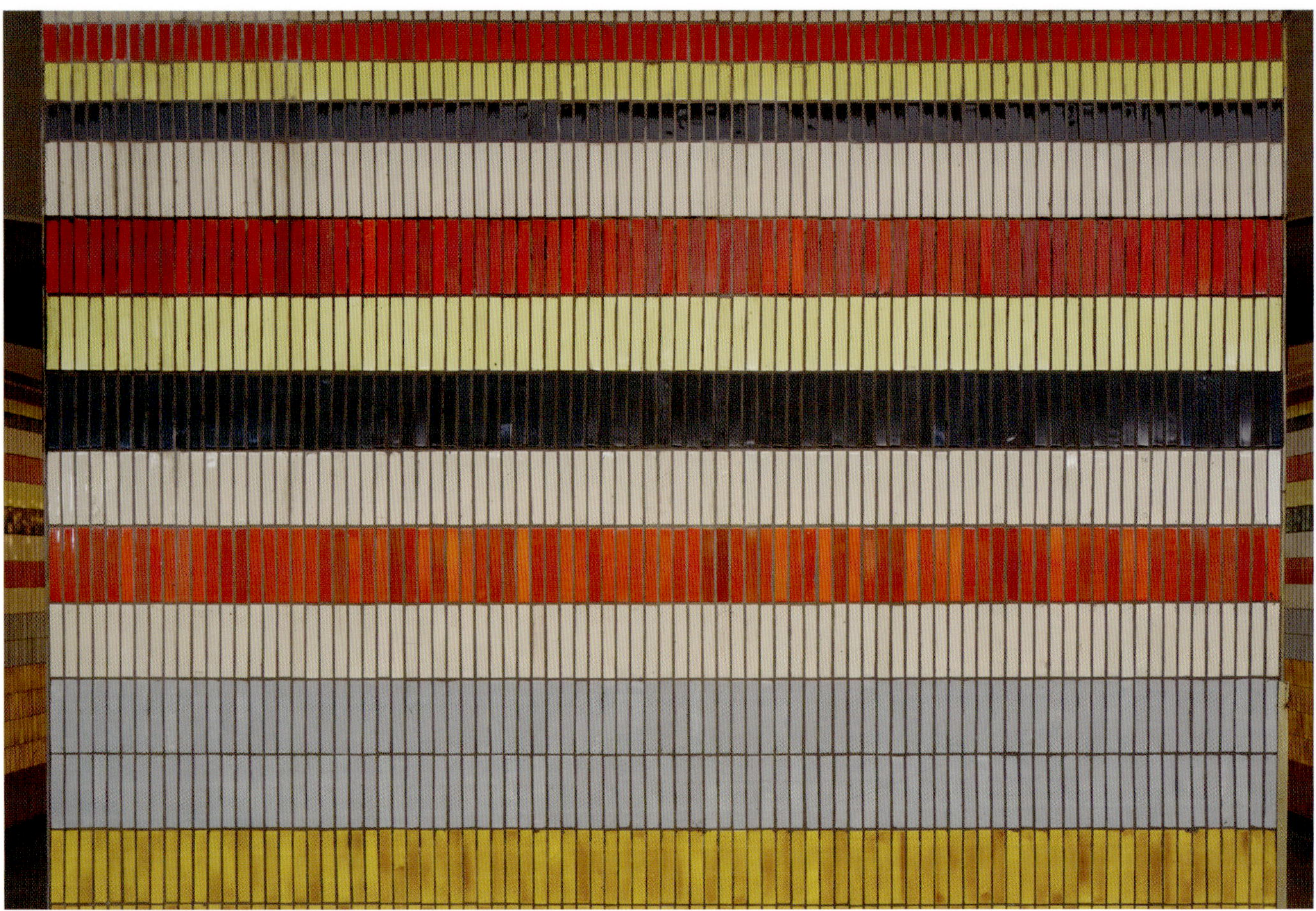

174   Shuliavska, KYIV

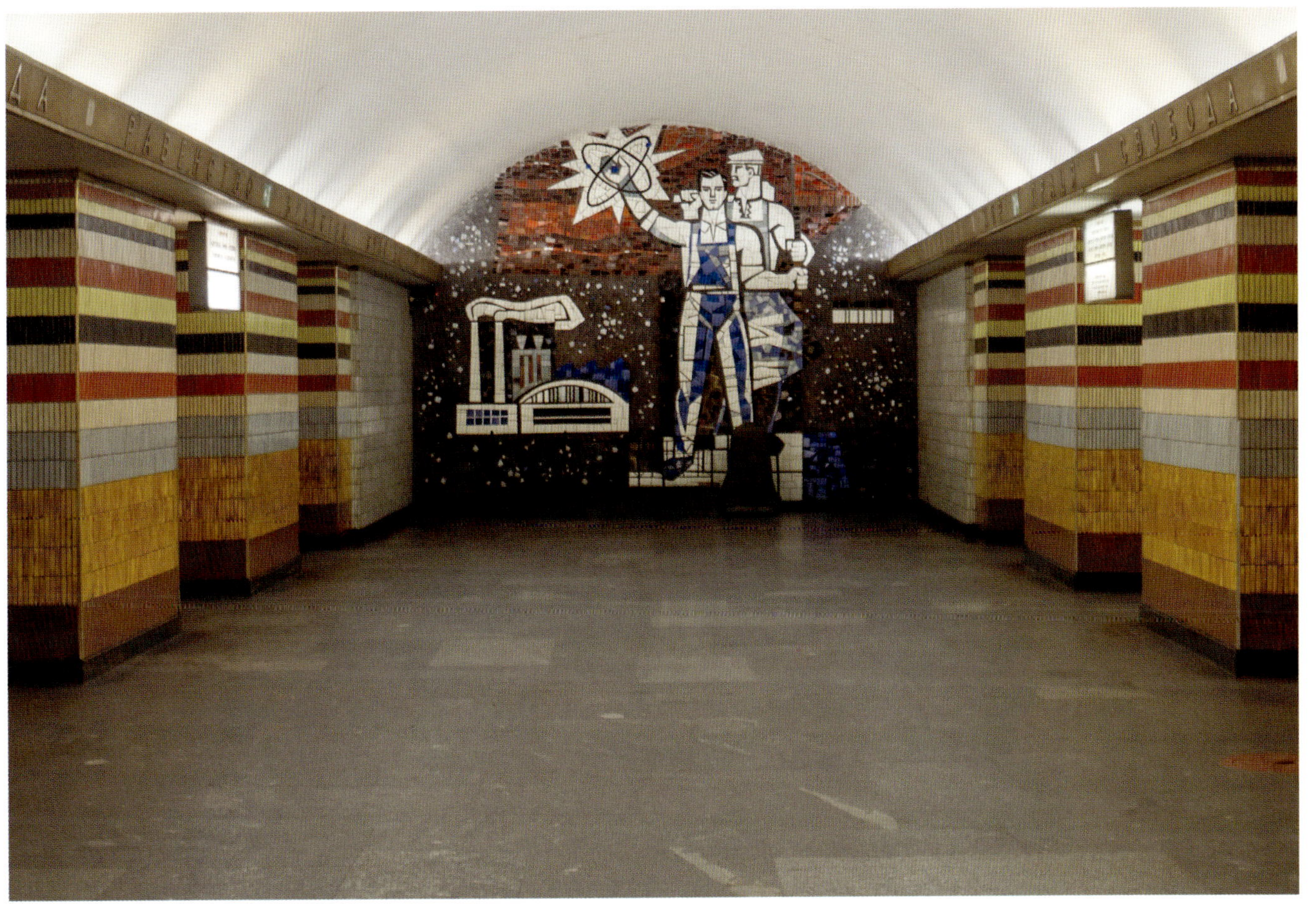

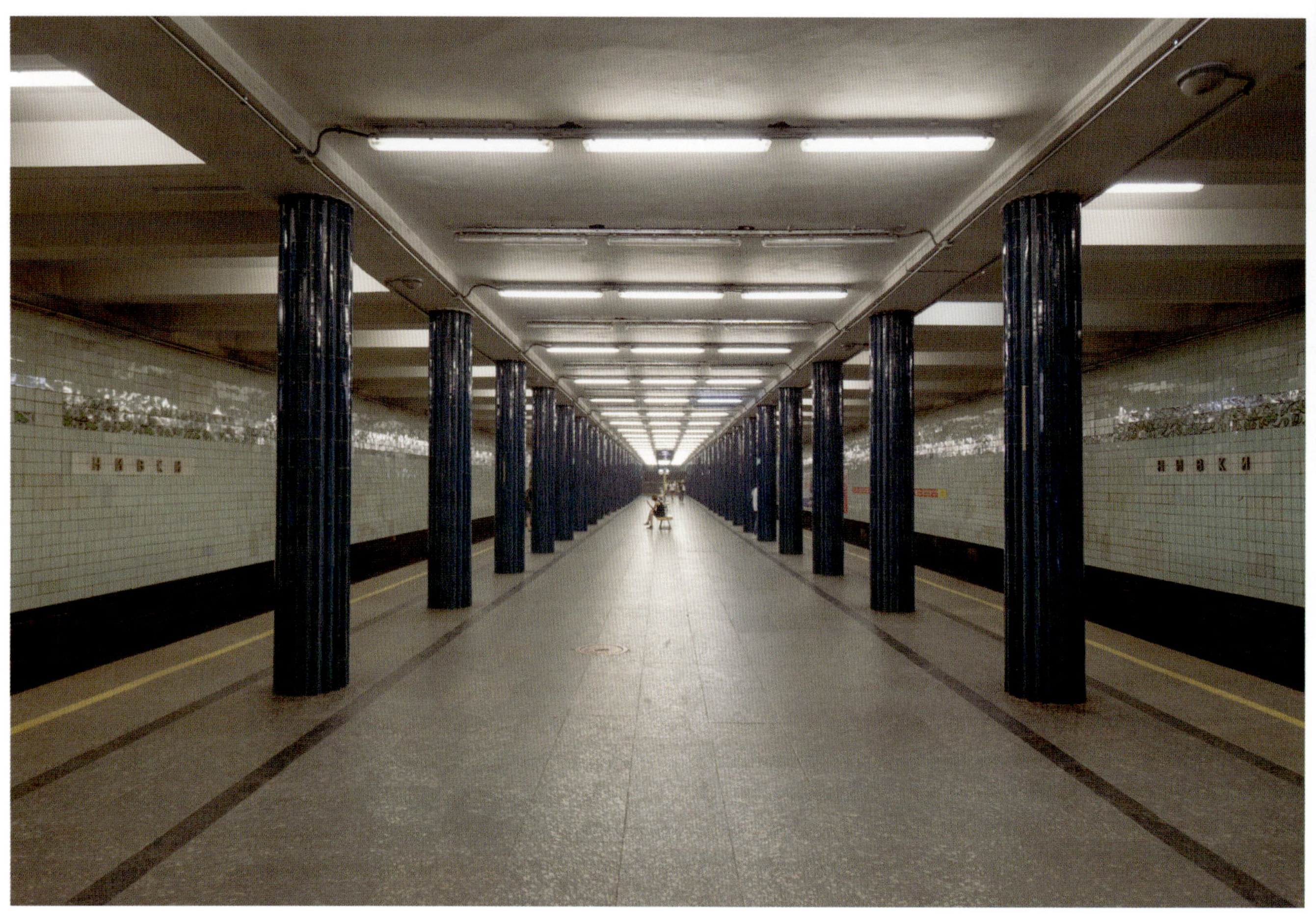

176   Nyvky, KYIV

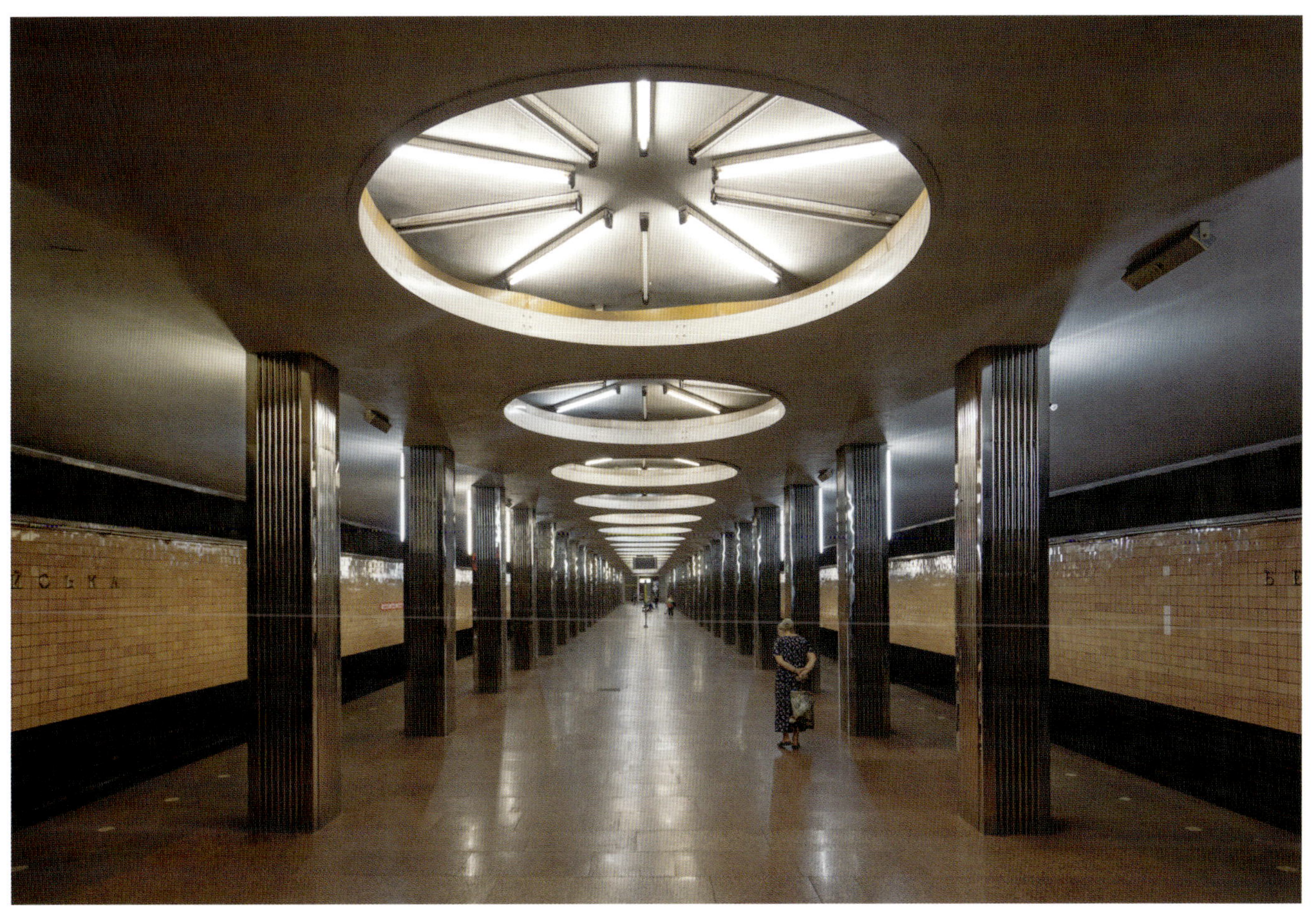

Beresteiska, KYIV   177

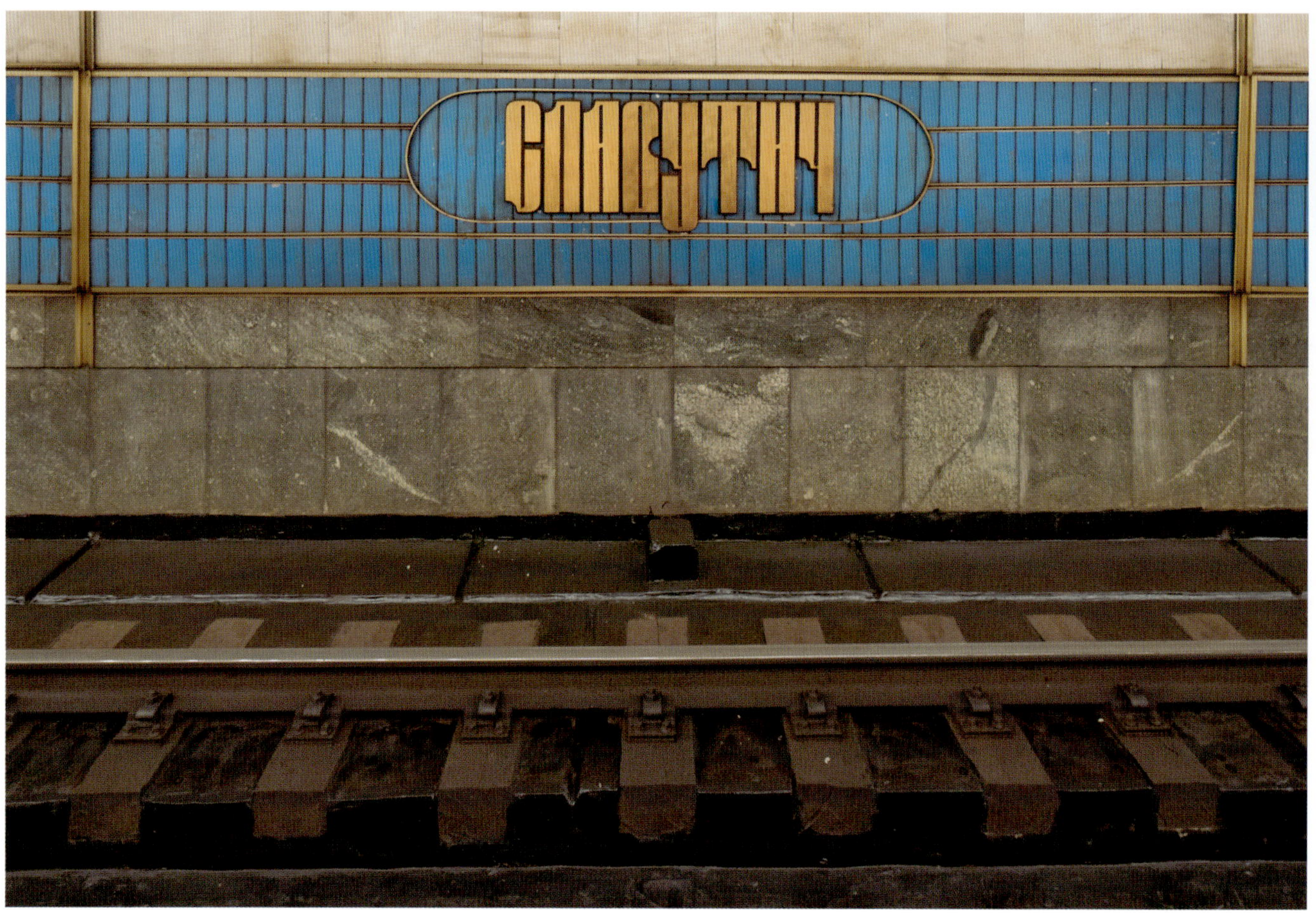

178   Slavutych, KYIV

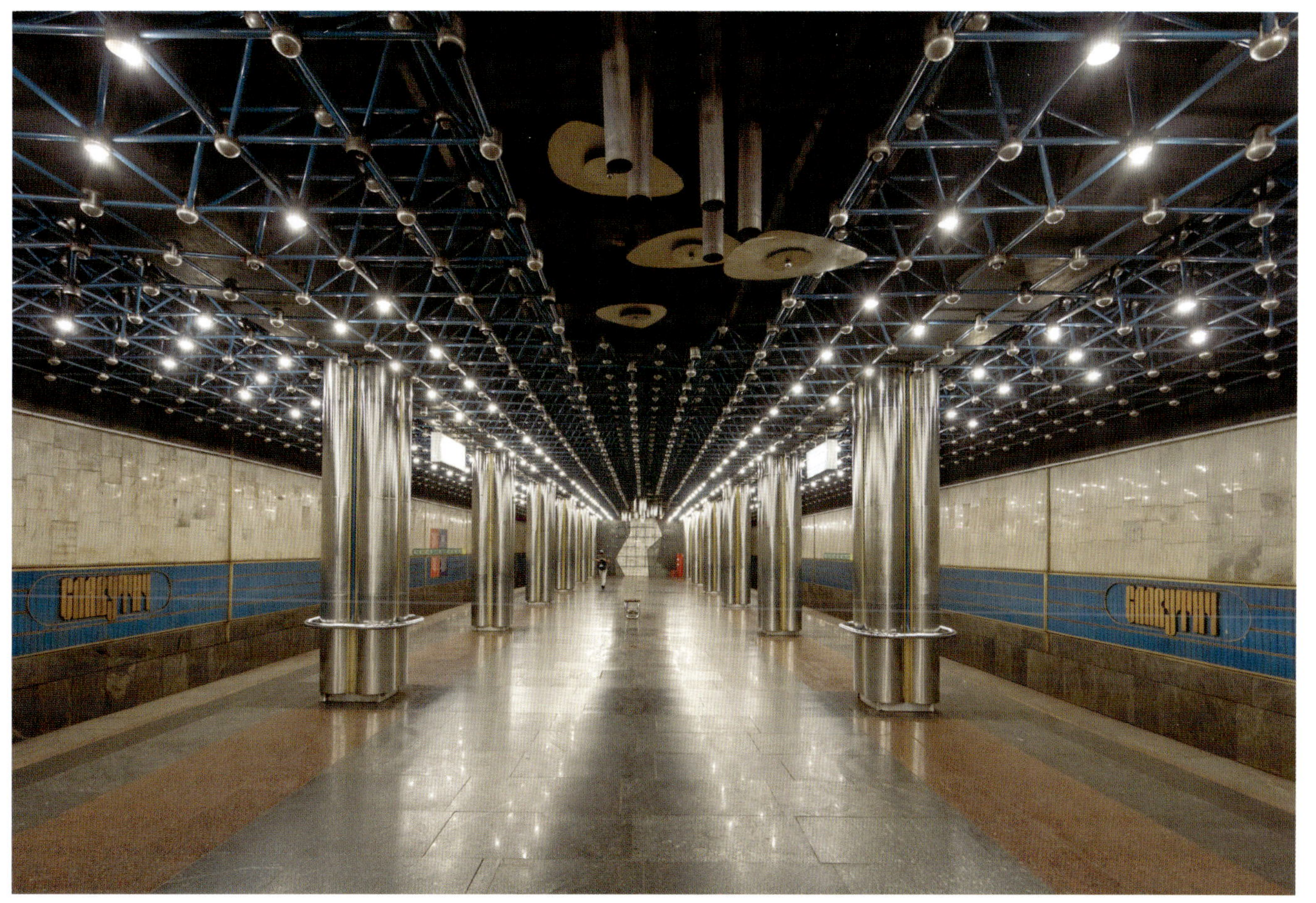

Славутич
Славутич

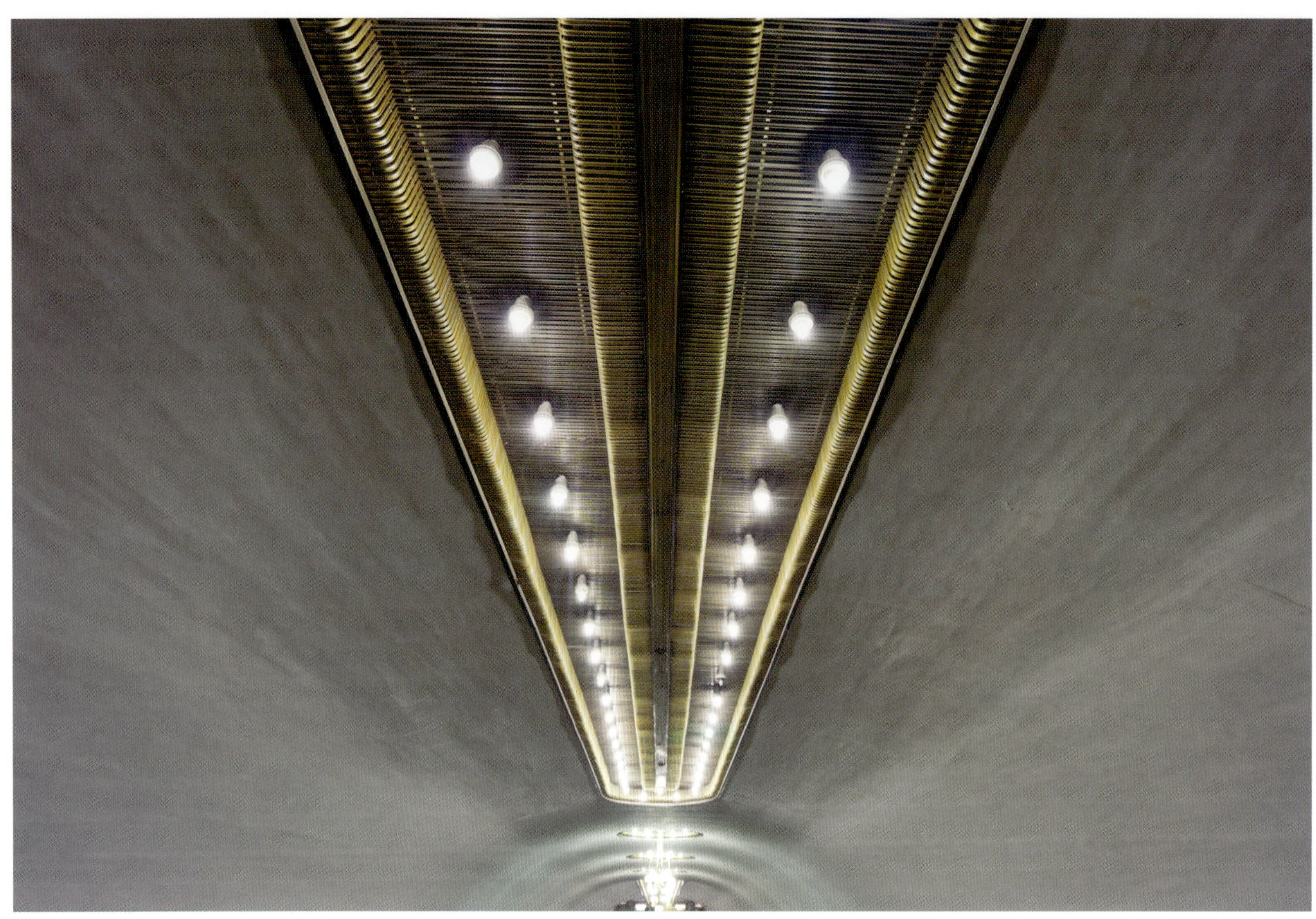

180   Kharkivska, KYIV

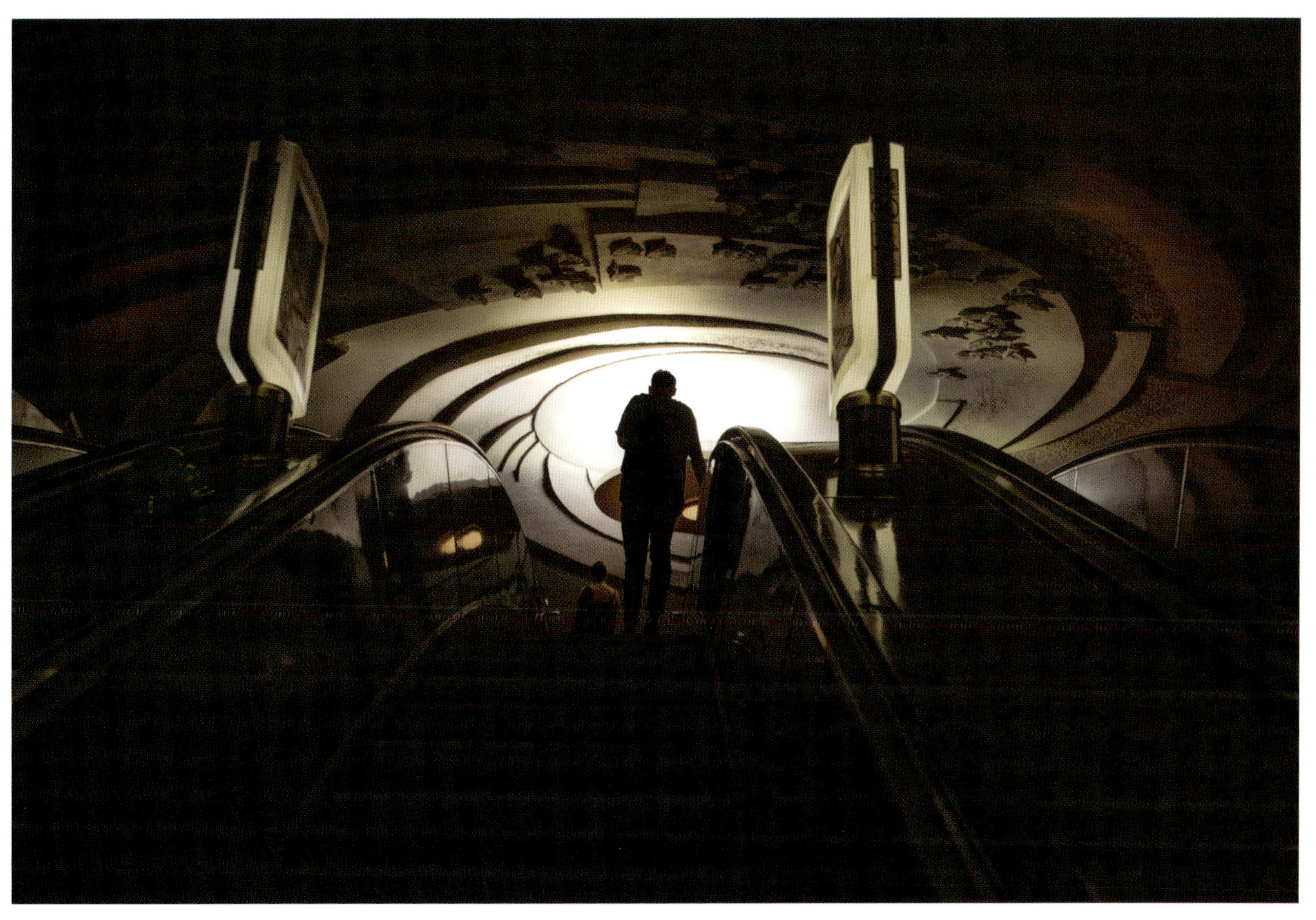

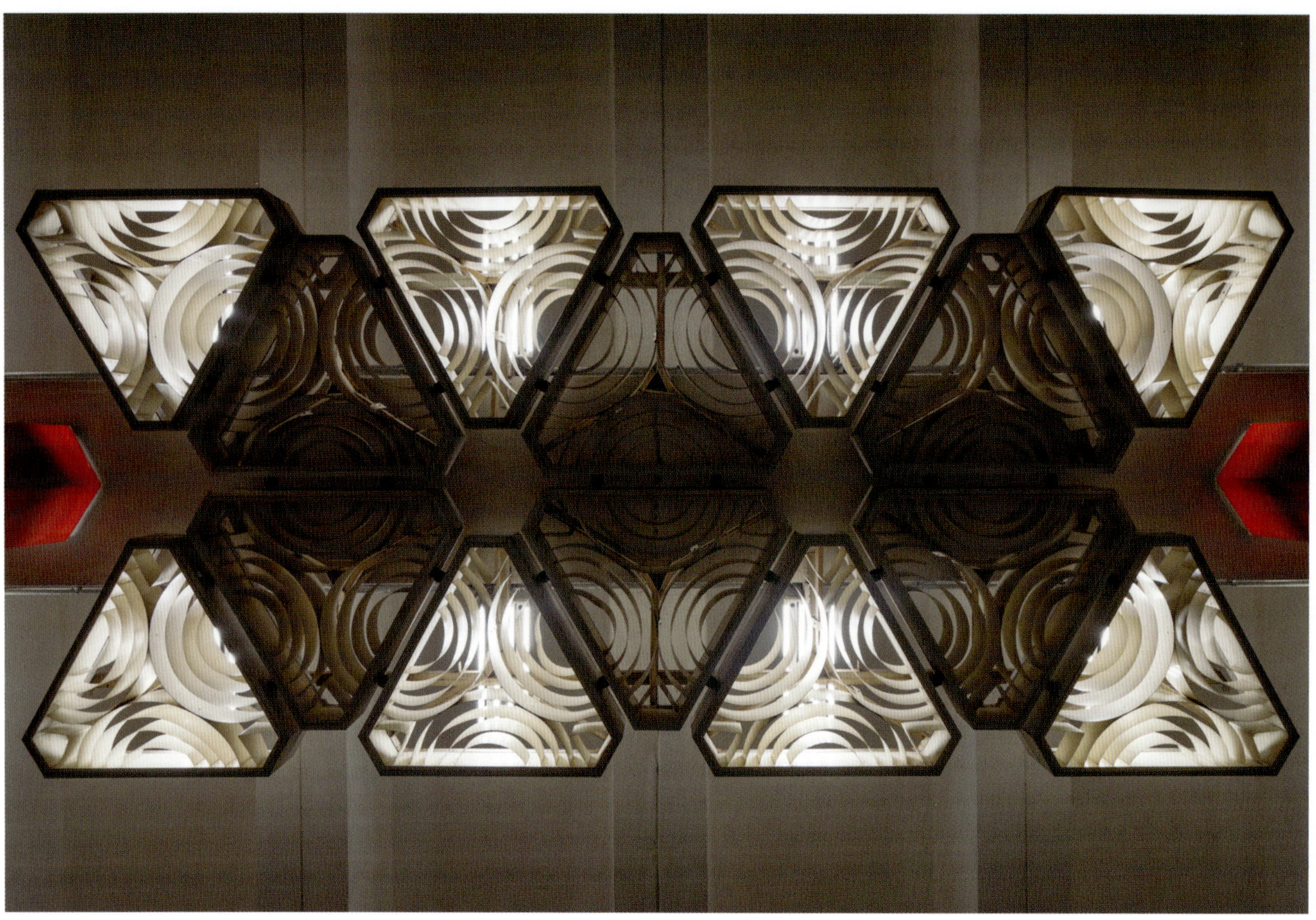

182   Obolon, KYIV

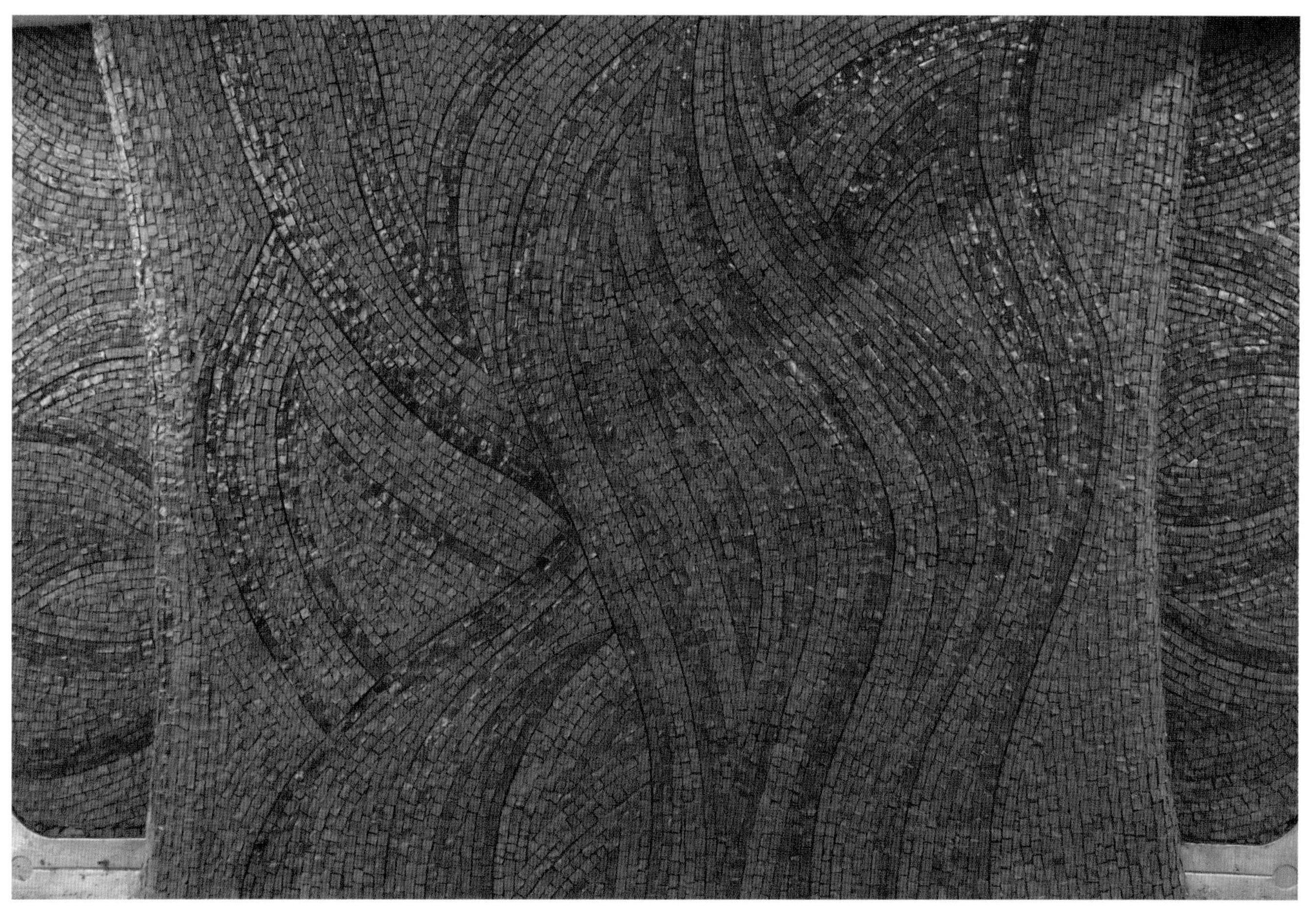

Palats Ukraina, KYIV 183

**САНКТ-ПЕТЕРБУРГ
РОССИЯ**

**SAINT PETERSBURG
RUSSIA**

OPENED 1955

    Ploshchad Vosstaniya, SAINT PETERSBURG

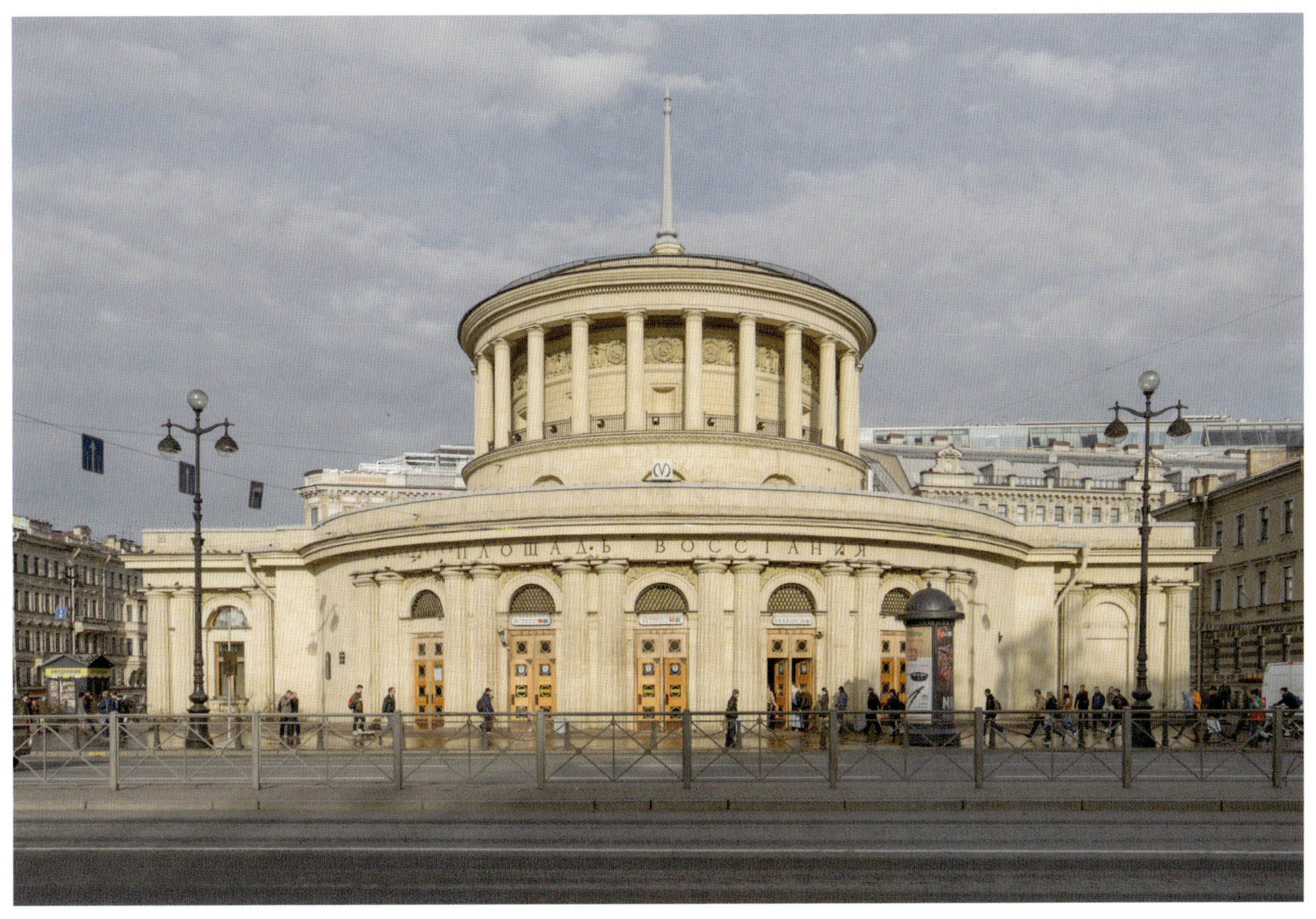

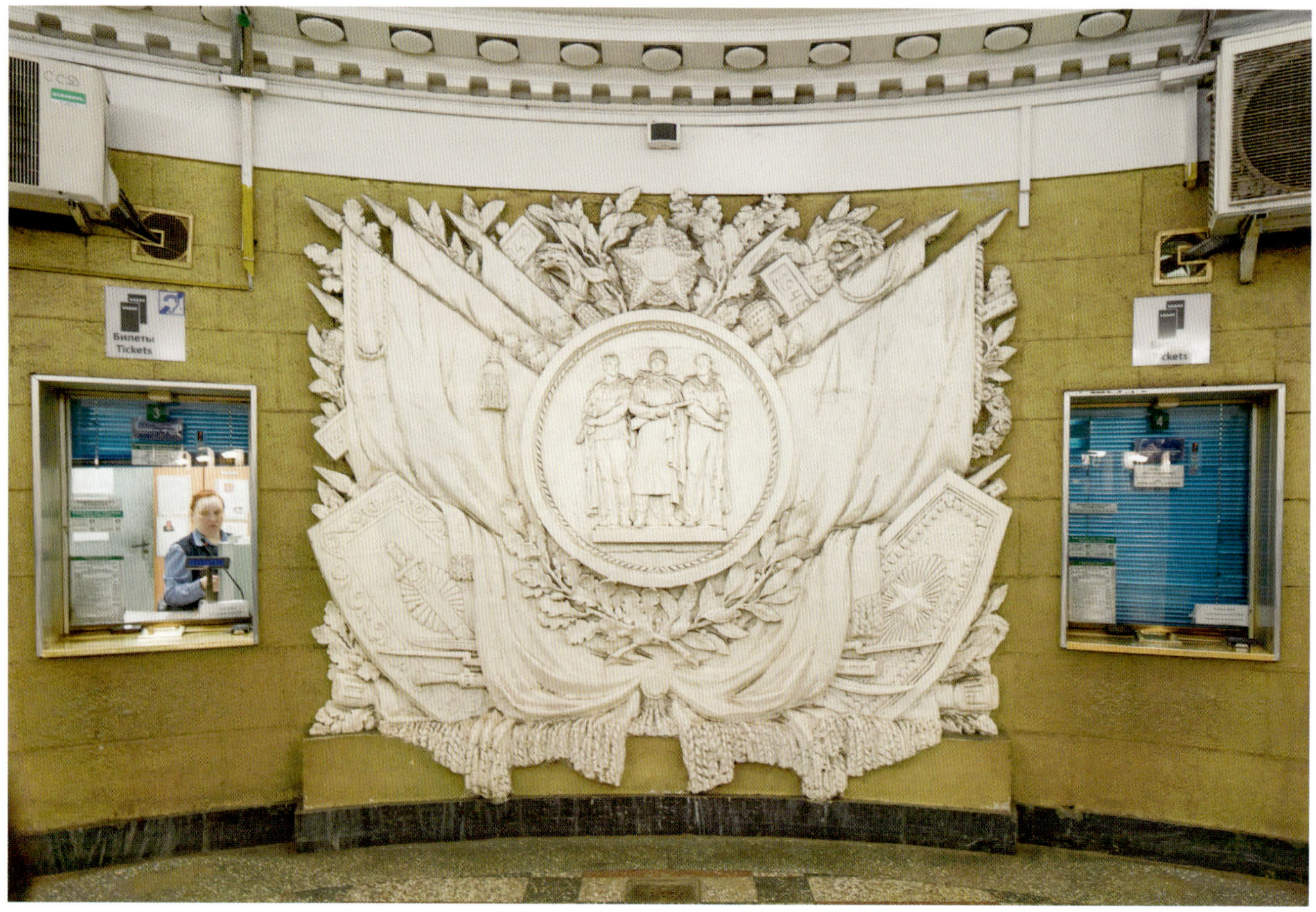

186   Avtovo, SAINT PETERSBURG

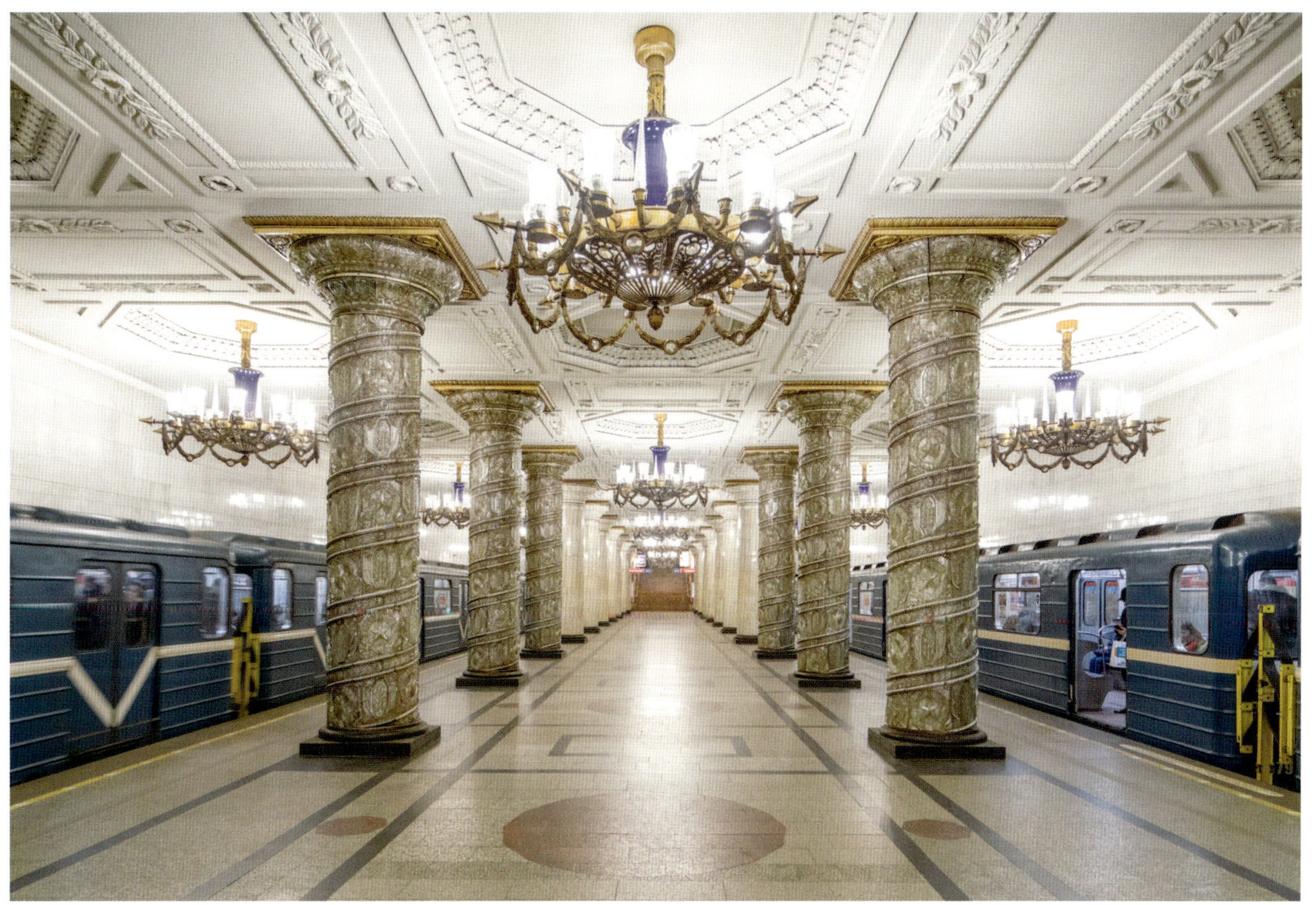

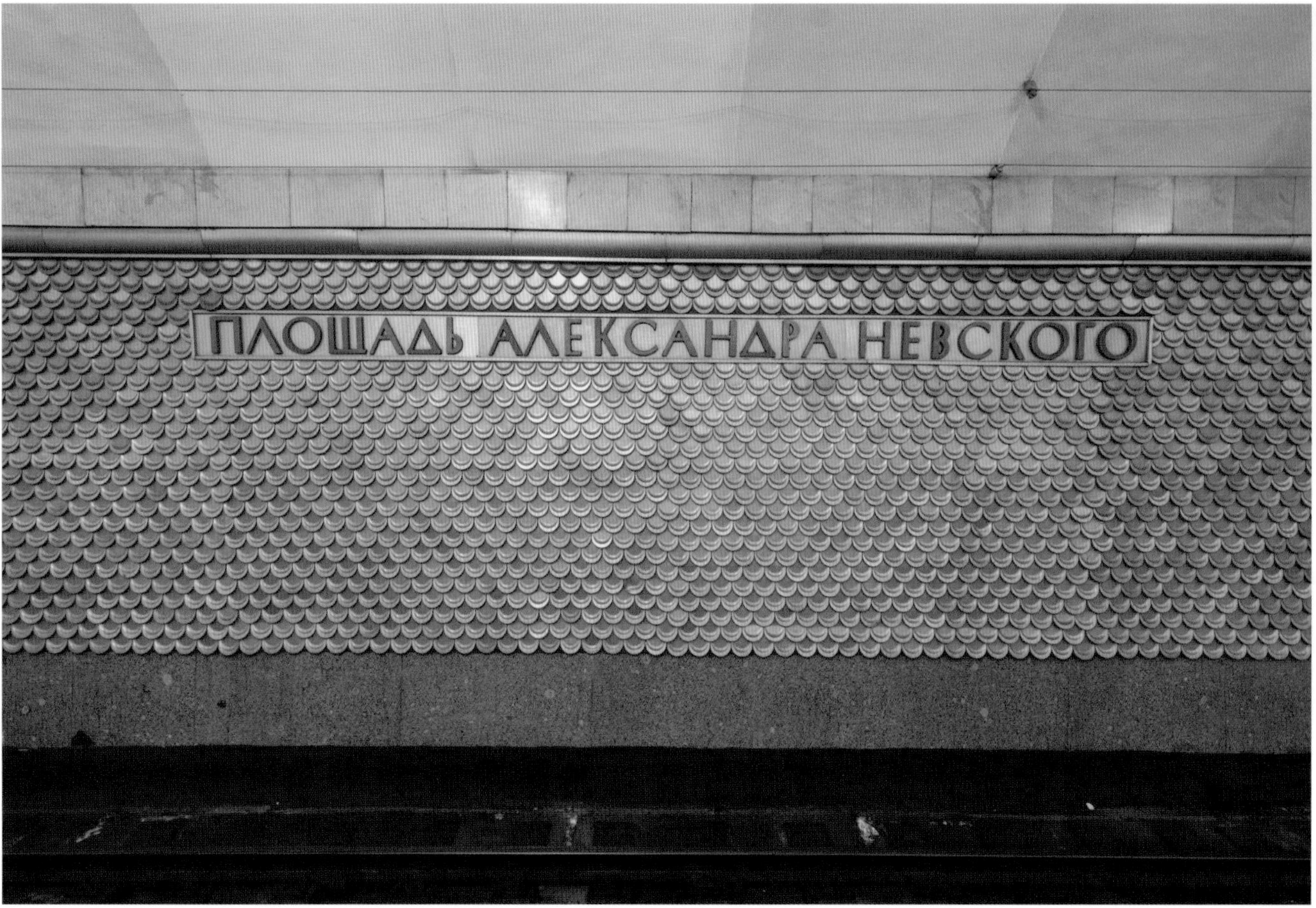

Ploshchad Aleksandra Nevskogo, SAINT PETERSBURG

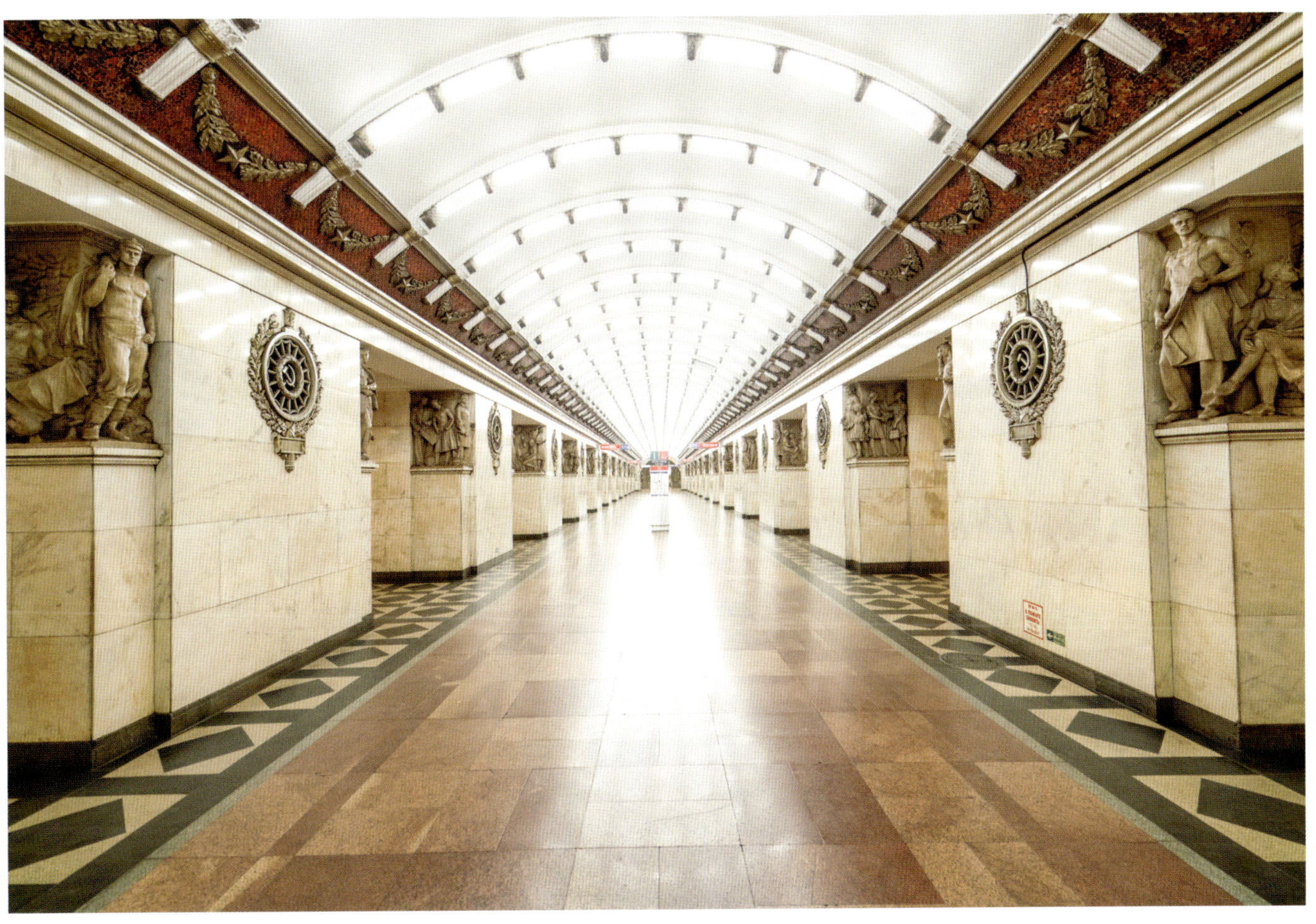

Narvskaya, SAINT PETERSBURG   189

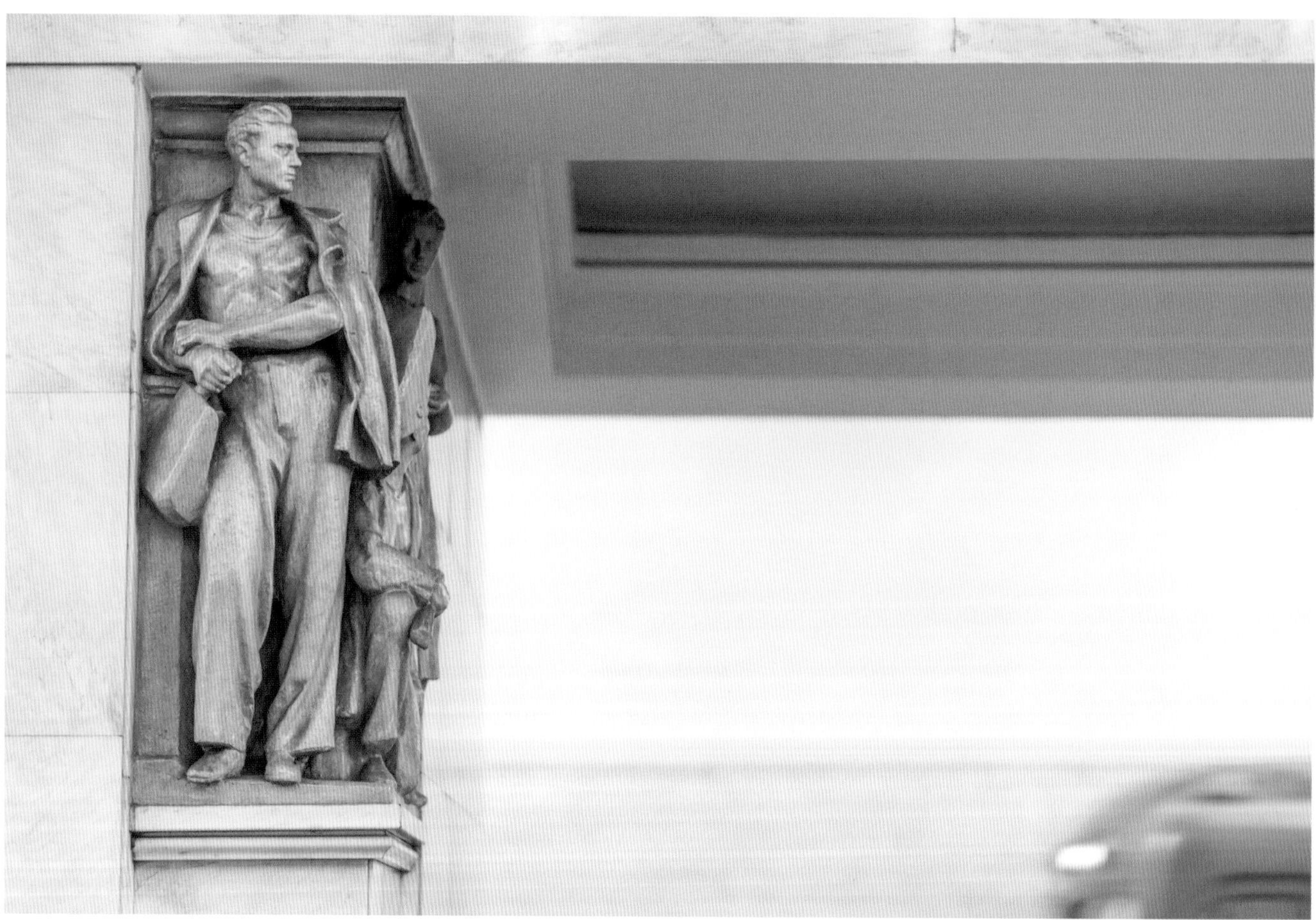

190 Narvskaya, SAINT PETERSBURG

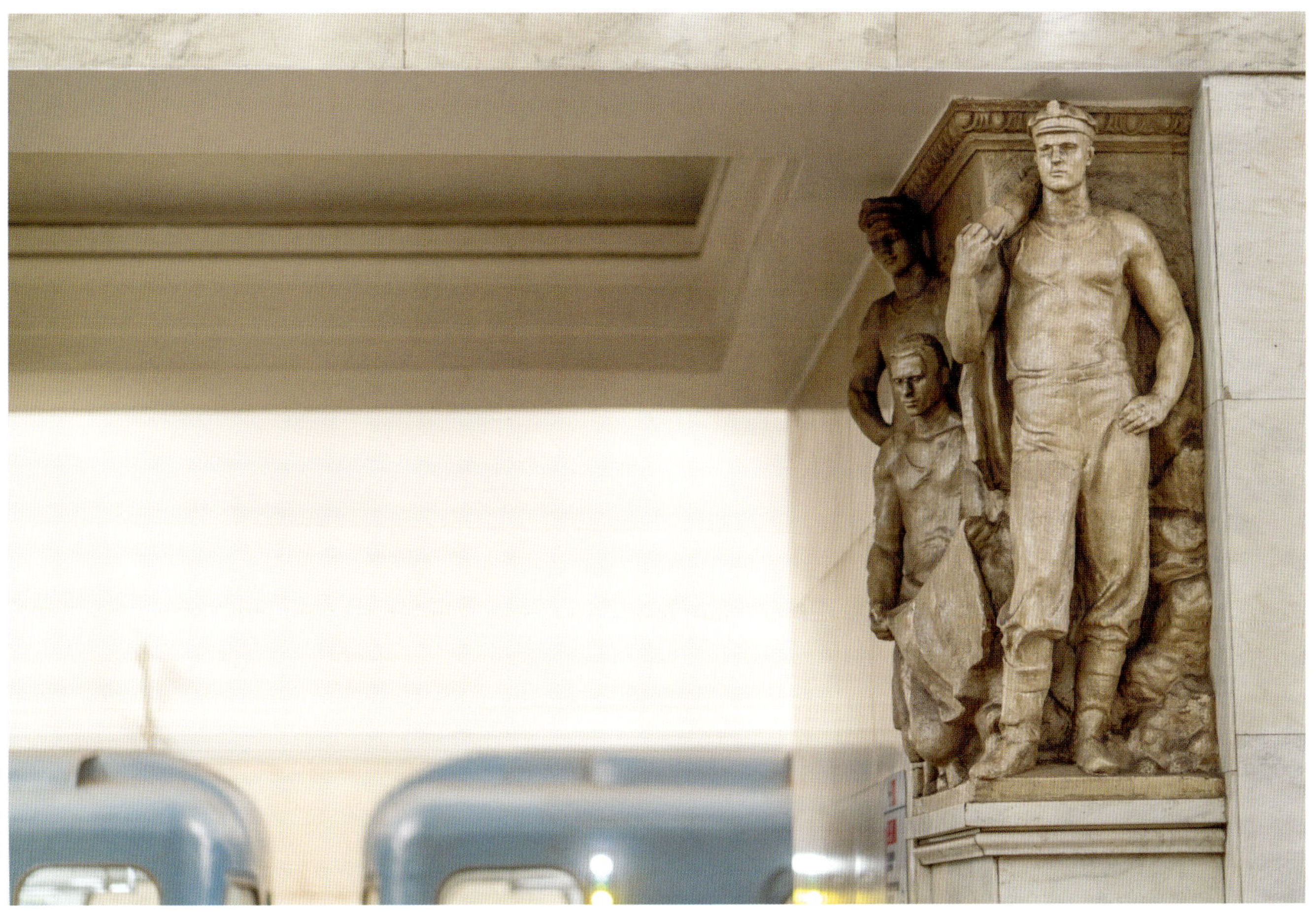

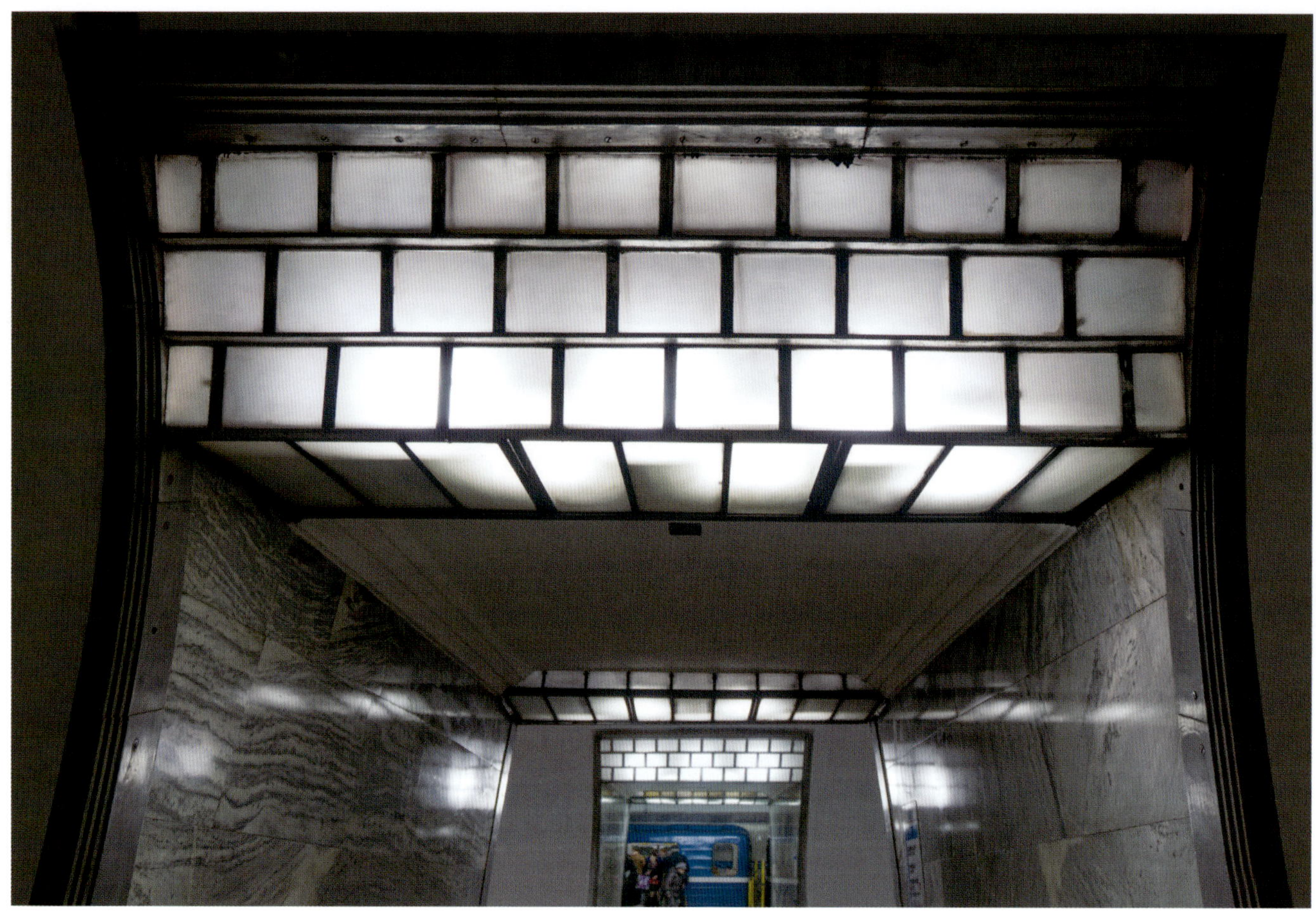

192 Electrosila, SAINT PETERSBURG

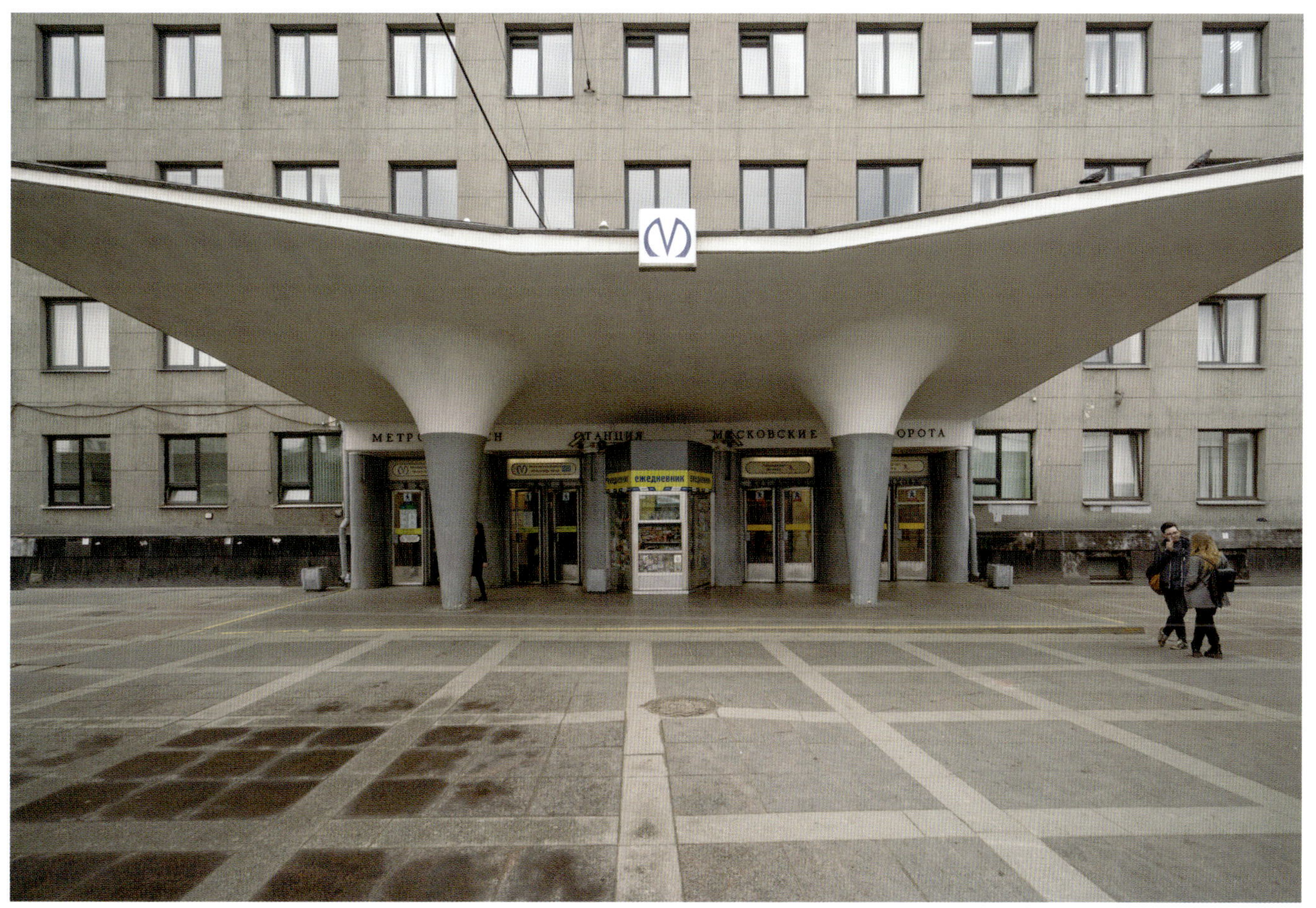

Moskovskiye Vorota, SAINT PETERSBURG   193

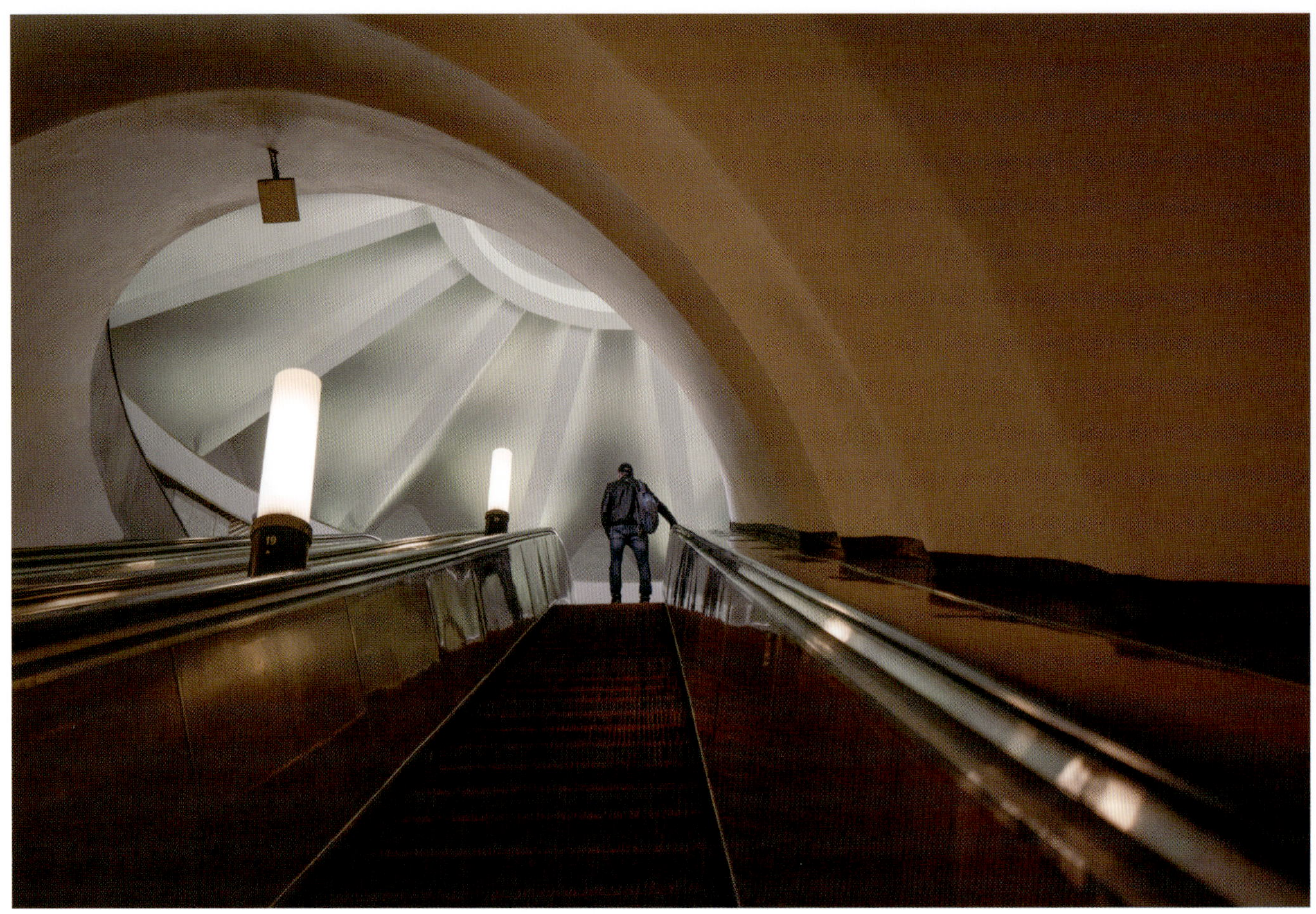

194   Ploshchad Aleksandra Nevskogo, SAINT PETERSBURG

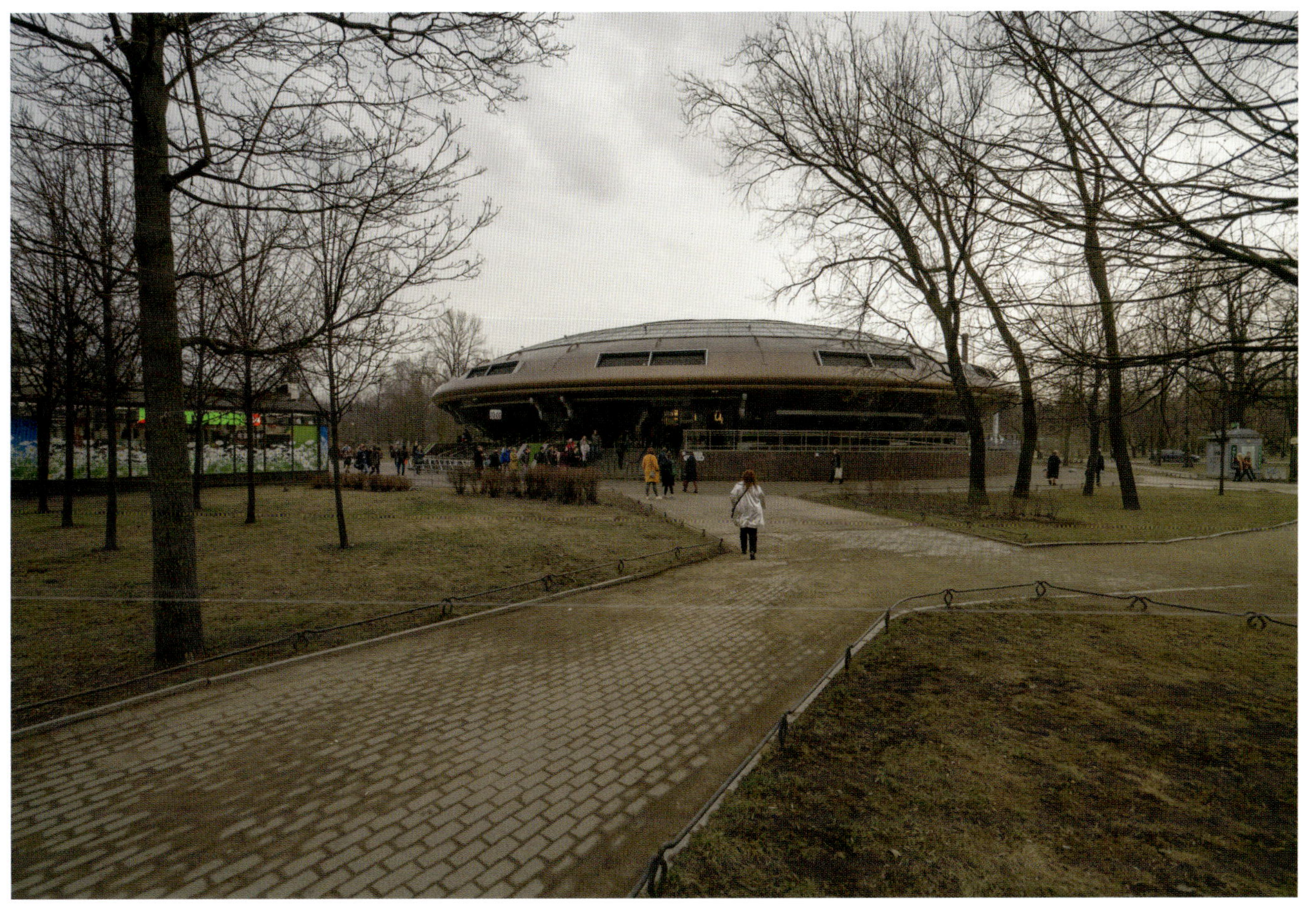

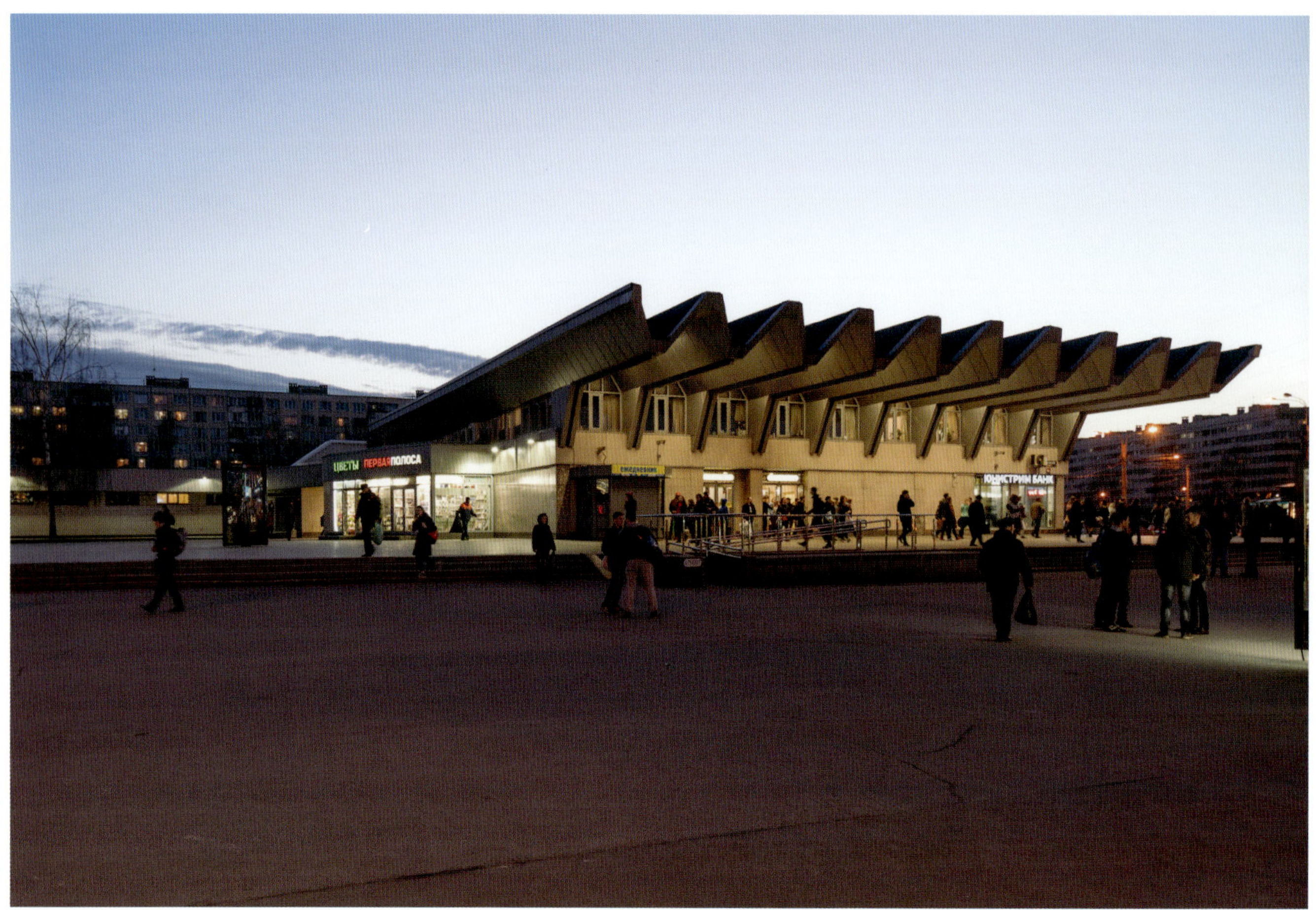

196   Pionerskaya, SAINT PETERSBURG

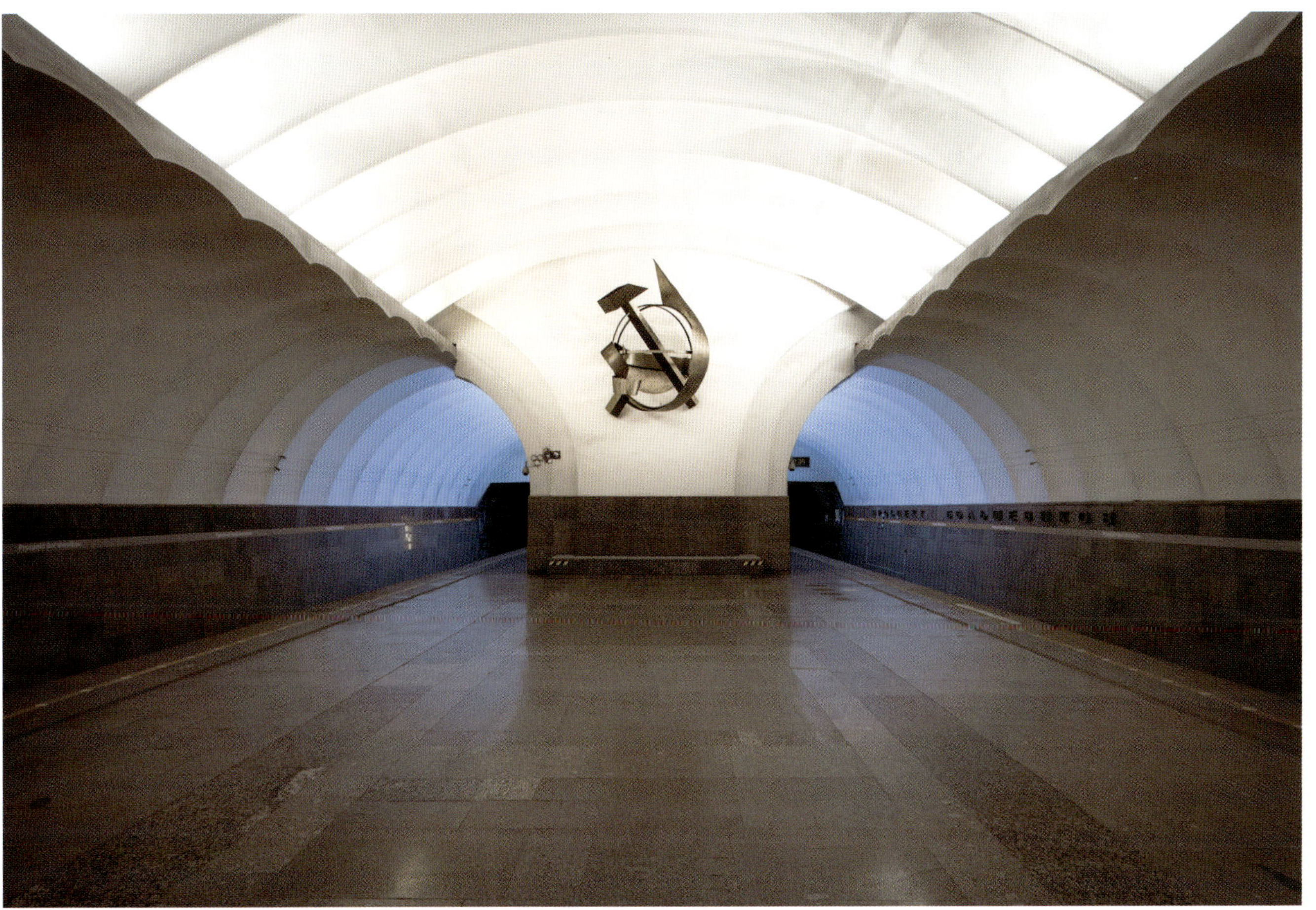

Prospekt Bolshevikov, SAINT PETERSBURG   197

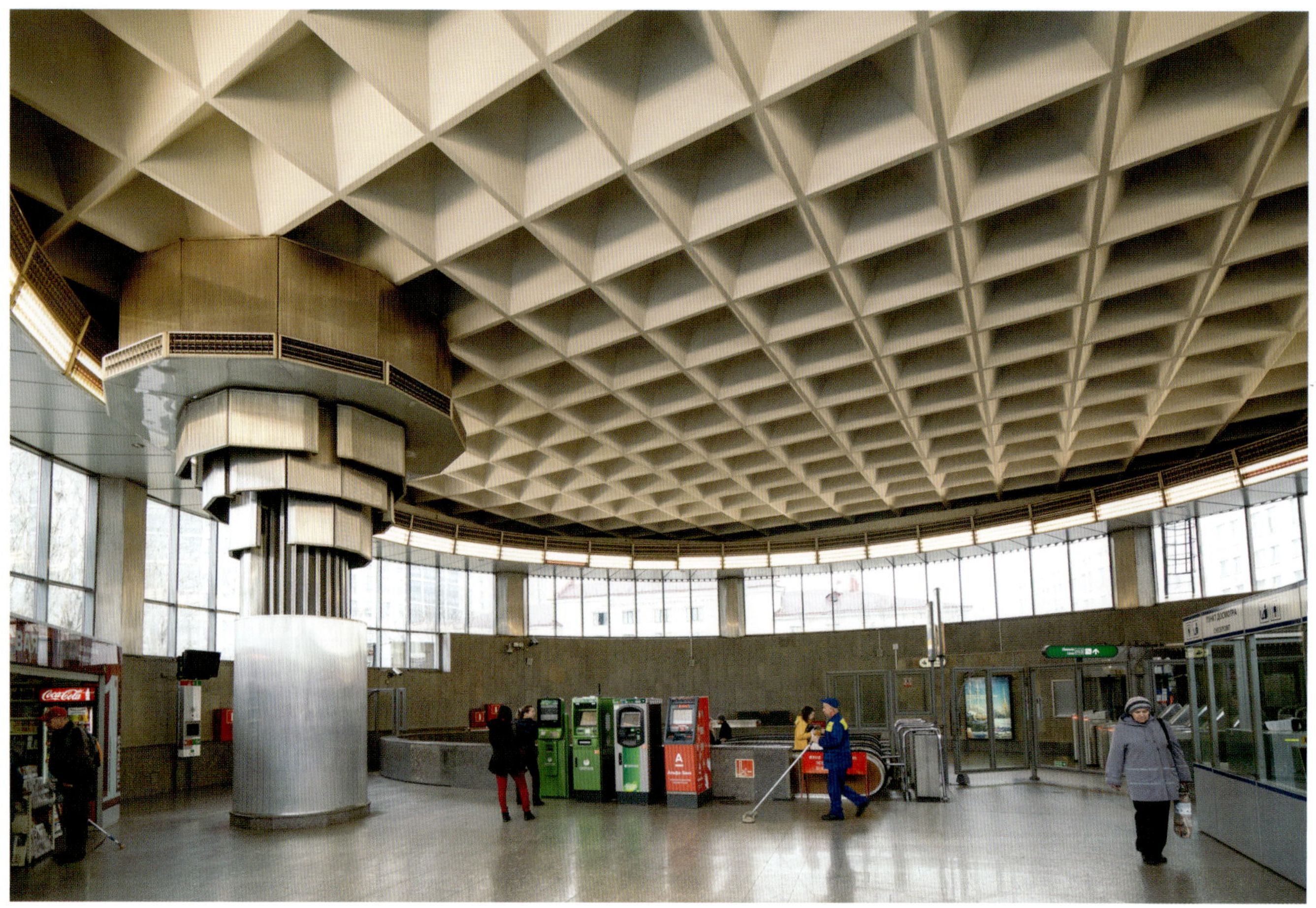

  Proletarskaya, SAINT PETERSBURG

overleaf left: Ozerki, SAINT PETERSBURG

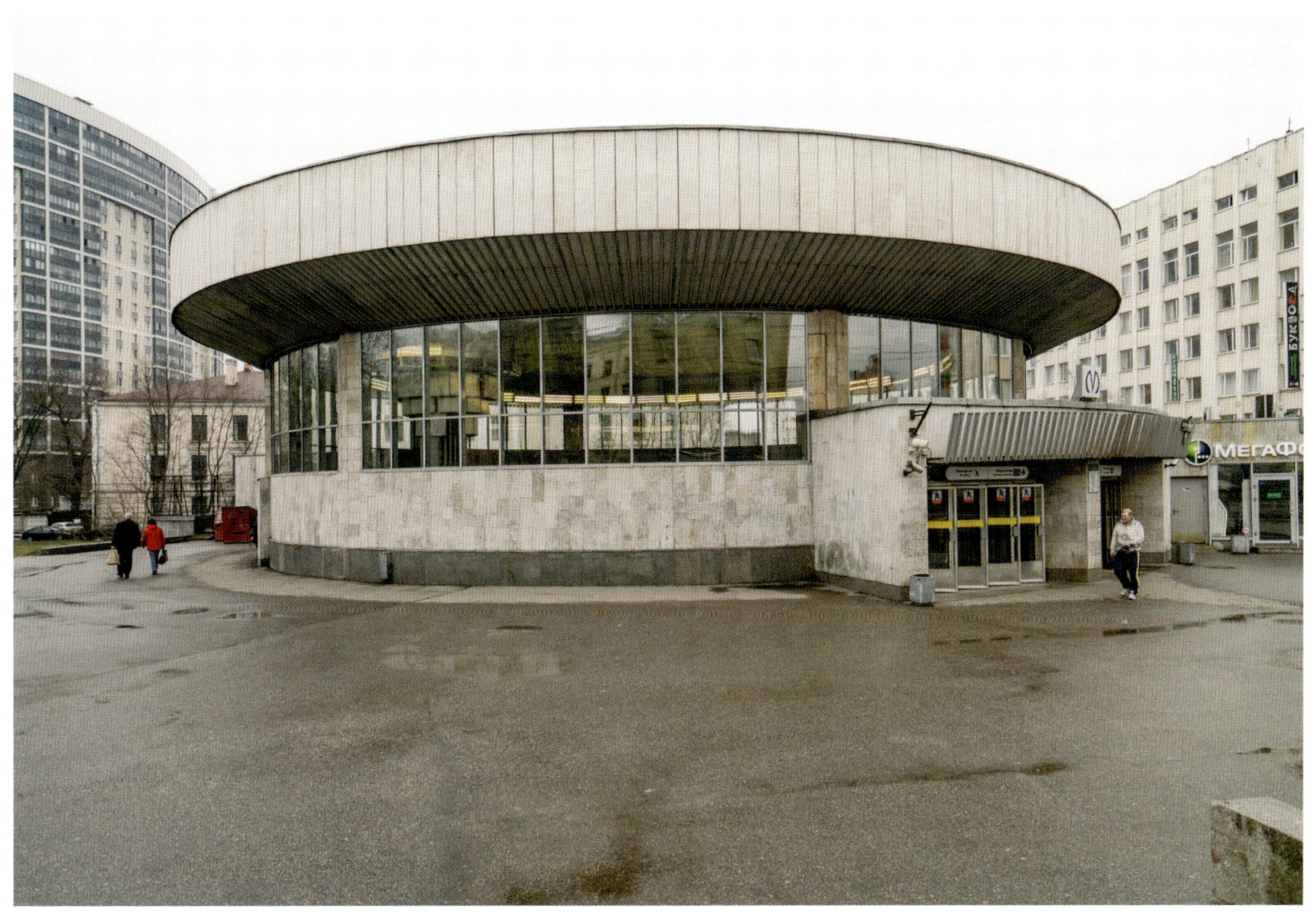

overleaf right: Novocherkasskaya, SAINT PETERSBURG

199

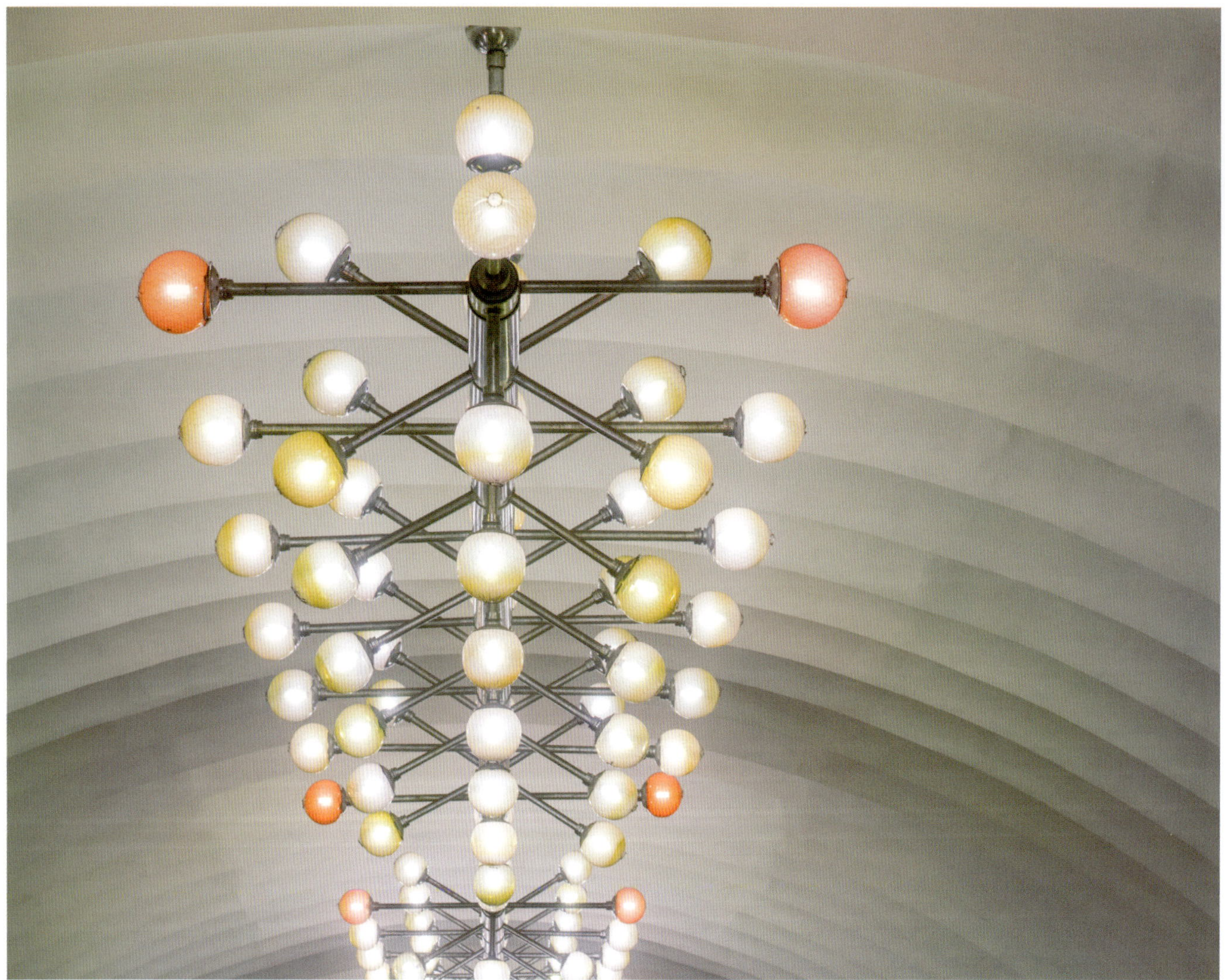

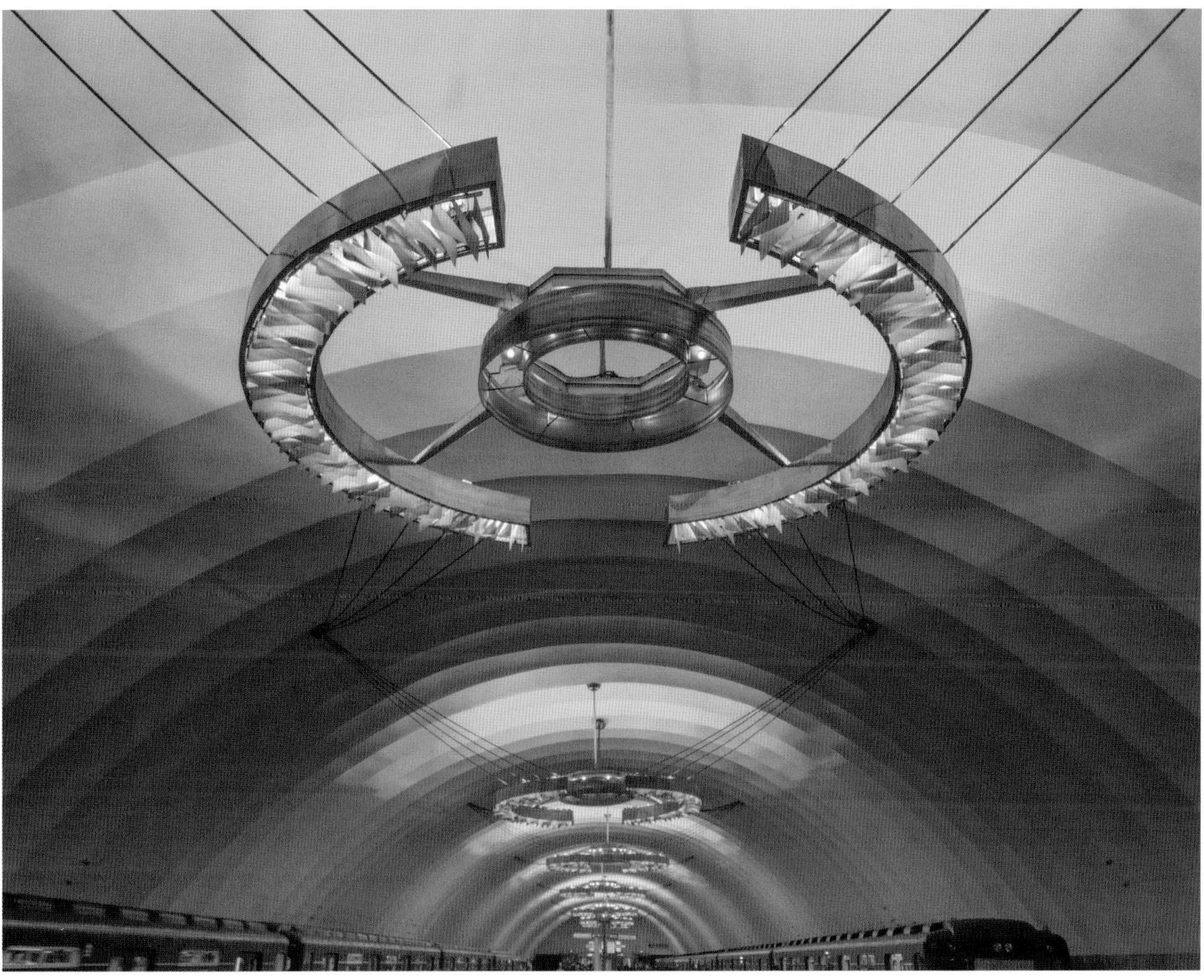

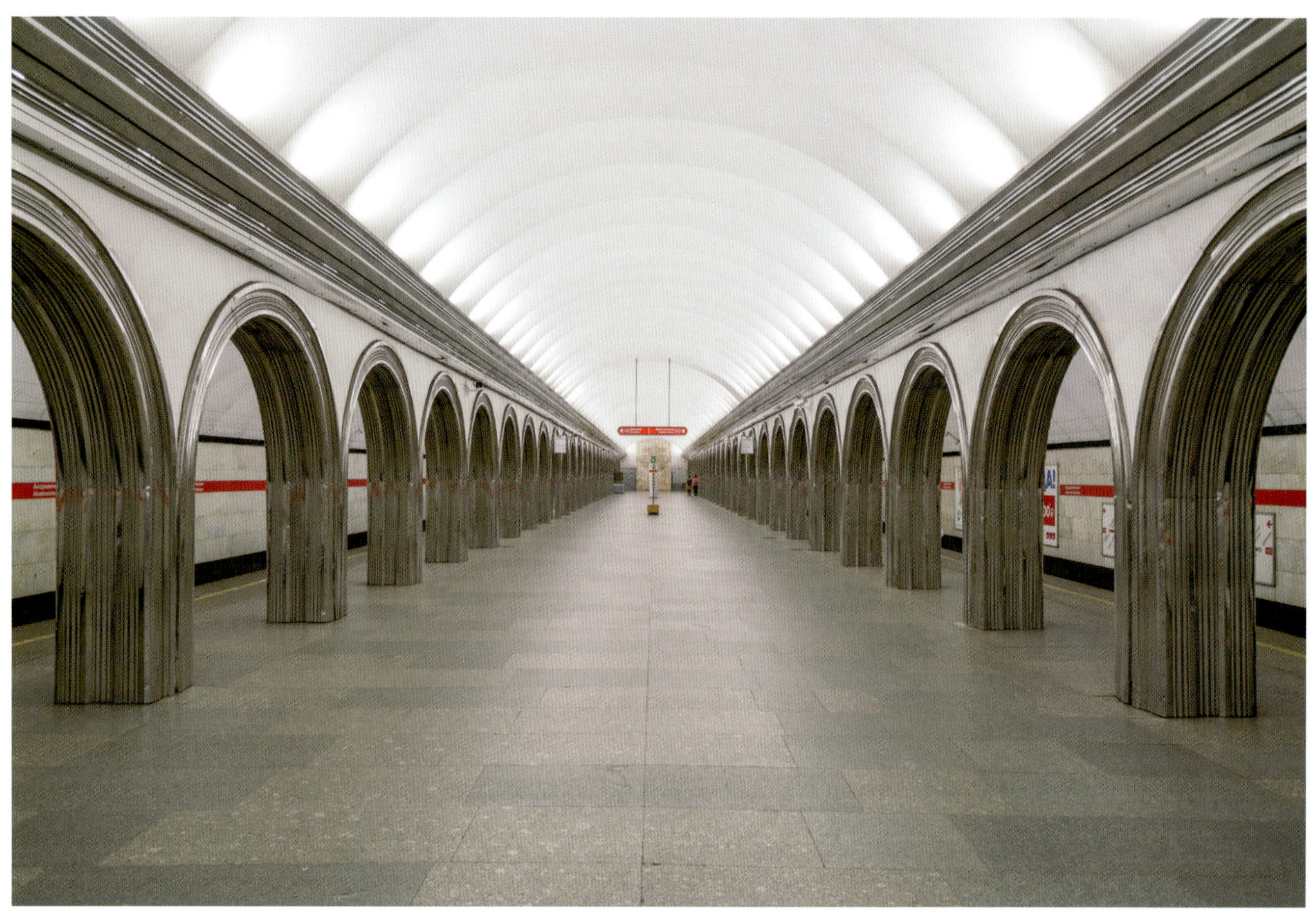

202 Akademicheskaya, SAINT PETERSBURG

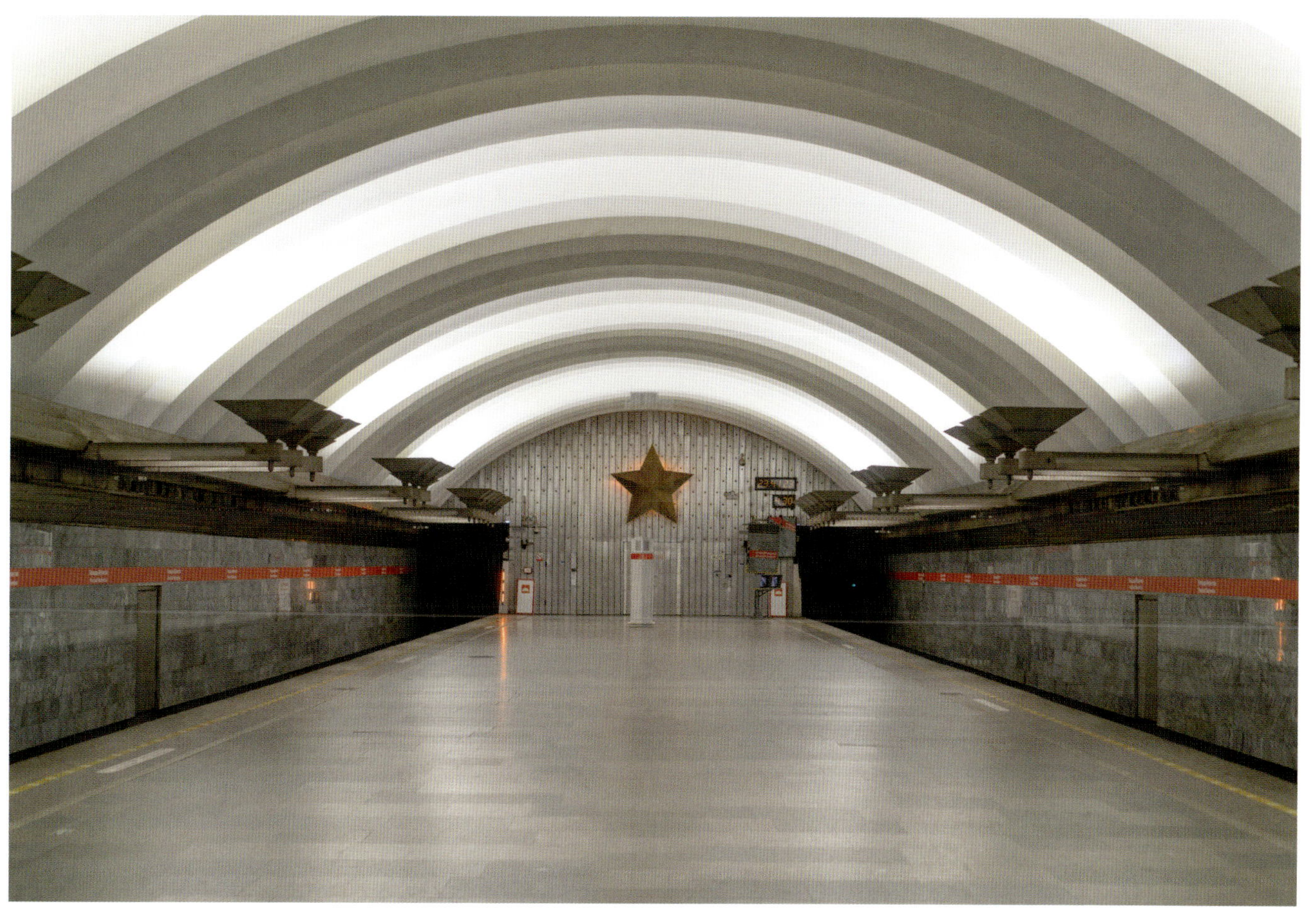

Ploshchad Muzhestva, SAINT PETERSBURG   203

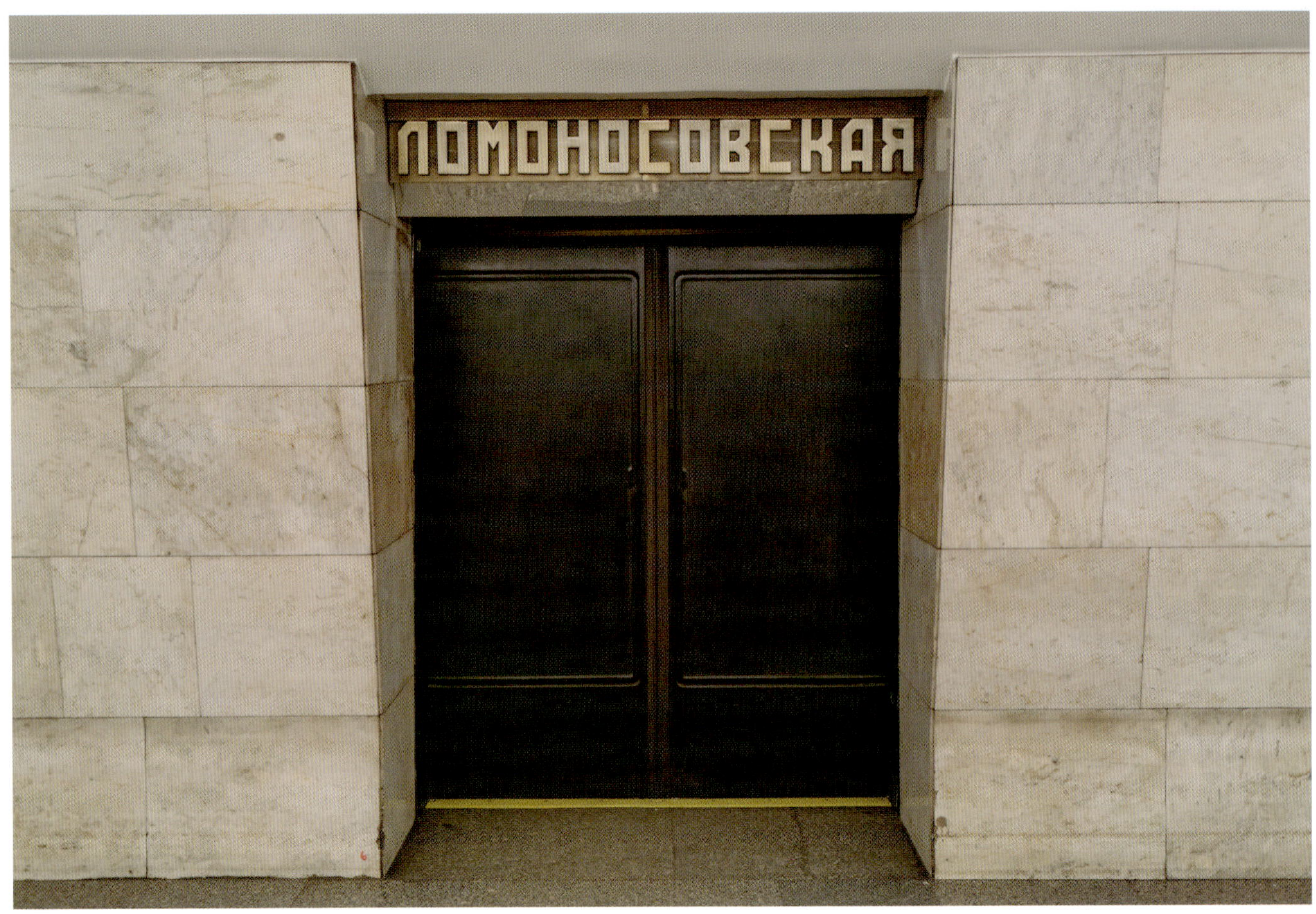

204   Lomonosovskaya, SAINT PETERSBURG

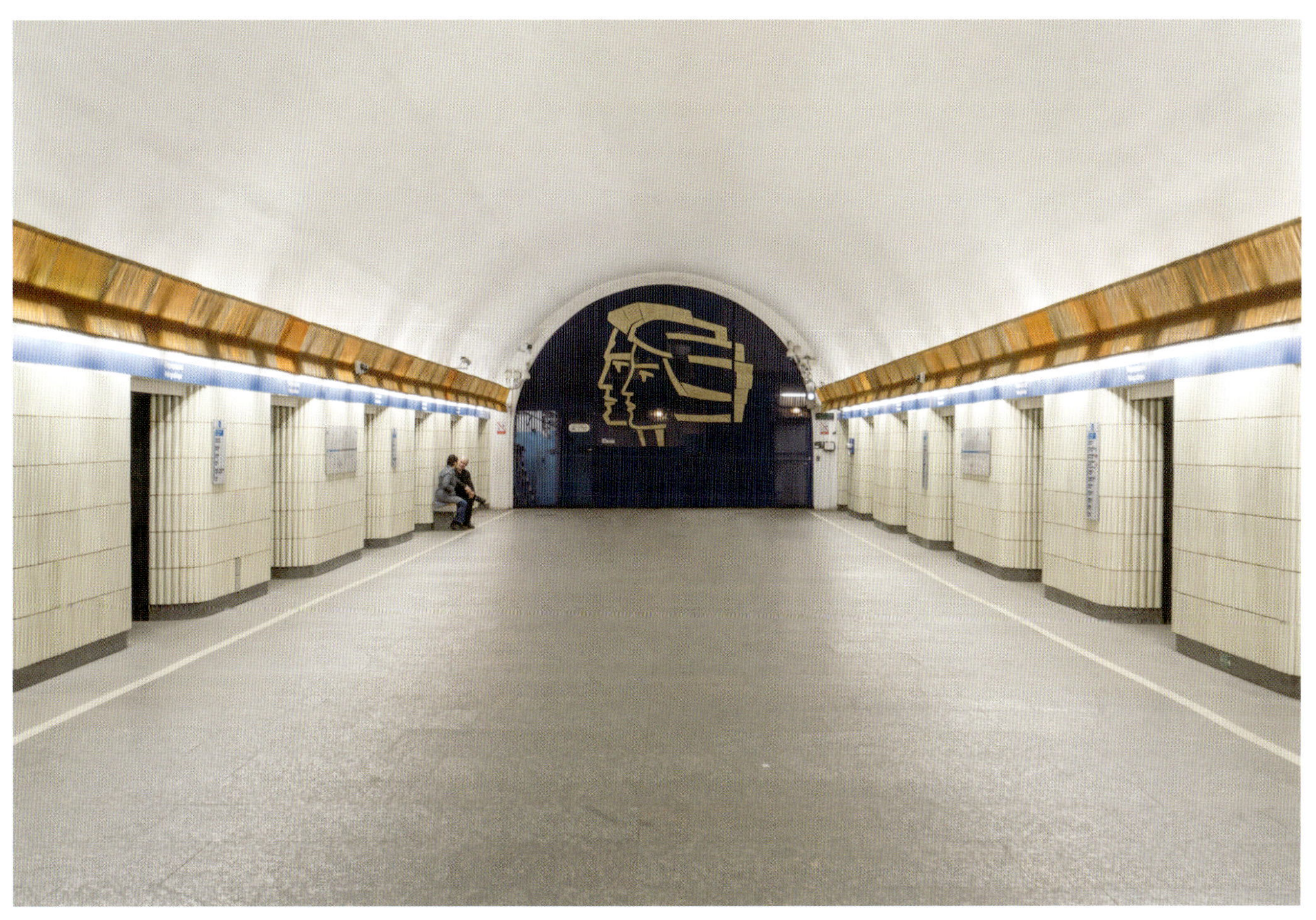

**МОСКВА МOSCOW
РОССИЯ RUSSIA**

OPENED 1935

    Aeroport, MOSCOW

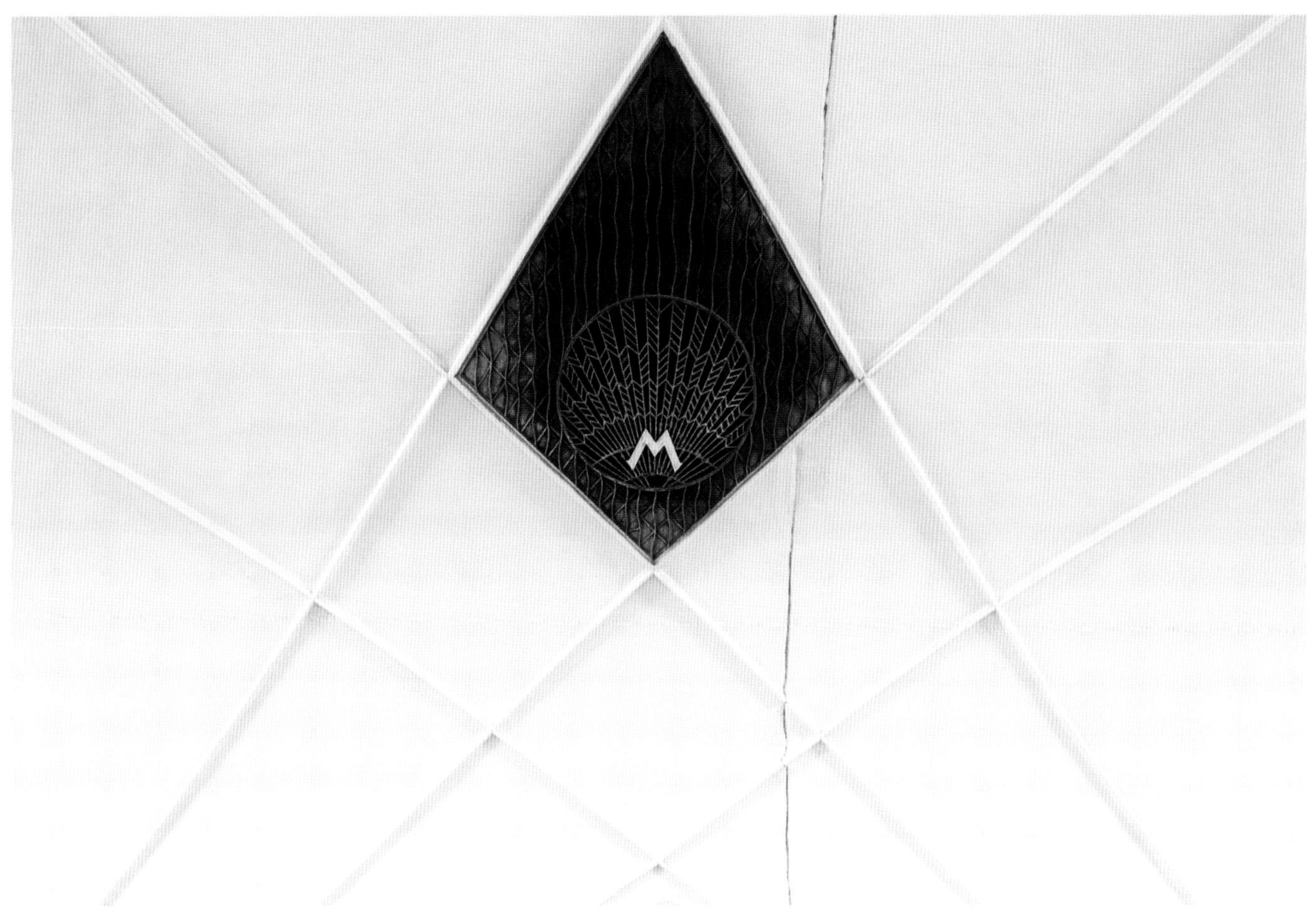

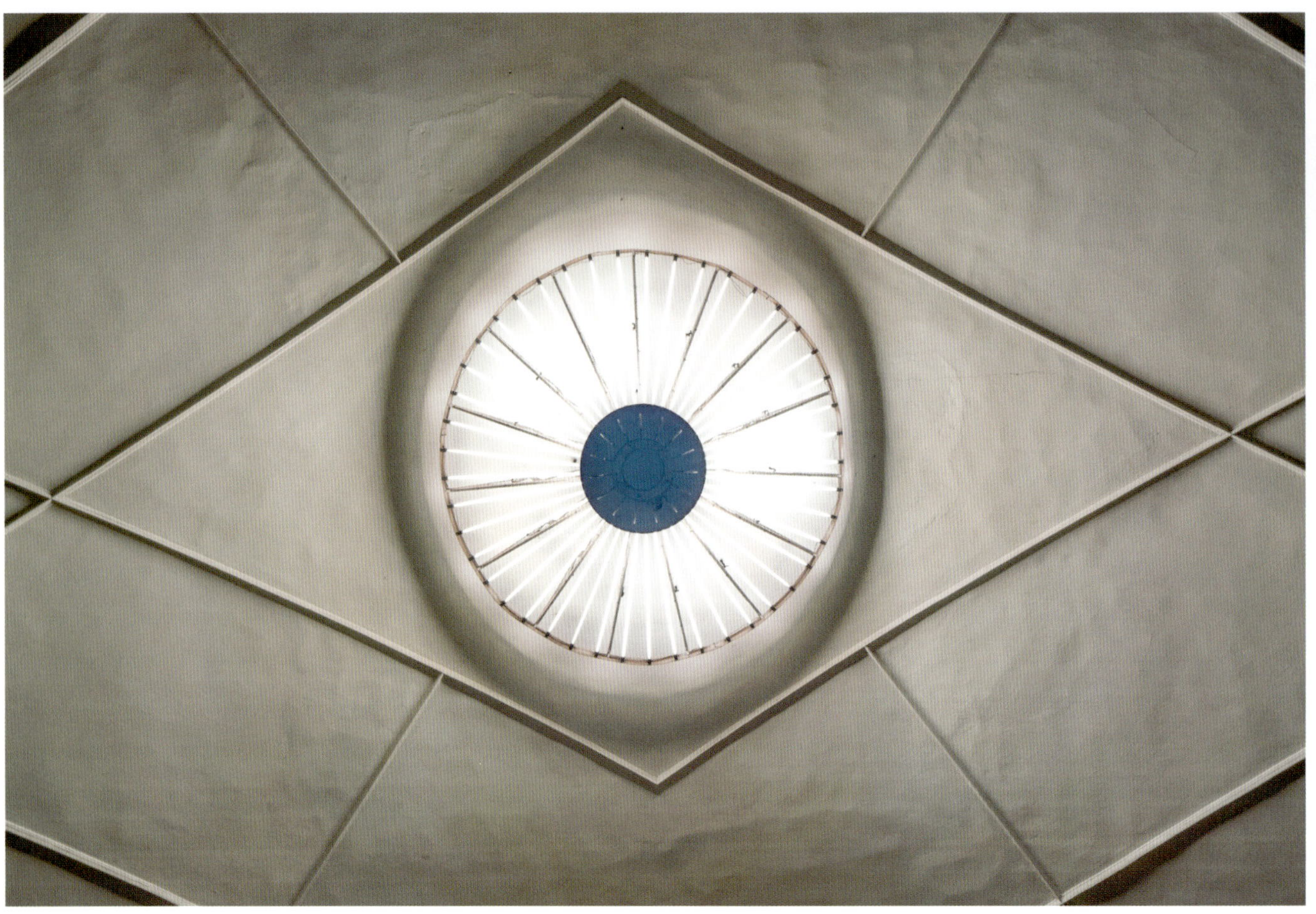

208   Aeroport, MOSCOW

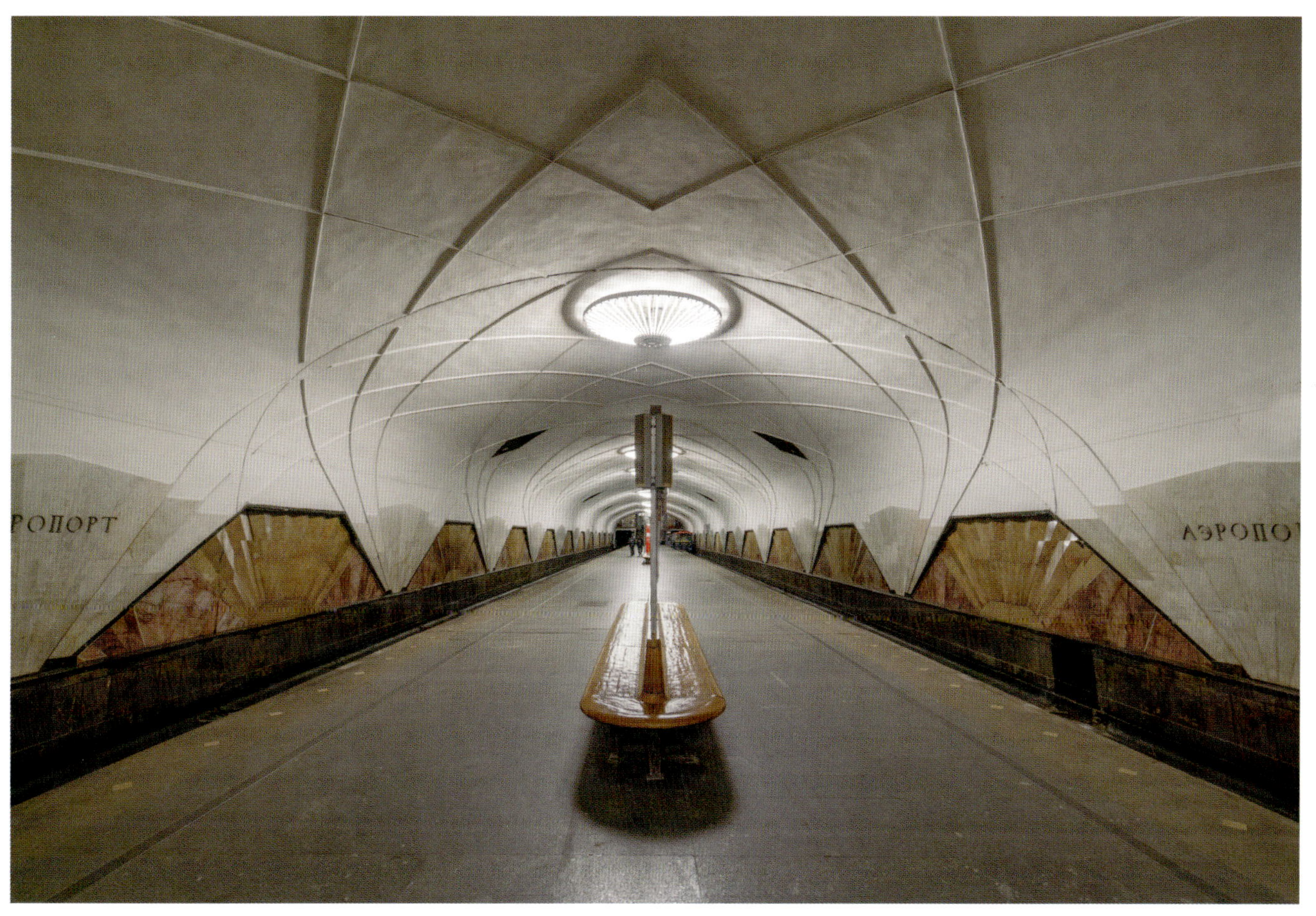

РОПОРТ
АЭРОПО

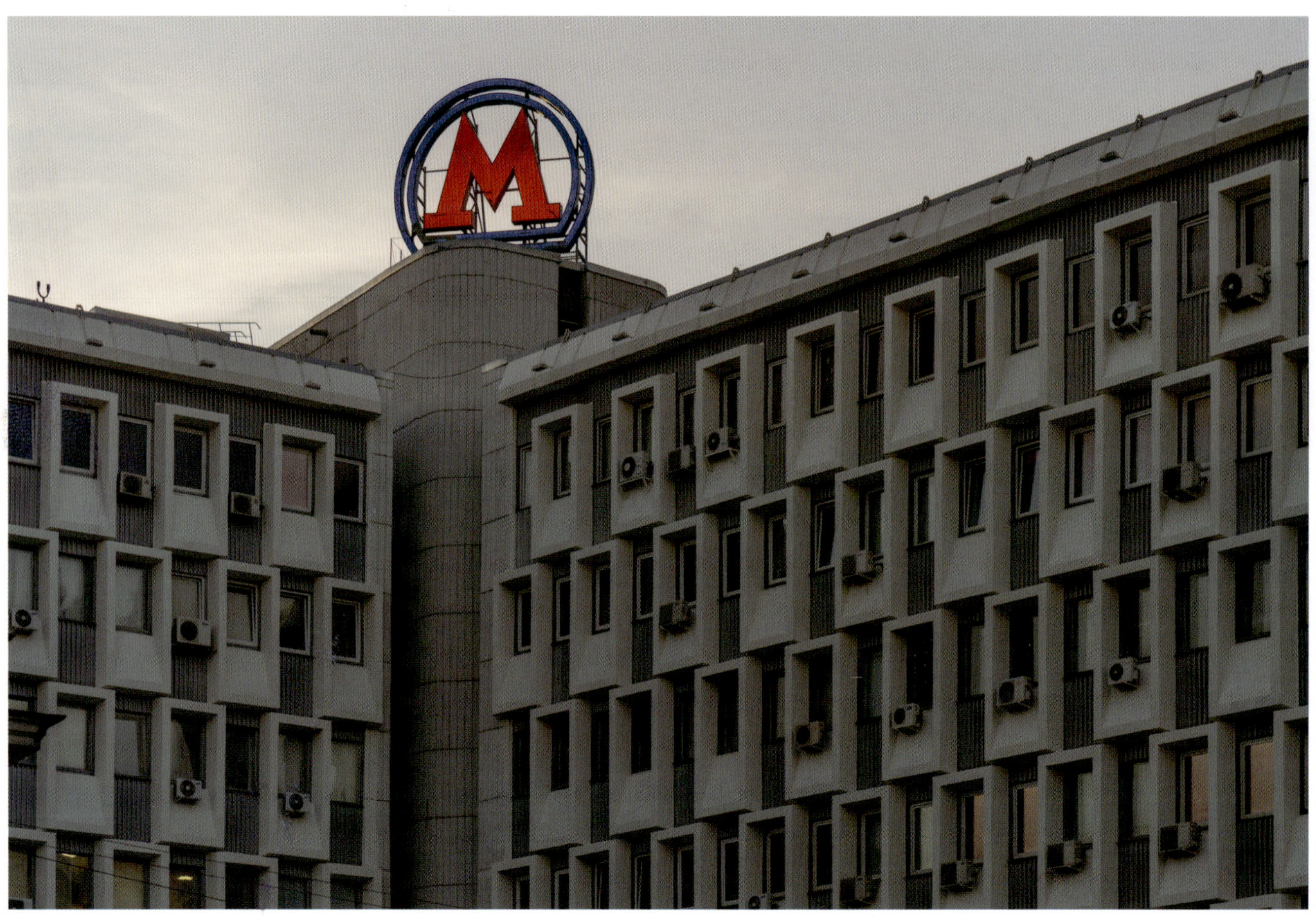

210   Prospekt Mira Metro Offices, MOSCOW

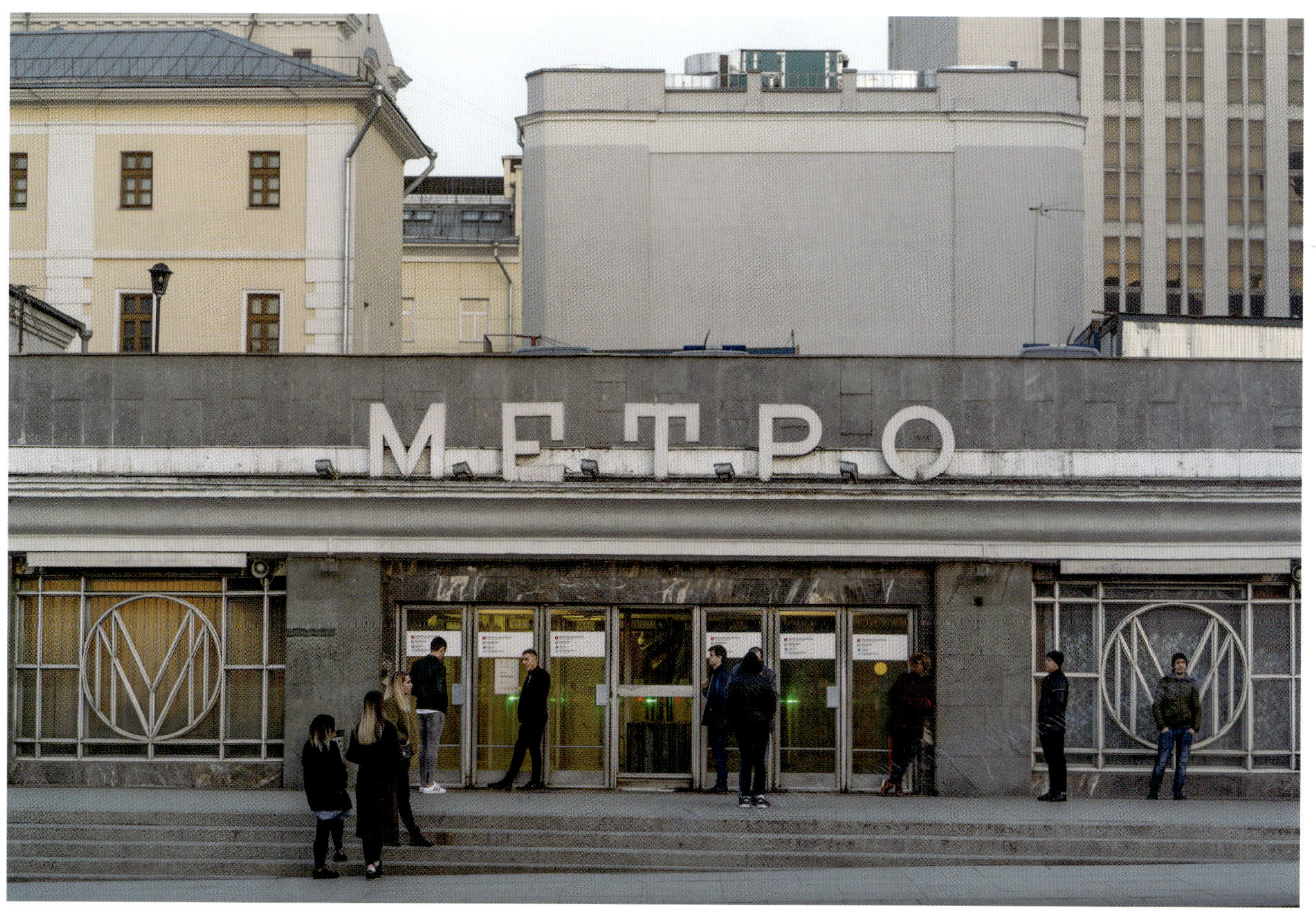

Biblioteka Imeni Lenina, MOSCOW   211

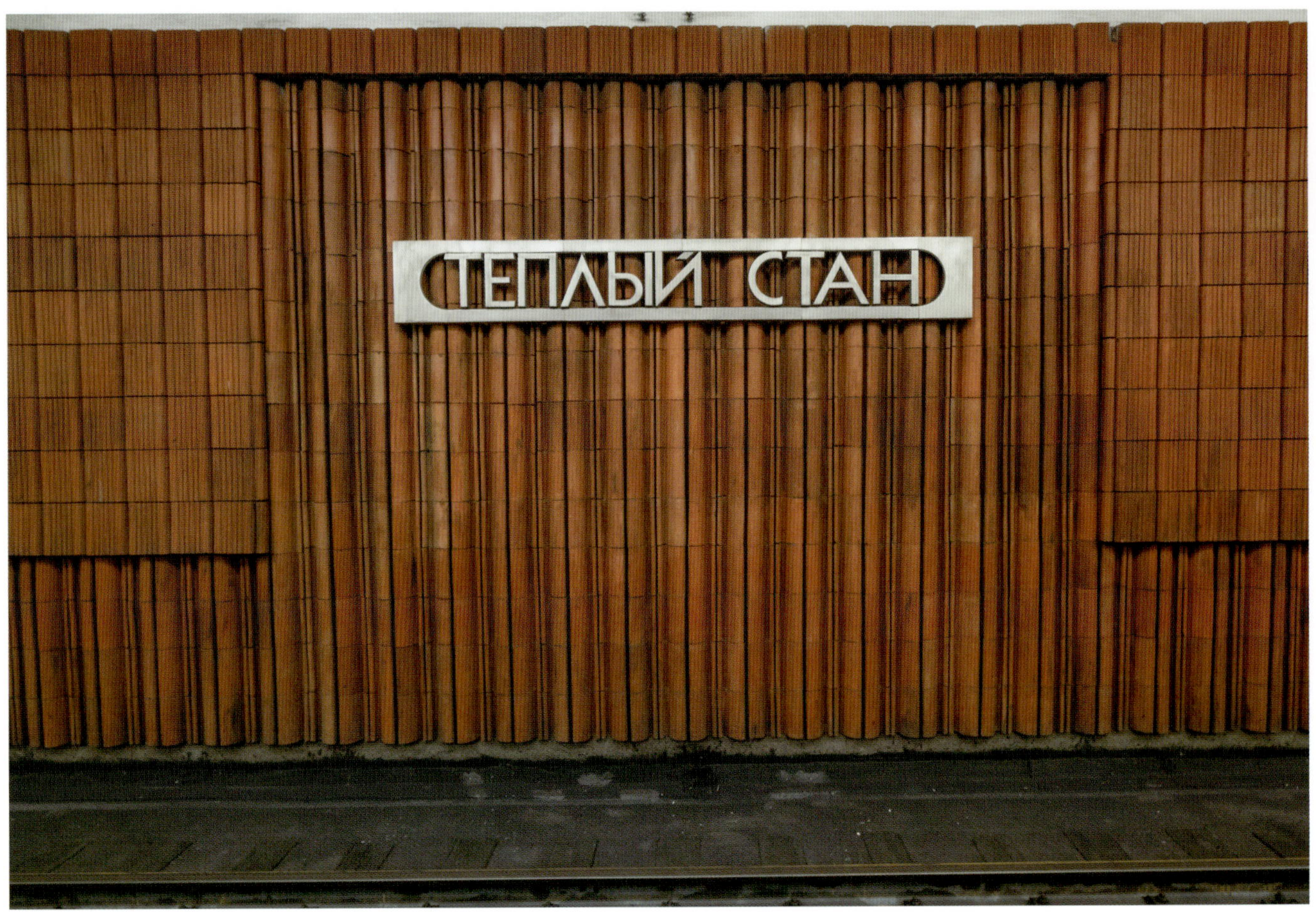

212   Tyoply Stan, MOSCOW

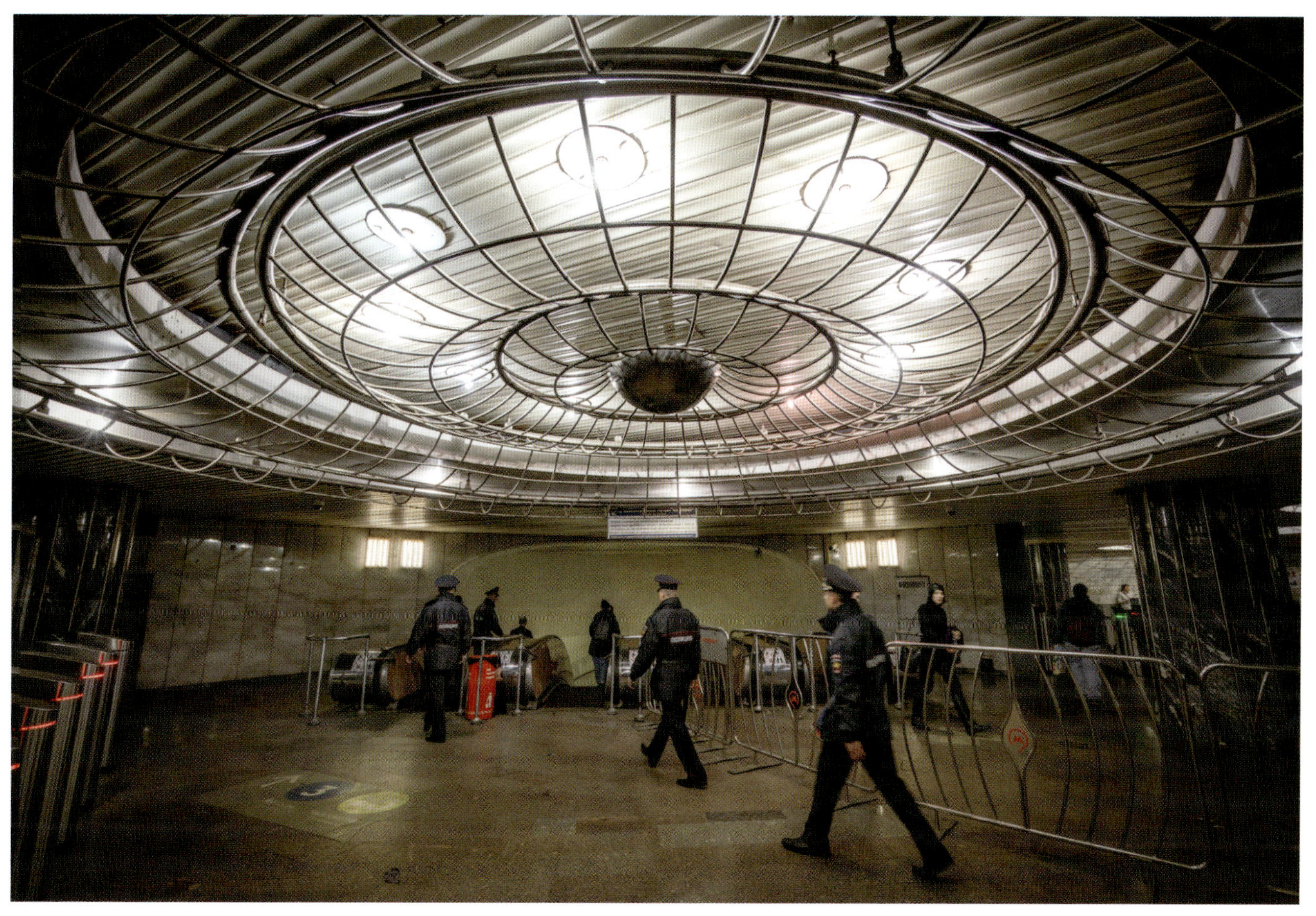

Kurskaya, MOSCOW   213

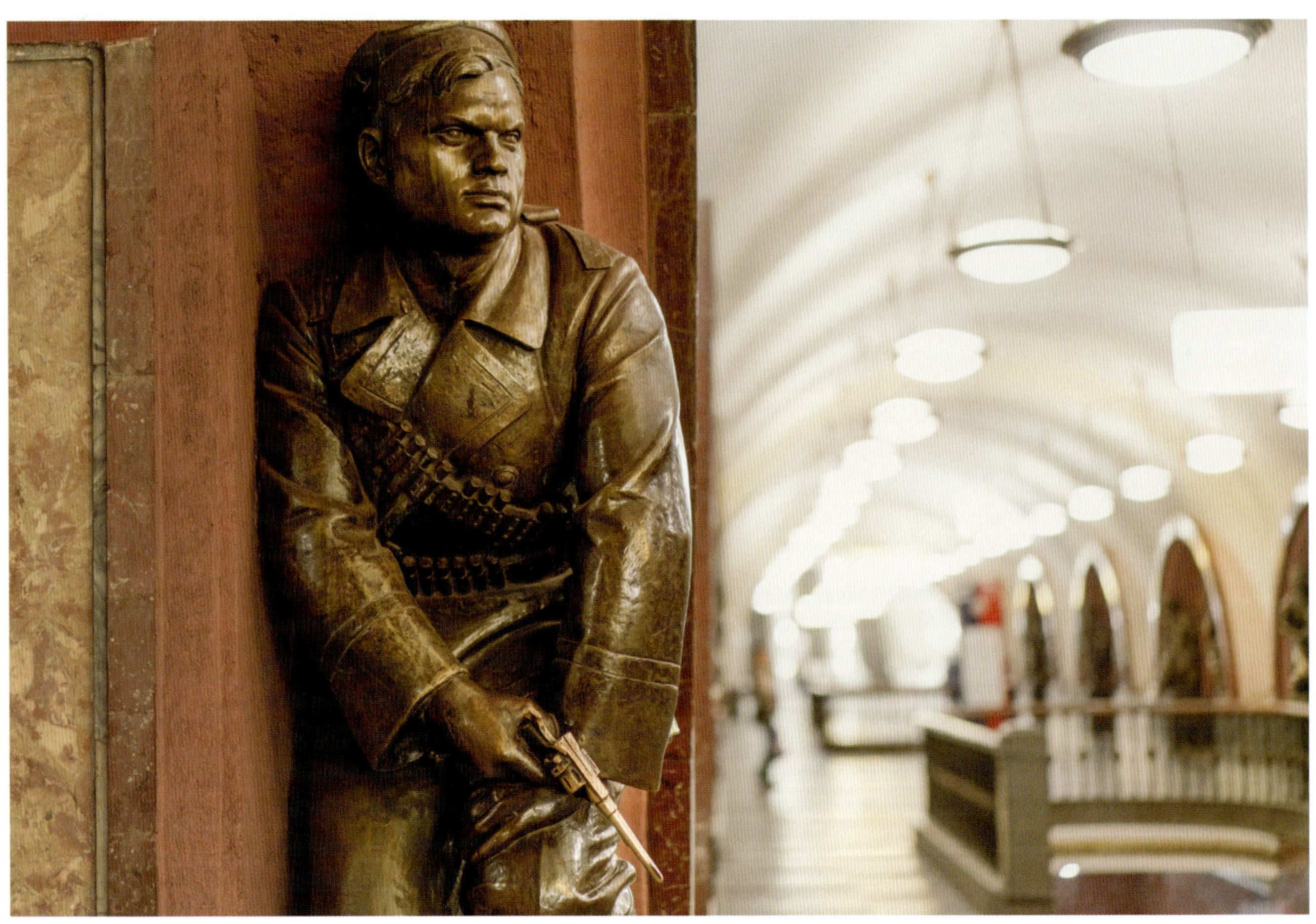

214   Ploshchad Revolyutsii, MOSCOW

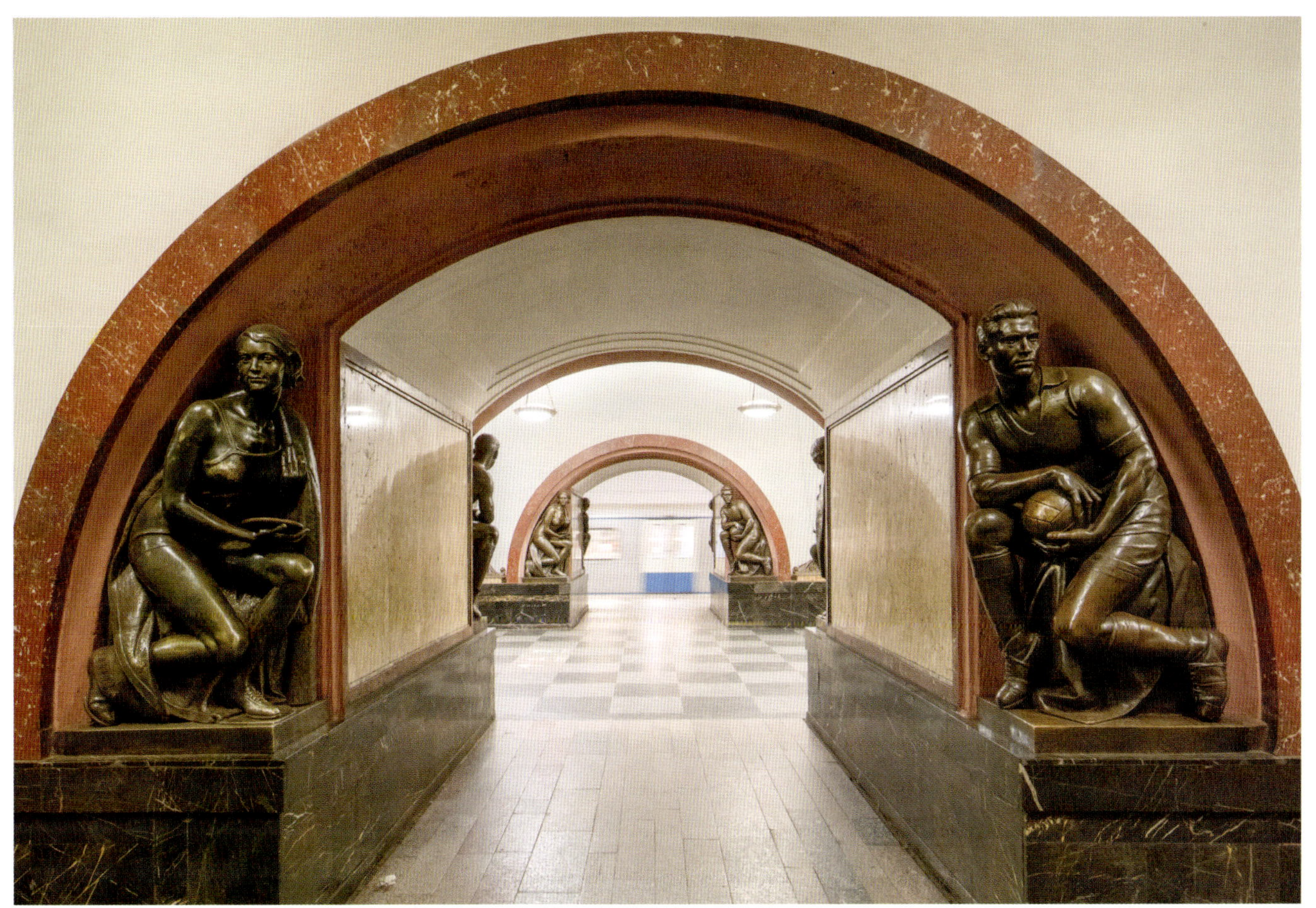

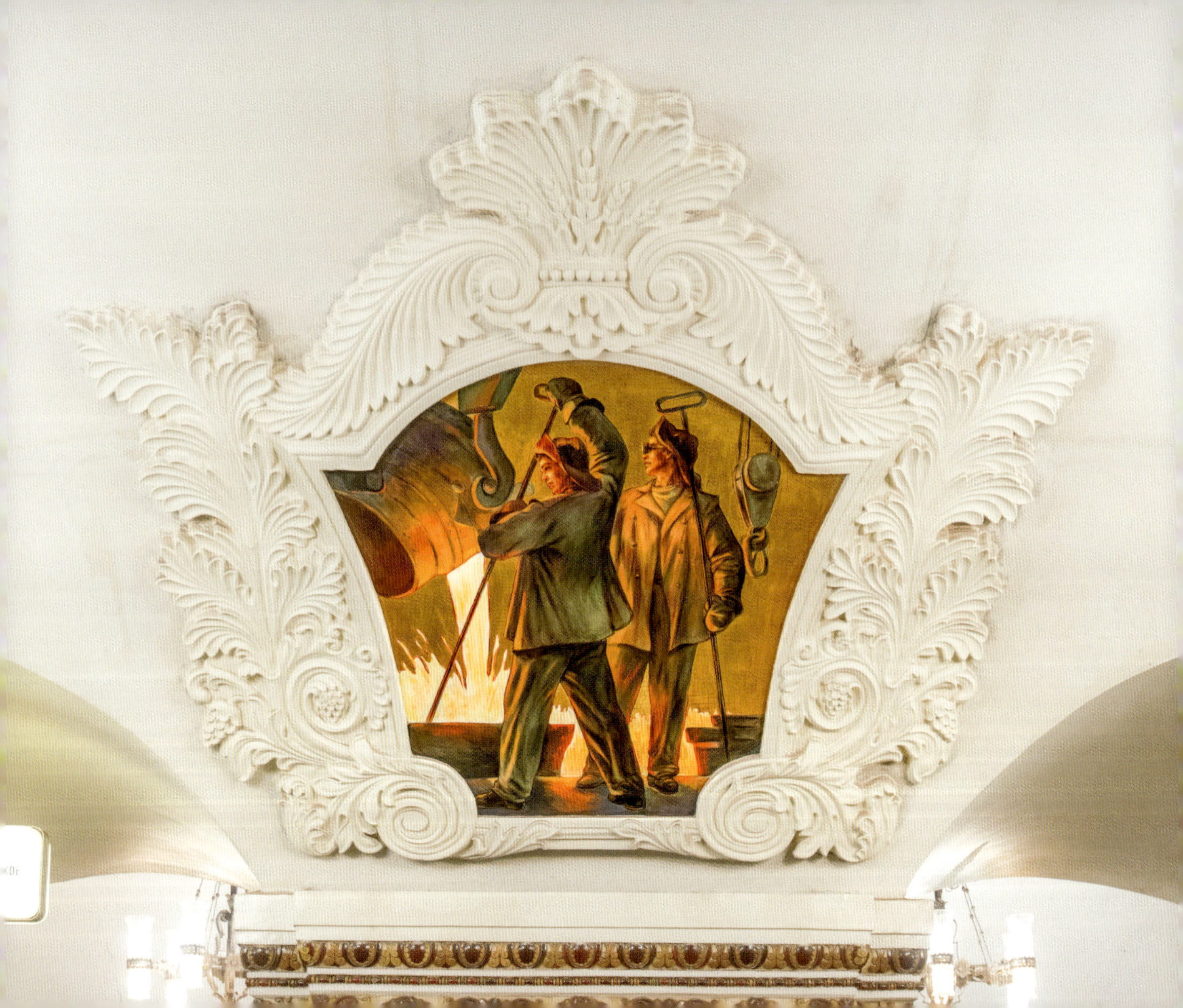

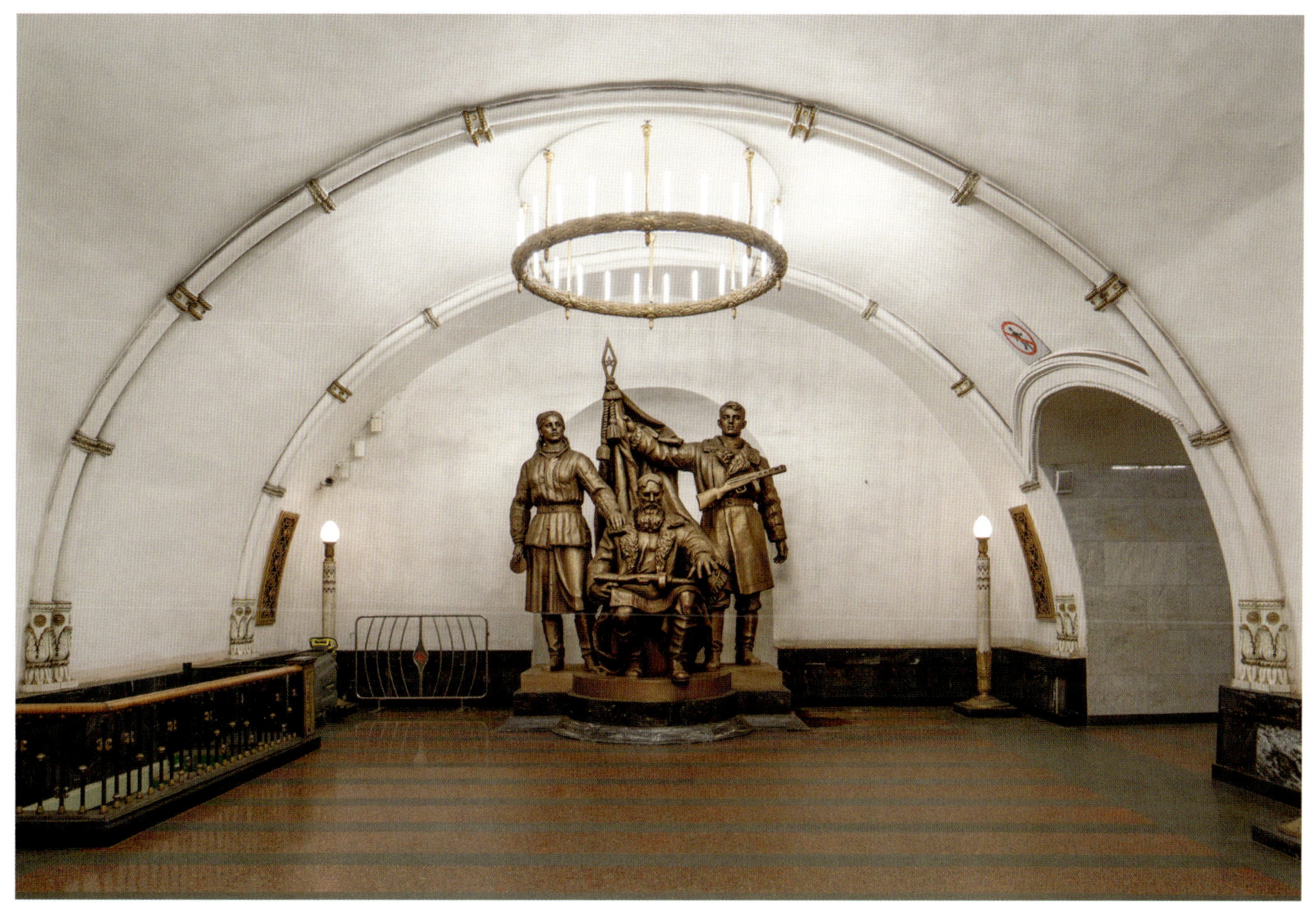

Belorusskaya, MOSCOW

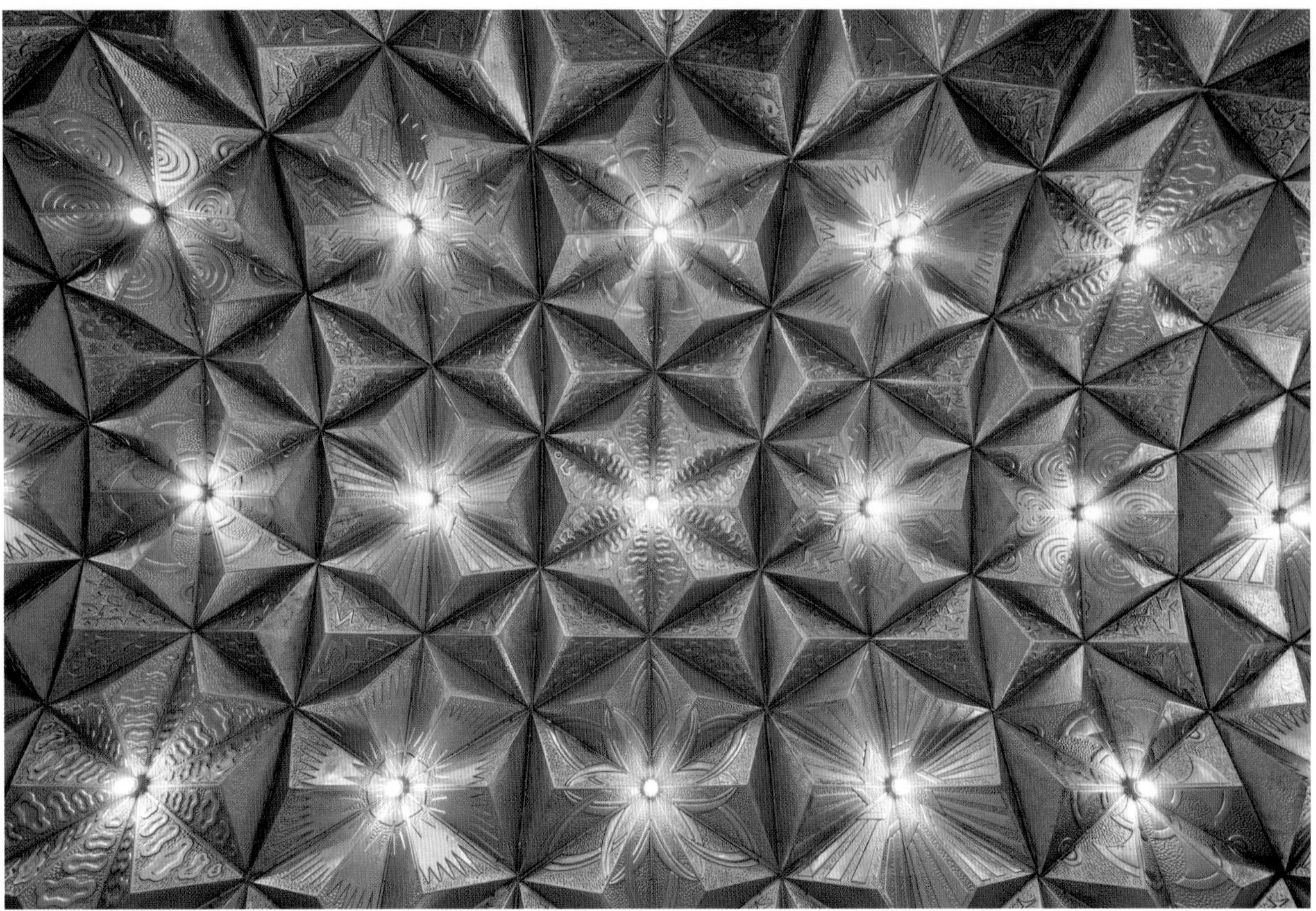

  Aviamotornaya, MOSCOW

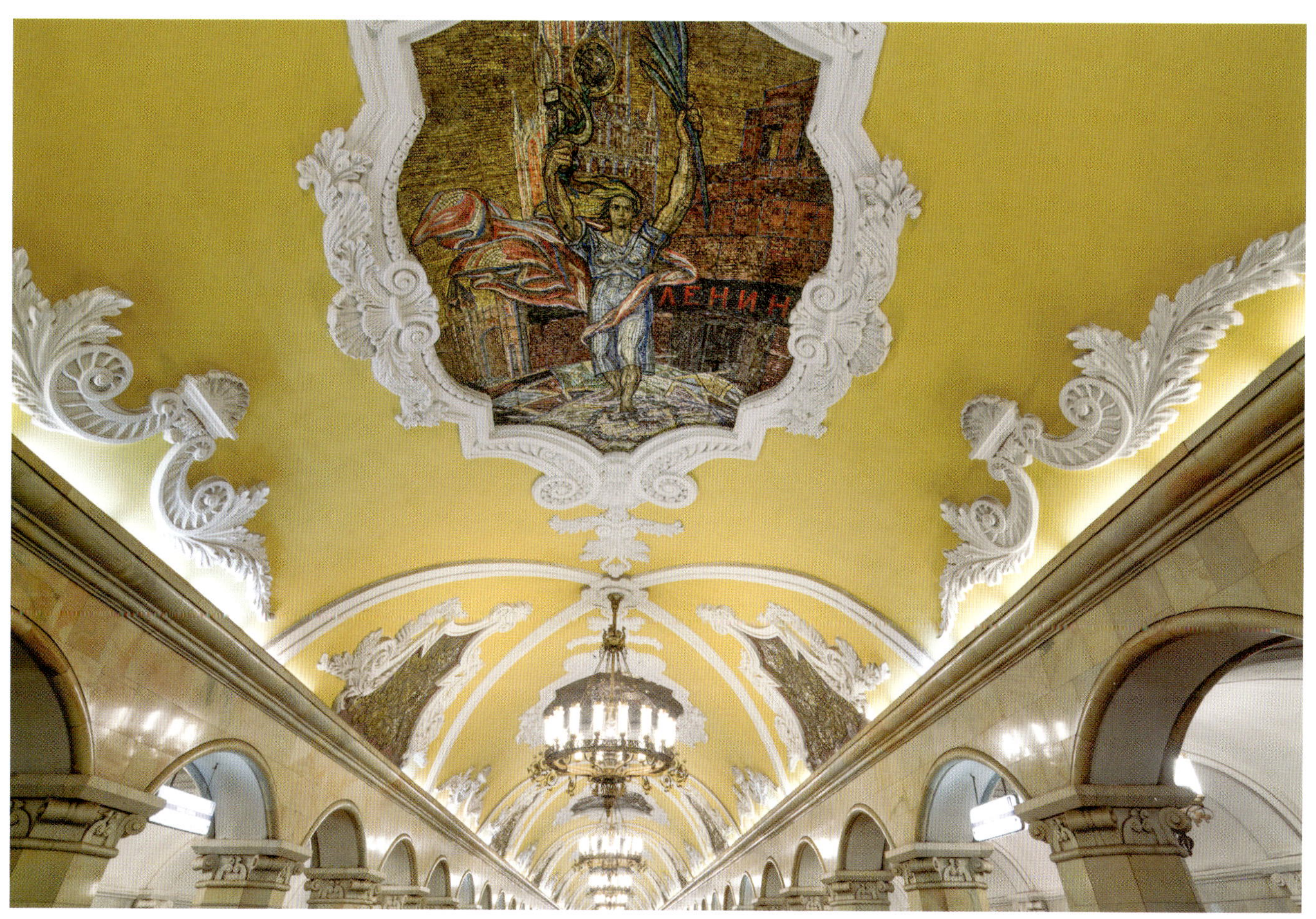

ЛЕНИН

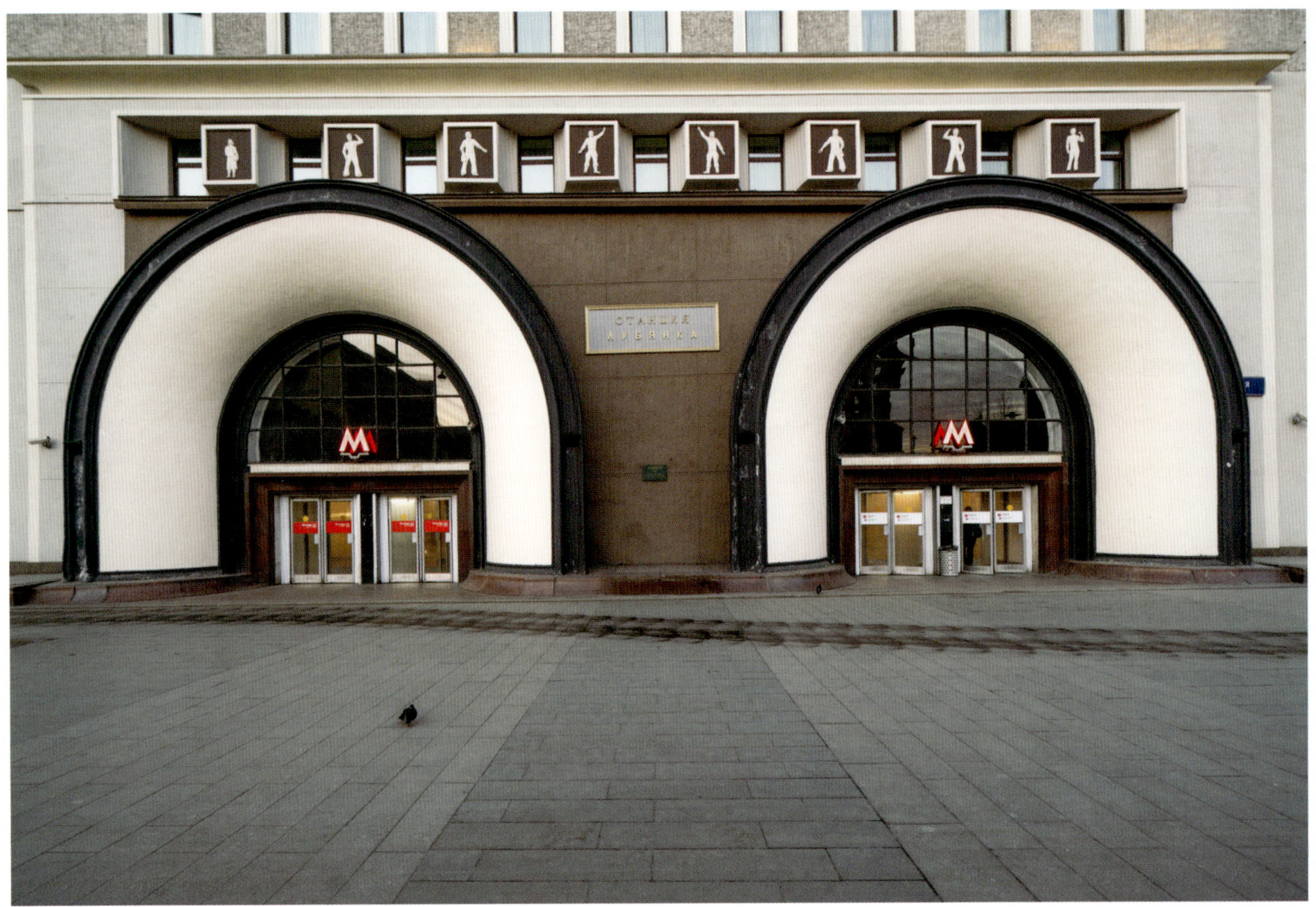

  Lubyanka, MOSCOW

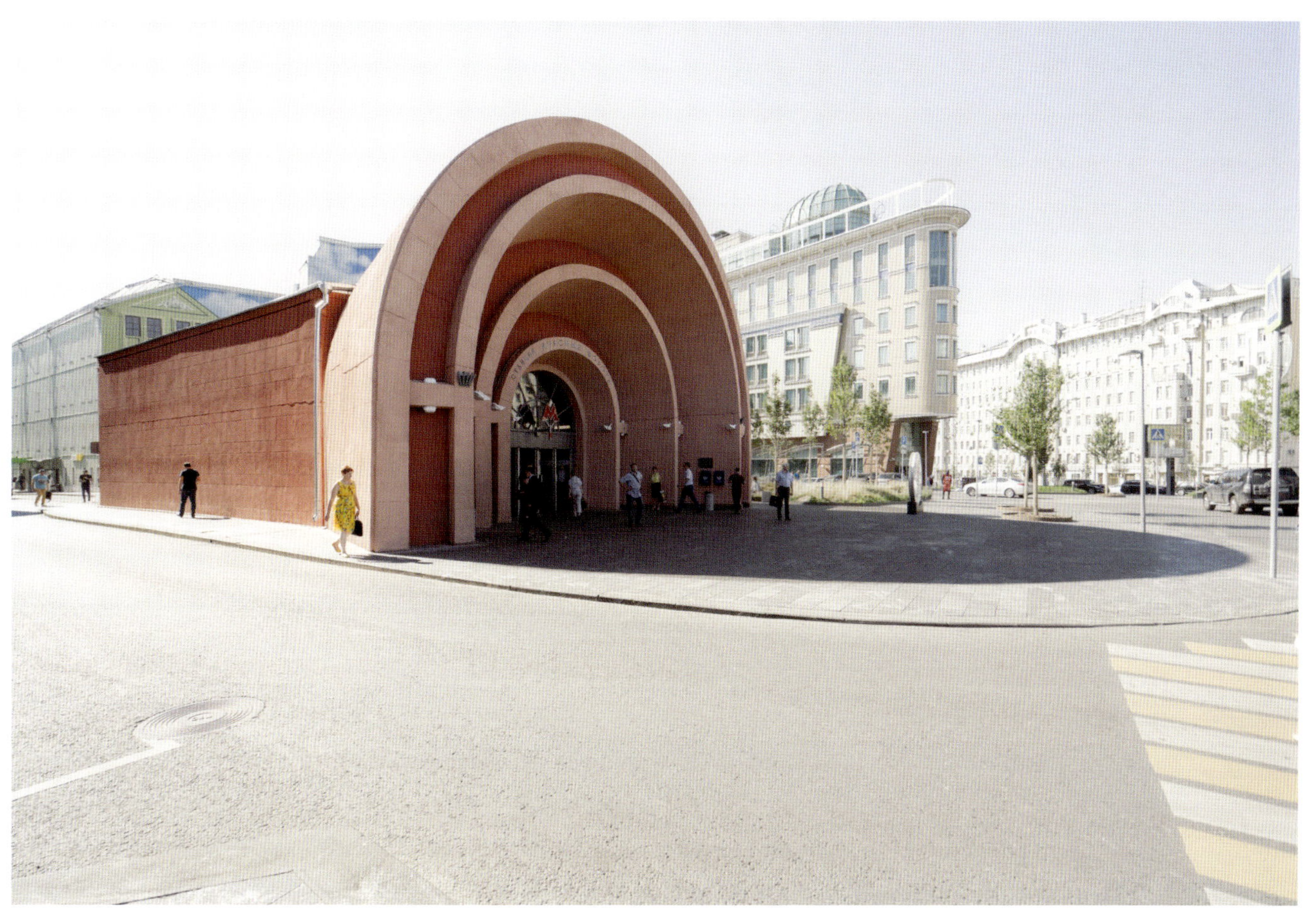

Krasnye Vorota, MOSCOW   221

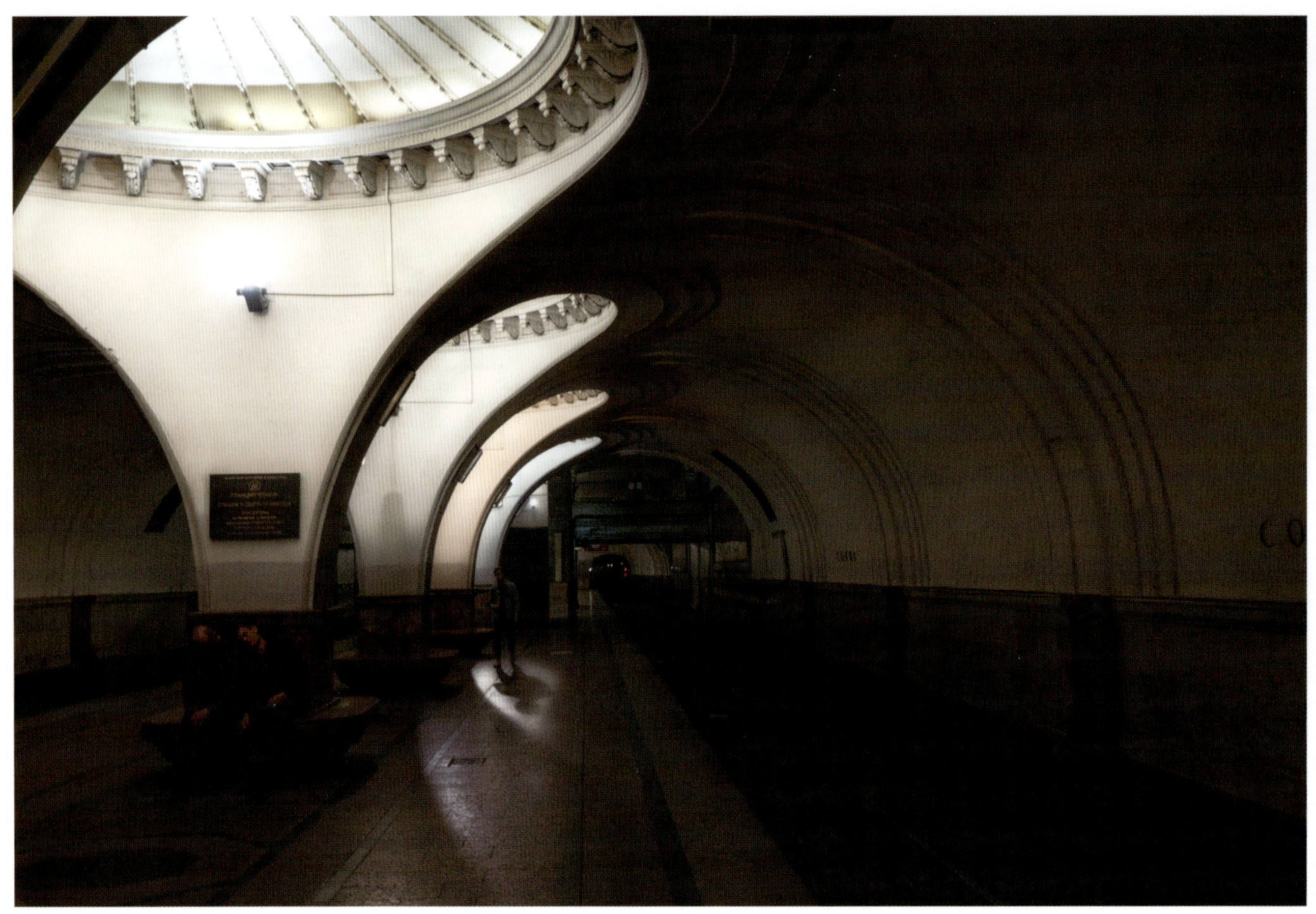

222   Sokol, MOSCOW

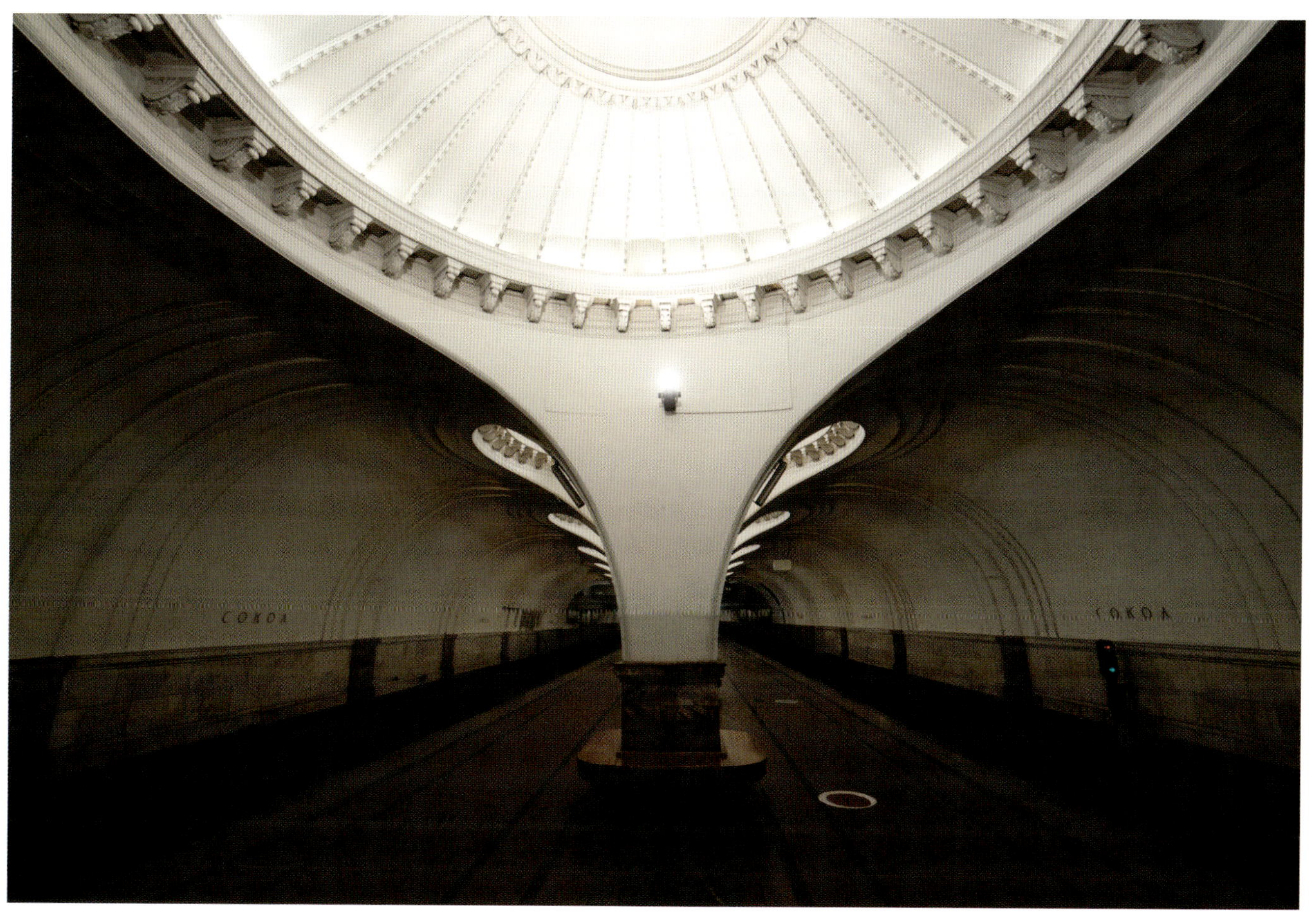

СОКОЛ
СОКОЛ

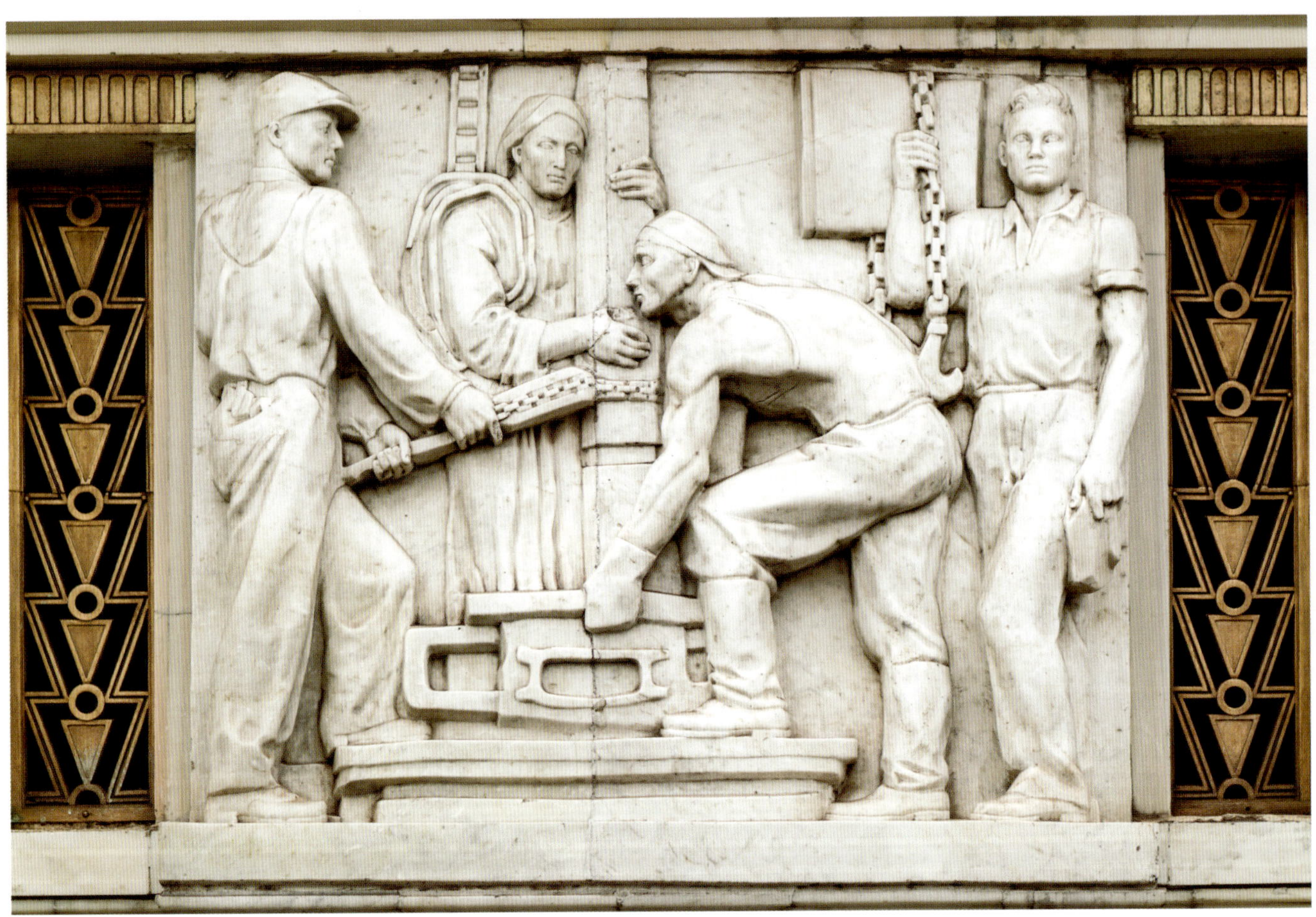

  Elektrozavodskaya, MOSCOW

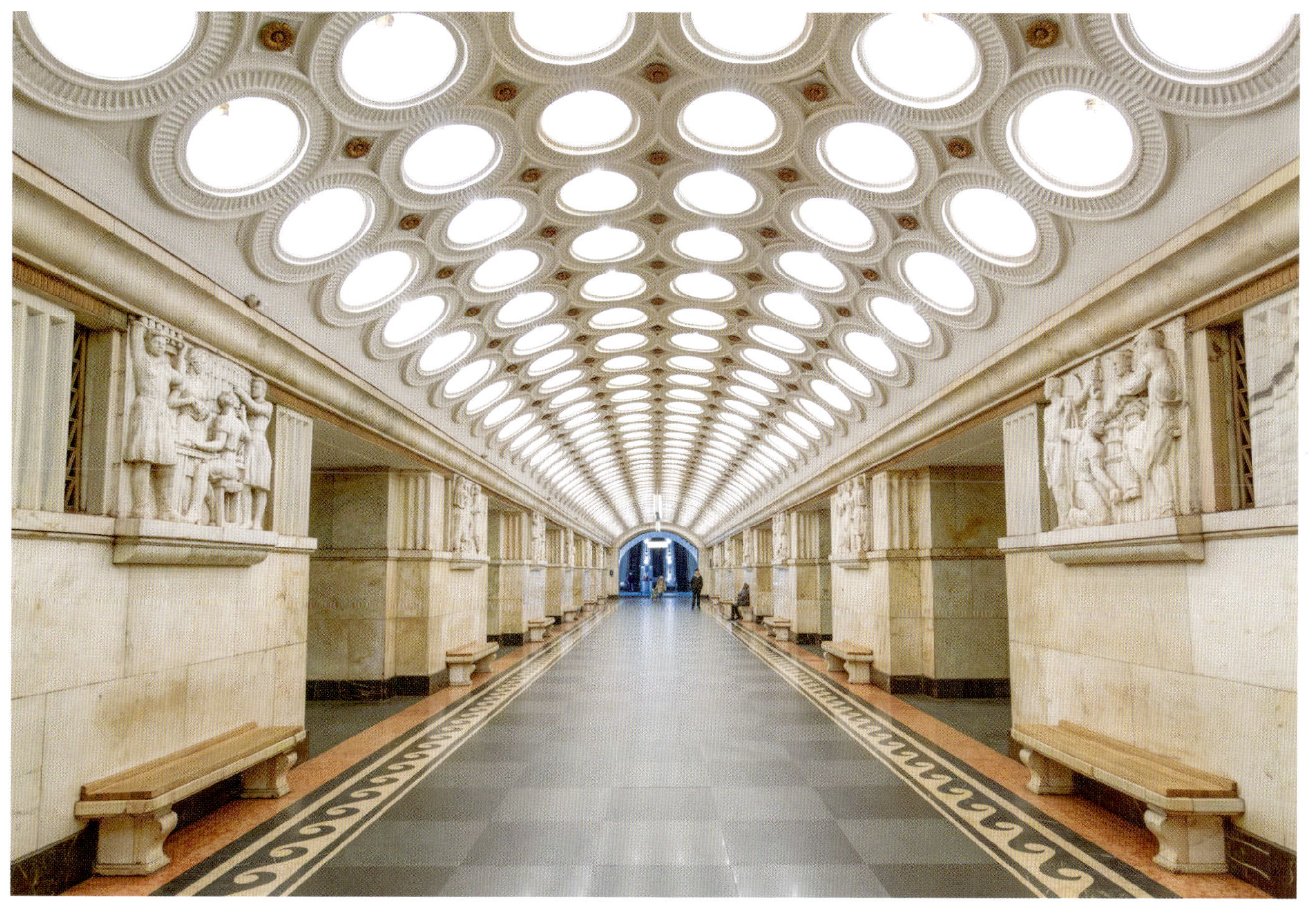

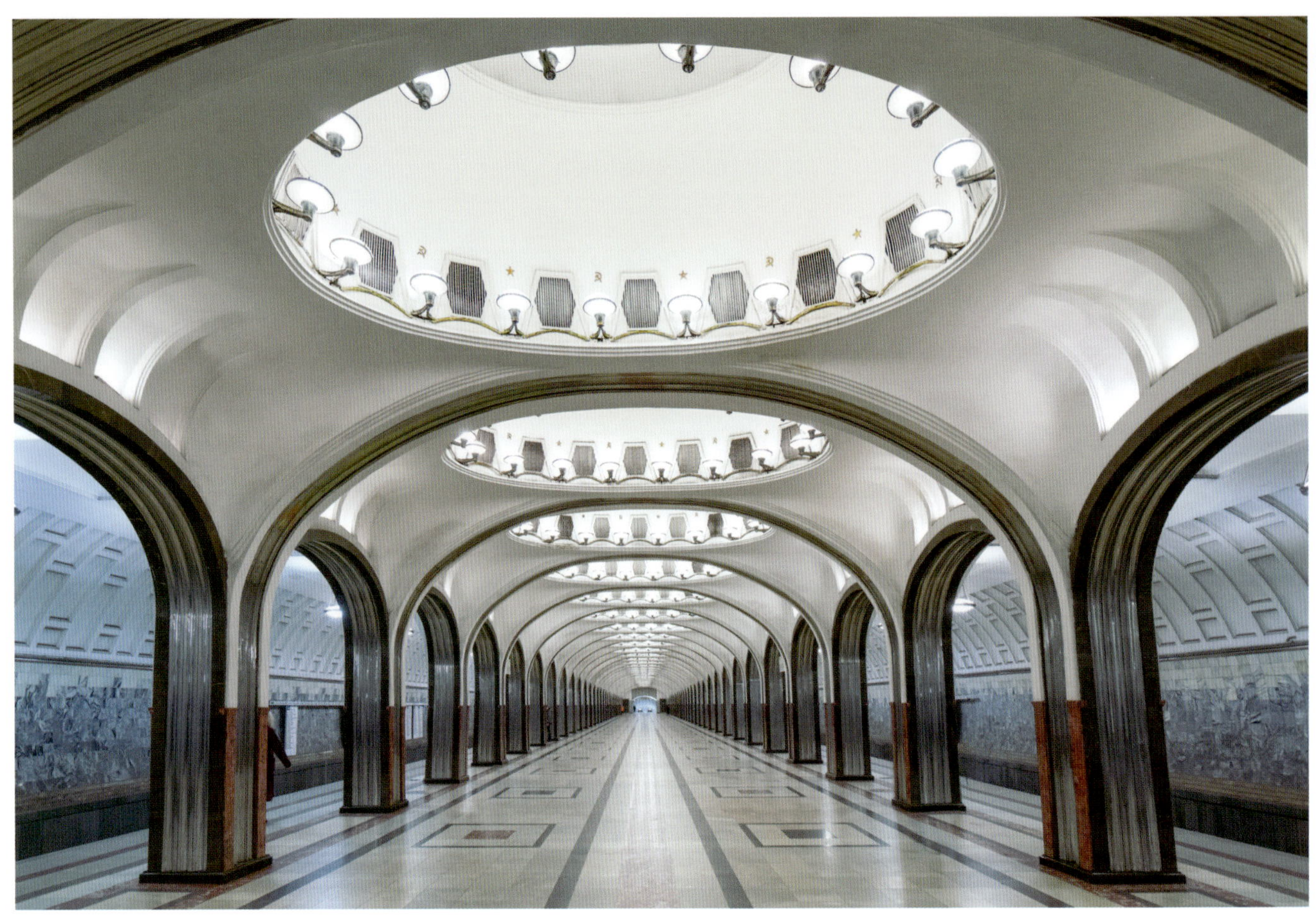

226   Mayakovskaya, MOSCOW

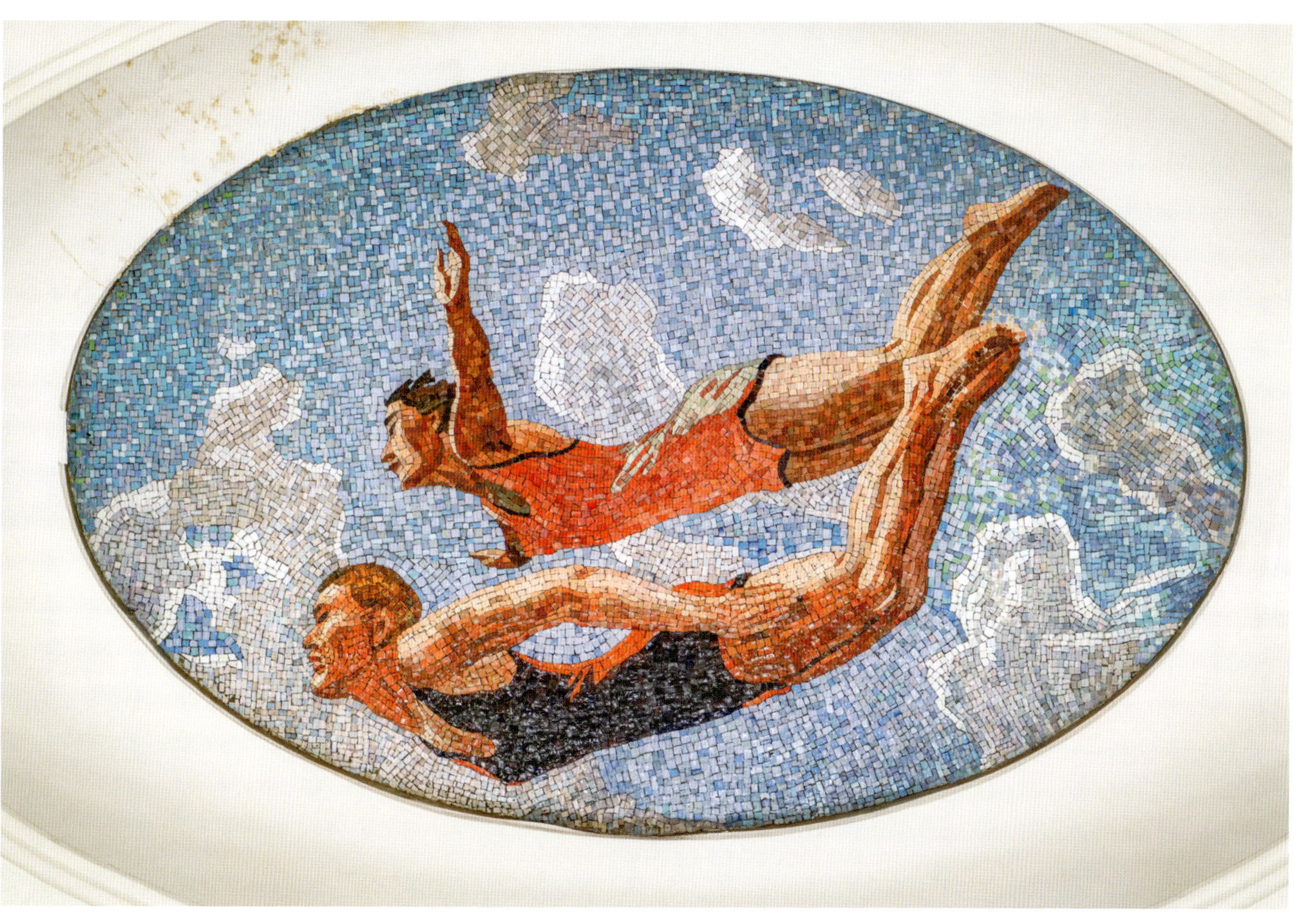

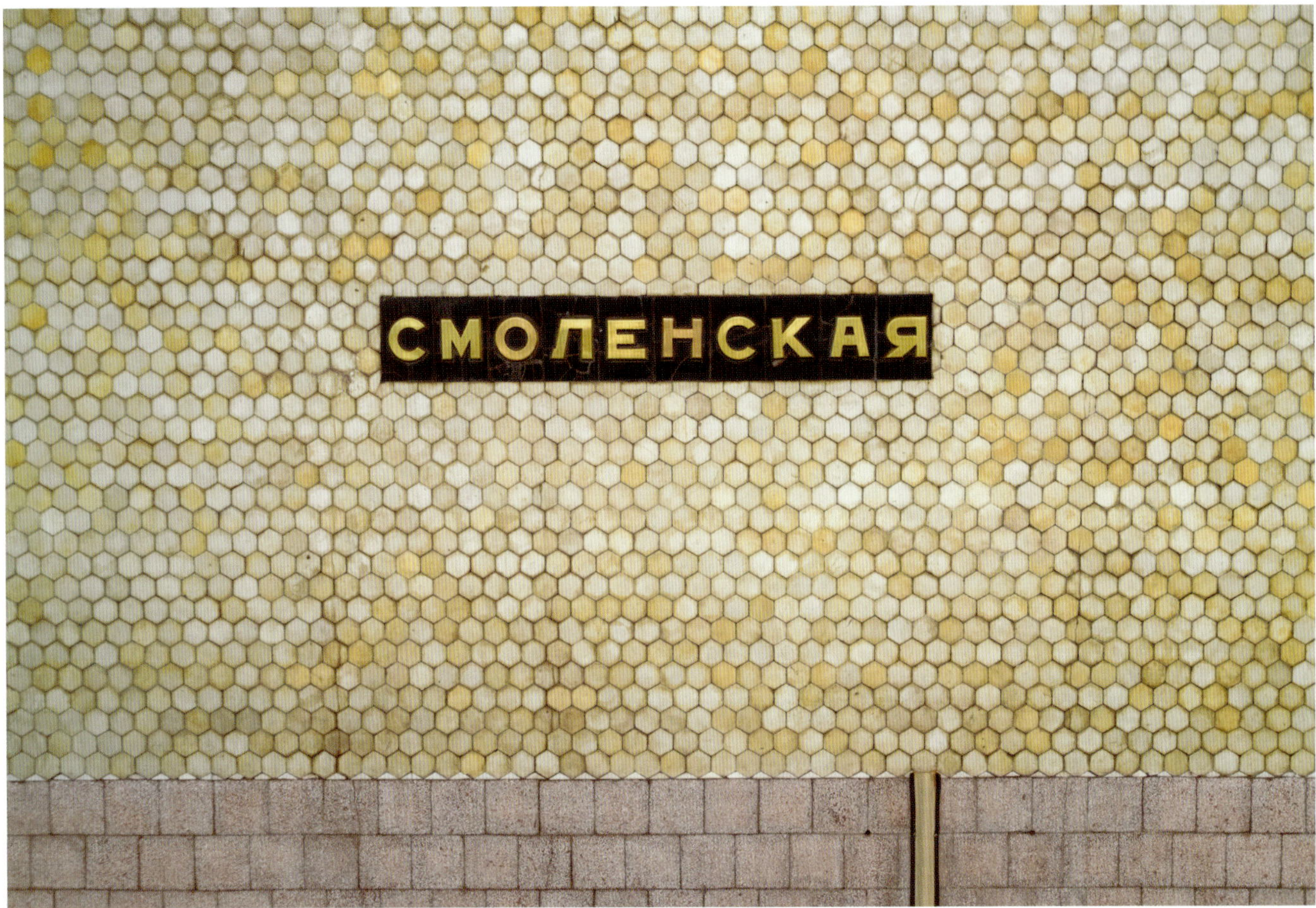

228   Smolenskaya, MOSCOW

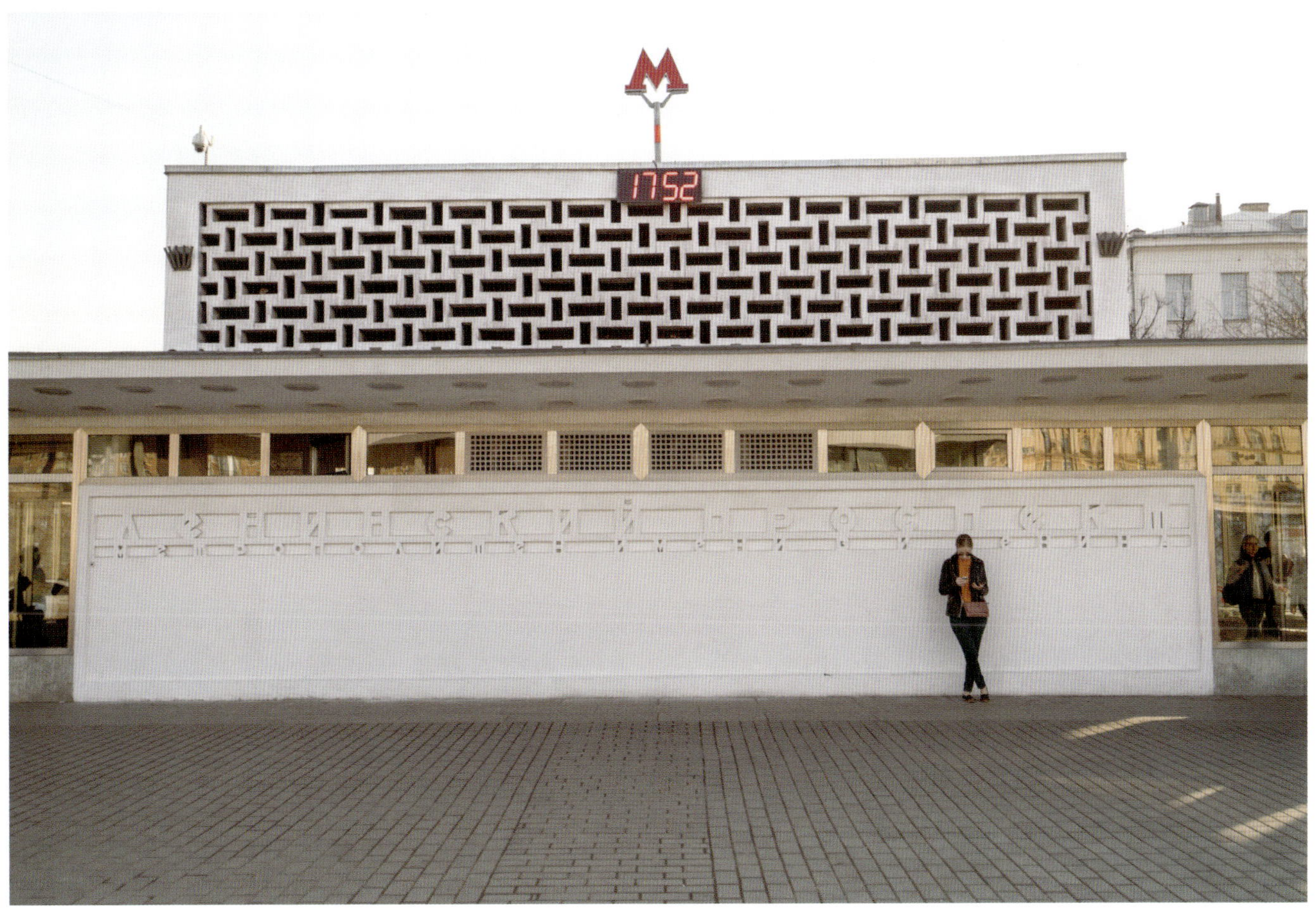

Leninsky Prospekt, MOSCOW   229

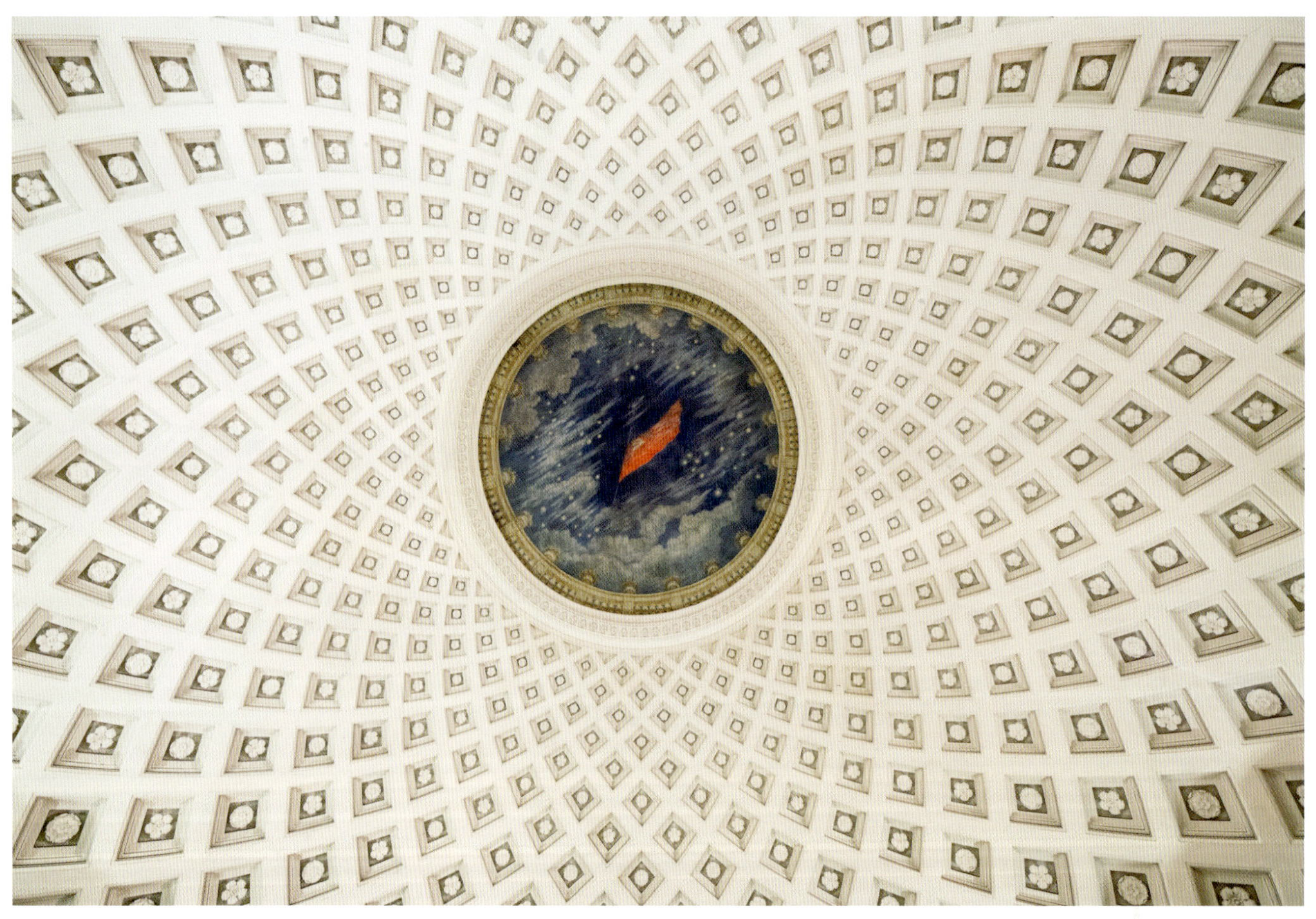

230   Taganskaya, MOSCOW

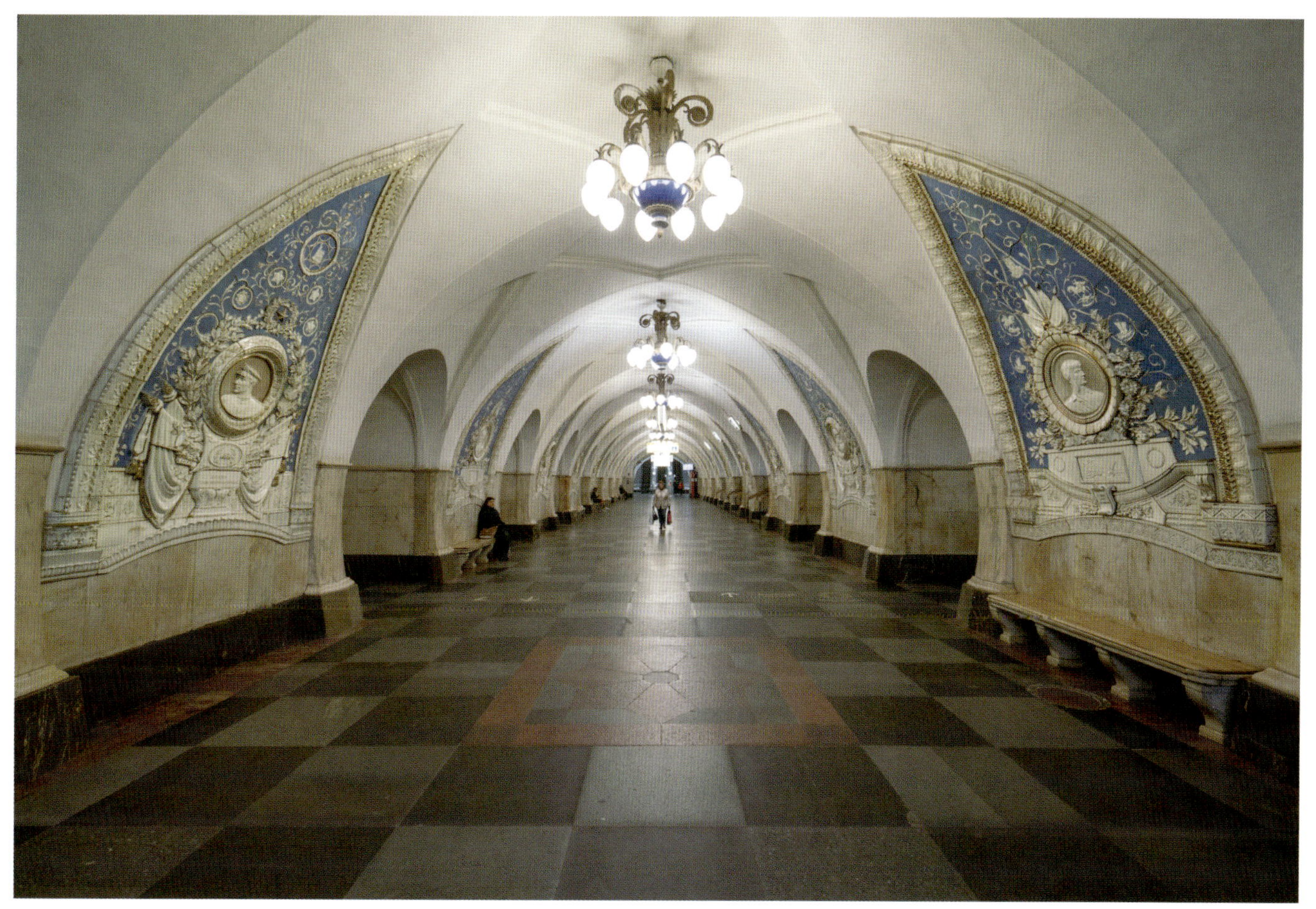

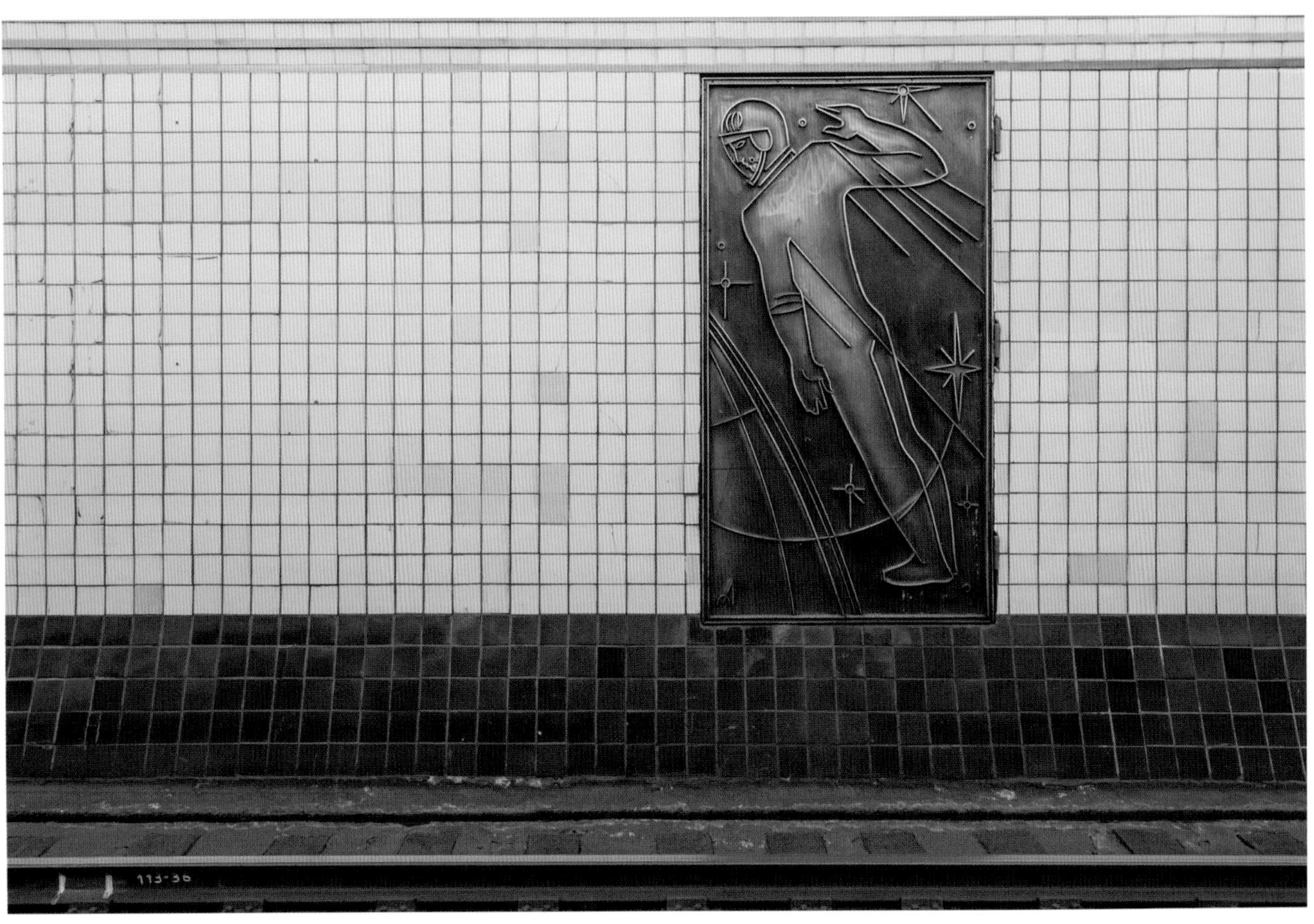

232   Taganskaya, MOSCOW

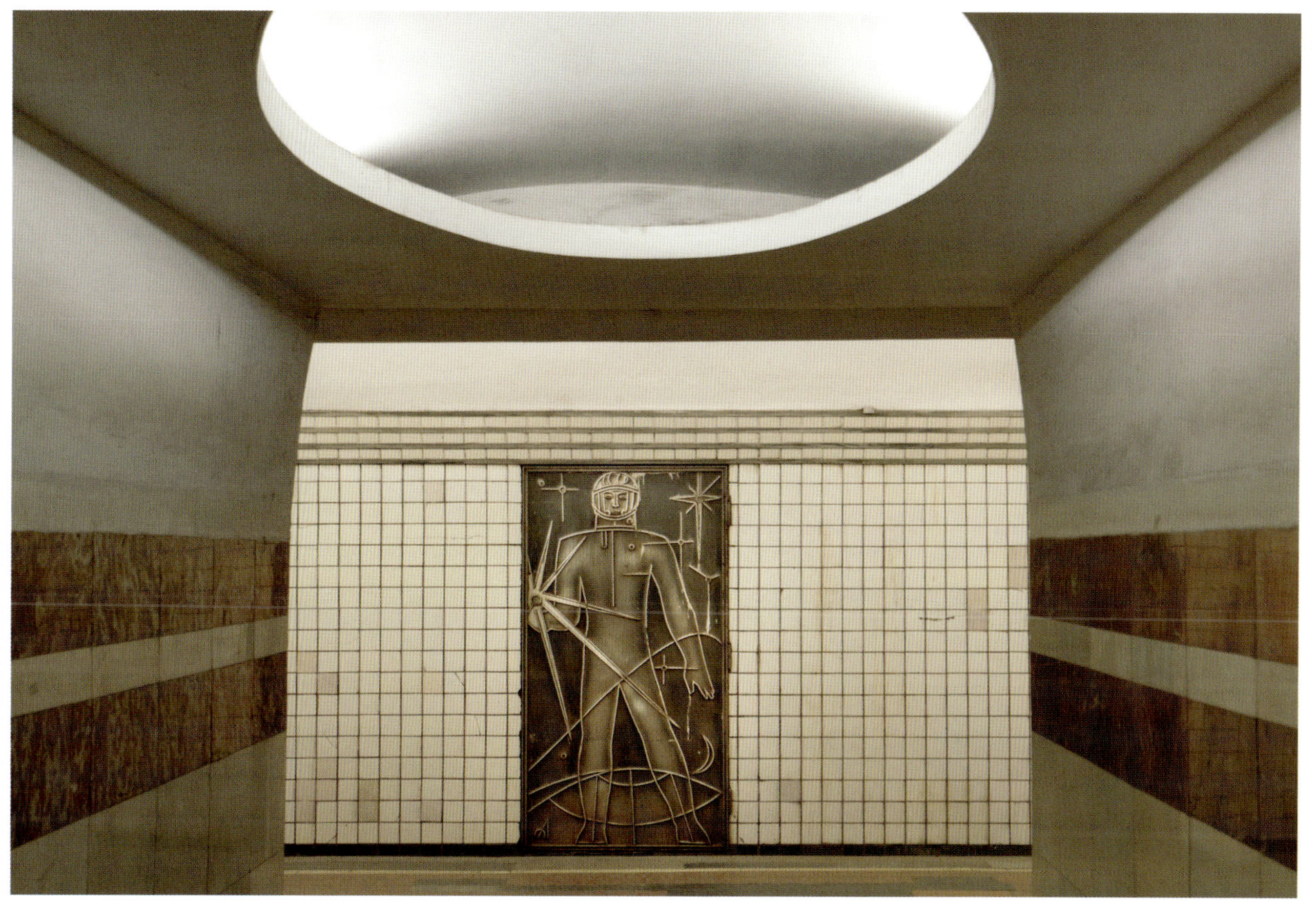

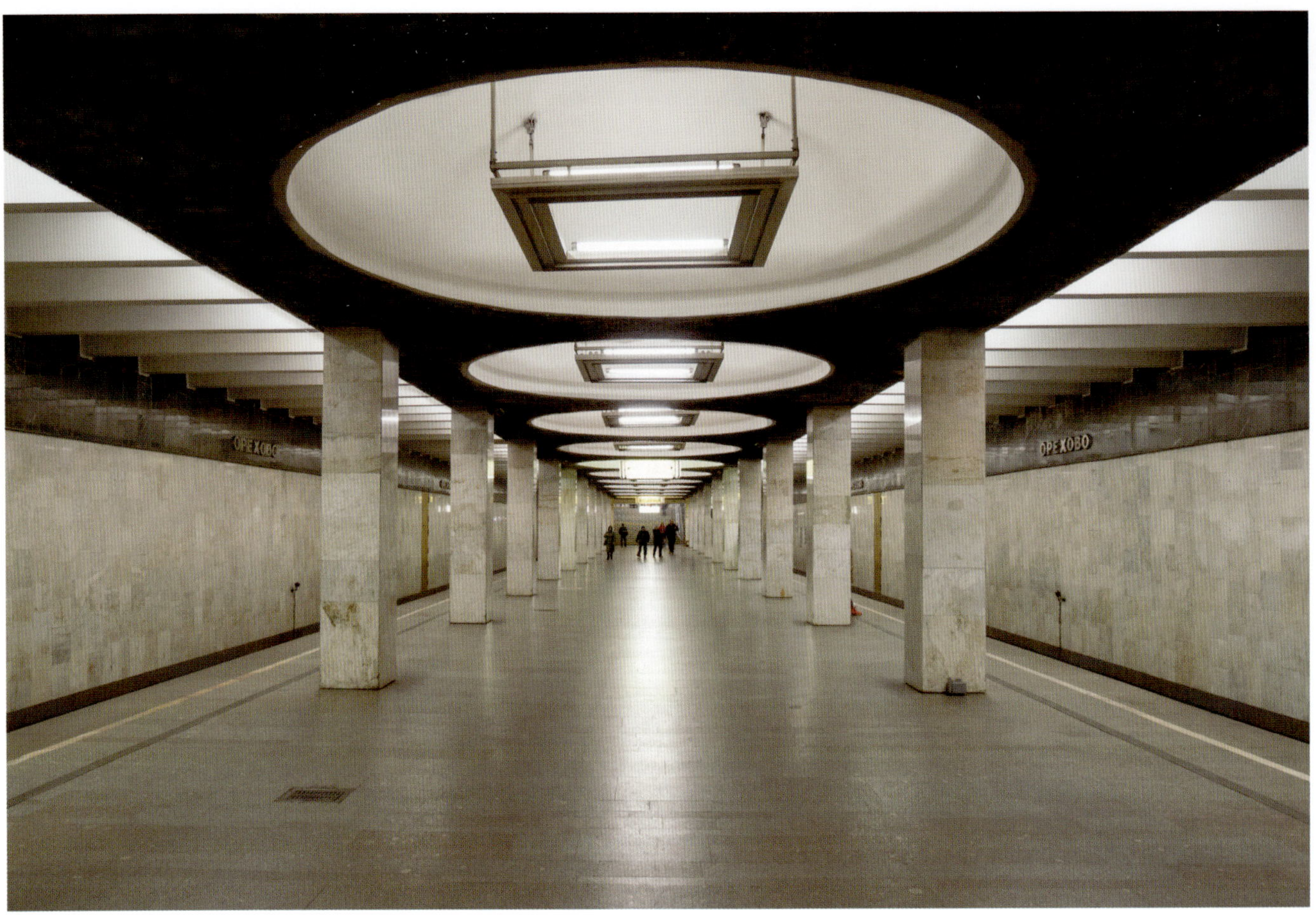

234   Orekhovo, MOSCOW

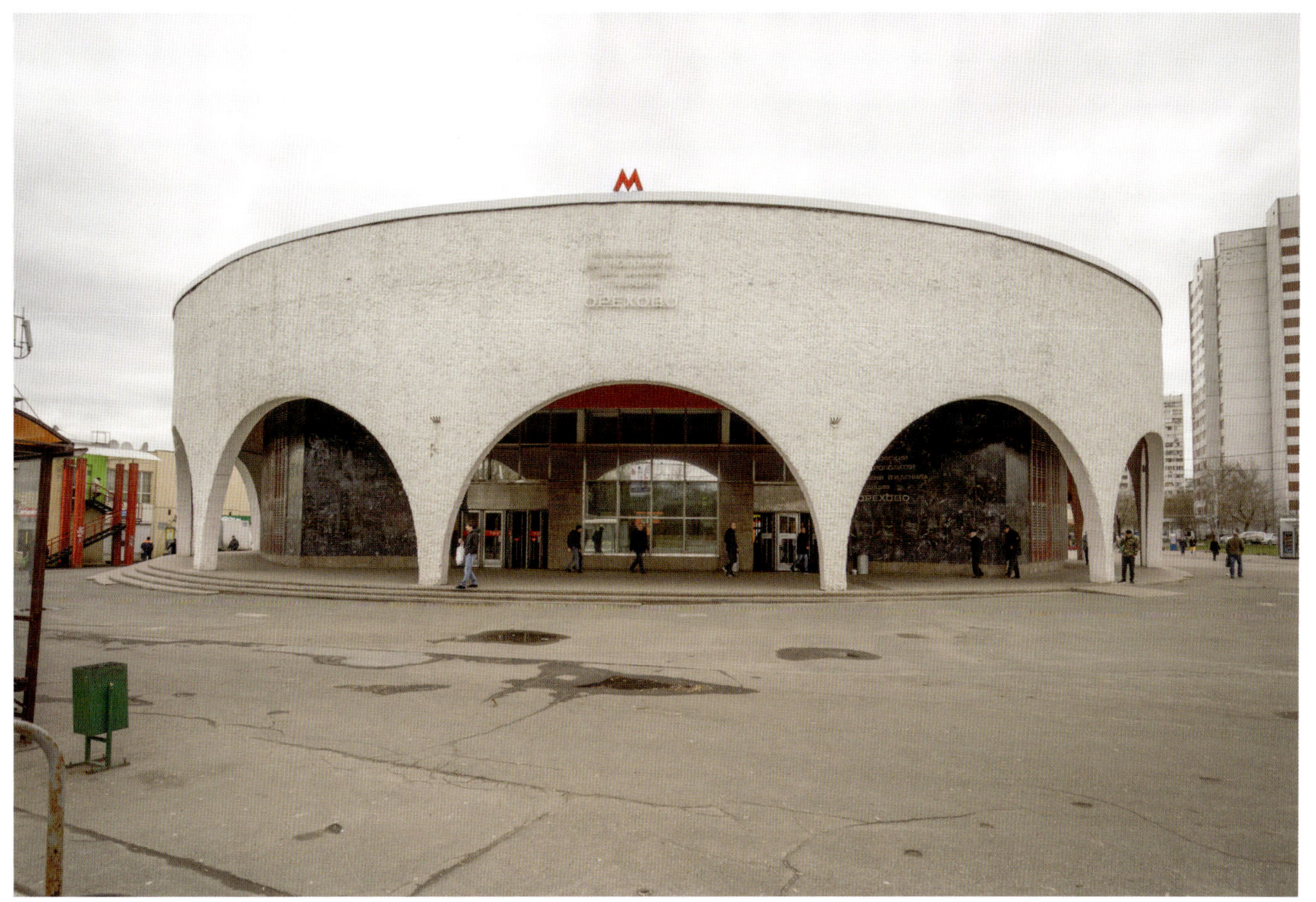

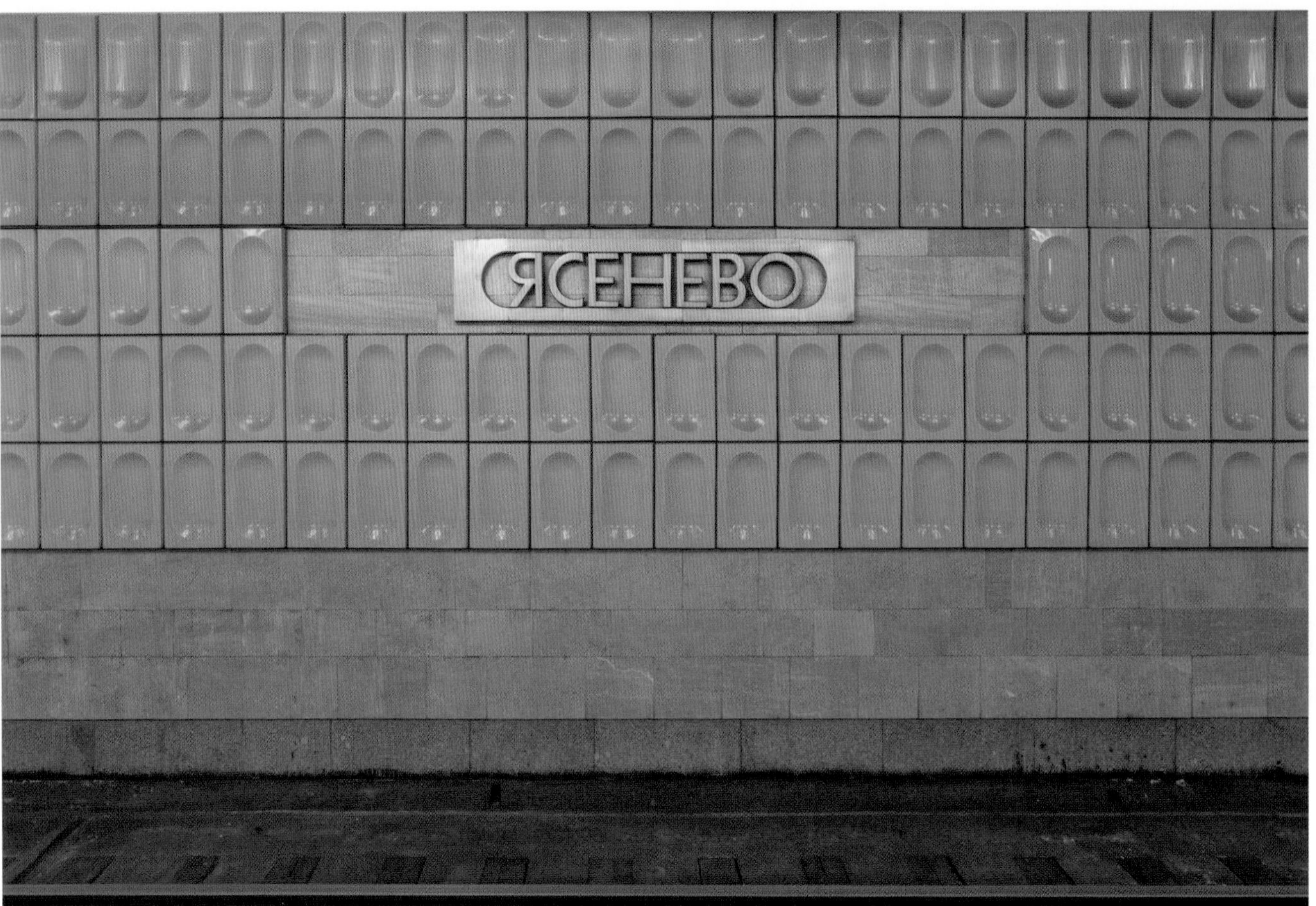

236 Yasenevo, MOSCOW

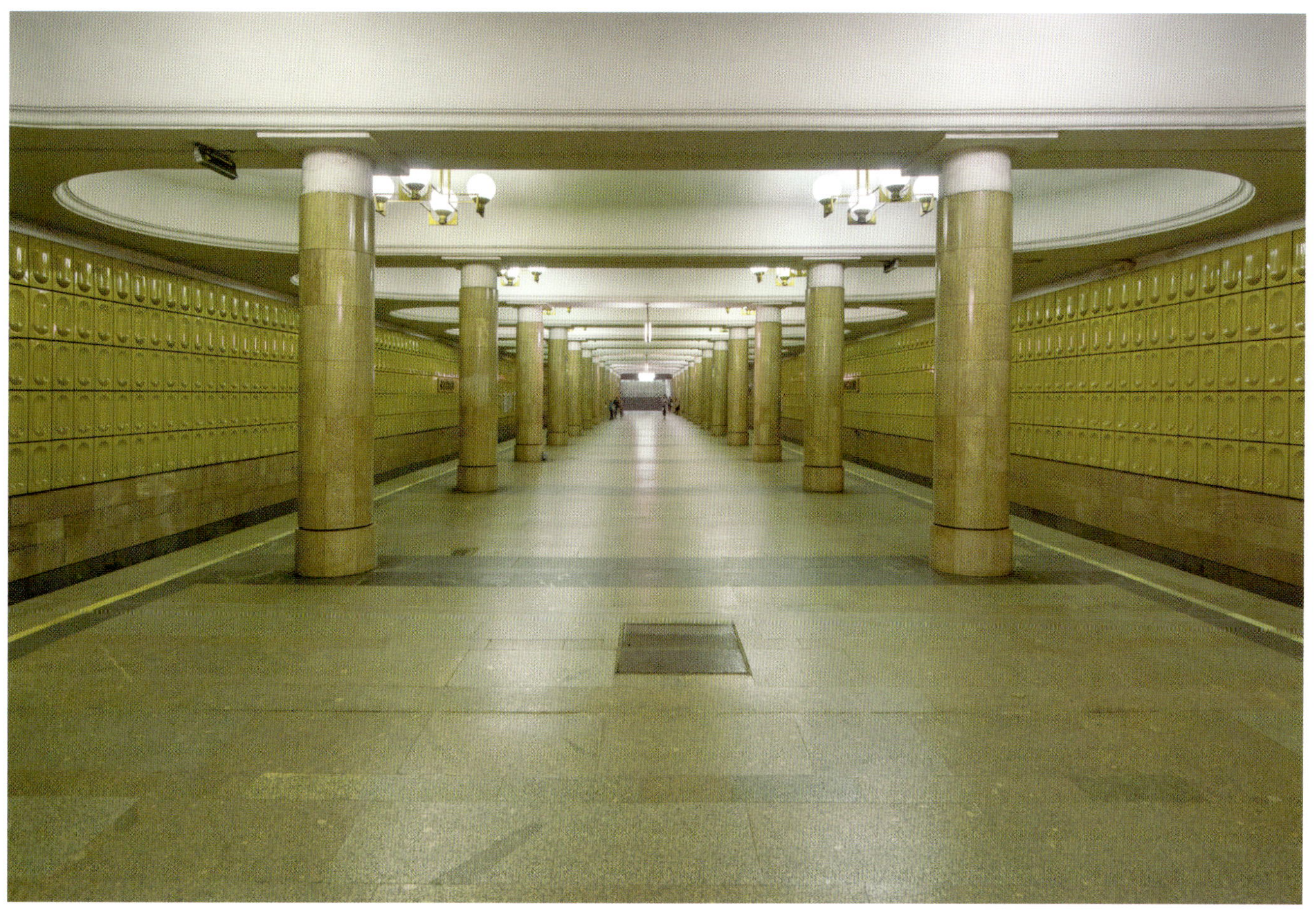

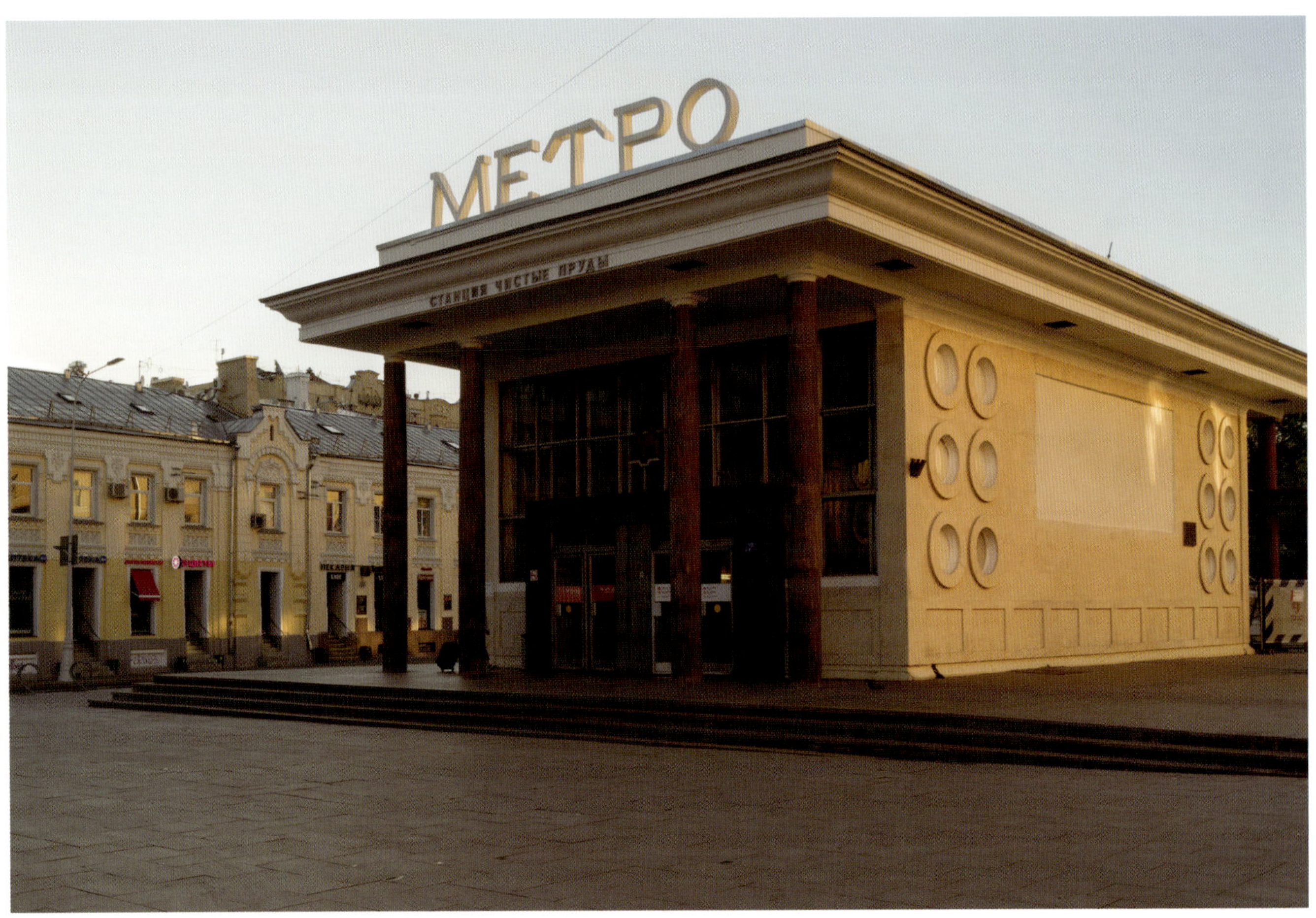

238   Chistyye Prudy, MOSCOW

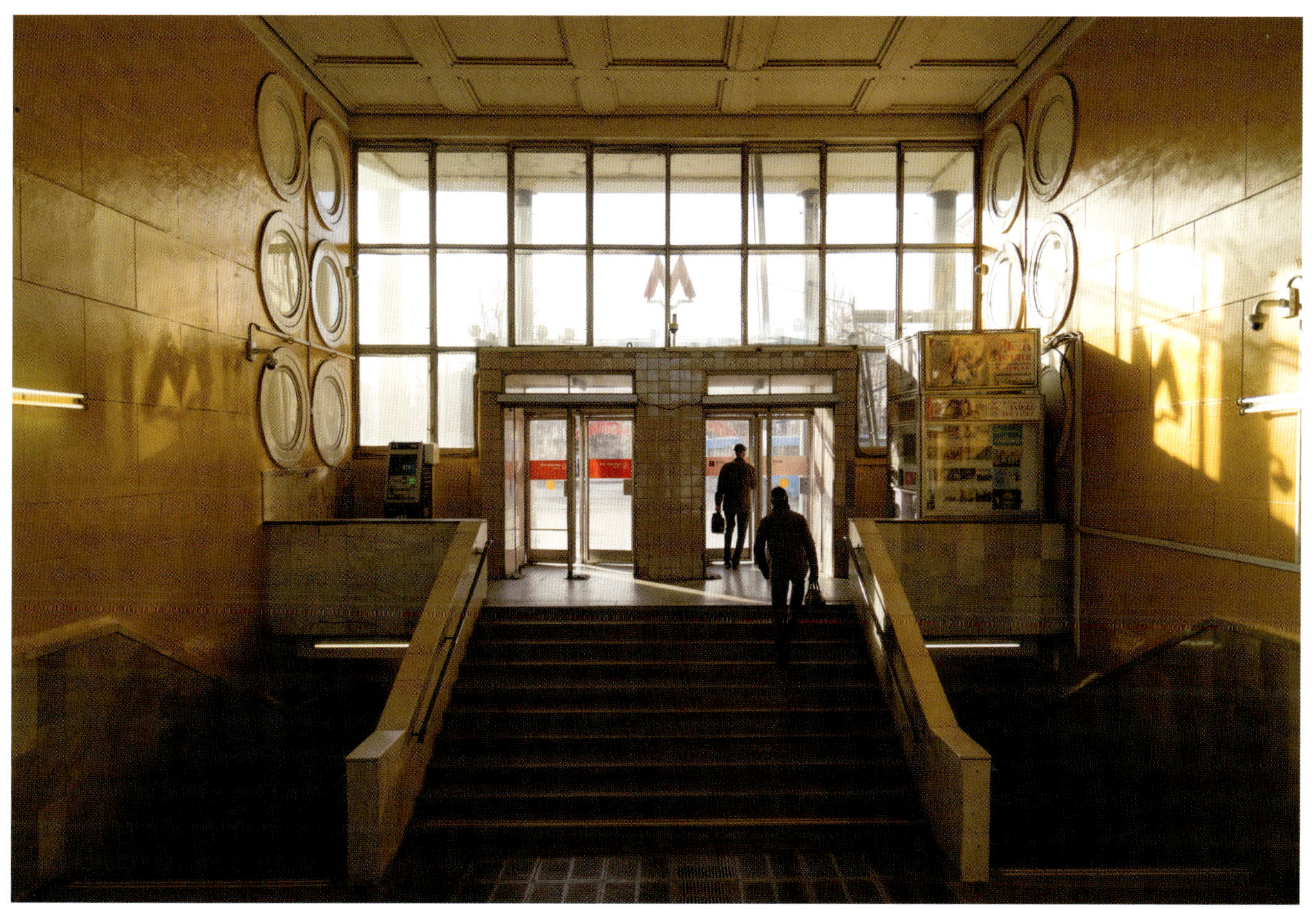

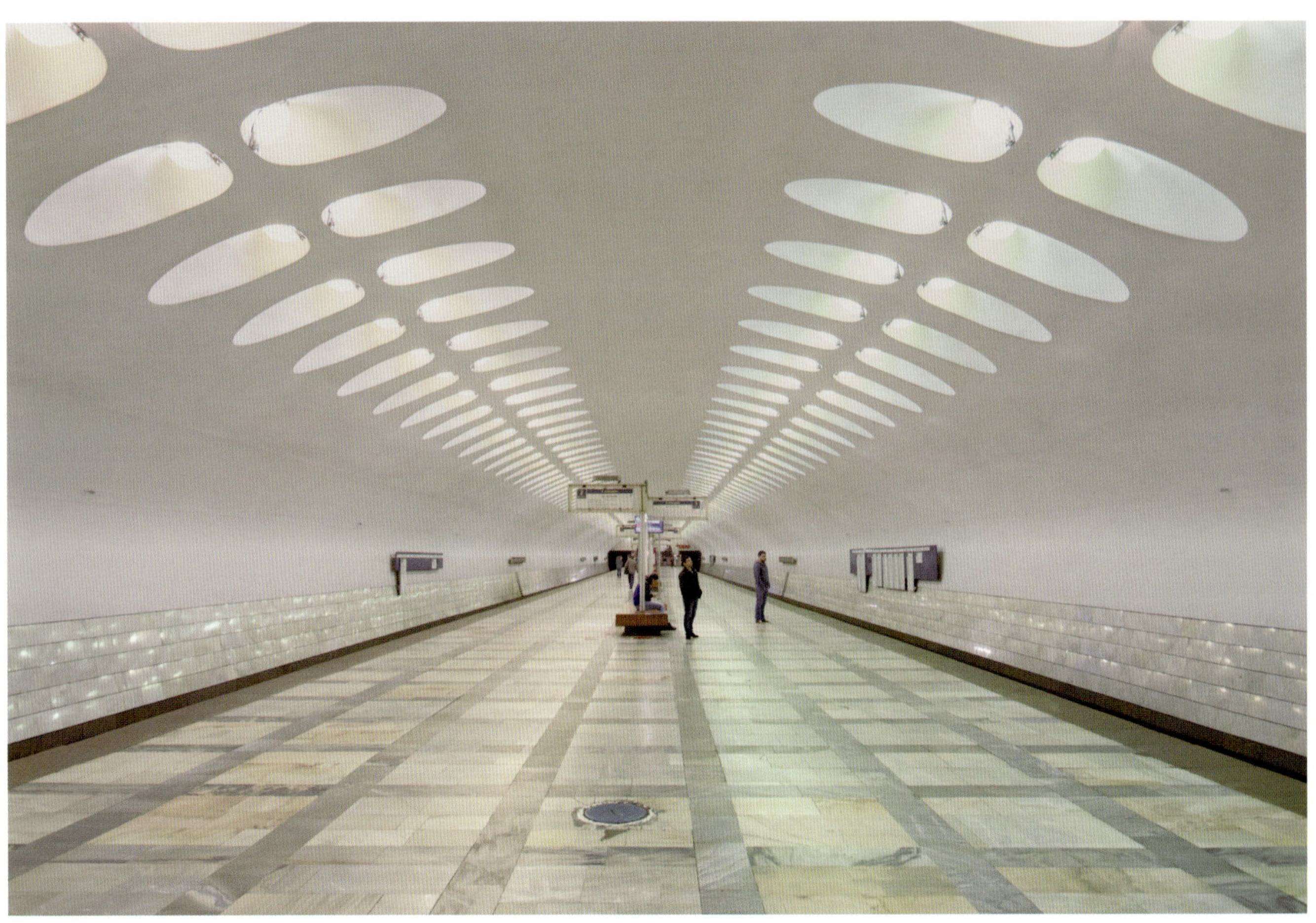

240   Nakhimovsky Prospekt, MOSCOW

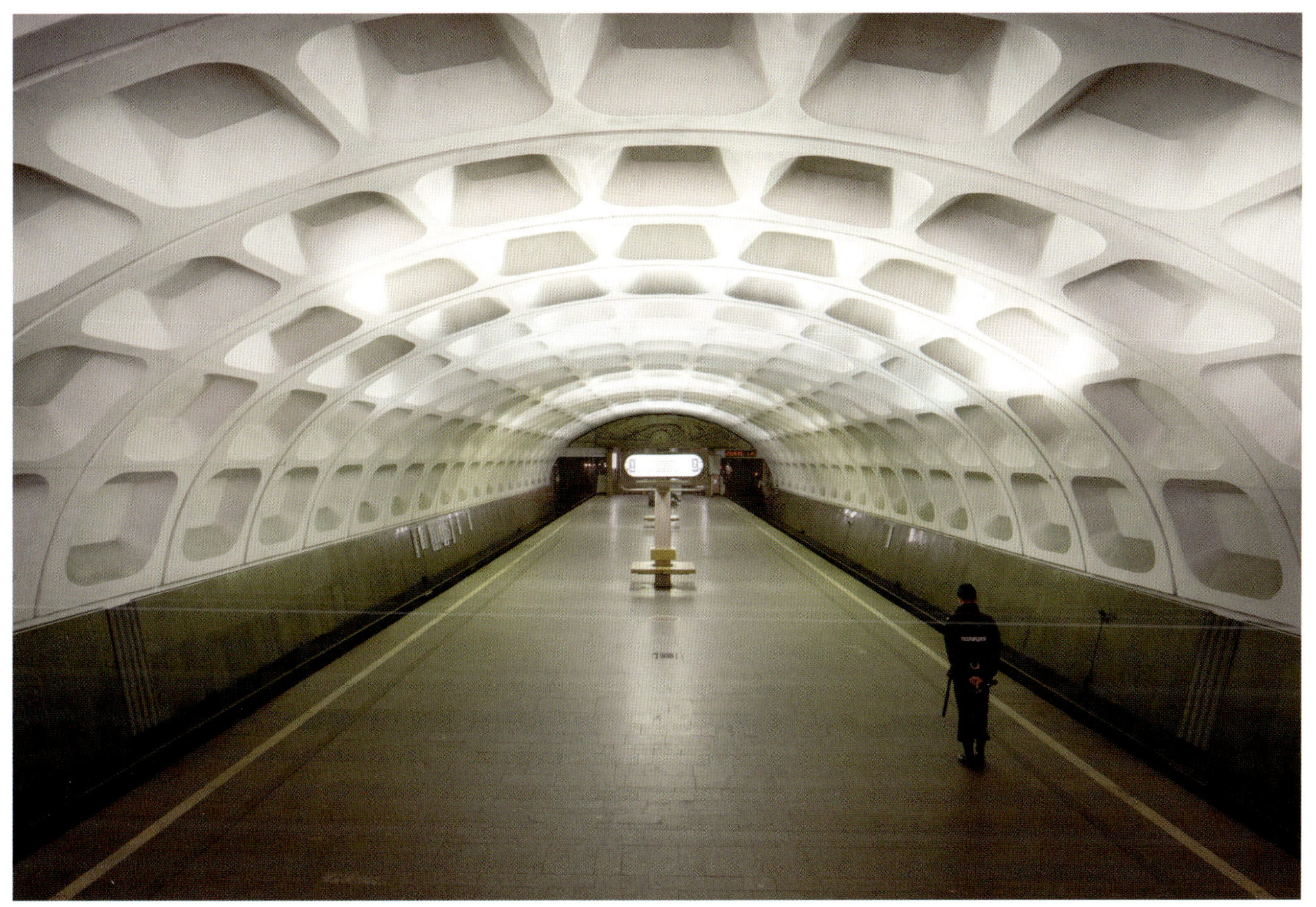

Krasnogvardeyskaya, MOSCOW   241

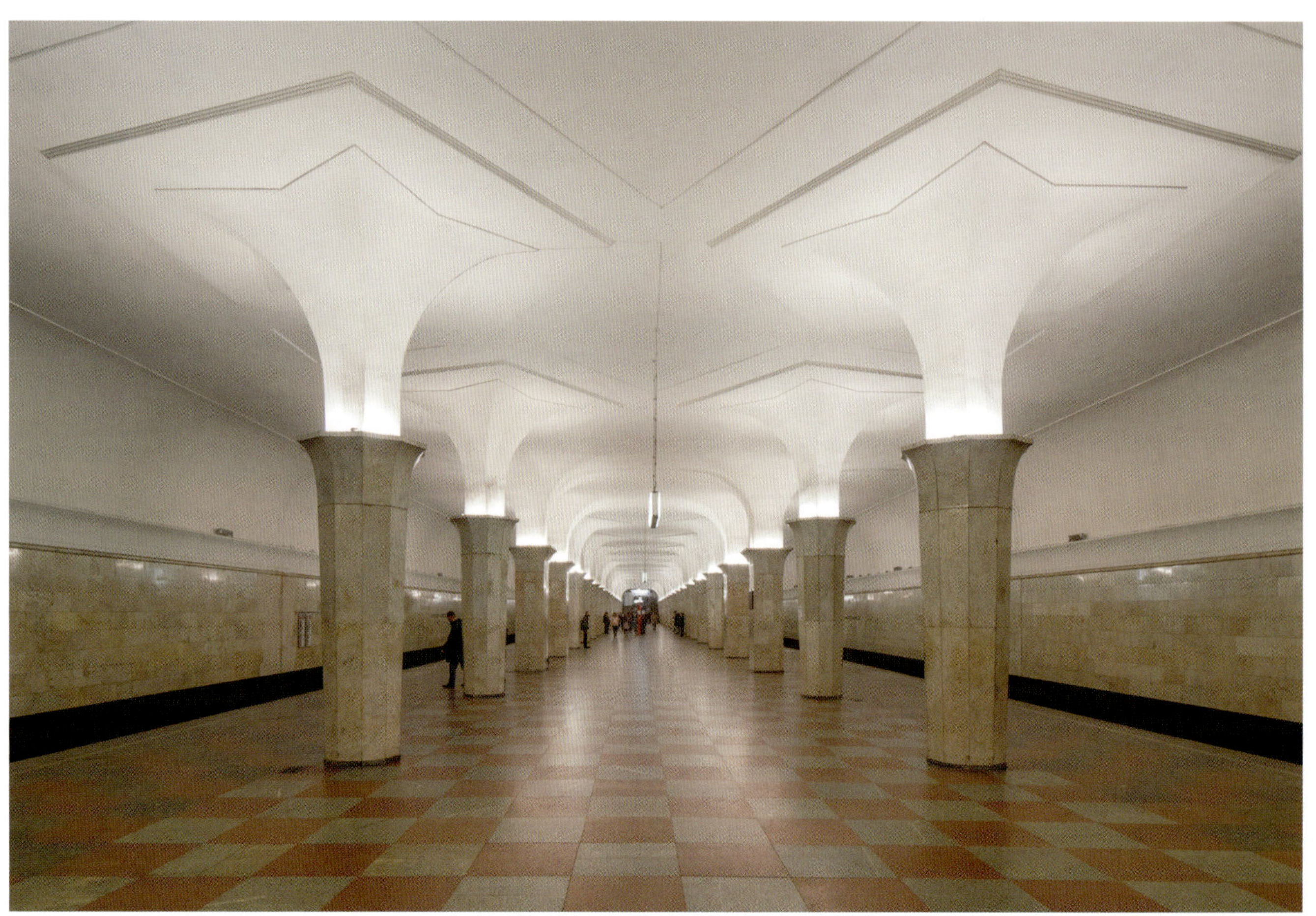

242 Kropotkinskaya, MOSCOW

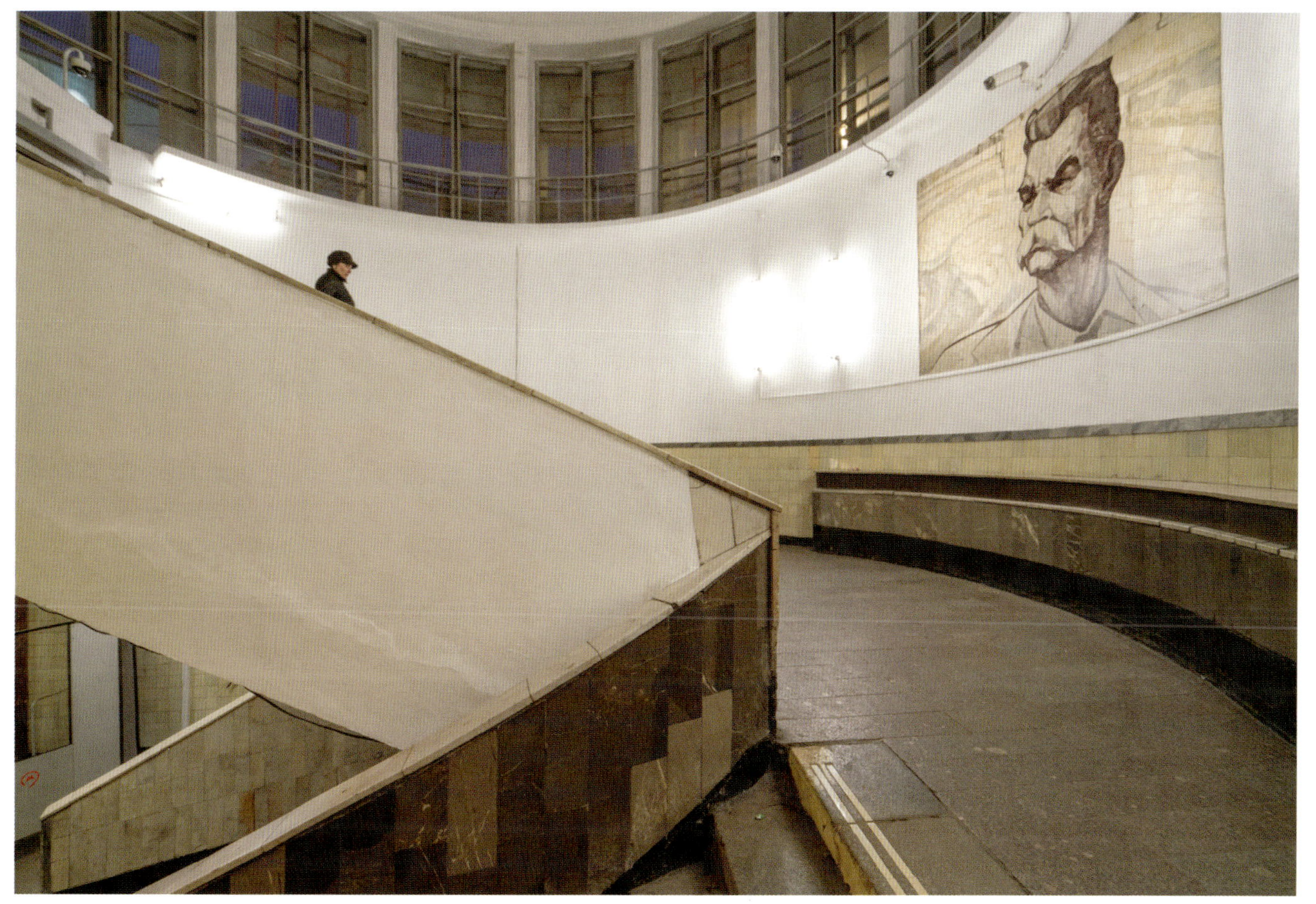

Park Kultury, MOSCOW   243

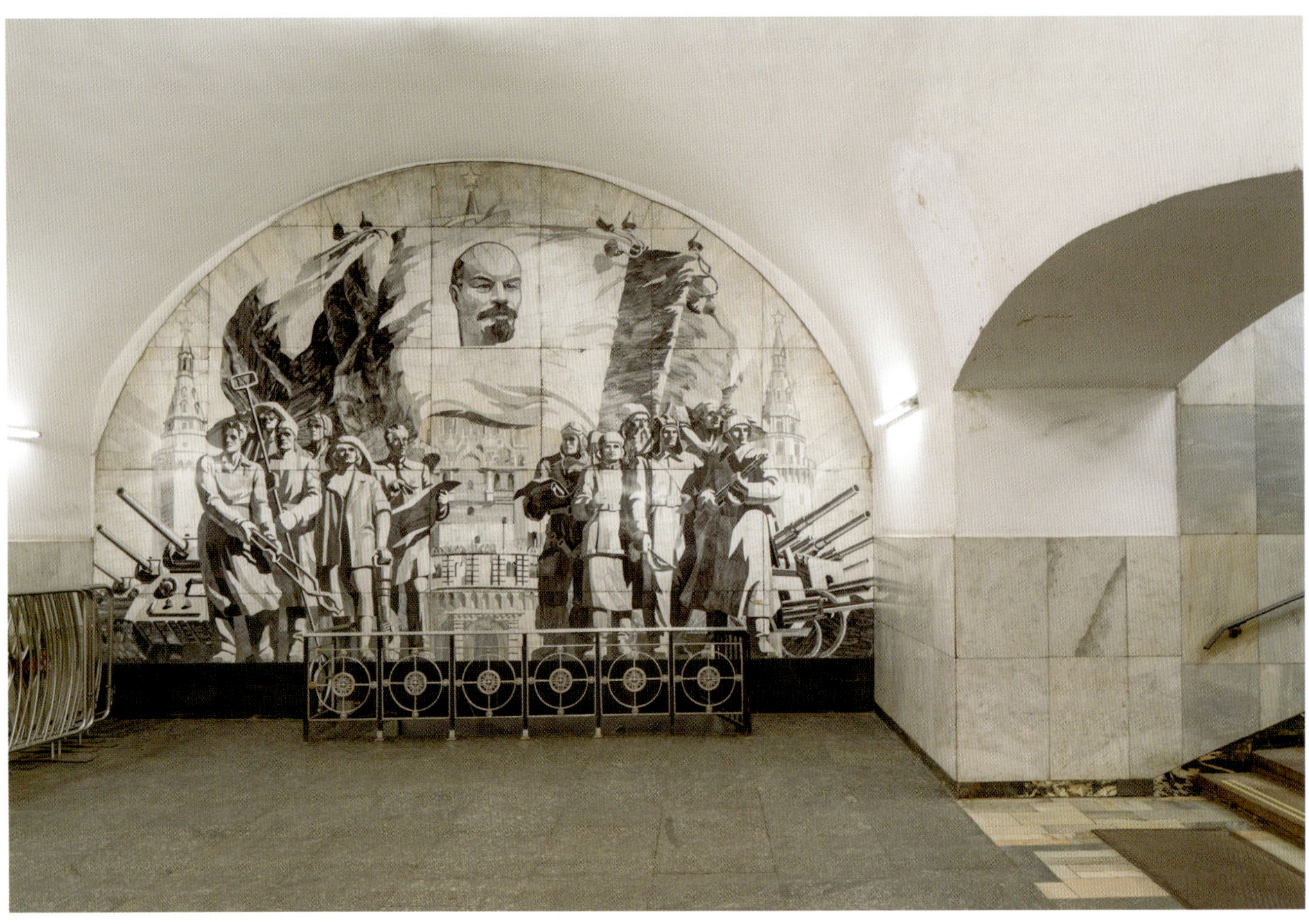

244   Novokuznetskaya, MOSCOW

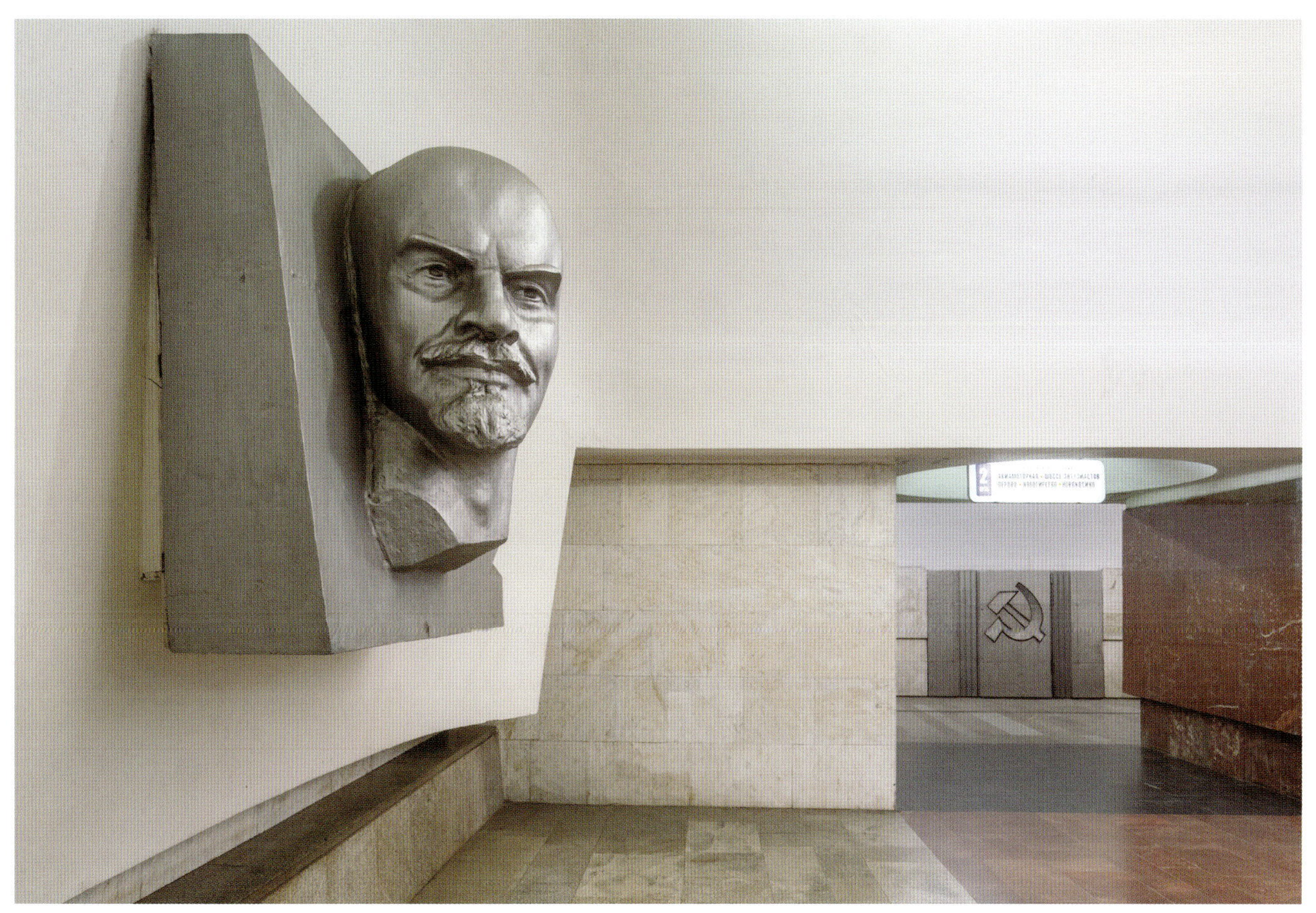

Ploshchad Ilyicha, MOSCOW   245

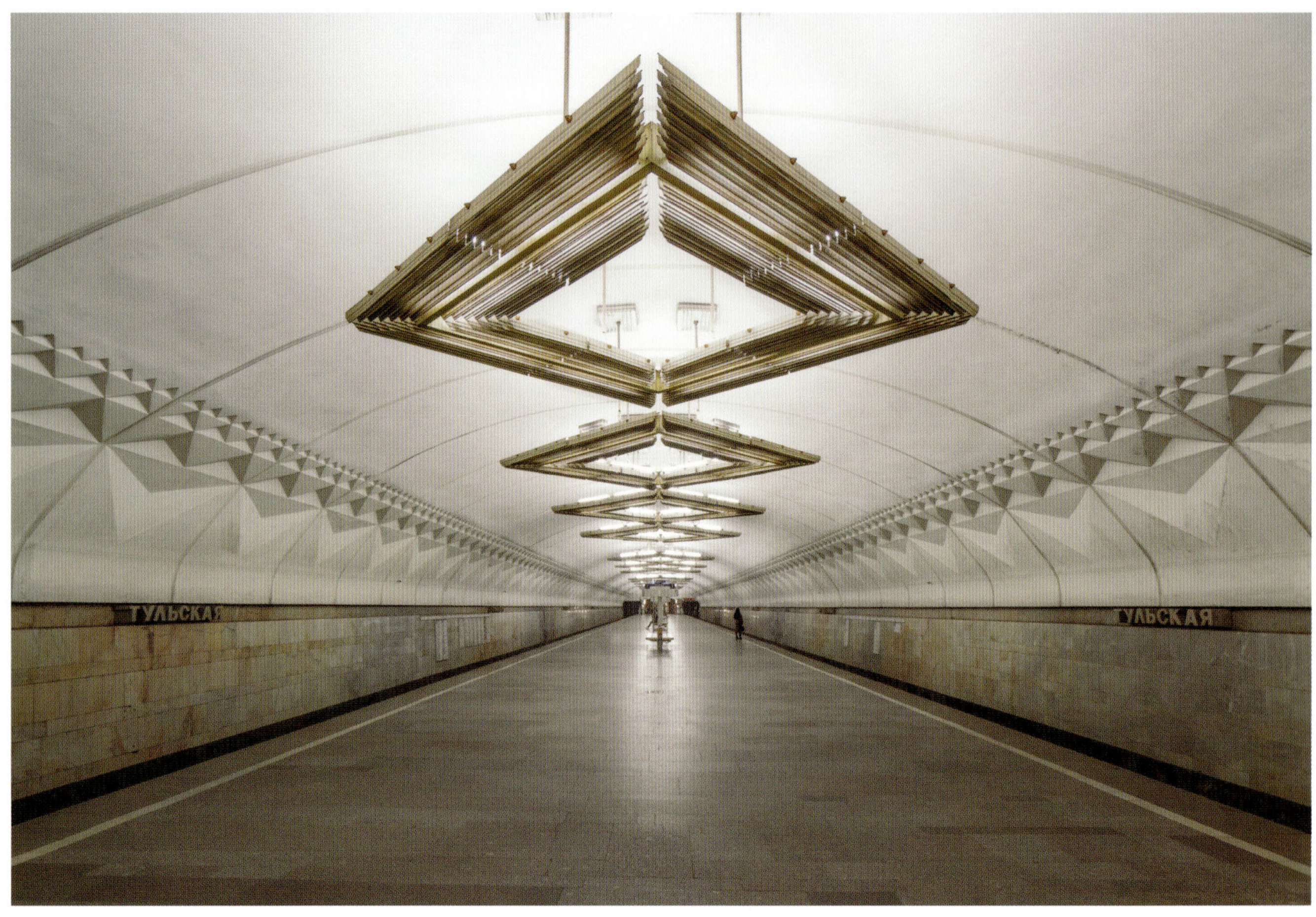

246   Tulskaya, MOSCOW

Afterword
Christopher Herwig

It's 5 am. I've only slept a couple of hours, but I drag myself out of bed. Like a zombie with a single goal, I'm drawn towards the illuminated 'M', where I descend the escalator deep into the earth. Some stations are so far down, the ride lasts five minutes. I arrive at the platform, wide awake and excited to photograph this breathtaking space: an underground world, with a distant horizon and a concrete sky. After weeks of early mornings to take advantage of the pre-rush-hour emptiness, I should be bored – but the unpredictable variety keeps the thrill fresh. I spent years photographing Soviet bus stops, which were monumental in a more humble way. By contrast, Metro stations are an exhilarating mix of propaganda, art and design. My eye is caught by quirky Cyrillic signs, exquisite mosaics and cosmic lighting fixtures. Then the serene calm is shattered by the crush of millions of commuters. I ascend to daylight and sleep.

To me, Soviet Metro stations have always been a secret place, unexpected treasures hidden underground. That photography was prohibited for military and security reasons only served to reinforce this feeling. The recent easing of restrictions in some stations allowed me to immerse myself fully in this project.

It's early afternoon and I wake up to get ready to go under again. Not the best time of day to photograph with the crazy crowds, but I need to scout out where I will be at the end of the day. I get off at each stop and walk around, taking notes, cursing the renovations or excessive advertising on the walls and wishing I could go back in time. My interest in the excessively ornate structures that caught my attention more than twenty years ago has steadily given way to a greater love for the more modern concrete and original creations.

It's past midnight but it feels like high noon in a cowboy film. I step off the train and walk to the top of the platform. Spinning around, I stand dead centre, waiting for the right balance of people and space. I may only get one shot. At the far end an official raises his baton and blows his whistle just as I manage to fire off a couple of frames. It turns out that not every city has relaxed its rules on photography. By the end of the project I've been shut down more than thirty times. Recognising my genuine intentions, this is usually a relatively friendly exchange, the harmless drama adding to the thrill of the hunt as I pass the time waiting for the last train.

With over twenty-five years of experience in more than ninety countries, Christopher Herwig is a Canadian-born photographer and videographer determined to find beauty and inspiration in all aspects of life. A firm belief that the thrill of exploration is still alive in the world has sent him hitch-hiking from Vancouver to Cape Town, across Iceland by foot and raft, and through Europe on a bike. Currently based in Sri Lanka, his previous homes have included Liberia and Kazakhstan. His photographs of some of the remotest regions of the world – from the Pamir mountains in Tajikistan to the rainforests of West Africa – have been reproduced in publications including *GEO*, *CNN Traveler*, *Geographical* and *Lonely Planet*. He has worked extensively with non-government organisations and UN agencies in some of the most challenging regions, to put a human face to their statistics and bring project proposals to life.

His best-selling books *Soviet Bus Stops*, *Soviet Bus Stops Volume II* and *Soviet Metro Stations* were published by FUEL in 2015, 2017 and 2019. The documentary film *Soviet Bus Stops* was released in 2022.

Endpapers: Medvedkovo, MOSCOW

First published in 2019
Reprinted in 2020, 2025

Murray & Sorrell FUEL Ltd
FUEL Design & Publishing
33 Fournier Street
London E1 6QE

fuel-design.com

Photographs © Christopher Herwig

Essay © Owen Hatherley
Archive material courtesy Owen Hatherley except page 21 Dmitry V. Aksenov, page 24 estate of Stepan Kyurkchyan, page 27 Troy Litten.

Design and edit by Murray & Sorrell FUEL

All rights reserved.
No part of this book may be reproduced without the written permission of the publisher.

Distribution by Thames & Hudson / Artbook D. A. P.
ISBN: 978-0-9957455-6-8
Printed in China

Printed with non mineral ink on FSC (Forest Stewardship Council) certified paper from responsibly managed forests and recycled materials, ensuring sustainable forestry practices and environmental protection.

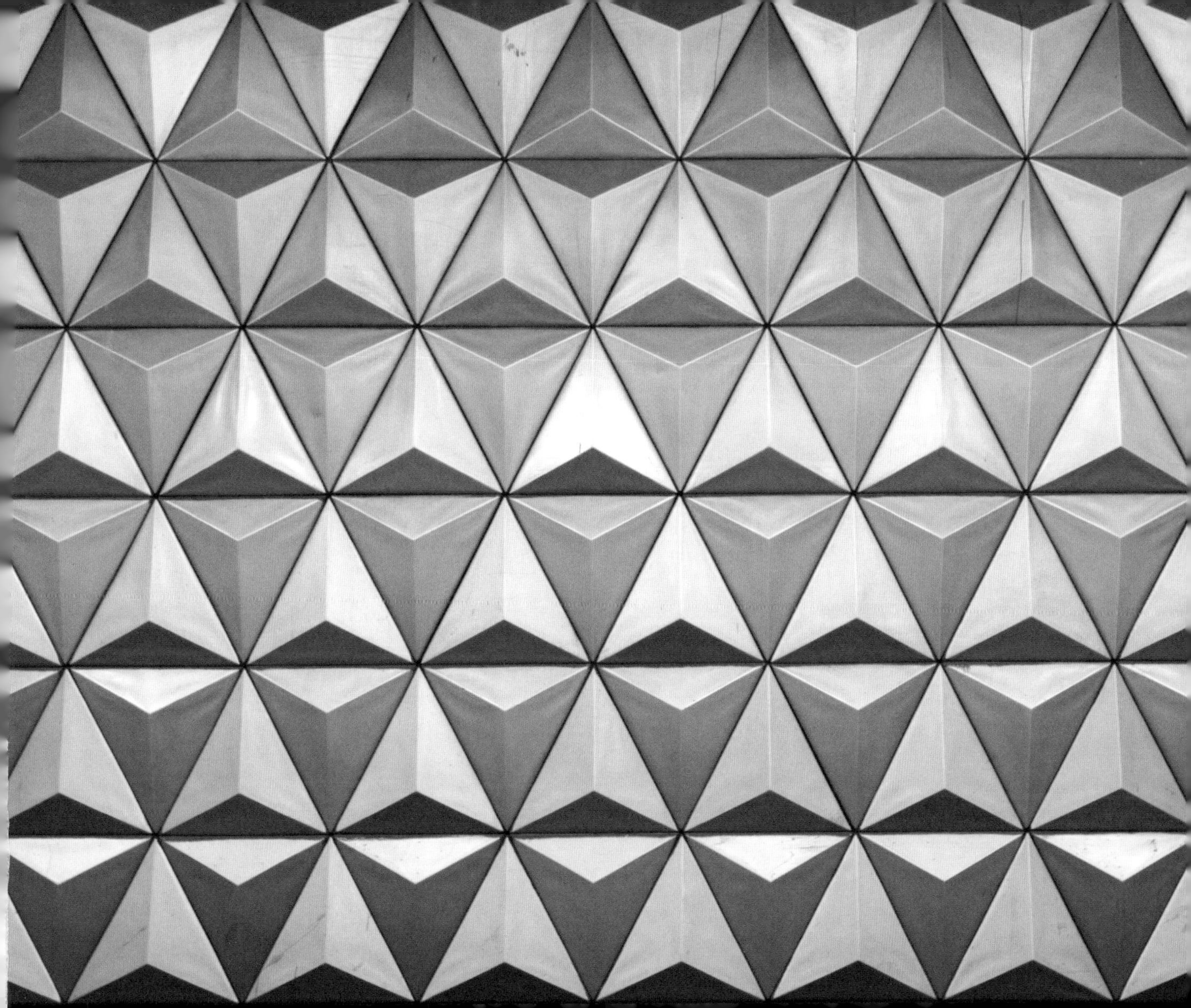

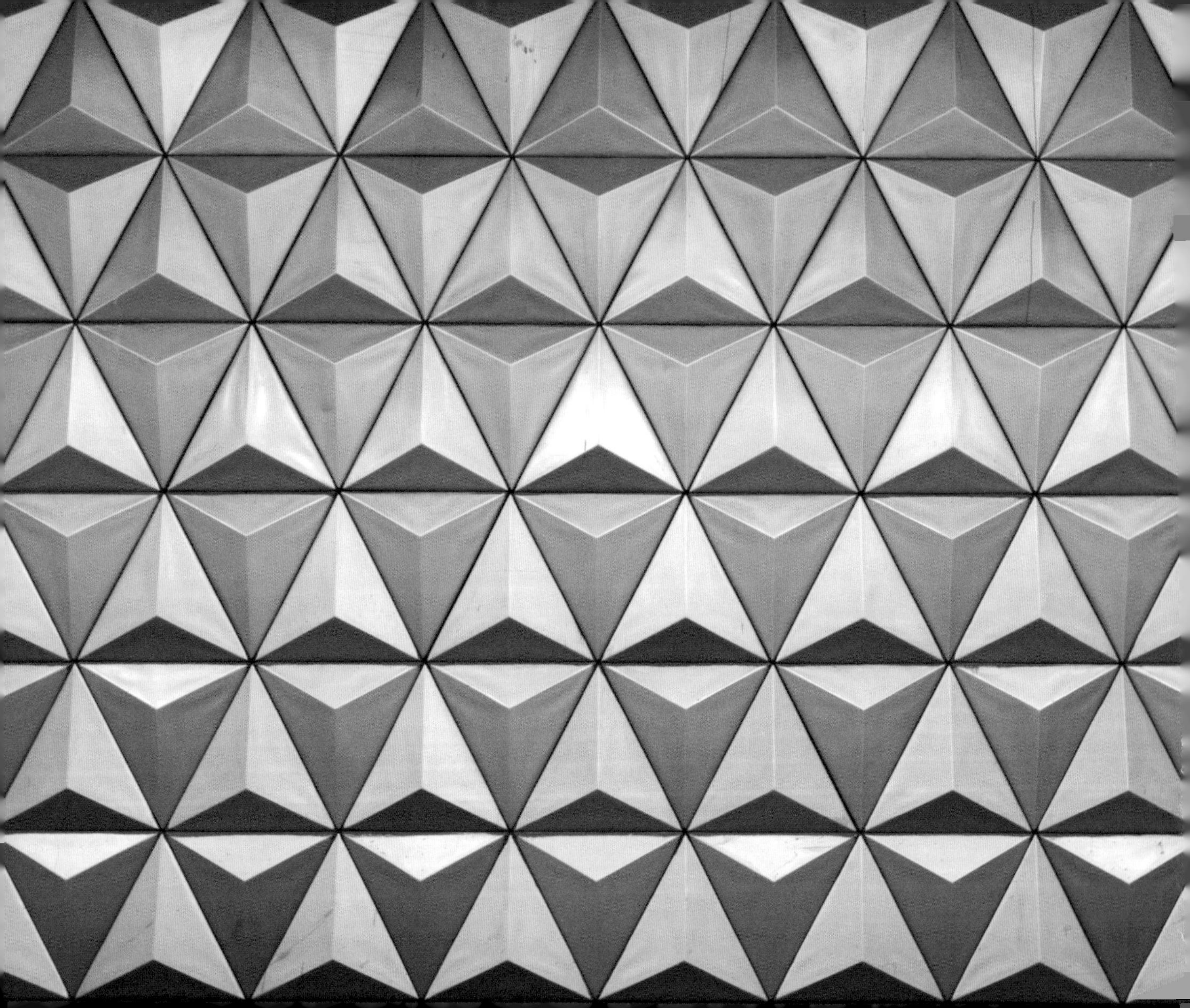